SELECTED LETTERS OF
E. M. FORSTER

Also by Mary Lago and P. N. Furbank

Selected Letters of E. M. Forster
VOLUME ONE: 1879–1920

SELECTED LETTERS OF

E. M. Forster

VOLUME TWO

1921-1970

EDITED BY

MARY LAGO AND P. N. FURBANK

The Belknap Press of
Harvard University Press
Cambridge, Massachusetts
1985

Library of Congress Cataloging in Publication Data

Forster, E. M. (Edward Morgan), 1879–1970.
Selected letters of E. M. Forster.

Bibliography: v. 2, p.
Includes indexes.
Contents: v. 1. 1879–1920 — v. 2. 1921–1970.
1. Forster, E. M. (Edward Morgan), 1879–1970—
Correspondence. 2. Novelists, English—20th century—
Correspondence. I. Lago, Mary. II. Furbank, Philip
Nicholas. III. Title.
PR6011.O58Z48 1983 823'.912 [B] 83–4376
ISBN 0–674–79827–9 (v. 2)

CONTENTS

ILLUSTRATIONS
Volume One

All photographs are the copyright of and published by courtesy of King's College Library, Cambridge, or the editors, unless otherwise stated.

Editors' Note
and Acknowledgements

This second volume of selected letters of E. M. Forster begins with his second trip to India, in 1921, and ends with a letter of 1969, the year before his death. Some cross-references to Volume One are essential; these are indicated by reference to Letter numbers for the most part, and we have tried to facilitate these by means of the Cumulative Index in this volume.

As in Volume One, spaced ellipsis points indicate editorial omissions; unspaced ellipsis points indicate a letter-writer's own ellipsis. Square brackets enclose editorial interpolations; angle brackets enclose material for which Forster himself used square brackets. Forster's spelling has been preserved; its frequent oddity became almost a hallmark of his epistolary style. Punctuation is again Forster's own except where meaning was in doubt: in such cases we have supplied missing punctuation in square brackets.

We have indicated the ownership of all letters quoted here, both in the numbered sequence and in the notes. The copyright in all of Forster's published and unpublished works, letters, and manuscripts belongs exclusively to King's College, Cambridge, Executor for the Forster Estate. Many of his letters (but by no means all) are in the Library of King's College; scholars who wish to consult them should make appointments in advance with the Modern Archivist.

The complete list of those who have assisted and encouraged us is again so long that it is impossible for us to mention all of them by name, but all may be assured of our continuing appreciation. We wish to repeat our thanks for the cooperation of the administrators of the Forster Estate, and for their continued interest in our work.

For approval of our use of Forster's letters, from sources other than King's College, we wish to thank the following: Alexander Turnbull Library, Wellington, New Zealand (to Frank Sargeson); Lord Annan; BBC Written Archives Centre (to Zulfikar Bokhari, Val Gielgud, John Morris, F. W. Ogilvie, R. A. Rendall, C. V. Salmon); Mollie Barger (to Florence Barger); Bancroft Library, University of California at Berkeley (to Frieda Lawrence, Stephen Spender); Beinecke Rare Book and Manuscripts Library, Yale University (to unidentified recipient); Berg Collection, The New York Public Library, Astor, Lenox and Tilden Foundations (to

Leonard Woolf, Virginia Woolf); Bodleian Library, Oxford, for Lord Bridges (to Robert Bridges); Boston University Library (to Santha Rama Rau); May Buckingham (to herself and to Robert J. Buckingham); Wallace D. Bradway (to Edmund Candler); Britten Estate (to Benjamin Britten, Eric Crozier); Bryn Mawr College (to A. E. Housman); Cambridge University Library, for Lord Kennet (to Edward Hilton Young); Lord David Cecil; Butler Library, Columbia University (to Duncan Grant, Lionel Trilling, unidentified recipient); Enzo Crea; Eric Crozier; Jill (Balcon) Day-Lewis (to Cecil Day-Lewis); Edward Arnold and Company (to B. W. Fagan); Eric Fletcher; Stephen Gilbert (to Forrest Reid); Harcourt, Brace Jovanovich (to John McCallum); Kenneth Harrison; The Houghton Library, Harvard University (to T. S. Eliot, Santha Rama Rau); Humanities Research Center, University of Texas at Austin (to J. R. Ackerley, Edmund Blunden, Dora Carrington, Malcolm Darling, Peter Gamble, John Lehmann, Lady Ottoline Morrell, J. B. Priestley, Hugh Walpole); Christopher Isherwood; Arthur Koestler; Richard Keynes (to Margaret Elizabeth Keynes); Timothy Leggatt; Irene Lightbody (to George Valassopoulo); Lilly Library, Indiana University (to Gerald Brenan, P. N. Furbank); Alice Mauron (to Charles Mauron); James McConkey; Shelagh Meade (to John Meade); Merton College Library, Oxford (to Max Beerbohm); Helen Moody (to Peter Burra); National Library of Scotland (to Naomi Mitchison); K. Natwar-Singh; William Roerick; Victor J. Rosen (to A. P. Herbert); George P. Savidis (to self and to C. P. Cavafy); The Society of Authors, London, and David J. Holmes (to Denys Kilham Roberts, Herbert Thring); Southern Illinois University-Carbondale (to Robert Graves); Wilfred Stone; George Thomson; Trinity College, Cambridge (to Robert C. Trevelyan); University of Arkansas (to Frank Swinnerton); University of Durham (to William Plomer); University of Hull (to Sir Thomas Inskip); University of Iowa (to John Collier); University of Sussex (to Leonard Woolf); Philip Whichelo (to Mary Ellen Whichelo); Basil Wright.

For permission to quote, in our annotations, passages from letters by writers other than Forster, we wish to thank Lord Annan; British Broadcasting Corporation (from George Barnes, Zulfikar Bokhari, Malcolm Darling, John Morris, Frederick Oglivie, R. A. Rendall, C. V. Salmon, Ormond Wilson); April Darling (from Jessica and Malcolm Darling); Livia Gollancz (from Victor Gollancz); Sir Rupert Hart-Davis (from Hugh Walpole); Frank Hauser; Lord Kennet (from Edward Hilton Young, Lord Kennet of the Dene); Trustees of the T. E. Lawrence Letters Trust (for quotations from T. E. Lawrence copyright © 1983); Irene Lightbody (from George Valassopoulo); Alexander Murray (from Gilbert Murray); P. E. N., London (from Hermon Ould); Santha Rama Rau; The Society of

Authors, London (from Denys Kilham Roberts); Wilfred H. Stone; Helen Strauss; Lawrence Toynbee (from Arnold Toynbee).

Many librarians and archivists have guided our research and answered our many questions. We wish particularly to thank E. G. W. Bill (Lambeth Palace Library); Richard Bingle (India Office Library); Kenneth Blackwell (McMaster University); Jeaneice Brewer (University of Missouri-Columbia); I. G. Brown (National Library of Scotland); John Burgass (Merton College, Oxford); David Burnett (University of Durham); Anthony Coulson (Open University Library); Ellen Dunlap (Humanities Research Center, University of Texas at Austin); Michael Halls (Library of King's College, Cambridge); C. W. Franklin (Wiltshire County Council Library and Museum Service); Colin Harris (Bodleian Library, Oxford); Norman Higson (University of Hull); Elizabeth Inglis (University of Sussex); Jacqueline Kavanagh (BBC Written Archives, Caversham Park, Reading); Trevor Kaye (Trinity College, Cambridge); Douglas Matthews (London Library); Elizabeth M. Moys (Goldsmiths College, London); D. S. Porter (Bodleian Library); D. Postles (City of Sheffield Archives); A. Raspin and Donald Ross (British Library of Political and Economic Science, London School of Economics); Kevin Stewart (Alexander Turnbull Library, Wellington); Rosamond Strode (Benjamin Britten Archives); Mary Thatcher (Centre of South Asian Studies, Cambridge University).

For their answers to our questions, for suggestions for further investigation, and for generous interest in our progress, we wish to thank all of those to whom we have applied, in many cases repeatedly. We wish especially to thank Donald Adamson, Richard Allen, Walter Allen, Lord Annan, Harold Barger, Michael Barrie, Victor Bonham-Carter, Laurence Brander, John Brinton, May Buckingham, Paul Cadmus, Alex Cain, M. V. Carey, Lord David Cecil, Lord Clark, Hilary Corke, Enzo Crea, Eric Crozier and Nancy Evans Crozier, Lady Knox Cunningham, Amlan Datta, Jill (Balcon) Day-Lewis, C. Emlyn-Jones, Howard Ferguson, Jared French, Veronica Groocock, Shyam Ratna Gupta, Lorna Hardwick, Sir Rupert Hart-Davis, Lord Harewood, Frank Hauser, Elizabeth Heine, Michael Holroyd, Samuel Hynes, Christopher Isherwood, Frank Jones, Lord Kennet, Francis King, B. J. Kirkpatrick, Lincoln Kirstein, Jane Lago, Joe Law, Timothy Leggatt, John Lehmann, Irene Lightbody, William McBrien, Frederick McDowell, Andrew McNeillie, Derwent May, Adrien de Menasce, Michael Millgate, Donald Mitchell, Christopher Morris, R. W. Pakenham, Elizabeth Paterson, Norman Prouting, Jan Reynolds, Alice Roughton, Sylvia Scaffardi, C. H. Sisson, Frances Spalding, Velda Sprott, Wilfred Stone, Julian Trevelyan, Diana Trilling, Marietta Voge, Glenway Wescott, George Weys, Philip

Whichelo, Donald Windham, Roma Woodnutt, Ormond Wilson, Oliver Zangwill.

We wish to thank Michael Halls and Elizabeth Heine for their careful reading of the proofs; and the English Department of the University of Missouri-Columbia, for the grant that made possible Joe Law's invaluable assistance in checking proofs and index.

We owe a particular debt of gratitude to our editors, for unstinted support in the form of editorial advice, technical assistance, and a heartening enthusiasm for our subject. One never knows, when beginning such a project, what problems and puzzles will emerge. We are grateful for Gillian Gibbins' help in dealing with them, week by week and page by page, and for Robin Baird-Smith's comprehensive guidance and advice.

Finally, we wish to repeat our thanks to the Open University and to the University of Missouri-Columbia for various financial aids during the course of this project; to the University of Missouri for ML's Research Leave in 1982–3; and to St Edmund's House, Cambridge University, for her appointment as a Visiting Fellow.

Mary Lago   P. N. Furbank

Cambridge and London
October 1984

ABBREVIATIONS

AH	E. M. Forster, *Abinger Harvest* (1936)
ALS	autograph letter, signed
ALU	autograph letter, unsigned
AMS	autograph manuscript
AN	E. M. Forster, *Aspects of the Novel* (Abinger Edition, 1975)
ATr	autograph transcript
BBC	BBC Written Archives Centre
Berg	Berg Collection, New York Public Library
Bodleian	Bodleian Library, Oxford University
BU	Boston University Library, Special Collections
CB	E. M. Forster, *Commonplace Book* (Facsimile Edition, 1979)
CSAS	Centre of South Asian Studies, Cambridge University
Durham	University of Durham Library, Special Collections
EMF	P. N. Furbank, *E. M. Forster: A Life* (1978–9)
EMOS	E. M. Forster, *The Eternal Moment and Other Stories* (1928)
GLD	E. M. Forster, *Goldsworthy Lowes Dickinson* (Abinger Edition, 1973)
Hansard	*The Parliamentary Debates*
HD	E. M. Forster, *The Hill of Devi* and other Indian writings (Abinger Edition, 1983)
HL	Houghton Library, Harvard University
HRC	Humanities Research Center, University of Texas at Austin
Hull	Brynmor Jones Library, University of Hull
IE	*Imperfect Encounter: Letters of William Rothenstein and Rabindranath Tagore, 1911–41* (1972)
KCC	Library of King's College, Cambridge
Kirkpatrick	B. J. Kirkpatrick, *A Bibliography of E. M. Forster* (2nd ed., revised, 1968)
LTC	E. M. Forster, *The Life to Come & Other Stories* (Abinger Edition, 1972)
LJ	E. M. Forster, *The Longest Journey* (1907)

MS	manuscript
PI	E. M. Forster, *A Passage to India* (Abinger Edition, 1978)
PP	E. M. Forster, *Pharos and Pharillon* (1923)
RWV	E. M. Forster, *A Room with a View* (Abinger Edition, 1977)
S. of A.	The Society of Authors (London)
Sussex	University of Sussex, Special Collections
TCC	Library of Trinity College, Cambridge
TCD	E. M. Forster, *Two Cheers for Democracy* (Abinger Edition, 1972)
TLS	typewritten letter, signed
TLS	*The Times Literary Supplement* (London)
TLU/cc	typewritten letter, unsigned/carbon copy
TS	typescript
TTr	typewritten transcript

A PASSAGE TO INDIA,
1921–4

Forster set off on his second visit to India on 4 March 1921, contriving on the way a very brief reunion with Mohammed el Adl at Port Said. It was a tense moment politically, for the repressive 'Rowlatt Acts' of 1919 had been followed by a bloody massacre at Amritsar in April 1919; and in September 1920 Gandhi, who had emerged as leader of the Congress movement, which temporarily united Hindus and Moslems, had declared a policy of 'non-cooperation' with the British.

At Dewas, the Maharaja welcomed Forster effusively, and it soon became plain that he wanted him more as a friend than as a secretary. However, Forster took seriously such responsibilities as he was given; these included care of the garages, the 'electric house', and the Palace gardens, and he looked about for further ways of being helpful. He felt happy in the Maharaja's friendship but surmised anxiously that the latter's extensive and ill-managed building schemes, and his passion for elaborate and expensive religious ceremonies, were bankrupting the State. Nevertheless Forster realised that, as a novelist, he was being offered the great opportunity of his life. In lengthy journal letters to his mother, his Aunt Laura, and others he recorded his day-to-day experiences of court life and court intrigue, and the festivities such as the great religious festival of Gokul Ashtami (evoked in the last section of *A Passage to India*). From the vantage-point of a princely state he was enabled also to see the British Raj, and the Indian political scene in general, from a fresh angle. He noticed a new and deliberate policy of politeness to Indians on the part of the British, although as the result of a supposed slight to himself by a visiting British official he in fact became the centre of a minor diplomatic fracas. He was involved as well in a quarrel with his predecessor at court, Colonel Leslie, who wrote accusing Forster of reading his personal mail. Forster also became involved in a sexual imbroglio with a court servant, and it was the Maharaja's understanding behaviour over this that gave Forster the belief that, though flawed, His Highness was a genius and a saint.

He left the Maharaja's service in November 1921, partly because of the expected return of Colonel Leslie, and partly because he felt himself of no practical use. His last two months were spent very cheerfully in Hyderabad, where Masood was now the Nizam's Director of Education. On the voyage home, Forster disembarked in Egypt to visit Mohammed el Adl and found him dying of consumption.

His attempt, after his return home, to resume his Indian novel precipitated a crisis of uncertainty and depression—overcome partly with the help of Leonard Woolf, who urged that he must at all costs finish the book, regardless of publication. The extended novel was now somewhat changed. As a result of recent public and personal history (and, in particular, it would seem, as a response to Malcolm Darling's personal account of the Amritsar massacre) it became darker in colour. Also, a deliberate ignoring of the 1914–18 war rendered it ambiguous as to period. In the writing of the last pages he was helped, according to his own account, by letters from Chhatarpur from his recently-acquired friend J. R. Ackerley, by reading Proust, and by the discovery of T. E. Lawrence's *Seven Pillars of Wisdom*.

Alexandria: A History and a Guide was at last published in Alexandria in December 1922, and in May 1923 the Hogarth Press published *Pharos and Pharillon*, a collection of his Egyptian journalism. Edward Arnold published *A Passage to India* on 4 June 1924. It was received with great acclaim, although it provoked some accusations of unfairness and inaccuracy from all the groups depicted in it: British, Hindu, and Moslem.

In May 1924 Forster's Aunt Laura Forster had died and had left him her house, 'West Hackhurst' in Abinger. After much indecision, and with reluctance on Lily's part, he and his mother moved there later in the year.

208   To Florence Barger

P.&O.S.N.Co.   S.S.Morea
17 March 1921

Dearest Florence,

I write in great peace of mind. Mohammed, in the face of great difficulties, pushed his way on board yesterday at Port Said: I was just starting ashore to find him, and the direction being inaccurate, should almost certainly have missed.[1] As it was, we had four perfect hours together. I found him more charming affectionate and intelligent than ever, and since the time was so short we decided only to speak of happy things. He asked after the children and you, and we indited a joint postcard to mother. He looked well and his clothes did him (and their donor!) credit; but says he has lost 4 lbs and has no job and that his father-in-law is bankrupt. It was, and still all is, dream like, and he too said it was a dream. He brought me some topping cigarettes, though the box was somewhat depleted by what he had given away as bribes. Thanks to our constant correspondence we met as we had parted, though there was much to tell that could not be put in letters. We spent part of the evening on the boat, but most on shore.

Well my dear that is my news. Would that I could think yours as satisfactory. I am so distressed at the drain on George's strength and at the wrecking of Italy. George wrote me a kind and interesting letter, for which please thank him, and I was very glad to hear from you—and the others—at Marseilles. Mother is fairly all right I think, though suffering from nerves and so inclined to be a trifle 'odd': she was almost ill when Agnes dropped a bottle! My present feeling is that as long as she does *anything* she is all right: it's only when she mopes and does nothing, that one will have to jog her. She has been in my mind whenever I go up a stair—except when M. is in my mind, as he has been almost without pause for the last 3 days!

I have had a happy day passing through the Canal and watching its live stock. Now we pound down the Gulf of Suez, and tomorrow I hope to think about India. I will write to you more on the spot when I arrive: this is to acknowledge your unwearying kindnesses to me, and to give you all my love, and my wishes for a speedy end to the miserable Dutch business.[2]

$$\mathcal{M} \text{organ}$$

ALS: KCC

[1] EMF left England on 4 March 1921 to take up duties as private secretary to the Maharaja of Dewas. On his friendship with Mohammed el Adl, see, particularly, Letters 168, 183, 187, 189, 192. Many important documents relating EMF's Indian experiences, including his Indian journal, are printed in *The Hill of Devi*, Abinger Edition (Vol. 14, 1983), ed. E. Heine.

[2] 'Wrecking of Italy', 'miserable Dutch business': allusions to Barger family plans.

209 To Goldsworthy Lowes Dickinson

[Dewas. c. 10 April] 1921

Dear Goldie
    It is most interesting and friendly, but very disjointed. Or, rather, I fear that I have lost my old power of joining it up. I'll pick from the confusion a few impressions of Holi, the Hindu Dionysia that coincide with our Easter and that few Europeans can have seen much. The evening I arrived I put on Indian dress and went to a party at the Cavalry Barracks a 'cha-pani' or 'tea-water' is its title. Troupe of dancers & actors from the Deccan—only one of the girls a girl, the others boys. There was a farce which I saw again at the Palace next night, so got some idea of. Husband & wife. She: 'Can I go and see my people?' He: 'Dangerous for you—and for

me—and morality generally.' She persists, and as soon as she goes the husband says 'I want a eunuch—*at once.*'—A tall scraggy man with a moustache then came on, in a pink sari, and paid attention to such members of the audience as His Highness indicated. (This is a recognised turn: the boy-dancers did it too). The 'eunuch' squatted beside his victim and sang 'do not hurt me'—or 'I am not too old yet to remember what we did as boys'—and tried to kiss him amid laughter from the court. Resuming the drama he danced indecently before the husband, made terms with him, bought him sweets, and was coming to a conclusion when the news is brought to the ill-advised wife. She returns from her parents. 'How can you ruin your health by such a proceeding?' is her arguement: and I think that's where this particular indecency ended. I was struck with the remoteness of their sexual gestures: in most cases I didn't know what was up. One 'girl' lay on her face and extending her hands before her clasped and unclasped them alternately. This indicated the act of copulation. 'If it had really been a girl' said H. H. 'it wouldn't have done, it would have been too much. But they have a boy which makes it all right.' I wonder! All very odd. I shall never feel the surety in these matters here that I felt in Egypt. The sphere of 'naughtiness' seems wider, and perhaps this it is that makes it faintly distasteful to me. And I rather fancy religion queers it. For: a few days later, I came in for more Holi in a village belonging to one of the nobles. We rested outside it while the villagers sang and tried to cover our clothes with red powder: and the women issued from a rent in the mud wall and sat twenty yards off. When we passed them they abused us ritually like the women at the bridge in Ancient Greece.[1] And I expect that queer superstitions are mixed up with the merriment and sex generally, & that's why we can't follow either.

This isn't as bright as it should be, but I was up at 5.30. and drove to Ujjain (23 miles either way) to show Masood the temples & ghats. M. couldn't meet me in Bombay so with energy got a week's leave and came all the way here from Hyderabad. His public deportment is too pompous for my taste, but probably goes down and he is as delightful as ever privately. His Highness very charming in all aspects: in fact all is well until I try to serve him or to cause others to do so, when I swim in the Ocean of Milk itself, where every one becomes anything or nothing.[2] It is impossible to get one thing done, and I feel in despair. Taps running. As Luard wittily remarked last week "As long as they do, India will never run herself." They symbolise to him her mentality. I should be resigned to the mess if so many of its ingredients were not European ~~articles~~. It does not seem right that a tap should run or a piano peel, or an electric fan be useless except as a perch for sparrows, or that 14 commodes should process past me in men's arms while I am drinking afternoon tea. But these are notes not a letter. Do write me a letter soon. My mother forwarded yours to her: it pleased her.

Address C/o T. Cook & Sons Bombay. But the name of the place is The Senior State of Dewas. No European within 20 miles. Which, speaking generally, I do like, without affectation. Scenery poor. Language a nuisance. I sleep on the roof, facing the Sacred Hill, and you can believe me or not as you like, but the air is so dry that when I get into bed the sheets emit electric sparks, and one night I got a shock.

There is a grotesque attack on you by Tagore in the April number of 'The Modern Review,' Calcutta. I have written a reply which, if it ever meets your eye you will think doubly grotesque. An organ note of pained surprise.—T. has gone to bits since Amritsar, I gather.[3]

Tea looms. The palace has been empty of attendants for hours—can't even get a commode emptied—but there has been abundant noise—the children of the day labourers squall, and a large rodent, thought to be a civet-cat, gnaws the canvas ceiling in my verandah. H. H. is at Indore, and will bring Luard back tomorrow I hope. L. goes on leave this month—possibly lending me his servant which'll be convenient. He is at present at the Sehore Agency (Bhopal) but frequently looks us up.

I think that's all I'll tell you. Except that the (morganatic) Rani is so nice. She doesn't live in the Palace, for reasons of state. I go to see her most days. She is expecting a 4th child and lies about on carpets in a farm yard, with men and lamps scattered around her. Having abandoned Purdah she has gone 'too far' in the opinion of a passing English doctor...

~~But I will end off charming letter from Egypt.[4] He feels as I did: that we had never parted, and he cannot think why he felt thus.~~

~~Much love   M.~~

ALU, incomplete: KCC

[1] See Sir James Frazer, *The Golden Bough*, I, Part One, p. 281.

[2] Ghats: steps descending to a river. Ocean of Milk: in Puranic geography, one of seven oceans composed, respectively, of salt, treacle, wine, ghee (clarified butter), milk, curds, and fresh water. See EMF, 'The Churning of the Ocean', *The Athenaeum*, 21 May 1920, pp. 667–8.

[3] Tagore's 'attack': his letter from London, 'Dr. Tagore on British Mentality in Relation to India', *The Modern Review*, 29 (1921), 527–8. In April 1919 he had resigned his 1915 knighthood, as his courageous protest against the Amritsar Massacre. In 1920–1 he undertook an ill-timed European lecture tour to raise funds for his international university in West Bengal. His 'going to bits' was the result of exhaustion, of lingering conservative resentment over the discarded honour, and of a rupture with William Rothenstein; see *IE*, pp. 190–1, 257, 267–97. Tagore's earlier admiration of Dickinson was soured by *Appearances: Being Notes of Travel* (1914), based on *An Essay on the Civilizations of India, China & Japan* (1914), Dickinson's report to the Alfred Kahn Foundation, on whose travelling fellowship he visited Asia in 1912–13. He found China more orderly, therefore more congenial, than India, and Anglo-Indians were 'an oasis in the desert, . . . ministers of the life within life that is the hope, the inspiration, and the meaning of the world' (*Appearances*, pp. 18–19). The book, Tagore told Rothenstein, 'made me feel sad' (*IE*, p. 50). See also Dickinson, 'A Personal Impression of Tagore', *The New Leader*, 2 (23 February 1923), 11–12.

[4] I.e., from Mohammed el Adl. EMF's letter redated 11 April in fresh ink. Presumed new conclusion now lost; letter further dated 14th.

210   To Florence Barger

[Dewas]   20 May 1921

My dearest Florence,

What a joy to see your handwriting again, though your news was not of the best. I don't refer to the actual death of Grandfather as a misfortune, but how much stupidity and selfishness always accompanies these events. I trust that George will continue to resist the expensive fetiches of Family: how expensive they can be no man can conceive until he has visited India.

The Tovey news is serious in a different order. It came as a shock to me, since I had heard no hint of renewed collapse. Since you say that Miss W. played no part in it, I am sure that she did not, though I should have leapt to that conclusion. My mind makes an unpleasant picture of that journey of the trio south. You don't indicate the Trevelyan attitude. Are they raving, or do they acquiesce, like yourself, because Tovey does?[1]

Yes, I read H. O. M.'s poem, about youth's exit, together with some others that were fastened up with it.[2] Powerful and gloomy stuff. I wonder what he *wants* us to think of it. Most writers have a secret wish that some particular judgment should be passed on their work, but in his case the wish is very secret if it exists at all.—Of course, like all writers, he wants to be praised, but I have in my mind a more interesting and subtle requirement.—I wonder what meetings will be effected this summer, or whether any. Damn Christabel and her inability or rather her ability to be moved. If she was fixed granite I shouldn't mind so much, but she reminds me of one of those heavy rocking stones on the Cornish Coast which do just nod their heads after immense effort has been expended. They nod and no more. As soon as the effort is withdrawn they resume immobility, and one has an uneasy and unwarranted feeling that a longer and stronger effort would have roused them to a merry dance.[3]

Your finances are an extra vexation. I certainly thought that if your continental tour were abandoned you would come out on the right side; but George's flits to Holland have no doubt made inroads.—How exasperating too about the farm. I wonder whether you can bring the villains to book.

I write without your letter. I will disinter it before this is sent off, in case there are other points. The last point in it—that about Mother—is of course clear in my mind. As I told you in England, I think you were wrong in supposing that there was anything special in her manner on my Grandmother's anniversary. Was there anything special in her refusal about Harrogate?[4] Here, probably, you were right, but it proceeded entirely from the low mental & moral state induced by my departure. She was of course 'naughty' with me during the last few weeks, not affectionate or considerate in manner, and I am glad that the weeks were so few, or I might have taken the 'naughtiness' seriously, which would have been wrong. I am not surprised, though of course sorry, that she should have reverted to old methods in your case too, and in your case, as we know, those methods always took the form of 'I know you will do anything for Morgan.' You must, as you say, 'live it down' though your phrase is much too solemn for the occasion. What you must really do is to treat what is superficial in her as superficial, until *she* has lived down the shock of my flight. Her letters to me still have the tonelessness that characterised her remark to you. It is all part of a new and I believe temporary atmosphere, and you must not for a moment ascribe it to any action (or absence of action) on your own part, or allow it to weigh more than is inevitable upon your mind. Steady affection acts as a dissolvent upon queerness in the end.

Well, my dear, I appear to preach. Let me turn to other memories of your letter and in particular to your sweet references to M.[5] I can more or less relate what happened. He got on board at once in the tow of Cook's man, just as I was struggling to get off: wore heavy great coat and blue knitted gloves with which he repeatedly clasped my hands, saying how are you, friend, how are you. I showed him the glories of 2nd Class P. & O. then we went off on a motor boat—not 5 minutes to the shore, and I had had my Pass Port visaed, nor did anyone ask for it. We went to a café and drank Turkish Coffee—I always make him pay. Then we walked down the Mole and saw the toes of the De Lesseps statue, the upper regions being invisible in darkness. It was cold and as far as I recollect cloudy. A stroll along the deserted 'plage' followed. We did not go down to the sea, lest the coast guard mistook us for importers of haschish, but kept to the road and sat down for a few moments at its edge—Back to another café (weak but costly beer) and his anxiety that I should not miss the boat began to wane before an anxiety that I should stop until the last possible moment. We went to the landing stage, arranged with a small boat and then walked up and down for a long time. He went off with me—we sat huddled up in the stern while the boat man made very slow progress owing to the trains of empty coal-barges that were drifting off the immense lighted Morea. When we reached, M. wanted to come on board again, but I did not think this safe, since the boatman had already had his money and might have gone off without him. So we parted at the gang way, and he receded into darkness and his Hotel, and spent, he writes, a very bad night, owing to the fleas and to thoughts of my foolishness at stopping for so few hours. I have had several letters from him, some typed. In the last there is an uneasiness lest I shall soar out of his sight in this regal atmosphere, but my reply should allay that. He gives me no news of Gamila's expected child. He still has no work.

News here is copious, but I don't know whether it would interest you. H. H. is very charming, considerate, & intelligent, and I wish he used his intelligence more. It is mostly employed on the detection of intrigues. The truth is that the fundamental in him is religious, not intellectual, and that I must understand his religion better before I can understand him. He will offer no obstacles, for he is in all directions devoid of reticence and pomposity, and treats me admirably well in small and great things. He has the security of the Autocrat without the arrogance, and such faults as he shows proceed from his position as he himself is well aware. In his social life (e.g. in the abolition of Purdah) he is most revolutionary. But in his politics, and particularly in his attitude to British India (which is spoken of as the home of all evil) he is conservativissimus, and I rejoice that the political problem is not urgent yet in Dewas. The population is purely agricultural and contented. There is absolutely no Constitution, though as always comes later talks of one, as there were 10 ten [sic] years ago, and I feel very uneasy as to what will happen when non-cooperation or some kindred movement lifts its head through the soil.[6] Indeed as soon as one thinks of what may be instead of what is, the picture is most black. The attitude to the English officials, to the 'Politicals' as they are called when they are concerned with Native States, is much more friendly than when I was here before and at the same time more independent: the explanation being that the ruling classes, whether English or Indian, find a common menace in Gandhi, and that the English have orders to treat the Native Princes with civility and to allow them—as far as is possible—a free hand. These aspects are in the background; in the foreground there is nothing that clashes too violently with my recent job as Literary Editor. I can live without constraint and may always speak my mind when I have one.

I have started a Literary Society which meets every Wednesday evening, but the attendance is slight and the enthusiasm slighter.[7] Very few of the nobility can speak or follow English. There are one or two exceptions and we have had an interesting but pious paper on 'Service' from a learned Brahman. Yesterday I gave an address on the Contemporary British Press, and next week is an address on
"   "   Indian   " , by the Chief Judicial Officer, followed by a discussion on both addresses. H. H. is behind my effort but does not openly appear. That is why it does not succeed. The direct interest in good stuff, indeed all direct interest, is weak in a court, and no one can cure this, not even the Ruler himself. All that happens in his absence is perfunctory and trivial. When he enters the room spurts of life enter each individual. He knows this as he knows most things, and it makes him sad. I have read him M. Arnold's Essay on Marcus Aurelius, and his comments were illuminating. 'Even in a Palace life may be well led— —'[8]

I have reread your letter—glad family is clear of coughs & colds. May it remain so.

Scindia (i. e. the Maharaja of Gwalior, a very big ruler) is expected to morrow for the night. I am curious to see him, but wish it could be done at less expenditure both of money and exertion. All real work gets postponed to these regal tomfooleries—red carpets, special dining rooms, dancing girls from Bombay. I wouldn't mind if the fellow would be surprised, but he is immensely rich, and will think nothing of whatever we do. The whole of this month has been wasted in cumbersome festivities; yesterday we had a funeral feast in commemoration of an aunt, before that 15 days on end to salute the arrival of a daughter.—How queer all this will read during a coal strike, I cannot imagine. Indeed I think I'll stop. But with the best of love to you all. I do hope you'll get a decent holiday. You speak no more of St Abbs, so I suppose there is some objection there of which I have not heard.[9]

When Scindia, and his reverberations, have died away we may go to the Hills. I hope not. Railways are torture, and the weather here is not. And from the Hills, we may descend direct to Bombay. I hope not again, though it will give me the opportunity of running down to greet Masood at Hyderabad.

Love & much love

M organ

ALS: KCC

[1] On Donald Tovey and Miss Sophie Weisse, see Letter 204. The 'collapse' was Mrs Tovey's; her mental health was rapidly deteriorating, and she was taken to a London nursing home. See Mary Grierson, *Donald Francis Tovey: A Biography Based on Letters*, pp. 183, 191, 195–6, 205–6. The Trevelyans, the Bargers, and the Toveys were old friends, and Tovey's letters to the Trevelyans and to Bessie Trevelyan in particular (TCC) indicate the extent to which they sympathised, and tried to help, with his troubles.

[2] Presumably poems written after Meredith's *Week-Day Poems* (1911), also 'gloomy stuff'.

[3] On Christabel Meredith, see Letter 109.

[4] The anniversary of her mother's death, in 1911, was always a bad time for Lily Forster. Apparently she had refused to go to Harrogate for treatment of her rheumatism.

[5] On EMF's visit to Mohammed el Adl, see Letter 208.

[6] Popular contentment, if prevalent then, progressively diminished. In 1928 there were complaints to the State Police of Indore that H. H.'s officials had kidnapped a party of Dewas cultivators en route to the Political Agent to complain of their ruler's exactions. 'No constitution': H. H. introduced one in 1922.

[7] EMF's prospectus, 'Proposed Literary Society at Dewas' (*HD*, pp. 302–4), states that the society recognised no barriers of race, creed, or class and was concerned with 'noble writings of the past and present'.

[8] In 'Marcus Aurelius' (1863), published in his *Essays in Criticism* (1865), Arnold discusses the relations between religion and moral authority, and sincerity and warmth of feeling as softening influences.

[9] St Abbs Head: promontory on the north coast of Berwickshire, site of an ancient monastery.

211   To Goldsworthy Lowes Dickinson

Dewas.   6 August 1921

Dear Goldie,

I have a spare moment, to speak importantly: means I sit in my office waiting for a chauffeur to come and be sacked, while a chuprassi flicks flies off me with a duster.[1] So will say that your letter, as usual, was a great pleasure. Do 'fondness' and 'love' lead to intimacies that are different in quality? The routes are different but I fancy the final state (providing one is lucky enough to reach it by either route) is the same. When I was with M[ohammed] those 3 hours in Port Said I was overwhelmed with a feeling of safety: overwhelmed on account of the route, but the *feeling* was identical with what I experience when I am with Florence or you, e.g.

I don't feel to be getting much here. If you are too old for travel, I am too old for quaintness and absurdity. The silliness of Indian life is presented to me in too large a beaker. At the bottom lies seriousness, religion, and this month we celebrate the birthday of the Lord Krishna and have already chosen for him 8 new suits of clothes and given orders for his bed and for his mosquito curtains. The clothes touch £30, although he is only 6 inches high, while the special electric light installation will exceed £100. We are thinking of closing the one High School in the state, on account of the expense, and we have dismissed the one man who could organise the garden. You can't be so silly and yet not go insane unless there is an invisible anchor. Which is to be found in, or below, the Lord Krishna. I am curious to see the celebrations, and shall take up my residence for part of the fortnight in the Old Palace, until the bugs and mosquitoes expel me or all my socks are worn out, for in the Old Palace it is not permissable to wear boots. But how will the externals help me to the underlying fact? I only want to touch the fact intellectually, in order to understand these folk and have done with them. I don't want the fact intellectually and emotionally, and there you are! therefore I shall never touch it, H. H. will say.

H. H. continues very good to me, very reliable and delicate. I am supposed to read aloud to him once a day. I read aloud to him once a month. We had 'John Chinaman' at a sitting last time. He understood and appreciated everything as usual, and has frequently referred to it afterwards. But note to what he refers. To your mischievousness in pretending to be a Chinaman when you were not, and to your success in deceiving people! Thus is his mind constituted. The intellect is in splendid condition but he does not want to use it, cannot see why it should be used.[2]

I am trying to get hold of the April number of the Modern Review (of Calcutta) which contains Tagore's attack. Meanwhile you had better enquire for it in England. He had been looking either at

'Appearances' or the Kahn report and had been upset by a comprehending reference to the English & their efforts. 'Mr Dickinson ignores the fact that gifts must be conveyed through sympathy & cannot be imposed by force.' I wrote to the effect that to write thus is to ignore Mr Dickinson—very polite to Tagore was I, but the editor returned my criticism as irrelevant and informed me that you and T. were friends. I might have pushed the matter further, but thought it wouldn't have been much use and that you wouldn't have wished it anyhow.

Have dismissed driver. He was dumb. A villain and will trouble us endlessly yet. Now I will go to the post with the new driver, and if we arrive you will receive this letter, perhaps. But I'll write again soon. Do the same.

Morgan

ALS: KCC

1 Chuprassi: messenger.
2 On Dickinson's *Letters from John Chinaman*, see Letter 156, note 1.

212   To Alice Clara Forster

Hyderabad.   1 December 1921

Well dearest, thanks for your letter, dated Nov. 7th. I am so distressed about the Morgans and wonder how much is true. They are very 'modern' and any arrangement they come to is likely to be by mutual agreement. That Agnew, who wants to get into Parliament, should involve himself in any scandal seems to me unlikely, since it gives such a weapon to the virtuous canvassers upon the other side. It is too too sad about Mrs Morgan. Yes, how happy she was, and how nice she was to me the day I called to say goodbye. Please tell me the actual facts, so far as you can pick them up during your visit. A. H. must be hired to run round.1

Faith-healer may do dear Maggie a little good.2 I hope he won't do her much good for then the improvement certainly won't last. I heard of him as in Calcutta but he has not made much stir.—By the way, dearest, I forgot to say how interested I was in all that you wrote about your visit to Salisbury. I wish that you would have had the nice expensive bedroom at the hotel. What is the use of Poppy sending you little presents on [sic] luxuries if you obstinately refuse to spend them? Masood says sadly "It is the same with my mother—they are alike in that."

I have booked my passage to Port Said—middle of January. C/o Messrs T. Cook Cairo is now my address, which seems nearer Mummy. Hassan evidently thinks I ought to have returned to her in

January, as I said I might, for he has done a most tiresome thing—said he wants to go back to Dewas instead of finishing me up in India. H. H. lent him me for the purpose, however long I stayed, but I have packed him off by this evening's train, as I can't bear any one by me who doesn't want to stop. So very inconvenient. He suited me perfectly, and I thought in my innocence he liked me, when this bomb fell. Never trust a servant to do the thing which is correct! Now I am left with no one, and we are just going on tour again, and I must get some one in a hurry who may steal all my things. I have given Hassan a tip but refused him a certificate. He looks dreadfully ashamed.

The enclosed will amuse you. Look at the dates, look at the distances! I offered to go, this time not in my innocence, for I felt sure that the scramble would fall through, and so it proved. Another wire followed "Deccan tour off."—'*Parcel*', is the old Colonel, of course! I hope that he hasn't had a fit—best thing for him, poor old thing, but H. H. will be upset and have some violent reaction. I have had a letter from Bidwai, but he gives no news of importance. The Colonel has not replied to my letter, or rather letters, for I sent duplicates to Bombay and London.[3]

As regards local news, we continue to have and to solve our little troubles. The Hydaris have come to an arrangement with their neighbours about the wall. The lady of doubtful character has consented to teach the little boys of Hyderabad instead of the little girls.[4] Sir Ali Imam continues to lie dangerously ill opposite, and as soon as he is a little better the Nizam comes and talks to him until he is worse.[5] The head of the Secret Police is accompanying one of the school mistresses to Australia. And so on and so forth. I have been to dinner with Nawab Nizameth Jung, a powerful and rather sinister official.[6] He takes no trouble with most people, but certainly put himself out to be nice to me, and I don't see what he will gain. We dined in his garden, where he is building a 'retreat' in the Classical Style, all the details being copied from the Parthenon, &c. It was a little pedantic, but in good taste. Like most things in India, it was not finished, so we had our dinner in a tent—masses of servants and delicious food, but quite informal; no evening dress and only 4 of us present. I did enjoy it very much. Nizameth knows English perfectly, and has even published a book of verses, very dull and correct in their sentiments and diction. He is an oracular and cultured talker, and his idea of happiness is to exclude reality, which may indicate a guilty conscience. We praised Marcus Aurelius and Epictetus and other celebrated back numbers and stuffed ourselves full of ~~wonderful~~ pilau, also discussing the stars.

My other chief festivity has been a night at Gulbarga. It was the seat of the Bahmani kings before they transferred to Bidar (cont[emporary] with Giotto, so to speak, whereas Bidar is cont.

The Maharaja of Dewas State
Senior, Tukoji Rao III.

The Hill of Devi, the sacred hill
of Dewas.

with the Medici). They did very well to transfer. The people, soil, and most of the architecture at Gulbarga are wretched, but I am glad to have seen it, as I am interested in these Mohammedan kingdoms of the Deccan—the first time I was in India I didn't realise their existence. There is much Persian influence—it is that that makes the work at Bidar and Bijapur so lovely. Now, if I have luck, I shall get during this tour to the Hindu city of Vijjanagar, which they all fought against and finally sat upon.[7]

Masood has a busy day. I must take myself out for a walk now. M[rs] Hydari, always kind, is hunting for a servant.

If this doesn't reach you at Xmas it will on Pop's birthday. Much Much love.

Pop

ALS: KCC

[1] Morgans, Agnew: Abinger neighbours. A. H.: Agnes Hill, Aunt Laura Forster's paid companion.

[2] I.e. Maggie Preston. On the Preston sisters, see Letter 3.

[3] EMF's predecessor, Colonel William Leslie (1861–1943) was feeling possessive about the Maharaja, the gardens, and the 'works' at Dewas and had written EMF an insulting letter; see HD, pp. 89–96. EMF told Florence Barger (13 October 1921. KCC) and H. H. was 'upset both for his own sake and mine, and doesn't want Leslie back, but all most complicated'. EMF anticipated trouble from Jessica Darling, 'who likes the dear old Colonel and will take up the line that he is ill and should be humoured. But sick men shouldn't write such good English. I have seldom read anything more carefully calculated to offend.' To his mother EMF wrote (24 November. KCC): 'What is now occurring at Dewas, Krishna alone knows. . . . O crimini what a muddle! I wish that, if H. H. intended to take up this line, he had cabled at once, but he reached the position gradually, and also delayed to get Malcolm [Darling]'s approbation, which he scarcely succeeded in doing after all. Malcolm says L. is the Soul of Honour, and will leave Dewas at once if he finds he's unwelcome. H. H. says (privately) No, he's a deep one, and will scheme to stop on at Dewas, even if an apology to me is the price: . . . How H. H. will get through the next 6 months from the financial point of view alone, I cannot imagine.' Bidwai: a Court official.

[4] Rt. Hon. Sir Akbar Hydari (1869–1942) came to Hyderabad in 1905 and advanced to become Accountant-General. He led the Hyderabad delegation to the London Round Table Conferences, 1930–2, inspired the founding of Osmania University in 1920, and was its Chancellor from 1925. The family were Masood's friends. They built a thirty-foot wall (with Government money) because new neighbours, strict Moslems, disapproved their relaxed observance of purdah and watched their garden through binoculars. EMF wrote to his mother (12 November 1921. KCC): 'M[rs] H. can't walk two yards without being fixed. I think she ought to stand it, but feelings are different in this land, . . . The strict Mohammedans are in a fury and tears, and the argument that the wall will make their purdah more complete does not appeal to them.' The second row involved Masood's refusal to appoint the lady in question as English Mistress at Mahoobia High School for Girls (see Letter 107).

[5] Sir Syed Ali Imam (1869–1932) was President of the first session of the Muslim League and in 1913 became an Ordinary Member of Council of the Government of India.

[6] Nawab Nizameth Jung: Sir A. Hussain; see Letter 278, note 3.

[7] EMF finally went to Vijayanagar on 15 December; see Letter 213. On 16 December he parted from Masood and proceeded on his own.

213   To Alice Clara Forster

Hyderabad.   20 December 1921

Dearest Mummy
    I returned to find your welcome letter, but will begin by my own
news, which is all pleasant. I have had such a wonderful time. The
Mount Everest explorers speak of visiting places where no white
man has been seen before, but I have had the same experience
without fatigue or expense at Gangávati. The remoteness and the
extent of Indian life are both wonderful. I described our journey
to Gangávati in a letter to Aunt Laura; our official tour ended there,
and very happily for Masood, who had a great ovation not only
from the officials but from the inhabitants. I thought it was mostly
the motor, but no; when we left in a bullock cart, the same crowds
accompanied us, and would have proceeded far into the mountains
but for his exhortations. We started late, because owing to the
rejoicings over the arrival of Education, the driver of the bullocks
was ~~could not be found had got~~ drunk and could not be found. Our
journey was to Vijayanagar, the great ruined city of which you have
heard me speak. Ali Akbar and myself walked for several miles
while Masood slumbered in the cart.[1] It was a solid but very
comfortable edifice, padded inside with good brown leather, and
decorated outside with paintings of cupids and sphinxes in the
Persian style and with Hindu smears of good luck. Over it was an
awning, you climbed in behind by a waggling leather step. One
bullock was large and white and its horns were painted vermilion
and studded with brass at the tip: the other was dark and wizen.
Although the country was perfectly safe, it gave the feeling of
Robbers at every turn, it was so wild and tropical, palms of every
description sticking up at every angle among masses of rock, and
swift canals, the remains of the old irrigation system, rushing by the
side of the track. The crossing of the Tungabhadra took over an
hour. It is the frontier between Hyderabad and British India, a great
rocky stream in a gorge. No boats in our sense of the word, but
immense bowls of wicker work, coated with leather and propelled
by a savage with a paddle. We stepped a-board, or a-saucer,
Masood's foot seemed to go straight through the basket into the
water and I thought we should sink. But we got across, revolving
slowly like the three wise men of Gotham, the bullock-cart followed
in another saucer—an incredible spectacle—then came two more
each towing a swimming bullock, then three more with servants and
luggage. The bullocks, especially the white one with scarlet horns,
were ~~highly~~ affronted at the experience, and stood gazing sadly at
the stream they had crossed and refused to eat. After they had rested
we went on to Vijayanagar.
    This is a wonderful place—a Hindu Empire, wiped out very

suddenly about 400 years ago by its Mohammedan neighbours, whom it had illtreated. The area is a rocky wilderness like Rustall Common on a gigantic scale, or Dartmoor, and between the precipices and boulders, the palaces and temples are fitted in. There were broad streets, too, but these have become rice fields, except the street leading up to the Great Temple of Hampi, which is still in use, like the temple itself; broader than anything we have in London, and still lined with deserted houses and shops. On the one side the Tungabhadra, among stupendous scenery, on the left, a covey of Jain Temples, perched on a long slope of rock like birds, closing the vista, the Great Temple; behind jagged peaks, supporting more shrines and reached by granite stairways. The architecture was often inferior and always ornate, but Mummy would have loved the situations, had she the legs or even the feet to reach them. Oh we were tired. The bullocks could go no further, and we three walked about 6 miles after our arrival, and the next day Ali Akbar and I walked quite 10, with a policeman, stolen from Hyderabad, to carry our books and bananas.[1] The most remarkable work is the Throne Platform a series of terraces carved with camels, elephants, dancing girls, &c[t], and at the top, with views in every direction, a level place where the king used to sit. The Hindus mess up most of their effects, and no doubt there was some ornate and fiddling canopy; but in its present desolation the Platform is wonderful. I may also mention a granite doorway, where the Kings of Vijayanagar were weighed against gold, and the colossal and hideous statue of the Man-Lion-God, with goggle eyes and a seven-headed serpent above him. But you will have done enough sight seeing. The Rest House—inconveniently situated at some distance from these great distances—was itself once a temple. Squatting creatures looked down on us while we ate and in the verandah, where I slept, lay a statue of Vishnu just my own size, with his two wives massaging his legs.

The bullock-cart—also stolen—took us at night to the R[ailwa]y Sta., whence M. and A. A. went east to Hyderabad, and I west for one more day's sightseeing alone. Nussu is excellent—so good that I think he is a spy; there are many in Hyderabad and I know that some of the officials are puzzled by the length of my stay. However, I am very glad to benefit at the expense of the Secret Service Fund. If indeed it does supply servants to globe trotters at less than the market rate, so much the better. My experiences—after reaching civilisation—were uncomfortable, bad food and much dirt, and Nussu was as willing as Hassan and far more competent, buying 14 bananas for 4[d] and carrying my bed endlessly about at night at Guntakal Station, in the search of some place which should be free from pilgrims, mosquitoes, mangy dogs, and the smell of oil. The people at Hyderabad are Telugus—black and thick, but not unattractive; at Gangávati we were among Canarese, many of whom had a wild beauty; at Guntakal I hit a new and most unattractive race, the Madrassi. They shave the front half of their head and greasy locks float behind; or they reverse the idea of the tonsure—i.e. shave all but the crown and in the middle of that, like a snake curled on a mat, lies a pig tail. They speak English in silken tones. Their bodies are weak and thin. Horrid Madrassis! Now the Bengalis, when one gets first hand accounts of them instead of the conventional gossip, seem to be nice—intellectual, imaginative, and manly. I wish I had seen something of them. Nussu and I returned on Sunday. Masood had a cold, but the Hydari girls very kindly met me in a car.—That concludes a most delightful time. I have missed out much and described the rest dully; I'll end by something very dull: a Time Table, so that you may see at a glance what we did.

Dec. 8th Hyderabad to Raichur (rail)
9th Raichur
10th to Lingsagur by car, which we took with us.
11th & 12th Lingsagur
13th to Gangávati by car, as described in letter to Aunt Laura
14th Gangávati
15th to Vijayanagar—car going back empty over 100 miles to Raichur, as roads gave out
16th to Ry sta—where we parted at night, I reaching Banni Koppa morning of
17th and walking to the lonely temple of Ittagi in the dawn; train to Guntakal
18th where I slept, and, travelling all day reached Hyderabad.

Politics here have unexpectedly turned to the worse. The boys at one of the schools never turned up the day the Prince landed.[2] The schoolmaster—so like a subordinate—never reported it to Masood, hoping to hush it up, and now the Police have found it out and—so like the Police—want a list of the boys who didn't come. Next step—all the scholars in Hyderabad will probably refuse to attend when the Prince processes here. The arrests elsewhere in India have exasperated everybody so much. I am very sorry for the authorities—except for those who invited the Prince to come. Now that he has come, they simply don't know what to do. If they do nothing, as at Bombay, there are riots. If they arrest right and left, as at Allahabad, the boycotting becomes more and more spontaneous, and the streets for seven miles are absolutely deserted by the inhabitants when the Prince passes. To the educated Indian, whatever his opinions, this ill-omened visit does seem an impertinence. You can't solve real complicated and ancient troubles by sending out a good-tempered boy; besides, this naive slap-the-back method, though the very thing for our Colonies, scarcely goes down in the East. People talk about his safety—but not about what he *is* or *says* or *does*; all that is ignored. He is just a piece of luggage that must be carried about carefully.—As for Hyderabad, there won't be ~~much~~ *trouble*, but the authorities were expecting enthusiasm and are agitated in consequence.

ALU, incomplete: KCC
[1] Syed Ali Akbar (1891–19??) met EMF in Cambridge in 1913.
[2] The Prince of Wales visited India 17 November–30 December 1921.

214   To Alice Clara Forster

P.&O.S.N.Co.   S.S.Kaisar i Hind
Red Sea.   19 January 1922

Dearest Mother

The Red Sea is its usual brilliant blue, rather rough, and quite cool. It always treats me thus. The voyage is unusually pleasant, few on board and they nice. I haven't much to say about it, in fact! I'll go back to Hyderabad. I told you, I think, of my foolish abandonment of Ajanta—I could quite well have gone and the last few days a frightful and upsetting intrigue against Masood broke out—I am writing to Lady Morison about it—in which I felt to be and could be of no help.[1] I was glad to see Sajjad however. I should have missed him otherwise. I met him at the Station and took him for a drive and walk next day. Poor fellow, he felt very low, and remarked that no Indian ought to go to England, too unsettling. When he arrived, he was whisked off to see a non-cooperative friend who was just going to prison, in the custody of another friend, a policeman. The three bewailed the times to one another, then Sajjad proceeded to the house of his brothers, where Abou Saeed lies sick.[2] Mess awful, medicine bottles &[ct] trailing, Abou Saeed's lip swollen till it touches his chin owing to incompetent treatment, his wife squatting grubbily on the floor, his child grubby and talking bad Hindustani with the servants, and while Sajjad, all spick and span, was conferring with the invalid, the younger brothers dashed at his boxes and routed out every secret place. "The custom officers were not nearly so searching—I had forgotten that Oriental family life was like this." In addition to the squalor at home, he has put himself wrong with Masood, to whom he had written an injudicious letter, asking for a specially high salary as a start because he is a friend. Masood furious and Abou Saeed makes matters worse by adopting a death bed tone "Oh help our brother in this our hour of misery" &[ct], when every one knows that his lip will be right in a few days. Masood says "This kind of thing makes social intercourse impossible" and scarcely thanked Sajjad for a pair of hair brushes brought from England, as he felt they were a bribe. S. has been excessively foolish. M., though he would give away all his personal possessions to friends, is not one to advance them at the expense of the public services. I have been old grandpa and probably helpful—can anyway have made the situation no worse.

Masood and the Hydaris saw me off. The latter have been so kind, Mʳˢ Hydari especially. She is serious and a little alarming, but a very nice woman with great character. Old Hydari is an able and honest official but pushful and inconsiderate and his poor wife gets the worst of both worlds, misses the peace of the Harem and doesn't gain in compensation the position of a European hostess. I left garlanded and be-nosegayed, and with a luncheon basket that lasted me and Nussu two days. Got to Bombay the morning of the 12ᵗʰ, where Camar and Rafi, two nice good boys, met me with a car—they are nephews of H.'s. In the afternoon we went to Elephanta in a sailing boat, a lovely expedition, and the sculptures though few in number very fine.³ The 13ᵗʰ I lunched with Mary Goodall, and with Camar in car afterwards to see his country estate about 10 miles out of Bombay, a desolate but lovely place.⁴ The morning of the 14ᵗʰ I sailed. The two boys saw me off, and would have been helpful had there been need, but all was easy and comfortable. Nussu perfect to the last, and I continue to find evidences of his care and prevision in my luggage. He has thought out every thing I could require for the voyage, and packed in logical order. It is well I didn't have him longer, he would have made me more of a fool than I am. I gave him a flaming certificate. He was unattractive externally—a coarse low face, but not vulgar in any of his ways, and massaged me with diligence and skill. My left elbow is still rather stiffer than formerly, but on the improve. My right wrist is all right.

I will leave this letter and finish it in a day or two, perhaps on your birthday.

Suez Canal.   22 January 1922

Yes! Oh how I wish you could have been with me—for all except the steps which always come into my mind when I think of Mummy. I brought out your photograph, which is now in Bai Sahiba's [sic] silver frame, and I set it up on the upper berth where I could see it and it could see Egypt.⁵ The atmosphere, temperature and colours have been so exquisite and fresh; compared to India, where all is aged and complex, it is like a world in its morning. I always did argue Suez is beautiful, and today it agreed with me, and hour after hour we have stølen through white desert, edged with pale pink or purple hills. We reach Port Said a day earlier than expected so I don't know whether Mohammed, who says he will meet me, will succeed. I shall settle plans as soon as I get my letters at Cairo. I am anxious to see something of Egyptians, so don't want to get entangled in Alexandria too much, except of course—always excepting!—dear Ludolf, and would also like to stay a day or two with Irene—will easily discover her and will tell her that your letter to her was returned to you.

This reminds me—on November 11 I drew a cheque for £6-6-9 in favour of Harper and sent it to you for him—you don't mention receiving it, and I know that one, probably two, of my letters to you have been lost. If cheque didn't reach, would Mummy very kindly write to H. explaining circumstances and remit him the amount, so that I may not be arrested by the police when I land on Albion's shore.

I shall stop 3 weeks or a month in Egypt if all is well in England, and shall come round by sea unless there is reason for the contrary, since coming through France would cost much extra, and I want, further, to keep with my luggage and see it through the English customs.

No word of farewell from sweet H. H. He has not done the thing that is correct, quite. He said he should see me off at Bombay if possible—I said "Oh don't do that" but he took no notice of me at all, though I continued to wire and write to him lovingly—and shall continue, for his silence means nothing. Did the photographs arrive? I have duplicates if they didn't, but you would prefer those he inscribed for you, of course.

I think that's all—I will try to get someone to post these in England, for there is no inserting them into the mail bags on board. Shuttleworth is ~~packing~~ married; a long story and a strange one: I know and like the lady.[6] They are to settle down at Cheltenham where his work goes well. I heard the news just before leaving Bombay.

Dinner—my last on board. The voyage has been unusually pleasant, and owing to the kindness of the Purser I have had a charming cabin all to myself. I was put into an inner one at first, which contained no porthole, ~~but~~ and an engine driver,—pleasant old man, but he seemed to have brought in a good deal of his engine, and he smoked cigars without stopping, so I took steps at once.

Goodbye my darling birthday one. I am very anxious for your news, your visit to Aunt Laura, how Mr Alford is, &^ct. I see it has been v. cold in England.

Your Pop

ALS: KCC

[1] The Ajanta Caves, near Jalgaon, in Aurangabad District, comprise Buddhist monasteries (*viharas*) and worship chambers (*chaityas*) and are noted for their wall paintings illustrating the life of the Buddha. The older caves probably date from the first to the third centuries, the second group from the sixth or seventh. On the Morisons, see Letter 100; on Masood's career, see Letter 64.

[2] On the Mirza brothers, Ahmed, Sajjad, and Abu Saeed, see Letter 92 and *HD*, e.g. pp. xxx–xxxi.

3 Elephanta: cave temples, probably dating from the eighth century, celebrating the god Shiva, on an island in Bombay harbour.
4 Mary and Charles Goodall: relations of Josie Darling, see Letter 102.
5 Bai Saheba: wife of H. H.
6 L. H. C. Shuttleworth: EMF's friend from the 1912–13 Indian trip, see Letter 149.

215 To Florence Barger

Alexandria.   28 January 1922

Dearest Florence

Thank you for your letter; my news in return is very sad—I have been writing a certain amount of it to mother. Mohammed collapsed under consumption about a fortnight before I landed, and though he is rallying from this particular attack I know that I see him for the last time. I stopped two days at Mansourah with him as soon as I got the news at Port Said, and may take him to Helouan near Cairo next week, if he has strength to travel. The horror of it makes him irritable and hard—it is an unhappy time for me in the local daily sense, but I am thankful to be on the spot since my money and even presence may be of use, and Ludolf has taken a slight and natural interest in my stray references which may be useful in the future; I mean he may remit monthly allowances for me and so partly solve my great need in this country—an agent. I don't want to give M. a sum down, as the doctors would simply take it at once from him, they are quacks and robbers, and pump tubes of useless stuff into his poor little arm. Gamila is A1. He speaks of and to her so sweetly, but she is no good at Helouan, of course.

I tell you as always what is most in my heart. He was mentioning you and the children the other day. If you care to write a line it would be appreciated. I have suggested to mother that she should. <Moh. el Adl, Mit Hadar, Haret Nefada, Mansourah.>

I am quite well and keeping my head. I don't expect to stop in the country long. The public situation is interesting and tragic.[1]

Furness and Mrs Borchgrevink, all animation, have just looked over the garden wall from their horses. F. asked me to stop with him at Cairo, she here; I have refused both. I am for the moment with the Ludolfs.[2]

Best love and I know that without hearing from you I have yours. These things are not sad really—there is incidentally some tears and indignation, but neither form part of the central truth. You may have to help me not to be queer, as you have helped Nancy, but my present belief is that I shall come quietly through.[3] I don't think he'll live as he has every bally symptom, but remember (if you write) that he is slightly more hopeful than I am, and not perfectly sure that it is consumption.

Love and prosperity to all

$\mathcal{M}$organ.

ALS: KCC

[1] Egypt was in a state of barely suppressed rebellion. See Letter 203, note 3 and Letter 205, note 1.

[2] In a lighter moment during this visit, EMF encountered his former landlady: 'Ludolf and I were walking aimlessly near here the day after my arrival when in a depression below the road, out of the lower story of a house, I saw a grey haired lady in spectacles leaning. I peeped, she peeped, I looked again, so did she. I said to L. 'I believe it's Irene', he said it wasn't, however I ventured the name and the head immediately uttered a piercing shriek and vanished into the interior of the building—it couldn't get out of the window because it was barred, or it would have. Then the noise was heard coming round the house, up a flight of steps—and then oh such a scene. She kissed my hand, I kissed hers, heaven was invoked, she said I was her son, we both nearly cried, then down we went—L. following all sympathy and amusement—and had coffee and cognac and cocoa-nut jam' (to ACF, 2 February 1922. KCC).

[3] Perhaps Nancy Catty: see Letter 251, note 5.

216   To Florence Barger

Helouan.[1]   11 February 1922

Dearest Florence

How wonderful money is, I said to myself, when the midday train drew up and out got Gamila carrying her baby and Ferida carrying her baby and Amin carrying a mountain of strange objects on his head. But for me they would never come, nor be established peaceably with Mohammed in a house about 100 yds. from where I write. I don't wonder people grow purse proud. It is a curious feeling. Ferida is a humble relative, Amin her even humbler little boy, a hideous child with a face like a tea pot and dressed in a pink nightgown and a purple cap and no more. They managed the journey not unsuccessfully. The train left Mansurah at 6.0 A. M. so they went to the station at 1.0. The porters told them 'too early' so they returned to the house and came at 4.0 again. At Cairo Ferida, who, owing to her low position, is accustomed to facing life and men, acted with some spirit and chartered a donkey cart which took them across to the station for Helouan. Where they failed was in leaving masses of things behind—cooking utensils, glasses, plates, knives, a great coat, a mosquito net, &[ct], all of which they were supposed to bring. Indeed no one knows what Amin did carry on his head. Mohammed angry, since same will have to be supplied here from shops. I had supper with them—not bad though floor was paved with babies. Gamila being out of Mansurah I am allowed to see her—she is such a dear; he is indeed lucky and he deserves a little luck.[2] Ferida any one may see. She goes back to Mansurah on Monday, but Amin stops to fetch and carry.

I thought you would like these scraps and they belong to a part of my life with which I particularly connect you and which is now closing. I don't feel upset at the moment of writing or even sad. I might if I had the least hope. My only anxiety is that he may suffer pain: the doctor only said "not necessarily." I stop on in this hotel, where he was with me for five days. I rather wish they had moved me into a single room as his empty bed faces me. Now I'll send this off, with much love. Your lost letter has not turned up yet.

Morgan

ALS: KCC

[1] In January 1922 EMF took Mohammed to the leading Cairo doctor, who pronounced his tuberculosis advanced and his case hopeless. EMF took him to Heulouan, a Nile health-resort, and found furnished lodgings where Mohammed's wife Gamila and their child joined him; see *EMF*, II, 103–4.

[2] Muslim custom would ordinarily forbid Gamila to show her face in public or before her husband's bachelor friends.

217 To Florence Barger

P.&O.S.N.Co.   S.S. Delta
25 February 1922.   Near Corsica

Dearest Florence,
I liked Mohammed's letter and hope you will. Yours to him incidentally gave me a happy day for he was in radiant spirits, and so charming and talkative. I am sure that I could have lived with him had he been in occupation and good health. I find him such a jolly companion, all else apart. He must be a lively talker in his own language: even in English, entertaining proverbs and anecdotes come lumbering out. He saw me off at Cairo. As we drove up to the station he interrupted my remarks (about a parcel!) and said "Don't let us talk of anything except you will see Mother soon, my respects to her, then you will see Mrs Barger, my respects to her, you will see Bennett. . . ." He sat by me in the R[ailwa]y carriage and said "My love to you there is nothing else to say" which is exactly the truth. I did not think him so well. I trust that the end will come without suffering poor dear little fellow. His face is unchanged. In the house he wears a yellow velvet cap, shaped rather like Goldie's, and folds his body up as only an Oriental can, so that the intelligent beautiful head seems to be resting on a pyramid of clothes. Ah me—but everything is bearable, it is the betrayal from within that wears away one's soul and I have been spared that. Happiness in the ordinary sense is not what one needs in life, though one is right to aim at it. The true satisfaction is to come through and see those whom one loves come through.

I should be home about March 5th. This will be posted at Marseilles.

Morgan.

TTr supplied by Mollie Barger

218   To J. R. Ackerley[1]

Harnham, Monument Green, Weybridge
26 April 1922

Dear Ackerly [sic],

I should have met you last week in town but have done so in the London Mercury instead. I wish it wasn't so hard to praise intelligently. Apart from liking your poem, what I like in your poem is its combination of the reminiscent and the dramatic—I mean one knows about it all in the opening lines, and yet it developes with the cleanness and unexpectedness of a play. Poe brings off the same combination in Ulalume—(so much so that he imposes on his readers a vision that verges on bunkum)—and I think indeed that this particular quality must lie very near the secret of poetry.[2] Without drama, a poem's a museum, without reminiscence it isn't a poem.

Reminiscence was probably the wrong word, because I want to use it again in another sense—i.e. in relation to your subject matter. This business of remembering a past incident. The horror, beauty, depth, emotional and mental insecurity, that is thus introduced into our lives, and that we can neither avoid nor recall. I have been reading Proust who knows all about it too and like you rejects the ordinary explanation. "Je trouve très raisonnable" he remarks, "la croyance celtique que les âmes de ceux que nous avons perdus sont captives dans quelque être inférieur dans une bête &ct...—perdues en effet pour nous jusqu'au jour, qui pour beaucoup ne vient jamais, où nous nous trouvons passer près de l'arbre, entrer en possession de l'objet qui est leur prison. Alors elles tressaillent, nous appellent, et sitôt que nous les avons reconnues, l'enchantement est brisé. Delivrées pas [sic] nous, elles ont vaincu la mort, et reviennent vivre avec nous."[3] It's just the same, he goes on to say, with our past; it's a chance whether we happen to hit upon the object that recalls it. I don't know whether you and Proust are right in your explanations. "Out of death lead no ways" is more probably the fact. But being right is of little importance. What you have done is to drive home the strangeness of a creature who is apparently allowed neither to remember nor to forget and who sees in the stream of his daily life, piteously disordered, the recurrence of something that was once beautiful and that passes as inevitably away now as it did then.[4] No—of course you don't quite do this, because your poem ends in unalloyed remembrance, if such a condition exists: but I don't suppose that you—i.e. the narrator—supposes that the remembrance is permanent. The moment a memory is registered by the intellect is its last moment.

I'm afraid the above is too long. I'd better just have thanked you for the pleasure you gave me, and stopped. But your poem set me feeling about, and thinking.[5]

Yours sincerely
EMForster.

ALS: HRC

[1] Joe Randolph Ackerley (1896–1967) was the son of Roger Ackerley, a director of Elder and Fyffes, the banana importers. As a young officer Joe was captured on the Western Front and interned in Switzerland. After the war he went to Cambridge University, then for some years lived on an allowance from his father while trying to write. He met EMF through the latter's unsolicited letter of praise for the poem 'Ghosts' (*The London Mercury*, 5 [1922], 568–73). A lasting friendship began, initially with much hero-worship on Ackerley's part, and for many years he was EMF's closest London friend. With EMF's assistance, he went in 1923–4 as private secretary to the Maharaja of Chhatarpur, an experience later evoked in his memoir *Hindoo Holiday* (1932). In 1928 he became a BBC Talks producer and from 1935 to 1959 was literary editor of *The Listener*. His father's death in 1929 brought Ackerley, his mother, and his sister Nancy the astonishing news that Roger had been supporting a second family, only a few miles from their Richmond home. Joe Ackerley, notably charming and amusing, had a promiscuous and disaster-strewn homosexual love-life. In later years he developed an obsessive attachment to an Alsatian bitch Queenie and grew somewhat misanthropic.
[2] Poe's 'Ulalume' ([1847–9]) is the expression of a lover visiting the beloved's tomb on the anniversary of her death.
[3] See Marcel Proust, *Du côté de chez Swann* (Pléiade Edition), I, 44.
[4] 'Out ... ways': see Thomas Lovell Beddoes, 'Dream-Pedlary': ' ... There are no ghosts to raise;/Out of death lead no ways;/Vain is the call.' In his *Works*, ed. A. W. Donner, pp. 110–11.
[5] In a note to this letter (TTr. HRC) Ackerley called this poem 'a not very worthy midwife [to their friendship], I fear. Years later I made an attempt to iron out some of its many and manifest crudities, ...'. See *Poems of Our Time 1900–1942*, comp. Richard Church and M. M. Bozman, pp. 182–5.

219   To Goldsworthy Lowes Dickinson

West Hackhurst, Abinger Hammer, Dorking
8 May 1922

My dear Goldie,
I go to Cambridge Sat[urday]. You said kindly that you would write about your rooms. I am so depressed that you won't be there, although I had no reason to think that you would be when I decided to go. I hope Lyme Regis'll be a success.[1] If convenient, you might call at Madeira Cottage and ask whether (from June onward) they have rooms in case I get my mother to come for a fortnight. Do you remember whether the bed in the room you occupied is soft? I can hardly ask you to go upstairs and punch it, yet the information would be welcome, since a bed of normal hardness now makes my mother ill: she gives no "trouble" in other ways.

Not to engage rooms of course, only to approfondir, as we call it here.

I hope you feel more—well you know what I mean; 'happy' is a silly word. I do, or at all events more master of my surroundings and time. I have actually written a little. It is a curious experience. Sometimes I am pleased, at others so bored that I could spit on the paper instead of inking it. I am bored not only by my creative impotence, but by the tiresomeness and conventionalities of fiction-form: e.g. the convention that one must view the action through the mind of one of the characters; and say of the others "perhaps they thought", or at all events adopt their view-point for a moment only. If you can pretend you can get inside one character, why not pretend it about all the characters? I see why. The illusion of life may vanish, and the creator degenerate into the showman. Yet some change of the sort must be made[.] The studied ignorance of novelists grows wearisome. They must drop it. Also they must recapture their interest in death, not that they ever had it much, but the Middle Ages had it, and the time for re[-]examination is overdue. I can't make out what I feel <about death> Mohammed is dying yet I don't care a damn so far. My mother's death would probably shatter me, but probably because of the alteration caused in my habits. All this needs mopping up by the novelists, and probably entails reconsideration of love and affection also, and fewer solemn powwows about the developements of character.

So you see I am more 'occupied' than usual and will be glad, though I can't tell yet whether my cloud of little thoughts has more than a defensive value. It's such a drawback having no message to give to the world, or knowing it won't listen to your message which comes to the same. There lies my aunt upstairs, entertaining and announcing the most ridiculous opinions and the most non-existent facts, and consequently convinced that she is an important figure. She is particularly remarkable about Ireland: in order to emphasise her right to condemn Sinn Fein she has taken to talk with a brogue. Mʳˢ Litchfield agrees with her, but sticks to pure English, her line being that, thank goodness, she hasn't a drop of Irish blood in her body, and has never set foot in the island, whereas Aunt Laura went to stop with a clergyman uncle when she was seventeen—a visit hitherto brief, but recently expanding into mystic dimensions. ("I ran in out [sic] of the cabins and so learnt what the Irish really feel, which Henrietta Litchfield with her Darwin downrightness cannot of course do").[2] Dear me, what odd fish we are, and how can we suppose that even the greatest of our catastrophes have a spiritual accompaniment of trumpets or violins. Celestial pom-pomming must also be dropped: in fact most of the problems of the future now present themselves to me as droppings rather than achievements, and whether the denuded little men who would result will sustain themselves sufficiently by laughing at each other, I can't be sure. It is so difficult to conceive of a rational being who will think it worth while to remain alive. Even if we try to acquire such opinions as are true, we end by believing them true because we have acquired them;

the instinct for self-preservation continually plays this trick upon us. I wonder whether science will ever discover anything about human nature that can be endorsed by writers and daily-livers (discoveries that ~~can't be~~ aren't endorsed and are ~~only~~ merely quoted aren't of course the least ~~good~~ use). We might get along a little if that happens.

Yours ever   E M F

Your card this morning: this incidentally answers it.

ALS: KCC

[1] EMF and Dickinson spent holidays there in 1919 and 1921.
[2] On Aunt Laura Forster's friend Henrietta Emma Litchfield, Charles Darwin's daughter and the Aunt Etty of Gwen Raverat's *Period Piece*, see Letter 28. Clergyman uncle: James William Forster (1784–1861), Archdeacon of Aghadoe, 1834–61, and Vicar-General of Limerick, 1823–61.

220   To Alice Clara Forster

The Mill House,   Tidmarsh, Pangbourne[1]
Reading Sta[tion].   29 May 1922

Journey very comfortable.
Dearest—Thanks for the 2 forwardings. I hope all goes well. The country has been exquisite as you may imagine—hedges and bushes so white with may as almost to alarm, and laburnum all along the banks of the Thames. Yesterday we motored to Garsington in response to a wire; except the Woolfs whom we had to leave behind and conceal because they had already refused a week-end invitation there on the ground of Virginia's health. Cars, many of them coronetted, blocked the entrance and a procession was just leaving, headed by Princess Bibesco.[2] Lady O. in bright yellow satin and a picture hat swam about with cries of joy and farewell, ~~and Tomlinson, Desmond and his wife therefore~~ and Lord David Cecil stayed a little longer on my account—at least so I was understood to understand.[3] He was a rabbity nervous undergraduate, very intelligent and polite. We got on quite well and he vows he will come out next Sunday for further conversation. Then Lady O. ~~detached me~~ shunted me on to another undergraduate, neither as high born nor as nice as the Lord, being an Alexandrian Jew who knew Cavafy.[4] They really are remarkable, those Sunday gatherings. The whole company had been bathing in the pond. Tomlinson and Desmond, both very dowdy, were there, also Desmond's wife, who like Tomlinson is deaf. Lady O. still dreads my visit, but I cannot put it off and will not! Wyndham Lewis is coming and she is surer than ever he isn't nice. Why ask such?[5]
    Tidmarsh very pleasant—lovely walk behind, hitherto concealed from me, and quite altering the capabilities of the country. Nice

young man named Brennan. Partridge and his wife also friendly & young.[6]

Will write again from Cheltenham. Love to Gerry.[7]

Pop.

ALS: KCC

[1] Lytton Strachey's home, near Oxford and near Garsington Manor, home of Lady Ottoline and Philip Morrell; on her role as patron of the arts, see Letter 80.

[2] Princess Marthe Bibesco (1887–1945), Rumanian-born novelist and biographer, friend of Proust. She was often in England in the 1920s.

[3] Henry Major Tomlinson (1873–1958), novelist, journalist, and travel essayist; literary editor, *The Nation and The Athenaeum*, 1917–23. Mary Warre Cornish (died 1952) was the wife of critic and editor Desmond MacCarthy. Lord David Cecil (1902–   ), younger son of the 4th Marquis of Salisbury; critic and biographer, and Goldsmiths' Professor of English Literature at Oxford, 1948–69.

[4] The friend of Cavafy is unidentified.

[5] EMF first met Wyndham Lewis in 1914; see Letter 134. Lady Ottoline had given EMF a choice of seeing either T. S. Eliot or Lewis. For his reply (13 May 1922. HRC) see *EMF*, II, 109–10.

[6] Gerald Brenan (1894–   ), historian and author of books about Spain, figures prominently in the complex relations among Strachey, his friend Ralph Partridge (1894–1960), and Dora Carrington (1892–1932), painter, companion to Strachey, and wife to Partridge.

[7] Shuttleworth became a schoolmaster at Cheltenham College (see Letter 149). Gerry: EMF's cousin Gerald Whichelo.

221   To Alice Clara Forster

The Manor House, Garsington, Oxford
4 June 1922

Dearest Mummy—I hope all goes well; was expecting letter from you here. Am having v. amusing time. I counted 30 people to tea yesterday and think there were more. David Cecil came to lunch—he is very pleasant and friendly, part of the aristocratic make up no doubt, but I prefer it to Mrs Buller's variety.[1] The dreaded Wyndham Lewis has worked out rather funnily. He is a curious mixture of insolence and nervousness, has been quite agreeable to me, and when Lady O. expected us both to be figuring separately at the tea-party drew me off for a walk. So we did cause her anxiety but not of the kind she ~~expected~~ anticipated. 'So like life' she murmured sadly. Goertler, another painter, is also of the party—a little East end Jew, very amusing and clever, exactly like a street boy who makes faces at the people in carriages and imitates their gestures.[2] He and W. L. were frightened of, and frightened, the high-born undergraduates, who motored out, gaping and undulating, from Oxford. Today the festivities continue, but on a smaller and more refined scale. Massingham has arrived and since Lewis has quarrelled with him that makes more trouble, and poor Lady O. drifts about wondering what will happen, wishes she could *understand* people, wishes they were more simple &^ct, clad the meantime herself in elaborate floating dresses of all the colours of the rainbow.[3] However all minor worries should vanish if M[r] Asquith should arrive this afternoon; it will give us something to think about, that will.[4] I have quite enjoyed myself. The house and garden are both exquisite in this lovely weather. I sit near the pond: croquet on the terrace above me: large happy horses among buttercups behind.

I had a pleasant time with the Gilletts.[5] We rowed down the river on Sat. then I walked up to Garsington—about 3 miles. Beautiful country, except for the smell, as I had to cross the sewage farm—like that awful walk near Tunbridge Wells. I arrived for dinner and exchanged suspicious and hostile stares with the other guests, but all that has thawed. There is also an old gentleman here, named M[r] Taylor, who never speaks and when he does inaudibly—a friend and patron of Goertler's, who frisks around him with exhortations of 'pipe up Walter, they can't hear you' which M[r] Taylor seems to like.[6] Julian (the Morrells' daughter) is sometimes a young lady talking highly about Thomas Hardy, sometimes a shattered child: rather pathetic.[7] She and her Ma don't get on too well. This morning old M[r] T. has given her a coral necklace and she is skipping about very happy.

You will have had enough of this silly-ish news. I will be in at 8.0. Tuesday *unless* I wire. Hope you have survived Phil.[8] Much love to dear Mummy from her Pop who longs to see her again and has often thought of her.

ALS: KCC

[1] Mrs Buller is unidentified.

[2] Mark Gertler (1891–1939) studied at the Slade School, 1909–10, and was for a time a member of the London Group.

[3] Henry William Massingham (1860–1924), liberal journalist, edited *The Nation*, 1907–23. As with so many of Lewis's quarrels, the origins of this one are obscure.

[4] Herbert Henry Asquith (1852–1928), Home Secretary, 1892–3; Chancellor of the Exchequer, 1906–8; and Liberal Prime Minister, 1908–16, responsible for the Parliament Act of 1911, which limited the power of the House of Lords.

[5] On EMF's friend Arthur Gillett, see Letter 62.

[6] Walter Taylor (1860–1943), himself a water-colourist, and a collector, met Gertler in 1919 and became his friend and patron. He lived in Brighton and often took Gertler abroad as his guest. Like Brenan, Gertler was long (but vainly) in love with Dora Carrington.

[7] Julian Morrell (1906–) became Mrs Igor Vinogradoff.

[8] Philip Whichelo (1864–1948), EMF's uncle.

222 To Alice Clara Forster

1917 Club, 4 Gerrard Street [London] W. 1
Tuesday   [early June 1922?]

Dearest Mummy
Poppy is safely arrived, and now he is going to write a disagreeable letter. He wants to ask Mummy to try not to interfere

with him so much. If he wants to take his clock to London, let him take it,—if he doesn't want to put little books into an envelope, don't put them back into it,—if he wants to give away his great coat, let him—if he loses his glove, accept the fact, &ct.—Each thing is so trivial by itself that it is absurd to mention it, but they all add up into a loss of independence.—I expect that if I was working properly I should see it all in ~~true~~ truer proportion, and should not make this tiresome fuss, but as it is, the [word inked out and illegible] criticisms, and still more the prohibitions, are rather on my mind.

Have just been having an Egyptian to tea, and am going on now to [Roger] Fry. I shall be back to-morrow night unless I wire to the contrary. Have taken my watch to the Haymarket Stores. Mainspring broken, alas. I wonder it went as well as it did. Have given myself a present—Hardy's Poems—and am ~~trying~~ going to try to make him write in it.[1]

> Ever love as ever from
> Poppy

ALS: KCC

[1] If the Hardy volume referred to is his *Late Lyrics and Earlier*, published in the first week of June, the year could be 1922. Cf. Letter 223. EMF later added to this letter the note 'Poppy kicks'.

223   To Alice Clara Forster

King's Arms, Dorchester.   19 July 1922

Dearest,

Brighstone ended well—I managed to call on Rev. Silver Tuesday morning; he had called Monday aft. on me but we were walking over the downs to Carisbrooke.[1] I thought him nice & sensitive & intelligent—and of course the visit gave satisfaction at the cottage. I did a little gardening for Maggie Monday and brought eggs and black currants Tuesday; having taken two lots of mushrooms previously. They and D. appreciated each other as well as can be expected: no hitches, I fancy.

I feel sleepy. The Carisbrooke walk Monday and the journey yesterday tired me. Miss Hawker drove us to Newport ("Take the greatest care of them, Maggie" said K. as we went off); crossed Cowes–Southampton, rather uncomfortable, with walks & bother with luggage each end. I changed again at Bournemouth reaching Dorchester 5.45. Mrs Hardy had called at the hotel Monday on the chance of my having arrived. I go there to tea in about ½ hour and will leave this letter open until I return. I went to a *Circus* last night; Lord John Sanger: an enormous oval tent, rather beautiful effects of light.[2] I only stopped an hour. This morning, since it was fine, I walked out to Maiden Castle—the greatest earthwork, I believe, in England, a most wonderful place, defended by three tremendous ramparts, &ᶜᵗ, now all solitude and grass.[3]

Wire was from Lady Colefax, whom I met and disliked at the MacCarthys'. I have had a letter too, and am sending a lying excuse.[4] I must take to lying more!

Simple, almost dull tea at the Hardys.—nice food and straggling talk. I am to lunch there to-morrow "but the cook only came to day I don't know what it will be like" says Mʳˢ H. gloomily, and then we proceed to a performance of Midsummer Night's Dream in the Rectory garden, of which likewise little is expected. T. H. showed me the graves of his pets, all overgrown with ivy, their names on the head stones. Such a dolorous muddle. "This is Snowbell—she was run over by a train...this is Pella, the same thing happened to her...this is Kitkin, she was cut clean in two, clean in two— — —" "How is it that so many of your cats have been run over, Mʳ Hardy? Is the railway near?"—"Not at all near, not at all near— —I don't know how it is. But of course we have only buried here those pets whose bodies were recovered. Many were never seen again." I could scarcely keep grave—it was so like a caricature of his own novels or poems. We stumbled about in the ivy and squeezed between the spindly trees over "graves of ancient Romans" he informed me; "sometimes we are obliged to disturb one." He seemed cheerful, his main dread being interviewers, American ladies, and the charabancs that whirr past while the conductor shouts "Ome of Thomas 'Ardy, Novelist." He went in a char a banc once, but "I didn't much like it—I was the last to mount and had to sit at the back and was thrown up and down most uncomfortably."—Thus the visit wore away, though he talked every now and then about his books: a sign of favour, I believe—I never pressed him to it. They were both very pleasant and friendly.

I will wire when I come—Saturday morning trains seem best; I can get one at 12.0. which will give me time to rest before the Play—so looking forward to it.

ALU: KCC

[1] EMF had been visiting the Preston sisters on the Isle of Wight. The Rev. Ernest Wollaston Silver (1862–1935) was Rector of St Mary Virgin, Brighstone, 1903–33.

[2] 'Lord George' Sanger (1825–1911) and his brother John had been proprietors of circuses and travelling shows since 1848.

[3] Maiden Castle, an impressive set of earthworks near Dorchester, is the site of Neolithic and Iron Age remains and was a principal town before the Roman occupation.

[4] Lady Sibyl Colefax (1874–1950), wife of the barrister Sir Arthur Colefax (1866–1936), was a tireless and resourceful London hostess.

224   To Virginia Woolf

[N. p.]   24 October 1922

Dear Virginia,

I like *Jacob's Room* and am sure it is good. You have clean cut away the difficulties that so bother me and that I feared in *Night & Day* were gaining on you—all those Blue Books of the interior and exterior life of the various characters—their spiritual development, income, social positions, etc. etc.[1] The danger is that when cut away these detach with them something that ought to remain—at least according to my notion of a novel, namely the reader's interest in at least one of the characters as a character—if that goes we merely swing about among blobs of amusement or pathos. You keep this interest in Jacob. This I find a tremendous achievement—the greatest in the book and the making of the book. I don't yet understand how, with your method, you managed it, but of course am reading the book again. Have only just finished it; and am confused by wondering what developments, both of style and form, might come out of it, which is of course outside the present point. The book was quite long enough—! this means not what it looks, but that some of your odd new instruments gave hints of scratches and grinds towards the end. e.g. the Proper Nomenclature. Having once taken such an instrument up you couldn't possibly lay it down, its occasional application to the surface was imperative. This is a minor point though, for the damage done by the scratches is too little to count. They disappear in the general liberation.—One very important thing is that most of the book is seen through happiness; you have got quite clear from the sensitive sorrower whom novelists cadge up to as the easiest medium for observations.

I will now say no more except that my favourite pages are 63–4. I will return Percy Lubbock next week.[2]

A muddle of plans seems ahead. I think I won't come to your old ladies this early November.[3] But I should like to, later. You may wear my pyjamas until I arrive.

I much enjoyed my visit.

Thank you very much for giving me the book. I do think it an amazing success, and it's full of beauty, indeed is beautiful.

Morgan

ALS: Berg

[1] Woolf, *Jacob's Room*, published 27 October 1922. *Night and Day* appeared in 1919.
[2] Lubbock, *The Craft of Fiction* (1921); cf. Woolf, *Letters*, III, 437.
[3] The 'old ladies' are almost certainly a reference to the Women's Co-operative Guild at Richmond.

225   To A. E. Housman

[N. p.]   22 February 1923

Dear Professor Housman,

I wish to thank you for publishing 'Last Poems'. When I read your other book, it promptly crossed the line that divides a book from a companion, and now, after twenty years, I have repeated my luck.[1] I am very grateful indeed to you—glad also that your genius has been recognised, but that is not why I am writing. Indeed I haven't anything to say at all—only thankfulness from the bottom of my heart and the wish that you may be happy.

We met once, but you will not remember me, and I have left out my address in order to preclude any question of a reply to this.[2]

Yours truly
EMForster.

ALS: Bryn Mawr College, Seymour Adelman Collection

[1] Housman's *Last Poems*, published in 1922; his 'other book': *A Shropshire Lad* (1896). Cf. *EMF*, I, 152–3. Housman (1859–1936) became Professor of Latin at Cambridge in 1911.
[2] They met at dinner at Harry Norton's house in Cambridge, Dickinson and Fry being also present: date uncertain. Housman replied (25 February 1923) and EMF stuck his friendly letter into his copy of *Last Poems* (KCC).

226   To J. R. Ackerley

Cheltenham.[1]   9 March 1923

Dear Ackerley

This is exciting and to discuss him & it with you is *both an interest and a pleasure*—do ram that into your head.[2] To discuss you & it with *him* is *not*. Ha capito?[3] Will you ring up Hogarth House on Tuesday about 9.0 A. M. on the chance of my being there?[4] It would be good to have a talk before you write to him—mail is not till Thursday.

Meanwhile I scribble a few notes.

I take back my advice to you to demand return fare in advance. I think it would create a bad impression—would look too much what it is in fact. Ask for £100 in advance (2nd class single P. & O. is or was about £66). The balance from your travelling expenses to count as advance of salary. Ask for Rs 400 per month and all found—i.e. full board & lodging, fully furnished house, conveyance & servants—with the exception of your personal servant (bearer) whom you had better engage & pay yourself, as he will then be ~~under your~~ wholly under your thumb. Agree for one year—at the end of which either party may terminate agreement. If he sacks you, he pays your fare back. If it's you who want to leave him, I think you might pay your own fare and I've put your salary at Rs 400 instead of Rs 300 so that it may accumulate out of the difference. <I had Rs 300 all found & fare both ways from Dewas>. At the end of two years, your fare back should be paid in any case. I would hold out no hope of stopping more than two years—say it is the Secretaryship which attracts you, also my accounts of Chhattarpur.

Your salary is very low of course—I've only in view that you shan't be out of pocket and have suggested more or less what I did in West's case.[5] Ask for better terms if you like: you're perfectly free to do so.

He appreciates a good letter as you may have gathered. He evidently would like you to come. I'll write to him this mail—a line!

I hadn't time to get the shirts, so if you pass a suitable trustworthy shop you might tell them to send him two. 14½ neck—to wear on bus. He expected to pay 3/– a shirt, so I suppose each will cost 5/– or 6/–, or more but I don't mind price if they don't *look* expensive. M[r] F. Palmer, Old Palace Gardens, Weybridge.[6] If not convenient to you, I will get them next week.

Morgan

He was glad of your success. 'That's something for him' or 'for England'—I didn't quite catch which.

I wish you had remembered to tell us that you are M[r] Aylward's g[t] grandson. Yes indeed! His wife (the one who was formerly M[rs] Synnot) was one of our greatest friends: her first husband was my first cousin once removed, so you and I are connections in consequence! Very nice. My mother liked your great grandfather so much, I remember: we often stopped at Holmleigh. I remember him more dimly myself. M[r] Fuller of course we know too.[7]

Yours ever
EMForster

ALS: HRC

[1] EMF is visiting Shuttleworth at Cheltenham.

[2] Him & it: the Maharaja of Chhatarpur and the invitation to Ackerley to be his Private Secretary. This came about indirectly through EMF, who prescribed a change of scene as a cure for Ackerley's writer's block.

[3] Ha capito?: Italian, 'Have you understood?'

[4] Hogarth House: Richmond home of Leonard and Virginia Woolf.

[5] West: unidentified, but apparently one of those EMF had already recommended as a secretary to the Maharaja.

[6] A bus-driver friend of EMF. See *EMF*, II, 133–4.

[7] On the Aylwards and Inglis Synnot, see Letter 3. Ackerley added a note to this letter (TTr. HRC) to the effect that his great-aunt Gertrude Fuller, Mr Aylward's daughter, had married a Dr Charles Fuller against her father's wishes and after declaring at a family council, 'I will marry him whatever you say!' Ackerley recalled her as an old lady.

227   J. R. Ackerley

[N. p.]   15 March 1923

Dear Cousin Joe (though the formula reminds me of 'dear Cousin Henrietta': Henrietta, as the sister of the first husband of your great-grandfather's second wife, was my first cousin once removed, and a terrific tartar. Indeed still is, for she actually lives, Henrietta does. However never mind her or even the closing of the bracket, but let us haste to the steps of the throne. I consider your letter a masterpiece. If anything could pin that queer wriggling little creature, it would. You were quite right to mention me about the £100—I made the same stipulation when trying to arrange for the going east of West. I return your fair copy, which you should keep. I don't think there are other points at present—except that you must realise (I dare say you have) that if you go you will have to hold up H. H.'s end against your own countrymen, even if you like them better as you well may. I had to do it for Dewas, but there it was not difficult because I didn't like them nearly as much. The English over at Nowgong will always be inviting you to side ~~with them~~ against him, or worming out of you stories not to his credit. His character, which is generally known, may also give you a little trouble at first—however don't take this last remark seriously. Your main job is to put up with him and to like him as far as you can, and indeed he has many endearing qualities. I meant to show you his photograph when you were over here. He is 5 feet high and has no bridge to his nose, and he usually wears a frock coat of magenta velvet, and earrings of diamond.

My mother much excited over the Aylward connection and wonders whose daughter your mother was—William's? and what is her Christian name.

Many thanks for your letter. Yes, I shall certainly visit you soon, either as caller or stopper. Very kind of you to ask me.

Yours ever
EMForster

Send on your MS or rather MSS. If you prefer me to read your Swiss play in silence I will do so—you told me you were off it, and when one is comments are tiresome.[1]

ALS: HRC

[1] Ackerley, *The Prisoners of War* (1925), three-act play about officers interned in Switzerland during the First World War. It was performed privately at the Court Theatre, London, on 5 July 1925, then opened on 31 August at the Playhouse, Hammersmith, where it ran for three weeks. It had a New York revival in 1935, when Brooks Atkinson found it dated, for 'the time machine was furiously clicking' (*The New York Times*, 29 January 1935, p. 24). EMF sent Ackerley an acute piece of advice ([?June 1924.] HRC): 'As to your play, I can only remind you what I felt about my novel [i.e. *Passage*]—namely, that it was dislocate and dead. Now people say it's good and I begin to agree. You can't tell what your work's like, and

you must not take any general *intellectual* view about it. Non-intellectual general views on the other hand are (I have the honour to inform you) all right: there will come moments when you will see it as a whole in a flash—i.e. see its faults and how to correct them, and then you must slap down your conclusions on the nearest piece of paper, because you won't have time to get to the MS, or if you do you will start reading it carefully, and be done for.'

228   To Gerald Brenan

Harnham, Monument Green, Weybridge
27 March 1923

Dear Gerald,

I am so glad that the Guidebook fetched you.[1] I hoped it might. I quite agree with what you say about flowers, but doubt whether the book will ever reach a second edition. It does not, and cannot, sell. The publisher will not let people who are not booksellers have it because they are not booksellers, and he will not let booksellers have it because booksellers are dishonest. It is my fate and perhaps my temperament to sign agreements with fools.

I would much like to see you and to pay £1 or even more for my food—'even more' because it sounds so little, not because the food I want is much.[2] I was always a coarse eater, and now am not even a large one. The worst of it is I don't feel to care for Spain. I invested in Italy, and though it has smashed cannot bear to sell out. If ever I go abroad again, it will be to Germania [*sic*] or North Africa—perhaps you will meet me in the latter place, or, better still, arrange for the Reconquest of Granada, when I will meet you there.[3] Are not the Spaniards ugly dirty surly superstitious?

This should draw a letter from you.

Leonard and Virginia should be just arriving now.[4] You will get all the news about me, and indeed others, from them. I had meant to write to you long ago, and thank you for your letter, which pleased me very much. I sympathise with your boredom over novels. I am bored with the one I am trying to get done now. And I expect even Virginia will get bored finally, though she has scooted down a very exciting passage of which I can't predict the end. I am looking forward with earnestness to her next book. It would take too long to explain why.[5]

Then your lust for facts. I have it too. But it is entirely different from dealing in facts. You and I have both sat gaping and listening to talk about cotton, and have occasionally, through our will, intelligence, and imagination, made a remark about cotton that passes muster with the company.[6] But we are outsiders, driven by desire, and desire makes us temporary and unreal. I daresay you are right, and books can be written out of the desire for facts, and my Alexandria may be one. But the practical man doesn't desire he possesses (just as Lytton possesses a good prose style). He deals in facts, we in words about them, and there seems to me this impenetrable barrier between us.

I should have liked to read Dante with you very much. I haven't read with anyone (on an equality) for years, and think it would profit me.

Carrington has sent me a card from Marseilles.[7]

Yours ever
EMForster

TLS: Lilly Library

[1] I.e. EMF's *Alexandria: A History and a Guide*, published by Whitehead Morris, Alexandria, in 1922.

[2] Brenan settled in 1922 at Yegen, in the Sierra Nevada. However, EMF's hints fell flat. Brenan then preferred inviting only writers whose works he liked. He 'could not bear' EMF's novels, which he thought 'woolly and sentimental, though, like his conversation, with sharp passages in them'. He invited the Woolfs instead, 'both of whom I liked and admired enormously' (Brenan, *Personal Record, 1920–1972*, p. 57). See Letter 220, note 6.

[3] Allusion to Dryden's play *The Conquest of Granada* (1672).

[4] On the Woolfs' visit, see *The Diary of Virginia Woolf*, II, 240–1; and her *Letters*, III, 23–9.

[5] Virginia . . . passage: the direction indicated by *Jacob's Room*; cf. Letter 224.

[6] See Forster, 'Cotton from the Outside,' *PP*, pp. 60–4; originally one of his 'Alexandria Vignettes': see Kirkpatrick, p. 115.

[7] Carrington was touring the Mediterranean with Strachey and Ralph Partridge. Her card is untraced.

229   To Robert Graves[1]

The Reform Club [London].   5 May 1923

Dear Graves,

Your comments on 'The Carpenter's Son' have just given me a pretty turn.[2] I thought you must be wrong, any how fanciful, then looked it up. This drove home what I had already suspected: How much you know about poetry! I call it 'poetry' because you use the word, but mean, of course something else. And I mean by 'know' the one kind of knowledge worth having, of which I get faint glimpses in myself, less faint glimpses in others, but never never enough. There are these shreds of Science about...among those loads of information that weigh your 'poems' down, you complain, and how much heavier do they clog all other forms of creation! I was very grateful indeed to you. I did not feel ashamed at having read Housman a 100 times and missing what he was after here. It turned me from your comment to the rest of your book, and then to the rest of what I think valuable in the world—a world I find smeared & bloody on the whole, and essentially so, yet it can't destroy our shreds of Science—they continue.—With very best wishes, and thanking you.

EMForster.

ALS: Southern Illinois University-Carbondale

¹ EMF and the poet Robert Graves (1895–) became acquainted about 1923 (cf. Letter 190). They were never close friends, but corresponded at intervals and had a mutual friend in T. E. Lawrence. EMF's recommendation in 1925 helped Graves to obtain a lecturing post in English at Cairo University, 1926–7. EMF described Graves as 'original to the point of wildness' and 'a lively lad and should make officialdom sit up' (to Cavafy, 12 December 1925, 2 January 1926. Savidis).

² A. E. Housman, 'The Carpenter's Son', No. 47 in *A Shropshire Lad*. On this lyric as an apocryphal account of the Crucifixion, see Graves, *On English Poetry: Being an Irregular Approach*, pp. 31–5.

230   To George Valassopoulo

(address)

The Reform Club, Pall Mall   [London] S.W.

18 June 1923

My dear George (as I always call you, I hope not impertinently).

I received your letter with great pleasure. To whom should I send a copy of *P. & P.* if not to you?¹ It is selling, you will be glad to hear, very well, and indeed we expect to sell out the whole edition by next month. We have broken up the type, so shan't be reprinting I fear but we may import some sheets from America, where Knopf is issuing it. (All my publishers are Jews).

Give my love to Cavafy and tell him he owes me a letter. If he writes to me I shall send him some reviews which will interest and concern him. And if he does not write to me, I shall not send him the reviews.

Speaking seriously (and to you) his poems have caught the reviewers['] attention. You can't imagine how happy this makes me. I regard it as *most important* that you should translate some more. You've not only the literary ability but what's as rare—the mental honesty. A really important piece of work which none but you could perform lies under your hand, and I do urge you to set a little time aside, either from your legal or your social obligations, and to perform it. I would try to get the poems published in Magazines (I am in with some of the editors) and if I succeeded we might then think of a book. I feel you owe this not only to Cavafy & yourself, but to Literature. If you don't do it, the (English speaking) world will be definitely poorer. I have long meant to write to you on this point, and the reviews have stimulated me.

I suggest you translate the poem about the poet who is finding epithets for the ancestors of Mithradates (?) and then learns that war has been declared with Rome. I forget the poem's title—am away from home. Start on this poem, and let me have it on or before July 10ᵗʰ when I shall be in town and can take it round to the editors.²

All good wishes from
EMForster

ALS: Irene Lightbody

[1] Forster, *Pharos and Pharillon*.
[2] Cavafy, 'Dareios', in his *Collected Poems*, pp. 78–9.

231 To W. J. H. Sprott[1]

Isle of Wight.   28 June 1923

Dear Sebastian,

Thank you for cheque; and for invitation, but I fear I cannot come. There is so much that I ought to do or try to do by remaining at home in the coming month. Will you not be in town? I want to see you. To thank you, even, for all the trouble you took over an oculist. I found traces of your activity throughover London, and am very grateful to you. I am so very sorry you are unhappy. I have given up expecting for myself happiness of the kind I want for you, but that is only because my friend went and died, it is no argument for general pessimism.—I am a little doubtful perhaps about your application of 'psychology' to your difficulties, though your psychology is of course better than other people's. Science, when applied to personal relationships, is always *just wrong*—I refrain from adding in booming tones, 'and always will be', but it is certainly always just wrong at present, and when you analyse the obsessions & reactions of D. W. and yourself, I'm not convinced that you have got on to either of the two people concerned.[2] Art is a better guide than Science. Ho! I wish I could expand that remark. Gracefulness is so important—I'll try that. We agreed that it wasn't graceful of me to send Alec & Maurice to a hotel after the British Museum, tho' it would have been 'sound' from their point of view.[3] We agree we want modern beauty—not yesterday's beauty which ranges us with schoolmasters & clergymen but a quality so up to date that no one has had time to note it down. That's the quality that makes a love-affair successful, and pulls it out of the pitfalls of logic—by which I also mean the pitfalls that logically await it, I am getting rather mixed and will go to bed. Good night dear Sebastian

Morgan

ALS: KCC

[1] Walter John Herbert Sprott (1897–1971), variously known as 'Jack' and as 'Sebastian', was the son of a Sussex solicitor. He went to Clare College, Cambridge, in 1919, joined the Apostles, and became friendly with the Bloomsbury circle. He was a demonstrator at the Psychological Laboratory in Cambridge, 1922–5, then went to University College, Nottingham, as Lecturer in Psychology, then was Professor of Philosophy, 1948–64. EMF came to know him in his undergraduate period, and they established a close friendship and corresponded continually. For some years EMF also gave Sprott a small allowance. Sprott was affectionate, loquacious, and witty. In Nottingham he occupied a large, very grubby house in a slum district and acquired a wide circle of working-class friends, some of them in and out of jail. His book *Human Groups* (1958) became widely known.
[2] D. W.: unidentified.
[3] In EMF's novel *Maurice*, Chapters 43 and 44.

232   To Constantine P. Cavafy

Harnham, Monument Green, Weybridge
5 July 1923

My dear Cavafy,

You are a bad poet. I have written to you and sent you, two copies of the book and a message via Valassopoulo. Do I get a word in reply? Not one word. You really must answer this. For things are rather exciting. The book has had a great success for a book of its type, 900 copies have been sold in 6 weeks, we are rushing out a second edition; a review of over a column in the Times Literary Supplement, long reviews in the Nation, the New Statesman, the Daily Telegraph and so on.[1] And the things that have attracted most attention in it are your poems. The reviewers have in some cases quoted them in full, and I have had private letters—e.g. from Siegfried Sassoon—anxious for more of them and for more about you.[2] And now I come to the exciting point. I was at Chatto & Windus' the other day—they are one of our leading publishers—and they began asking me about you, and whether more of your poems couldn't be translated.[3] I didn't mention you, they did. Of course they made no promise to publish and I don't want to raise hopes that may be dashed. But seriously my dear Cavafy, if you could get G. V. to translate *at once* half a dozen more poems, I could then take them to Chatto & Windus and talk over the matter again. If they were still encouraging, we would add some more, and the end might be a nicely got-up book. It's not much of an end, I know, still it would give you and G. V. and me pleasure, and it would certainly give great pleasure to the discriminating who read it. I hoped[?] hate it when beautiful things are kept from places where they are needed. It makes me angry.

Do you want to see some of its reviews? If you will be a good poet instead of a bad one I will lend you them. The Times [*Literary Supplement*] (by Middleton Murry I fancy, but it's unsigned) is really rather beautiful—semi mystic, semi humourous, and I think has 'got' us rather well.[4] It sold us anyhow, like hot cakes.

Your expectant friend
EMForster.

ALS: George P. Savidis

[1] The Hogarth Press printed 1,000 copies of *Pharos and Pharillon* in June and another 1,500 in March 1926. See John Middleton Murry, 'A Vision of Alexandria', *TLS*, 31 May 1923, p. 369; G. Lowes Dickinson, 'Mr. Forster's New Book', *The Nation and The Athenaeum*, 33 (1923), 273; R. M., 'Things That Have Interested Mr. Forster', *The New Statesman*, 21 (1923), 302, 304. There was no review at that time in the *Daily Telegraph*.

[2] Sassoon's letter does not survive.

[3] Forster's letters to Chatto and Windus (University of Reading) do not include correspondence about Cavafy's poems.

[4] Murry used the same review, with the title 'The Magic of E. M. Forster', for *The New Republic*, 35 (1923), 293-4.

233   To Malcolm Darling

The Reform Club [London].   18 July 1923

Dearest Malcolm,

Josie and I should meet on Friday and this should loose my pen and bestow on you the really long interesting letter that I feel to have been your due these 18 months. This will have the jejune merit of catching the mail.

I read all you said about Bapu Sahib. (Of course I read it!) Could you give me any more details of the Conspiracy? Was young Waghalker implicated? Hints always were given me that he was a villain and I could never believe them, indeed the only friction I had with Bapu Sahib while there was about him.[1] Awful awful about Bai Saheba. Awful altogether the sudden gibber and horror-stricken[n]ess of the East. I have heard nothing from Bapu Sahib, save a brief wire, since I sailed. I fear I may have chilled him by two articles I wrote about the Native States, though no names were mentioned therein.[2] I wish now I had not written them, but it is difficult to strike a balance between self-expression and personal loyalty: it is one of the difficulties that holds up my Indian novel. Of course I have this odd feeling about Bapu Sahib, that if one wrongs him (in his opinion) one is yet, sub specie aeternitatis, forgiven. I have not this feeling with any one else, or with scarcely any one else. I don't believe in immortality for myself. I can't feel it possible for others, and yet my *relation* with him has this immortal quality. You will know what I am trying to express and could express it better. I am paying a distant and roundabout tribute to him as a saint. I am not intimate with him, and have never in ~~more~~ my own mind claimed intimacy. It is something else I am trying to say. I wonder whether I shall ever see him again. Any how he remains one of the great spiritual experiences of my life, and of the depths of his goodness to me not even you can have any idea. Malar Rao and Deolekr. And I daresay Nadka.[3] Well, well. Strange are the sweets of mediocrity. I could wish him better attended, but so it ever will be and amen. I see no end to the chaos, architectural and otherwise, that informs his state. In the language of common sense, he won't stick to any thing, and that's what's wrong. I am glad you did not go, and I think it quite possible that though nothing could diminish his love for you, you might have caused him much pain. Dewan and Brother would be bound to receive some nasty knocks, however carefully you plied the broom, and as for the smaller obstructionists—I tremble to think not of their feelings but of his.[4] Dewas, you see, as it recedes, seems to me a mystic country where all we are accustomed to regard as important is performed as a game, and where we seldom grasp and never ~~appreciate~~ enjoy what *is* important. How I wish I knew what India is after! When I am there, she seems to me up to nothing at all, and so she will seem to you as you read this letter, because you are there. And she hasn't the lure of beauty. But when I get away and am vexed no longer by her incomparable fatuity, my notion is that all the judgements I came to on the spot were wrong.[5]

Well dear Malcolm I'll stop now. One of the old gentlemen is coughing himself inside out in a leather armchair, and I fear that my opinions are killing him. Josie meets me in the National Gallery, and I am giving her lunch at my anarchist club.[6]

Morgan

Pharos & Pharillon has sold well.

ALS: HRC

[1] The young Sardar Sahibrao Waghalker, descendant of a branch of the Puars, from the village of Waghale, was in disfavour with H. H. and was generally excluded from the Dewas court. EMF thought him 'about the only nice and intelligent young man in the state . . . He is practically an outlaw and is snubbed and held back by his cousin (H. H.) who hates & fears him. I have had it out, but to no effect. It is one of those family quarrels that poison the best of Orientals' (to Dickinson, 30 August 1921. KCC). H. H. had put his son and heir Vikramsinharao Puar (1911–83) in the charge of a tutor named Sharma, thought to be a Kolhapur spy. The Darlings turned Sharma out when Vicky was with them in 1916, but H. H. rejected their entreaties that he sack him. Consequences were serious, for Sharma became a leading actor in the drama of Vicky's flight from Dewas in 1928. In 1924 Josie Darling, visiting Dewas, found H. H. drinking rather too much. She wrote: 'Vicky is still at the guest house, with his three elder sisters. He is being taught by the high school master, and two other masters. Sharma is still in charge' (to Malcolm Darling, 16 [?   ] 1924. CSAS). State finances were in a bad way, largely owing to the expense of the secret service. Conspiracies centred upon rival dynastic claims, since H. H. now had children by his 'Diamond Concubine', Bai Saheba.

[2] See [EMF], 'The Mind of the Indian Native State (by Our Indian Correspondent)', *The Nation and The Athenaeum*, 31 (1922), 146–7, 216–17; reprinted in *AH*, pp. 332–43.

[3] Sirdar Malaraw Pawar was Chief Secretary at Deas Senior, and a Major, 'innocent of warfare and almost of English' (see *HD*, p. 303). M. Deolekr joined the court in 1915 as Secretary to H. H. and remained throughout the scandals that began in 1928. EMF came to view him as an adversary. Deolekr told PNF in 1970 that EMF's post as Private Secretary was purely nominal: some rivalry plainly existed. Nadka (Nadkarni?): a Dewas court functionary. On the history and politics of Dewas, see Manohar Malgonkar, *The Puars of Dewas Senior* (1963).

[4] Dewan: Pundit Narayan Prasad, a Malwa Brahmin, previously tutor to H. H.; see Darling, *Apprentice to Power*, p. 158. Brother: H.H.'s brother 'Bhau Sahib' (Jagdevrao Puar).

[5] EMF's musings about India were related to resumption of work on *Passage*. He wrote to Ludolf (13 June 1922. KCC): 'I am working at my old Indian novel (don't tell anyone this—secrecy conveniences me) but without enthusiasm; my additions are not bad yet I can't convince myself that the thing will ever be finished. If I could convince myself once, even for a second, it would be all right. Also there is a fundamental defect in the novel—the characters are not sufficiently interesting for the atmosphere. This tempts me to emphasise the atmosphere, and so to produce a meditation rather than a drama. And I work terribly slowly.'

[6] I.e. the 1917 Club.

234   To Siegfried Sassoon

[N. p.]   21 July 1923

I'm particularly glad you like the story as it is the last I wrote.[1] I think it good too. Why can't I always be writing things like this—it is the only freedom. I shouldn't want friends or bodily gratifications then.[2] This endless wanting, and dependance [sic] on the opinion and behaviour of others—it begins to bore me so, though it is preferable to resignation, it's [sic] detestable alternative. Just for three or four hours in a year, perhaps, I escape both and become a god.

I wish the story could have another ending, but however much skill and passion I put into it, it would never have satisfied you. I tried another chapter, it is true, in the forests of the Underworld 'where all the trees that have been cut down on earth take root again and grow for ever' and the hut has been rebuilt on an enormous scale. The dead come crashing down through the foliage, in an infernal embrace. Pinmay prays to his God who appears on high through a rift in the leaves, and pities him but can do nothing.[3] 'It is very unfortunate' says God: 'if he had died first you would have taken him to your heaven, but he has taken you to his instead. I am very sorry, oh good and faithful servant, but I cannot do anything.' The leaves close, and Pinmay enters Eternity as a slave, while Vithobai reigns with his peers. I hear rejoicing, inside the hut, to which occasionally the slaves are summoned. I see them come out again broken in spirit and crouch outside the entrance or lie like logs under the ice-cold flow of the stream. A gloomy prospect you see—except for Vithobai, who has won the odd trick.

I enclose my own experiences among savages—though not all of them: Egypt was a very different story, which I recall with thankfulness and pride.[4]

EMF

ALS: George Sassoon

[1] Forster, 'The Life to Come' (1922), first published in *The Life to Come and Other Stories* (1972), pp. 94–112.

[2] EMF had written to Florence Barger (17 June 1922. KCC): 'I have become a friend of Sassoon's, and he of me. It is difficult to make real intimacies at my age—and I remember George [Barger] saying that he has only added one friend—(Sydney [Waterlow])—since the war. I am very glad about Sassoon, though I don't expect to see much of him. I could talk quite freely to him if ever I wished.'

[3] Pinmay: the missionary in the story.

[4] EMF sends his memoir, 'Kanaya', about his involvement with a palace barber at Dewas in 1921. See *HD*, pp. 310–24.

Siegfried Sassoon.

With Forrest Reid.

At Ham Spray House. Left to right: Jack Sprott, Gerald Heard, EMF, Lytton Strachey.

235 To Siegfried Sassoon

Weybridge.   1 August 1923

I don't go to Scotland till the 15th and should much like to see you first. Lunch or tea on the 9th? I detect however in your letter the tone of one who is determined to be indeterminate, and such are difficult to cope with, I am well aware.[1]

I tried to write that thing without either self-pity or swank, and think it has some value in consequence, though it is anxious work showing it to anyone else.[2] Register it back here, and if you should wish to make comments on it, they would interest me.

Since you are interested in The Life to Come, its genesis may interest you also. It began with a purely obscene ~~vision~~ fancy of a Missionary in difficulties. The obscenity went and a great deal of sorrow and passion that I have myself experienced, took its place. The personages are imaginary. I rather think good work can come out of some such processes as the above. 'Lóvely story.' Yes, I thought so. I wish my novel was. I shall never write another novel after it—my patience with ordinary people has given out. But I shall go on writing. I don't feel any decline in my 'powers'.[3]

Morgan.

ALS: George Sassoon

[1] EMF more than once reproved Sassoon for being unreliable, nor was he the only one to do so; see, for instance, Harold Owen, *Aftermath*, pp. 7–8, 16, 61.

[2] I.e. 'Kanaya': see Letter 233.

[3] His feelings on this subject fluctuated a good deal. He had written to Sassoon (12 June 1922. George Sassoon): 'I continue to try to write, and though not dissatisfied with what I do have never the faintest conviction that it will be finished. Now I must get the conviction. How does one get a conviction? By looking blandly ahead? By screaming? How? By Living? But if you Live you can't go on with your writing, because you are in a train or a prison at the time.'

236 To Constantine P. Cavafy

Reform Club   [London] S. W.
11 November 1923

Dear Cavafy,

All mourn, all deplore,
    Both Gentile and Jew,
That they hear no more
    From you.[1]

Yours inconsolably
Fellow-Poet.

ALU: George P. Savidis

[1] EMF wrote to Leonard Woolf (1 August 1923. Sussex), submitting a group of Cavafy's poems to *The New Statesman*: one in Cavafy's original Demotic, the others translated by Valassopoulo, one of which had 'literary revision' by EMF, and with notes by Robert Furness. EMF seems to have been more eager than Valassopoulo and Cavafy himself to capitalise upon the initial success in England. Translations either did not arrive, or came in bunches, in the manner of London omnibuses. EMF wrote to Sprott (24 January 1925. KCC) that 'the translator of Cavafy has been in England and left me 50 more poems "and there are 8 more which I have not translated, and please do not press me to translate." General excitement, involving even the Hogarth Press, and I see a pleasant piece of niggling work ahead, for I am to be allowed to tinker up the English. Some of the poems are marvellous.' Valassopoulo had written to EMF from Paris (20 January 1925. Irene Lightbody) that he was 'writing this evening to Cavafy and am pressing him urgently to accept the terms that were offered to him by your friends. I think that he would be ill-advised to refuse them now that people seem interested in his poetry. They might forget all about him later on.' Much later, EMF sent Plomer a long summary of frustrations in his efforts to organise a volume of Cavafy's complete poems (2 July 1945. Durham); he concluded, 'Deep behind it all is Cavafy, whom I loved, and what is best done for his immortality. If only Capetanakis was here!' Demetrios Capetanakis (1912–44), a friend of Plomer and a devotee of Cavafy, left Greece to go to Cambridge in 1939, and his promising career was cut short by his early death.

237   To G. H. Ludolf

[N. p.] 27 January 1924

My dear Ludolf,

My sole political activity has been the enclosed poem, nor have I any useful information to accord to you.[1] What leads you to want to take an interest on the subject of English politics? If gossip aids your course, I can tell you what Mrs Barger tells me. She is an old friend of the MacDonalds, and found all in confusion at Belsize Park, the children and the general servant radiant at the prospect of the move, but the Lady-housekeeper in despair. The Baldwins seem to have been very nice. B. said to Mac. 'For Heaven's sake take the whole of your salary—I spent £400 over mine' and has left them a Ford down at the Chequers. But the Downing Street butler was even nicer saying 'Miss MacDonald, better not say anything to anyone, perhaps your father wouldn't like it.'[2] I suppose a torrent of venom is poured by Rotherbrook & Beavermere, but I don't see their papers—Morning Post, Times, Spectator, &^ct are courteous, and Aunt Laura announces from her bed that she would far rather be under MacD. than either Asquith or Lloyd George. The latest Foreign Office mot is 'Thank God, we've got a gentleman over us for a change.' What do you think about it all? I confess to elation. I want Labour to be in power if only for a little—it will teach them a lot and teach the country a lot—knock away some of the snobbery that seems to me so much more harmful than this or that political opinion. The thing I dislike about them is their disregard for individual liberty, but since Sir William Harcourt I don't think any statesman of importance has tried to protect it.[3] It is bound to decline when the sovereignty of the state is exalted.

Well, here is almost a whole page political in tone, and really a few graceful words are now in place. Thank in the first place Mrs Ludolf for her letter. I shall write to her later on. I valued her birthday wishes. I often think of the birthday and other meals I wolfed at Giannaclis.[4] Then you—You have given me two letters, both long and interesting and the first of which I lost, and a pendent but not pensive Alighieri. I appreciate all but feel rather too strongly that you and you your [sic] wife have behaved better to me than I to you. I must try to get over this— — — Thank you very much, both of you.

My chief news is that the novel is done at last and I feel—or shall feel when the typing's over—great relief.[5] I am so weary, not of working but of not working; of thinking the book bad and so not working, and of not working and so thinking it bad: that vicious circle. Now it is done and I think it good. Publishers fall into ecstacies! But I know much about publishers (toujours excepté Monsieur Homme [Mann]) and sent them those chapters that are likely to make them ecstatic, concealing the residue in the W. C. until the contracts are signed.[6] They unite, though, in restraining their joy until the autumn. I'm afraid it won't come out till then.

Mother's remembrances to you both. She is fairly well—rheumatism *has* been much better and even now is better than a year ago. January is always a trying month with one thing and another—the worst month in the year—and I'm thankful it is ending.

How do you spend your days—besides dressing your staff in curtains? Do you read much, and if so what? Does the climate suit your health? Are you making money for your brother and yourself? And are the general expenses of an Italian residence not unpleasantly surprising? All that sort of thing. I hope to arrive sometime. Thank your wife very much for so warmly encouraging me.

I feel I ought to get in some more news, but what will interest you? Do you remember longing to go to Hassan? I found it enjoyable rather than[7]

ALU, incomplete: KCC

[1] Probably the poem 'A Voter's Dilemma', *New Leader*, 30 November 1923, p. 8.

[2] Ramsay MacDonald (1866–1937), England's first Labour Prime Minister, and Tory Stanley Baldwin (1867–1947) played musical houses at 10 Downing Street for thirteen years. Florence Barger had known the MacDonalds since the early 1900s. They moved to Downing Street from Belsize Park. Ishbel MacDonald was her father's hostess at No. 10.

[3] Sir William George Harcourt (1827–1904) served in five Liberal governments. He wrote in *The Times*, as 'Historicus', on questions of international law.

[4] Giannaclis: tram-stop in the Alexandria suburbs.

[5] Novel: *A Passage to India*.

[6] Mr Mann: at Whitehead Morris, Alexandrian publisher of EMF's *Alexandria*.

[7] *Hassan* was a poetical play by poet and diplomat James Elroy Flecker (1884–1915).

238   To J. R. Ackerley

[N. p.]   29 January 1924

My dear Joe—have had two letters from you and must get off a line this mail tho' I don't feel communicative. I may write to H H also though I have not heard from him. I can't imagine you will be poisoned. I never was. Still, it was bad policy on his part to warn you, and this I shall gaily indicate. You, in a sort of way, ask my advice over one or two points, more particularly over a certain cultivation of a certain transplantation.[1] Fortunately, long before this letter arrives you will have decided for yourself. *I* should probably cultivate. But I should do so with the knowledge that nothing I ~~did~~ meditated in a Native State will be hid from that Native State, and might possibly trickle through to the Agency.[2] From the Agency I should not expect it to reach India as a whole, nor Europe from India, nor Heaven from Europe. These are Geographical considerations. Your conduct, like every one's, is a mixture of imprudence and suspicion, and consequently general rules are useless.—As for being bored, don't mind it—more than the unpleasantness I mean: don't think you are wasting your time. You will never get hold of anything in India unless you experience Indian boredom. There is Hell of a lot to be found out at Chhattarpur, and it will only come gradually. Insist on seeing as much as you can. It's a good sign that you got so soon onto the gods. Much in India is more striking, but nothing I have ever come across is so odd as your corner. You don't say whether you like Khajraho or the scenery[3]— in fact you don't say a lot of things, but some of them may be in your letter to E. K. B[ennett] which he has promised to let me see.[4] Dirt is a delicate question, certainly. I recognise the brand your torn sheet indicates, and it fails to mix with my own. Quot homines, tot immunditiae, perhaps.[5] Like you, I got timid or depressed.

Glad Camar & Co played up.[6] But I can't think who my beautiful Arabian admirer is unless she is notably plain and 3/4 Indian with a stentorian voice.

Any news of the Teverino. Or is that all over.[7]

Your letters were a godsend to my etiolated novel.[8] I copied in passages and it became ripe for publication promptly. I appreciated them myself very much too.

Write again—so will I

EMF

What of the P[olitical] A[gent]? Also, do you see any of the Court Officials? I was much with them at Dewas. My first visit to Chhattarpur I saw a good deal of Fazl-i-Haq, then Private Secretary, but think he is out of favour now. Give him my regards when you meet. He was sent from Aligarh by Morison, if my memory holds.[9]

ALS: HRC

[1] Ackerley's note on his typewritten transcript (HRC): 'Who was the "certain transplantation"? I have forgotten.'
[2] Agency: office of the British Political Agent at Nowgong. The Maharaja was always in difficulty with the agents, of whom there was a long procession during his reign.
[3] EMF saw the Hindu and Jain temples as Khajraho during his second trip to India; see his 'The Art and Architecture of India', *The Listener*, 50 (1953), 419–21.
[4] This is EMF's friend 'Francis' Bennett: see Letter 203.
[5] 'To each his own kind of dirt': cf. Terence, in his play *Phormio*, line 454: 'Quot homines, tot sententiae' ('There are as many opinions as there are people').
[6] Camar Tyabji: a nephew of Sir Akbar Hydari.
[7] Ackerley's note on his typewritten transcript (HRC): 'The "Teverino" was an Italian merchant seaman cadet whom I met on the *S.S. Teverino* on the way to India. He stayed a night or two with me in my Bombay hotel.'
[8] I.e., *A Passage to India*.
[9] Fazl-i-Haq was a Hinduised Mohammedan who was educated at Aligarh, an 'able and entertaining man, and, being Chief Magistrate as well, is very important in the state' (EMF to ACF, 9 December 1912. KCC). On Sir Theodore Morison, see Letter 100.

239 To Alice Clara Forster

Harnham, Monument Green, Weybridge
Friday [mid-March 1924]

Dearest Mummy,

Thanks for your letter. I am just off to town, but not on pleasure bent, for Ian's tooth has kept me awake the whole night. I have wired to David begging him to see me. I expect that it will have to come out.[1]

That however is a trifle beside the fact that *Agnes has just given me notice*.[2] 'Like to leave in a month, is not very comfortable here.' I said she must write to you. I hope that she will not, but if she does the facts are as follows.

Last night I had coffee up here in my room, and as she was carrying down the tray she yelped and shouted 'Ruth, Ruth, turn on the light' in an extraordinary voice. She had been altogether rather uppish, though aimiable, and I thought you would not like her screaming about the house as if it belonged to her, so I told her this morning that I was sure she had forgotten, and would not do it again. (Quite gentle!) Notice followed when I descended to breakfast. Ruth tells me that her leg hurt her last night, and that was why she screamed. That of course I did not know and have sent A. a message to that effect. I have not talked to her, as she is not a fit receptacle for speech. When it is suitable, I will apologise ~~or do~~ to her if you like, or do anything else. I expect it will blow over—Ruth thinks so.

Now I must to the dentist. Sorry not to write Mummy a more cheerful letter. I sent off the parcel. I will post this in town.

I shall return to dinner here, and in no case go to Dorset until Monday. Have not heard from Shaw yet.

Pop.

ALS: KCC

¹ David Thompson, EMF's dentist.
² Agnes Dowland's giving notice was a common occurrence, but it was a generally tense time at Harnham (see Letter 243), and the letter might be dated from EMF's visit to T. E. Lawrence (pseudonym: T. E. Shaw) at Clouds Hill, Dorset (Letter 240).

240   To Alice Clara Forster

Black Bear, Wool.   Sunday.   23 March 1924

Dearest Mother—

Thank you for letters &ᶜᵗ. I am having a most interesting time, so much so that I feel somewhat fatigued. Yesterday, I sightsaw in Wells all the morning, Glastonbury all the afternoon, and Poole part of the evening. I reached here at 8.0. and found a little private soldier awaiting me in the inn. This was the romantic L.[1] He was rather shy and so was I. He had to go at 9.0. Today I went out to his cottage by car. He shares it with two other private soldiers—also little. They spend their leisure there but have to sleep in camp. A charming place in a hollow of the 'Egdon Heath' described by Hardy at the opening of The Return of the Native. It is all among rhododendrons which have gone wild. We worked for a couple of hours at his book, then had lunch on our knees—cold chicken and ham, stewed pears and cream, very nice and queer; a fine log fire. I like L. though he is of course odd and alarming. In the afternoon the man who is about to print his book came down from town, so I suggested to one of the other soldiers we should go a walk. A cockney youth, intelligent and musical. We got on well.[2] L's identity has leaked out of course, but as the cockney said 'People aren't so interested as soon as they are sure—it's a doubt that excites them so.' We returned to tea and a most beautiful gramophone. I walked back to Wool (about 4 miles) and got wet crossing 'Egdon Heath' though not to the skin. Tomorrow I go into Dorchester to call on the Hardys and (I hope) get some money.[3] If I fail in the latter quest you may receive a wire. I leave here Tuesday or Wednesday, and will go to Plymouth since you think it would be useful I will write a line to Aunt E[liza], to reach her before I call, otherwise it will startle her so. I will be back by the end of the week. I have much enjoyed my fly-round.

I am very anxious you should go to Wells. It seems quite easy, and in early May the tourists have not begun to arrive. I enquired for lodgings in Vicars Close (which is much lovelier than the p. c. suggests) and the little Restaurant which I tumbled into is very clean and comfortable for a night, but has no proper sitting room. The

Cathedral is superb, and the gardens of the Bishop's Palace most lovely, and everything is so close together—no toiling: and motor buses to Glastonbury, &ᶜᵗ. Glastonbury—except for the fine ruins—is not attractive, though.

I became intimate with the Bishop's Butler at Wells. He took me round the garden out of the stated hours, and afterwards we met on the Glastonbury train and had much Egyptian conversation. A nice young man. He says 'the bishop is a jolly fellow, all for games.'[4] My landlady and I also got on well. Her little boy (a wolf cub) helped me to transfer my luggage from one station to another.[5]

I must draw to close and retire, but will leave this open till tomorrow and post it in Dorchester. Thank you about Hashim. He had better come at the end of his holiday—i.e. *about* April 14ᵗʰ for 3 or 4 days, but I will fix up the exact date in a day or two.[6] Poor fellow, he has no where to go to, asks do I know of lodgings near London. It is really very sad. He will appreciate your goodness, and I hope mine, for I too shall find him a sad weight. Quant à Rosie, elle est impayable! What must the Knights think of us! But I wonder whether she (R.) would be kind enough to ask Hashim to tea one afternoon. Or will this too result in some unforeseen and unbelievable mess?

The somewhat shattery inn has filled my bobbie and I will follow it. The place is full of reincarnated Gippies who flounder into the bedrooms and run out with shoes and socks in their mouths. The inn people say they never saw such dogs!

Love to R. I look forward to seeing her Jean on my return.

~~I will tell Hashim to write direct to you—that will save time.~~

Dorchester. Monday [24 March 1924]

Your agitating letter received.

I will stop at Wool till Wednesday for certain, by which time your plans will have cleared. Let me know by wire or letter whether I should proceed to Plymouth or to West Hackhurst on Wednesday. I will not let Aunt E. know I am calling until I reach Plymouth. If I go to P. I will try to pick you up at Aunt L's on Friday or Saturday, provided you will travel latish in the day. So sorry you are having all this worry.

I have just rung up Mʳˢ Hardy and she has asked me to lunch. I spend the end part of the day with the Soldiers. Weather better. I hope tomorrow to get to Lulworth.

Sad about piece of land. It certainly sounds unfavourable.

Love from
Pop

ALS: KCC

¹ In February 1923 T. E. Lawrence, enrolled as 'T. E. Shaw', was sent to Bovington Tank Corps Depot, near Dorchester. He and EMF first met in February 1921; see *EMF*, II, 119–21. On Lawrence's Dorset cottage, see EMF 'Clouds Hill', *The Listener*, 20 (1938), 426–7. 'Two . . . soldiers': presumably Edward ('Posh') Palmer and another named Russell.
² His book: 'Oxford edition', *Seven Pillars of Wisdom*. Cockney soldier: probably Palmer.
³ EMF wrote to Siegfried Sassoon (25 March 1924. George Sassoon): 'Max Gate seemed very thin. The "latest trouble" there is the roots of the trees, which have pasted themselves beneath a parsnip bed and have had to be extracted. "Now who could have foreseen a thing like that?" But the old man was in superb form, I have never seen him better. Floods of talk. He seems rather sick that I have finished a novel.' Money: presumably from a bank. Max Gate: the Hardys' Dorset home.
⁴ Rt. Rev. St John B. W. Willson (1868–1946), Lord Bishop of Bath and Wells, 1921–37.
⁵ Wolf cub: most junior grade of Boy Scout.
⁶ Syed Hashim Muhammed Ali (1900–76) was a relative of Masood. He studied engineering in England, 1923–4, and EMF took a fatherly interest in him.

241   To J. R. Ackerley

Harnham, Monument Green, Weybridge
1 April 1924

My dear Joe,
Thanks for your last letter—the one that terminated at Lucknow. Faint and unfavourable are my recollections of that city.¹ Moslem society there is witty and degraded, but of that, alas, I saw none, being in the grip of an Anglo Indian acquaintance whose square jaw was further distended by too large a set of false teeth. He was a Mutiny expert, and drove me for miles along the road by which Havelock advanced to relieve Ellis.² The natives did not get quickly enough out of his way. He was not brutal towards them, but chanted drearily 'they used to be quicker, they used to be far quicker than this'—while buildings of bad architecture fled past, chased by monotonous maidans.³ Also don't I remember a blue and white club, and the sound of the teeth twice at breakfast, twice at dinner, and once at lunch? To the Residency they did not accompany me. I was bored at finding this so small and trim: a pernicious little memento which ought to have been mislaid. "Well do I recollect my mother saying as a girl— —" taking down, as he spoke, the Residency at Lucknow from the mantle shelf: or: unhooking, with a sigh, the Residency at Lucknow from his fob: "well do I recollect her saying that her own mother, my grand-mother, that is to say, — — —" Most certainly let us return to Chhattarpur. But I wonder how Agra struck you. I do find it superb. And what Luard showed you of Gwalior.⁴
Thanks for telling me about R[aghunandi].⁵ Yes, a lovely name and an interesting reaction. I hope things are better by now, or

perhaps by now you have ceased to mind whether they are better or worse. You sound awfully understanding of those people: indeed your letters are all those of one who has lived in the country for years: not Anglo Indian years, but the years of reality that seldom get lived anywhere and scarcely ever in India. I am longing to hear everything as soon as you return and while it is fresh in your mind. Remember this, and do not suddenly feel that you ought to go for a solitary walking tour in Denmark. H. H.'s letter to me was a gem, and of a pellucidity that completely deceived me: composed, I thought, in a mood of unsullied and transparent trustfulness. Did it therefore fail of its purpose? Or did it succeed? I cannot decide. As far as I can make out, the Indian is disappointed if he succeeds at producing the effect he aims at producing. He feels that the universe has played him false by responding truly, and I see him edging to try and peep round its paper-hoop, and detect the next surprise. While he is engaged in this, Havelock relieves Ellis, of course, to every one's amazement, throwing at the same moment 80000 Lancastrian troops into the upper valley of the Imambara.

Perhaps I ought to go to bed. I have had a fortnight's varied and really very good holiday in the west of England[.][6] My MS. is with the printer's, but I hope to piddle a little urine over the proofs. I have a ~~little~~ pleasant piece of editing to do—18th century letters—and I am going to Wembly as the special correspondent of the Nation.[7] I meant to go abroad, but really don't think my state of mind necessitates it——a dreary remark, but Europe always presents herself now to me as a necessity or a superfluity, never as a romance. Perhaps if I got down into Italy, all might be wonderful again, though I doubt it, I do so deplore the Fascisti. And for Jerusalem, Azaz, Rum, and Jeddah, which I do want to see, I have not yet the money or time. The East has spoiled Europe for me, though not England. I wonder what it will do to you.

My best wishes to H. H., thank him for his letter, I shall be writing. Tell him I am jealous of you.—Wait a bit—is that right?—can't think it out. Drop in something or other, any how, listen carefully, and report what you hear.

I forget whether I've written to you since your father, very kindly, let me read a letter of yours in which you described the birth of the Princess. Why at Dewas we had the hell of a fuss over one—slept in a farmyard for eight days, cows positively puffing in my face, and she—so unlike yours—was not legitimate.

How did you manage for a servant during your tour? I had a horrid old man, I loathed him.

Well that's enough. Best wishes,

ALS: HRC

[1] EMF's Lucknow host in 1913 was Barré Cassels Forbes (1879–1946).
[2] On 25 September 1857 Sir Henry Havelock (1795–1857) relieved the British garrison in the Lucknow Residency. Lt.-Col. John Eardley Inlis (not Ellis) (1814–62) took command there after the wounding and death of Sir Henry Lawrence (1806–57), the Resident. EMF is no doubt punning on the name Havelock Ellis.
[3] Maidan: an open space in the middle of a town or city.
[4] EMF had met and liked the archaeologist C. E. Luard; see Letter 162. Luard became a Political Agent in 1909 and was EMF's host in Indore in December 1912.
[5] See Ackerley, *Letters*, pp. 11–12.
[6] This was the trip to visit T. E. Lawrence and the Hardys; see Letter 240.
[7] EMF edited *Original Letters . . . Eliza Fay* (1925). Wembley: see Letter 242.

242   To Constantine P. Cavafy

Harnham, Monument Green, Weybridge
14 April 1924

My dear Cavafy,

Your welcome letter of March 14th took some time to reach me: it was delayed my end, not yours, apparently, being hidden under some papers by mistake, with the result that I have only recently opened it——should have written to you before, otherwise.

I hope that The *Nation* sent you the copy containing *The City*; also that you did not too strongly disapprove the slight modifications I made in the translation, with Arnold Toynbee's authority. But I have written on these & other points recently and at some length to Valassopoulo, so won't recapitulate.[1]

I quite agree with you that Valassopoulo is your ideal translator if he would but translate! The British public won't know you as I wish, if he only sends a poem a year. Do urge him. The *Demaratus* was (from the English point of view) not quite as successful as the others, because the subtlety of the character didn't quite come through.[2] But nearly all the rest he sent are excellent. I think I told him how much Colonel T. E. Lawrence admired your work and his: and L. is a good judge of literary matters.

More poems, then.

More poems.

I have at last finished my novel. It will come out next month.[3]

Tomorrow I am going to the Wembley Empire Exhibition to write an article for the Nation. I believe it is all pools of water and open drains. I hope I shan't fall in, like—well, let us say like Sappho.[4] His Majesty the King follows me there next week.

With all good wishes from your friend and admirer

EMForster

ALS: George P. Savidis

[1] EMF placed 'The City' and 'Theodatus' in *The Nation and The Athenaeum*, 35 (1924), 16, 380. T. S. Eliot asked for a poem and published 'Ithaca', *The Criterion*, 2 (1923–4), 431–2.

EMF wrote to Eliot (11 March 1924. Houghton Library): 'Valassopoulo is honest, but clumsy and not always impeccable, and your ideal course, if you could persuade him, would be to get Arnold Toynbee to go through the poems. . . . (I don't know him personally.)—(Failing this, I would gladly try trimming them myself: for which I have no qualifications, but C. & V. do not mind.)' The historian and classicist Arnold Joseph Toynbee (1889–1975) was Koraes Professor of Byzantine and Modern Greek Language, Literature and History at London University, 1919–24. He wrote to EMF (12 June 1924. Savidis): 'The poems fall into two distinct groups—erotic & historical, and I suppose he would say that these two motives, between them, make Alexandria. / He does seem to have got Alexandria into his bones, and I think it has inspired true poetry in him—not bastard stuff, like most of the historical poems that one knows. / He is an adept at the dramatic monologue, without Browning's over-emphasis and elaboration. I admire the way in which he makes his point by a series of flat colourless statements. / As to beauty of sound, I have come across nothing quite so fine, (at least, to a foreigner) as ἡ Πόλις ["The City"].' Cf. Letter 246.
² 'Dimaratus', in Cavafy, *Collected Poems*, pp. 109–10.
³ I.e., *A Passage to India*.
⁴ See EMF, 'The Birth of an Empire', *The Nation and The Athenaeum*, 35 (1924), 110–11. The Greek poet Sappho committed suicide by drowning.

243   To T. E. Lawrence

W[est] H[ackhurst].   3 May 1924

Yes, we're different all right, and your admission that you laughed at 'The Life to Come' makes me laugh and laugh.¹ The laughter of Hut G. 25 at 'The Birth of an Empire' was, on the other hand, perfectly in order.² I don't understand much of your letter. Points that I do:—"Story too short...shadowy physically...passage of time not naturally felt": with this I agree, and will try to make improvements.—"Of god-like beauty" was deliberate. I wanted heavy colour, overripeness almost. It is a premature touch of cynicism. Still you are probably right, and I will take it out.—I don't agree about the final violent spasm. I had prepared for it all along and given a rehearsal of it in the cart.

What I don't understand is that my 'two victims make no bones about what happened to them.' The savage didn't want to, but the missionary made bones for both.—And 'voluntary parallel'—I should have written 'emotional tangent.'

I am glad you wrote, as I had assumed you were disgusted, and was sorry, though I knew that in such a contretemps neither the disgusted nor the disgusting party would be the least to blame. I think the story as good as any I've written, so does Siegfried.³ Lowes Dickinson doesn't like it. Scarcely any one else has seen it.

I am having an awful time—not blood-poisoning or trifles of that sort, but alone with seven elderly women, one of whom has had a mental breakdown.⁴ I hope to get home in a day or two and send off your book to Doughty.⁵ I will keep this letter back.

I am grateful to you for starting me on D[oughty]. He gives me a good deal of pleasure, and I can see why he might mean a great deal more to others.

6 May 1924

Just sent off book. Don't like being without it. Perhaps you will let me read it again when I have finished Arabia Deserta. I might then begin to get some notion of the geography.

My remembrances to Russell and Palmer. Thank the latter for his message—I appreciated it—I may call again at Clouds Hill later in the year if it suits all your plans.

E M F

ALS: KCC

[1] Lawrence had written (30 April 1924. KCC): 'Comment? Oh, it's very difficult. How much, you will see by my confessing that in my first avid reading of it I ended it, & laughed & laughed. It seemed to me, in the first instance, one of the funniest things I'd ever come across.

'It's abrupt, beyond grace & art: but at my second reading what came out of it strongest was a feeling of pity for the African man. You cogged the whole of life against him. . . . . . and he was no good to wait all that while. None the less his illness was overdone, or his sudden spasm of strength at the end of it. It was too unexpected. Couldn't you have led up to it by some careful hints of force & sinew in the last pages?

'Then there were things which grated on me. "Of god-like beauty" a hateful careless worn-out phrase. The tale itself is too rare to be spoiled by a gash like that across it: and across its most beautiful opening too. The passionate & the pathetic are beautifully done; but the two main figures, while very complete in character, are only shadow-drawn physically. Can't you make them flesh & blood. V[ithobai] only came to shape lying on his roof just dying naked. Before that he'd not been embodied. And the missionary never, except in that hacked phrase of the first page.

'The thing is too short. The passage of time doesn't make itself felt naturally. Perhaps paragraphing might bring this out.

'Is breaking the neck necessary? It is brutal, snatching, a spasm of agony. I'd rather have had a slower clutching killing. However you are the artist, & the emotion charged in it all makes me feel that it's very uncommon art. Contrary to your opinion I incline to consider it quite fit to publish. Perhaps other people's improprieties come a little less sharply upon one? It doesn't feel to me nearly as bad as my true story. Incidentally we're different, aren't we. I make an awful fuss about what happened to me: & you invent a voluntary parallel, about which the two victims make no bones at all. Funny the way people work.'

[2] Forster, 'The Birth of an Empire', *The Nation and The Athenaeum*, 35 (1924), 110–11; on the British Empire Exhibition at Wembley.

[3] Sassoon wrote to Lawrence on 13 November 1930: 'The problem of writing about life becomes more & more difficult. The only solution seems to be—writing for oneself (& someone, like E.M.F.—if there are any more people like E.M.F.—& he is in the same dilemma, I suppose)' (*Letters to T. E. Lawrence*, ed. A. W. Lawrence, p. 156).

[4] The breakdown was his Aunt Laura Forster's. It was a particularly trying time, for 'unluckily mother both wants and is wanted to be "in" the thing [the nursing] too, though I can see no necessity for it, and the fact that she and Aunt L. have never been friends makes it all rather artificial and painful. . . . I am surrounded (in that direction) by the contending cries of the elderly. It is queer—I don't feel any affection or tenderness for my aunt so far, though she has always been so good to me. My chief feeling is intense irritation at her for having—quite wantonly—dismissed a reliable servant who would have taken much of the anxiety off one's hands' (to Florence Barger, 22 April 1924. KCC). Laura Forster died on 6 May, having left West Hackhurst to EMF.

[5] Your book: the privately printed 'Oxford' text of *Seven Pillars of Wisdom* (1922), a copy of which Lawrence had lent to EMF in December. In February EMF had written Lawrence a long commentary that tells as much about his own methods of composition and criticism as about Lawrence's; see *Letters to T. E. Lawrence*, pp. 58–63. Charles Montagu Doughty (1843–1926), the Arabian traveller and geographer, was author of *Travels in Arabia Deserta* (1888).

244   To George Valassopoulo

Harnham, Monument Green, Weybridge
17 May 1924

My dear Valassopoulo,

Many thanks for your two letters and the three poems.[1] I should have written before, but owing to the illness and death of an aunt have been greatly occupied. Now I have much to say.

I think the three poems *superb*. I have submitted them to the *Nation* which wants to publish them all, but asks me to do a little 'polishing'[.] I know that neither you nor Cavafy have any objection to my doing this, and have indeed instructed me to do it. But I am always rather nervous in case I carry the process too far. I will do my best. Possibly I may not let the *Nation* have all the poems after all, because it can only publish them with long intervals between. It may be better to arrange for them with the *Criterion*—which is a high-class literary quarterly. I will exercise my discretion.

The *Nation* has just sent me the proof of 'Theodatus' and please tell Cavafy that I will post him a copy of the number that contains it. Here, ~~not only have I polished~~ in my polishing, I have consulted Arnold Toynbee, formerly professor of Modern Greek at London University, so we are jointly to blame for any misinterpetation.

You and Cavafy wonder how I can be paid for my labours. I can tell you! For each poem I succeed in placing, will you please send me translations of two more. This letter announces to you that I have placed four poems. So will you, my dear Valassopoulo, kindly send me by return of post translations of eight, and when I have placed these—and I rapidly shall—I shall require translations of sixteen. This will keep you nicely busy.

As for de Menasce, the situation is a little difficult, because I sent him (with two or three exceptions) all the translations then in my possession, since I gathered from him that this was Cavafy's wish. He has duly returned the translations and has always behaved with complete civility towards me, but he has made typescript copies of the translations, and I don't know whether he intends to make any further use of these, either in the *Oxford Outlook* or elsewhere.[2] If Cavafy is disinclined for him to do this, he had better write to him direct I think: I can't very well make any suggestion to him myself.

You ask about the erotic poems. But you've never sent me any! at least nothing that I recognised as erotic. I quite agree with you that they ought to be published, and I don't think that the British Public is as silly as it used to be on this point. It stands Aldous Huxley and D. H. Lawrence, and I don't imagine Cavafy will be hotter stuff than they are. Please let me know their names, because I rather fancy that, in the past, a letter of yours to me may have been lost, and that the poems to which you refer may have been included in it. Some of the poems you've sent me, I have not pressed on editors, it is true, but only because I felt the Greek did not probably quite come through in a translation[.] I have never held up ~~any~~ a poem because I thought it voluptuous or sordid.

Is not MIA NYXTA (the poem on page 5) erotic? I have an idea that some one told me so.[3] If it is, would you please send me a translation of it.

Arnold Toynbee has my duplicate copy of the poems, and he has promised to give me a list of those which are, in his opinion, particularly suitable for an English audience. I will forward this on to you, in case it is any help.

Is there no hope you may come to England on your travels? I wish you would. You could meet the Hogarth Press people, and a discussion with them might prove very useful. If you don't come to England, what are your Continental plans? I have a faint hope of getting abroad also. A German friend (a Pastor!) has asked me to stop with him in August in Berlin, and conceivably I might come south afterwards, and meet you.[4] I am very busy at present with family matters, so can't be certain of my movements, and my work has been knocked on the head entirely. It's lucky my novel is done.[5] My publisher is giving me a dinner on May 28th. All the leading booksellers of London are to be invited, and I am to make a speech, and the booksellers are to be so delighted with my speech that they are to order more copies of my book than they will be able to dispose of. At least that is the publisher's idea. Whether it will work, we shall see. Immediately after the dinner the book is to come out. In fact, it will correspond to the part played in a Roman Banquet by the emetic!

Please write to me, and at length, and so much the better if you send in your letter the eight new poems. I enclose an article which has just reached me from an American paper, and in which Cavafy is mentioned.[6] I don't want it back. I will try to send you some more reviews of Pharos & Pharillon, but have none to hand. They have brought it out in quite a nice form in the States.

You will be about sick of this letter. I want in return for it all the Alexandrian gossip and news.

Yours ever
EMForster

ALS: Irene Lightbody

[1] Apparently, the same poems about which EMF wrote to Cavafy: Letter 242.

[2] 'Four Poems by C. P. Caravy [sic] (Translated from the Greek by George Valassopoulo)', appeared in Oxford Outlook, 26 (1924), 94–5: 'Ionicon', 'The Ides of March', 'Manuel Comnenus', 'Come Back'. See Cavafy, Collected Poems, ed. Savidis, pp. 32, 29, 61, 41. Jean de Menasce (1902–73), son of an Alexandrian banking family, joined the Dominicans in France and became a noted Aramaic and Persian scholar.

[3] MIA NYXTA: 'One Night', in ibid., p. 41. EMF's reference to p. 5 (numbering altered)

from p. 12): a collection (KCC) comprising broadsheet publications, 1915–21, of Cavafy's poems.
    [4] This was Herr Steinweg, EMF's fellow tutor at Nassenheide in 1905; see Letter 49.
    [5] *A Passage to India*.
    [6] This American article is untraced.

245 To Florence Barger

West Hackhurst, Abinger Hammer, Dorking
9 June 1924

Dearest Florence,

I sent Harold a copy of my book, and expect a critique from him in return.[1] The sales have begun well.

I am here alone for two nights, rather to mother's distress. I thought I would like to feel what it is to be in my own house, for a minute, and I cannot do that while she is in ~~con~~——! command! Then I take her to Brighstone.[2]

Much water has flowed under the bridge since you left—and flowed back too, for ~~a~~ mother's mind closely resembles an estuary. Things are not as straightforward as you thought, for you had scarcely quitted the estate before she violently contradicted all that she had said or implied to you, burst into tears, and said she could never live here. I think that she is terrified of death, and that the conviction the house would be her 'last home' overwhelmed her. I don't think it would be, for the lease has only 13 years to run. So round and round we go. Her suggestion this morning was that we should keep *both* houses! I don't think any one can ever have got so little satisfaction out of Property as I am doing. My consolation is that as soon as I leave either of our abodes my mind becomes perfectly free; the knack of a double life grows.

I had four very happy days in Gloucestershire with Vicary.[3] Unsuccessful in that ~~we~~ I did not find him a house, but very very happy. I was received straight into the bosom of village life. His father, who has a wooden leg, breaks stones, but drives to and from his work behind a donkey called Richard. After I had left him he said to V. 'Frank, hasn't that fellow rather narrow feet?' adding 'But he is a nice young chap any how'. V. is salmon fishing now, and in lodgings until some ~~land~~ house turns up. I condemned the one he was after, and Mrs V. agreed with me when she arrived, so I am glad I went down. V. has a younger brother who is very good looking, but bad health—bombed in France. Also another brother and a sister. The whole family, including father & mother, are unbelievably witty. I laughed the whole time. Housing conditions filthy: I stopped at a decent little hotel. It was altogether a great experience—and I was a thundering success, especially with a rather drunken man who wanted to give me a dog that really belonged to his brother: a dear dog. The basis of society is agriculture, but most of the younger men bicycle out to work in some small locally owned mines. The mixture seems to have a good effect on their mentality. It was a great emotional relief to me to be there.

I have also managed some things in town—Götterdämmerung & Rosenkavalier, both superbly performed: and the Bookseller's Banquet: and the Aquarium at the Zoo.[4]

You are sure to be doing and seeing heaps. I hope all goes well.

Love from
Morgan

Address: c/o Mrs Whitehouse
    Hunny Hill
        Brighstone
            Isle of Wight

ALS: KCC

[1] He had sent Harold Barger a copy of *A Passage to India*.
[2] EMF had a general sense of disequilibrium. He wrote to Sprott (16 June 1924. KCC): 'It is very queer at such a moment to have been the author of that striking novel on India, and only through the letters I receive am I reminded of the fact.'
[3] Frank Vicary: see Letter 155.
[4] The operas were at Covent Garden. The Banquet was Edward Arnold's. (Letter 244).

246   To Constantine P. Cavafy

[Clouds Hill, Moreton, Dorset]
<'as from':   Harnham, Monument Green, Webridge>
23 June 1924

My dear Cavafy,
    Thank you for your letter of June 11th. I must apologise for my silence of late, but the illness and death of my aunt—followed by much business, and coincident with the appearance of my book—has left me very little time for my friends. Valassopoulo, to whom I wrote the other day, will perhaps have told you this, and he will also have given you certain messages from me.

Thank you also for the two poems you enclose (the 'Envoys....' and '..... the Achaean League'). They interested me much, though I do not think they are as suitable for an English audience as the two superb examples of your irony I last received (namely 'Emilianus ....' and 'The Byzantine grandee...'. I hope to place these with *The Nation* when it has published the 'Theodatus').[1] The problem of suitability is rather a difficult one, and in this connection in the list made by Professor Toynbee may be useful. I sent it to Valassopoulo.[2] The Demaratus—which I understand, and can well believe, to be among the sub[t]lest of your works—did not really get through in the translation, I felt:—[3]

I am stopping with T. E. Lawrence for a few days, and have brought down all your poems with me, that he may read them through. He has done so (all) with enormous enthusiasm. He said "A very great achievement—work modern literature of the very highest order in its class." Since he is well read in French and English—besides being a most remarkable personality and a fine scholar—his praise is worth having, I think; any how it gave immense pleasure to me. He also spoke highly of Valassopoulo's translations—though he added "But why doesn't Cavafy, with his perfect knowledge of English, do his own translating?" He liked your 'flatness' as he called it, your 'chronicle-method' as I call it, and he compared your final retrospective effects with the methods of Hérédia.⁴ He said "I like the African & Asiatic poems best". I agree as you know, but I should like to have some examples of your erotic poetry also, so that all aspects may be represented.—By the way, when sending in the future, do not trouble to enclose the originals, because, when last we met, you very kindly gave me two complete sets. One I keep at home, the other I lend about.⁵

You were kind enough to enquire about my book. I am glad to be able to tell you that it has made an excellent start. Both the press and private criticism has been favourable, and the sales go well. My publisher gave a dinner, at which various booksellers and myself were present; somewhat of an innovation, but it has worked quite well from the advertising point of view. He has also brought out a special edition of 200 signed copies, in the hope that we shall find 200 rich men who are sufficiently foolish to buy them. I fear not; wealth finds other outlets for its imbecility. It is more to the point that Thomas Hardy was over here yesterday and cheered delighted me by a word of praise.⁶

I must conclude this scrawl. Thank you very much for your thanks!⁷ It makes me very happy to think that I may have been able to introduce you to a few new readers. I am sure that your work will have a European reputation in the end, but it will take time. All good things take time.

Believe me with admiration and affection.

Yours ever
EMForster

ALS: George P. Savidis

¹ Cavafy, 'Envoys from Alexandria' and 'Those who fought for the Achaian League', in *Collected Poems*, pp. 62, 86. 'Aimilianos Monai, Alexandrian, A.D. 628–655' and 'A Byzantine nobleman in exile composing verses' (in *ibid.*, pp. 65, 80) did not appear in *The Nation and The Athenaeum*. However, it published 'Theodatus', 35 (1924), 380.

² On the connection with Arnold Toynbee and on the list of poems in Toynbee's letter of 12 June 1924, see Letter 242.

³ On 'Dimaratus' see Letter 242.

⁴ José María de Hérédia (1842–1905), French poet of the Parnassian tradition, noted for his sonnets.

[5] Surviving typescripts of translations, and the two 'complete sets' of printed poems in Greek, are at King's College.

[6] Cavafy wrote later (15 October 1929. Savidis): 'At least, during these few hours I had the opportunity to express to you fully my admiration for that beautiful book "A Passage to India", to explain the reasons for my admiration. They have become, ever since 1924, companions of mine:—Mrs Moore, Fielding, Aziz, Adela, Heaslop, the Nawab Bahadur, MacBryde.'

[7] Cavafy had written (11 June 1924. Savidis): 'I am very, very thankful for the interest you take in my poetry, and the pains you take to make it known.'

247   To Edmund Candler[1]

Harnham, Monument Green, Weybridge
28 June 1924

My dear Candler,

I am so glad that you think the book good. You are the first critic of it who *knows* India, and I feared that the solecisms and absurdities a globe-trotter inevitably commits, would have stuck out too much, and made the sum-total unreal. I sent it in some fear and trembling indeed.

I must firmly if gaily indicate the gulf between us! We both amuse ourselves by trying to be fair, but there our resemblance ends, for you are in the Club trying to be fair to the poor Indians, and I am with the Indians trying to be fair to the poor Club. By busting our respective selves blue, we arrive at an external similarity, but that's all, and I really don't endorse anything you say in your letter! Anglo-India—and still more Anglo-Indians—bear to my mind the greater share of the blame in this gathering tragedy, and were it my object or duty to distribute marks, I should say so. I have almost always felt miserable in a Club, and almost always felt happy among Indians, and I want to go back among them. They won't like my book, I know, because they don't like fairness; dislike it fundamentally, and here something in my own heart goes out to them again. God preserve us from cricket in Heaven!

Yours ever
EMForster

ALS: Wallace D. Bradway

[1] Edmund Candler (1874–1926), journalist, novelist; foreign correspondent and observer in North Africa, the Middle East, Tibet; Director of Publicity, Punjab Government, 1920–1. On his interpretation of India, see Benita Parry, *Delusions and Discoveries*, pp. 131–63. His letter to EMF does not survive.

248   To Malcolm Darling

Harnham, Monument Green, Weybridge
15 September 1924

Dearest Malcolm—I will keep thy Sir Walter in this country, since there is hope of your coming to it before long. Is there no chance of settling permanently? For I badly want several talks. Do you, as you get on in life, formulate anything like a philosophy about it? I ask because you are one of the few people I know of who have done practical work and continued to think dispassionately. The thoughts of people who have not done practical work don't seem to me so valuable. I heard a nice story yesterday of Gerald Balfour, who returned to France after Cambridge "to think out the secret of the Universe." He was absent several years, and on his return was greeted by J. K. Stephen with the ~~frivolous~~ enquiry: 'Well Gerald: did you think of anything?' Freezing and frozen silence.[1] Quite how the mind is to be nourished through the experiences, I don't know—sometimes it is stifled, at others starves—yet there certainly is some process, or what is the difference between philosophy and mathematics?

This is a priggish start to a letter, but I have been thinking over a remark of yours, that my last book might be called The Infernal Omnibus, and I have wondered—not whether I was getting ~~bet~~[ter] down or up, which is too difficult, but whether I had moved at all since King's.[2] King's stands for personal relationships, and these still seem to me the most real things on the surface of the earth, but I have acquired a feeling that people must go away from each other (spiritually) every now and then, and improve themselves if the relationship is to develope or even endure. A Passage to India describes such a going away—preparatory to the next advance, which I am not capable of describing. It seems to me that individuals progress alternately by loneliness and intimacy, and that legend of the multiplied Krishna (which I got, like so much that is precious to me, by intercourse with Bapu Sahib) serves as a symbol of a state where the two ~~are~~ might be combined. The ~~Cambridge~~ 'King's' view over-simplified people: that I think was its defect. We are more complicated, also richer, than it knew, and affection ~~is~~ grows more difficult than it used to, and also more glorious.

Here again it occurs to me whether the above is not the philosophy of a bachelor—conditioned by the accident that I haven't married, and that yours (whatever it is) is conditioned by the accident that you have. Happily-familied, is it not probable that both the universe and personal relationships will appear to you as steady, rather than intermittent, progressions? There is no discounting one's experiences. But as I implied early in the letter, I feel dear Malcolm that you are one of the few who have worked in the world without being worked *into* the world, and that you have got some wisdom out of life which might be very useful to Morgan—! Who will go to bed now, having made this modest request, and who will tomorrow be in such a different mood that he will scarce understand what he himself has written.

---

16 September 1924

As I anticipated, my vein of lofty obscurity has petered out, and I must end with news. There is not much. We still hesitate between the two houses, and my mother—I fear to avoid making a decision—clings to the hope that we can keep on both.[3] She is well—very well—and quite a good little walker again, but all this worry for her makes me anxious. I am well also. So is Goldie Dickinson, who was down here for the day last Sunday, and nearly walked me off my legs. The lawyers continue their cold courses, sometimes stealing one's money openly, sometimes nibbling it away from below. Doctor Robert Bridges, the eminent metricist, will be 80 this October, and I have sent him 5/- to buy a harpsichord.[4] And so on and so forth. I will close now, with very much love to Josie and yourself. Before long I will write again.

Morgan

I enclose a letter about my book, for I think it may interest you. A very good and fair attack, I think.[5] I replied privately—I know H[orne] a little, a nice fellow. 'Burra Sahib' crops up again—How tiresome memory is, for I could have sworn I had heard the phrase used (with a touch of archness perhaps) to and of a Collector by other English people. Was of course wrong.[6]

ALS: HRC

[1] Rt. Hon. Gerald William Balfour (1853–1945), Conservative politician and active member of the Society for Psychical Research. James Kenneth Stephen (1859–92), barrister and author of light verse; Virginia Woolf's cousin.

[2] The Infernal Omnibus: an analogy from *The Celestial Omnibus*.

[3] Two houses: Harnham and West Hackhurst.

[4] Robert Seymour Bridges (1844–1930), retired physician and active poet noted for his innovative metrical theories; Poet Laureate, from 1913. The harpsichord was made by Arnold Dolmetsch (1858–1940), an important figure in the revival of interest in old music. Sassoon organised the presentation, which attracted much publicity. The five shillings is a joke: each contributor gave a pound.

[5] See *EMF*, II, 128–30, for part of this letter from Eric Arthur Horne (1883–1930), formerly of the Indian Educational Service, author of *The Political System of British India* (1922). His letter first appeared in *The New Statesman*, 23 (1924), 542–4. Horne, despite his strictures, wrote a very interesting one-act play, 'In His Own Country' ([n.d.] Typescript, CSAS); the three characters are Ronny–Adela–Aziz counterparts in that they too come to the conclusion that British–Indian rapport is a long way off.

[6] 'Burra Sahib': in Sanskrit-based languages, literally, 'big [English] master'. EMF intended to delete this reference in subsequent editions. Ronny Heaslop uses it, of Turton, in *PI*, p. 23. Several readers had told EMF that he used the phrase incorrectly.

249 To Florence Barger

Harnham, Monument Green, Weybridge
2 October 1924

Dearest Florence,

This is strictly non-official and confidential, but I *think* we shall live at West Hackhurst. I have put the screw on and told mother she must decide one way or other in a fortnight's time, and fortunately I am coming off very badly over the Death Duties on my aunt's estate—an extra £400 to pay, which has touched her and caused her to want to save me money. But she is upset at the thought of action, of course. I left her this afternoon, and called in at E. C.'s: the whole family pleased with your greeting and excellent short bread of which I partook. I can't stop them calling you Mrs Barger![1]

A curious and touching little thing has just happened—connected with Mohammed, so I should like to tell it you in brief. Do you happen to remember my telling you that one of the motor drivers here reminded me of him? No real resemblance, beyond smoothness and darkness of skin, and similarity of profession? The young man in question disappeared to some other job some months ago. I had never spoken to him, and began to forget him. Last month he reappeared, driving the station bus. It was like a return from the dead, and upset me. I talked to him in passing (ordinary civility I thought—no more) and once or twice gave him a cigarette. He gave me one too, and then surprised me by presenting me with a cigar one evening—quite a good one. But stranger was to come—my desire to know him must have 'got through', for he asked me rather shyly whether I'd care to come round to his place one evening and 'have a crack'. I said I would, and went last Sunday. He and his wife and child live in part of the big house in Palace Gardens; it has been converted into flats. She was a very nice woman—better educated than he—and we all had biscuits and coffee, and I nursed the cat. The man is not intelligent and rather rough, and I don't think anything important will come from it. But he is perfectly straight—a simple response to friendship—so I mean to go on. I told mother about it <in passing>, for now I must ask him here, and I had to get her leave. She thinks he hasn't placed me socially, and will collapse when he sees the splendours of Harnham. I'm not sure. I must arrange that Agnes doesn't open the door to him, however! I shall pretend he is coming for a French lesson—he did talk of it, he learnt some strange sounds in France which it pleases him to repeat. I am moved by the whole episode in ways that you will understand; I find references in my diary—to his similarity with M.—over a year ago. They are not alike really, and now I have come to think of him as himself. The 'lower classes' especially near London, seldom ask strangers to their houses. That he has done so, and introduced me to his wife quite simply, does suggest something rather remarkable and perhaps rather loveable. I had better have such adventures while I can, for there will be no place for them in the pseudo-feudalism of West Hackhurst.

Another matter about which I told you, led to a second meeting without difficulty or uneasiness. In several ways, life has been more interesting of late, but I wish I didn't feel so rootless. It will be better when I know where we are to live. I have written again to Lord Farrer asking for some arrangement by which we should not be turned out of W. H. during mother's life time. I will let you know his reply. She does not know I have written.

Ruth has said definitely to mother: 'Wherever you go, I should like to come too—you have always been so good to me.' Mother touched and relieved. Aggie couldn't be trusted to stop 2 seconds if something affronted her. She is at present all smiles '*Lovely vegetables.*'

3 October 1924

Lord Farrer's rather unsatisfactory reply has just come in.[2] Let me have it back—but don't bother to write until you have leisure. When you have, I shall of course love to hear all your news.

Love from

Morgan.

ALS: KCC

[1] Perhaps Edward Carpenter and his ménage: he had recently moved to Surrey.
[2] These letters do not survive.

250 To Florence Barger

In the Train from Gomshall [Surrey]
24 October 1924

Dearest Florence

Glad of your letter. Things have been bad at W[est] H[ackhurst] but seem now on the mend. Just as I thought mother had settled to come, and I had had up the builder about repairs and had despatched an additional appeal to Lord Farrer on her behalf, she turned round and said she should not feel independent in the house—had been too used to a house of her own to live in some one else's, also said I was 'difficult'. I had a slight nervous breakdown an hour or two afterwards, which caused her to withdraw what she said. I have told her this morning that W. H. is to be hers in every sense except the legal sense, and that I shall live there in the same relationship as I did at Weybridge. She does not like this or anything else I suggest, but in view of her conduct yesterday it's the only course open to me. I am going to have two rooms in town. I am going up to town now in the hope of some music—there is no chance of doing any writing in the midst of such worry and storms, so pleasure seems the only course.

ALU, incomplete?: KCC

251   To Florence Barger

Harnham, Monument Green, Weybridge
23 December 1924

Dearest Florence

Many thanks for the Legenden Vol I. It is very nice having the whole series. I will practice them as soon as opportunity offers.[1] Thank you for your letter also. I will try to keep patient, but I have had seven months of it.[2] Your George boy would have crumpled in 7 days I bet!! We are off to the above address in an hour or two. It is lovely to know that I shall see you ere long.

Egypt seems to me awful, and I have felt relief that Mohammed is dead. Sydney is a Gov^t official, and all Gov^t officials are Tory.[3] I am rather bitter about over [sic] the Boxer indemnity committee, as he has (he tells me) either caused or permitted B[ertrand] Russell & Dickinson to be turned off it. Soothill (who knows China educationally and is an Oxford Professor) goes on instead of B. R., and there may be something to be said for that change. Goldie's substitute is a man who is in favour of British commercial interests; this is particularly disgusting.[4] God knows, officials have to do things they dislike, and one wouldn't blame Sydney on that account—but he appears to feel merely mild amusement at shelving the humanists and humanitarians and that did make me wild. The exact extent of his responsibility no non-official will ever discover. His mentality is unmistakable.—Goldie himself doesn't mind a dam of course.—I had quite a pleasant time with S. otherwise and of course it is only his friendly naivety that gives me my information.—

This letter seems all politics. I learn now that the Gov^t are upset about the sales of A Passage to India. They did not mind until it sold. I shall hear more shortly, and will pass it on to you if it is sufficiently interesting. The American sales are about 30,000 and still going strong: nothing can stop them there. The English is not more than 13000—I wonder whether they will ban it at this point. All this fame and money, which have so thrilled me when they came to others, leave me cold when they come to me. I am not an ascetic, but I don't know what to do with them, and my daily life has never been so trying, and there is no one to fill it emotionally. I am at

Weybridge now. Mother's here, and sweets, calendars, &ᶜᵗ, have all arrived safely, and she will be writing.

I agree with you that the news about Doctor U. is far from reassuring. I wonder what Nancy really feels—or whether she feels as we all must, that it is better to speak cheerfully.[5]

I saw Goldie at Roger Fry's. Also Malcolm Darling, who is just the same as ever. So frank, friendly, and charming.

How I do long to see you. You will like the rooms, I think. Love to all at 48.

Morgan

ALS: Mollie Barger

[1] Antonin Dvorak, *Legenden*, Op. 59, in two volumes, 1880–1.

[2] I.e. seven months of upheaval about where to live. EMF wrote to his mother (30 September 1924. KCC): 'I am sure I shall settle down in whichever house you decide on, and if it is West Hackhurst I shall probably take interest in the garden. Your decision to keep *both* houses surprised me very much, and the more I thought over it and discussed it with people the less practical it seemed. The expense—the double servant difficulty: . . . however much you reminded yourself that I could do what I like at West Hackhurst, you would not have been able to refrain as soon as you ~~saw~~ knew of me doing anything you considered unwise or unsuitable—at the very moment you suggested I should have a free hand in the place, you were dreadfully worried because I had the gorse cut down!'

[3] Sydney Waterlow, who had been instrumental in EMF's going to Nassenheide in 1905 (see Letter 49), was now a Counsellor in the Foreign Office.

[4] Bertrand Russell and Dickinson were invited to sit on a Statutory Advisory Committee, to advise Sir Austen Chamberlain (1868–1937), the Secretary of State, on disposition of China's Boxer Indemnity payments. The invitation was cancelled when Chamberlain, who declined to discuss Russell's and Dickinson's qualifications, stated that the proposed eleven-member Committee represented too little 'practical experience' of education in China, to which it was proposed to apply the money. MPs got nowhere with questions as to whether the cancellation suggested vindictiveness toward the Labour Party affiliations of Russell and Dickinson or whether it smacked of a class war. The Rev. William Edward Soothill (1861–1936), United Methodist missionary in China, 1882–1911, and President of the Imperial University of Shansi Province, 1907–11, certainly represented educational experience. But 'practical experience' apparently meant also commercial influence. The Committee as finally constituted included Sir Charles Addis (1861–1945), who had wide international banking experience and was connected with the Hongkong and Shanghai Bank; and Sir Christopher Needham (1866–1944), Manchester banker, chairman of rail, canal, and insurance companies, and an advisor on reorganisation of the Board of Trade in 1917. See *Hansard*, s. 5 (c), 179 (1924), cols. 961–2, 1261; 181 (1924), cols. 283–317; 186 (1925), cols. 2177–8.

[5] Dr U: John Frederick Unstead (1876–1965), Professor of Geography at the University of London, 1922–31, and author of textbooks on the teaching of the subject. He was a friend of Nancy Catty (1873–1959), a fellow-educationist and friend of the Bargers. She joined the teaching staff of Goldsmiths' College when it opened in 1905 as a Training College for teachers.

A FLAT IN BRUNSWICK SQUARE,
1925-30

In 1925 Forster, feeling increasingly imprisoned by his life with his mother, took a flat at 27 Brunswick Square, in Bloomsbury, and he formed the habit of spending a night or two each week in London. It enabled him to see more of his London friends, and a small group of these, among them Joe Ackerley, Gerald Heard, and Leo Charlton, would meet regularly at a favourite Soho restaurant. He had no plans for another novel, but, having in the past written some indecent stories of a facetious kind, he now wrote several serious stories on homosexual themes. These were not intended for publication in his lifetime, but he put much creative effort into them, and when T. E. Lawrence told him that 'Dr. Woolacott' was the best thing he had ever done, he was inclined to agree. In 1926 Trinity College, Cambridge, invited him to deliver the annual Clark Lectures. He chose as his subject 'Aspects of the Novel' and took the opportunity to catch up on his readings of 'modernist' contemporaries such as Gide and Joyce. The lectures, published in 1927, were a great success, and on the strength of them King's College offered him a three-year fellowship, which he accepted on the understanding that he need reside for only six weeks in the year. In 1928 the action of the Home Secretary in banning Radclyffe Hall's lesbian novel *The Well of Loneliness* prompted Forster and the Woolfs to organise a vigorous but unsuccessful protest campaign.

Despite these activities he felt somewhat at a loose end at this time, and in 1929 he went with his friends the Bargers on an extensive tour of South Africa, organised by the British Association. He found it a dispiriting experience, but on his homeward journey he paid an enjoyable return visit to Alexandria and surviving friends there.

Joe Ackerley, whose flat was in Hammersmith, had various friends among the Hammersmith police. With one of these, a talented and reckless figure named Harry Daley, Forster had for a year or two a rather chequered affair. Then, in 1930, he met a policeman friend of Daley's named Robert Buckingham. It was an important event in his life. He established with Buckingham the most intense friendship of his later years.

252   To Alice Clara Forster

c/o C[harles] Mauron, Mas Blanc, par Tarascon,
Bouches du Rhône[1]
5 March [i.e. April] 1925

Dearest Mummy,

Thanks for p. c. which I received soon after my arrival at this lovely place yesterday. I hope you got my wire, also my card from Paris. I had a most successful journey after leaving England—the French trains are now much better than ours. I travelled in an express from Paris to Tarascon (12 hours) in the greatest comfort and luxury for under £2. Prices are very cheap—even the swindling type of Hotel at Paris was not much, and my bill at Tarascon for dinner (soup, whitebait, oeuf sur le plat, cauliflower, mutton chop, fruit, biscuits, cheese, wine) bed, and café au lait in the morning was 20 francs in all—i.e. little more then 5/–. Taxi across Paris ($\frac{1}{2}$ hour's drive) was 7 francs.

Many things happened—my arrival here the most amusing perhaps. I got to Tarascon Friday night and could not make anyone understand where I wanted to go to, because I did not pronounce the s in Mas Blanc, which is apparently necessary. We got it right at last by going to a café where the entire public took part in the discussion—Provence is more like Italy than France. I took the early train Saturday and then a polite young lady introduced herself to me—the temporary schoolmistress of Mas Blanc—and we travelled together. Mauron met us at Mas Blanc—quite young and not altogether blind: very nice fellow and so intelligent. They live in the Mairie. His wife is the (permanent) village schoolmistress (having a holiday), and also secretary to the Mayor, who is a peasant and only comes in when people marry or die. She (Madame) is full of energy and ability—cooks, discusses literature, &ᶜᵗ, all the time looking so smart. A servant comes in occasionally but does not do much. I have a big and clean room containing *only* a bed, 4 chairs and a table. Nothing else at all. Windows opening in two directions on to the most heavenly country—short hedges of cypresses, standing up like black cardboard, pink flowering trees & green fields between them, and behind, hills covered with rocks and pines. There are lovely wild flowers—bee orchids and grape hyacinths—and innumerable birds make remarks both by day and night. Brilliant sun, but not at all hot—indeed on Friday it was colder than England. I sit in the garden now, accompanied by two black cats who would not make up Verouka between them.

Lucy's telegram—that she despatched for me Monday—created a great sensation, it seems. Telegrams are rare, and this was taken over the mountains to the wrong destination—a peasant, who was horrified when he saw it approach and began to cry 'Qui est mort?'

On opening it, he saw that it was in English and contained the word 'Arrive' so concluded it referred to an American agricultural machine, which he had decided not to order, and therefore was again plunged in despair. When I did arrive, the whole of the children in the village rushed to look at me, also some grown ups, and the Mayor's wife walked in (while we were out) to enquire if it really was true that an Englishman had come to stop. "Mais il est comme les autres" is the verdict on me.

We eat deliciously, but there looks likely to be very little washing. There is a pump in the kitchen for hands and a saucer of cold water in the cabinet de toilette. I must go away for a bit & do some. I shall probably come back, as much remains to be done to the translation—so continue to address here. On my homeward way I must stop in Paris to see publishers.

I sit in the garden—itself a sorry patch, but lovely spikes of cypresses surround me—all different heights. The highroad passes the gate and occasional cars rush past, but all is peace otherwise. It is altogether a charming & placid country. The Maurons are 'of it'—peasant stock both sides I think—but so lively & up to date that they must find it rather dreadful to be dumped here. He was to be a Gov^t chemist & had a good post—then came this catastrophe of his eyes.

I suppose Rosie will have gone by now—love to her if she hasn't.

ALU: KCC

[1] Charles Mauron (1899–1966), French critic and translator, was born in Provence, the son of a peasant farmer who wrote Provençal verse. Incipient blindness prevented Charles, originally trained as a scientist, from taking up a government post abroad and turned his interest to literature and philosophy. Roger Fry came to know him and his first wife Marie (later well known as a regional novelist) and introduced Charles into Bloomsbury circles. At Fry's suggestion he undertook a translation of *A Passage to India*, and Forster, who went to France in order to discuss the translation, became very friendly with him. He later translated other novels by Forster and by Virginia Woolf. His own principal contribution to literary criticism was a theory of *psycho-critique*, expounded in books on Mallarmé and Nerval. During the war he was active in the Resistance, and at the end of the German occupation, although by now quite blind, he was elected mayor of St Rémy, as his father had been before him. EMF wrote to Ackerley (6 May 1925. HRC): 'The Maurons are a great find—he & she both young, gay, and intelligent. They have no furniture and the most exquisite food which Madame cooks and serves with gestures of despair.'

253   To Dora Carrington (Partridge)

West Hackhurst, Abinger Hammer, Dorking
13 April 1926

My dear Carrington—Thank you for your loving letter. I did like it very much. I sail from the Tower Bridge for the Chapon Fin on Saturday.[1] The latter is probably very costly, but I shall only be there a night or two. The voyage takes three days. I should like to come and see you on my return.

Human beings cannot be dull if I find them interesting, because if I find them interesting I am interesting, and if I am interesting they are. Twiggez-vous?[2] Or supportez vous the still more interesting proposition that I am dull whenever I am interested?

I am glad about Lytton's Edinburgh degree. But may not the students laugh at him when he takes it?[3]

Much love from
Morgan

ALS: HRC

[1] Hôtel du Chapin-Fin, Bordeaux: EMF had asked Carrington's advice, saying that he 'thought of going off there (as soon as I have served on a jury), and ending up in Provence, which I know' (26 March 1926. University of San Francisco).

[2] 'Twiggez-vous': borrowed from Kipling; cf. *Stalky and Co.*, (1899), Chapter 2.

[3] On 20 July 1926 the University of Edinburgh gave Strachey an honorary Doctorate in Law.

254   To Hilton Young

West Hackhurst, Abinger Hammer, Dorking
28 August 1926

My dear Hilton,

I wonder where you are—well and happy I hope, and all of you also. There is nothing at all in this letter. I only had the impulse to tell you my news. Nothing the least exciting: I am merely happy and well too. I have just come back from Sweden and Denmark as well, and liked them very much.[1] The further north I went the hotter it got, and the more the people bathed. At Stockholm I attended a physiological congress, and for this I was given a medal, but could not attend a banquet in the City Hall, owing to absence of clothes. This absence was bravely born[e], a fortnight later, by the widow of a margarine millionaire in Jutland. Towsled but respected, I sat by her side, while down the centre of the enormous table stretched the national flag of Denmark, executed in dahlias. How very nice the Danes are! I am so used to travelling in countries where the English are hated and where one has to be unduly affable or intelligent in consequence, that is a real rest to rely upon the Nelson touch.[2] I liked the Swedes too, but many of these were physiologists and therefore sources of anxiety.

Earlier in the year I went to France—the man there who translated a Passage to India became my friend during the process.[3] He is going blind. He is a very wonderful fellow, Provençal: he and his wife are of peasant stock. But it rained in France. What was good was the voyage out—London to Bordeaux.

This is all very well, but what about one's work? Oh God. Well, I have got a thing called the Clark lectures, and no doubt you have got some thing important too. On hearing from you what it is, I will try to settle on something more important still. My lectures will be entitled "~~Some~~ 'Aspects of the Novel', and indeed I was preparing them when suddenly I was obliged to write to you. Analysing 'The Ambassadors' had been too much for me. Everything so perfect and apparently so noble, and then you look in the dust bin or the W. C. and find that H. J. has very quietly pared off and thrown away, for the purposes of his damned pattern, all that *really* makes life noble, all that's interesting too, all that's exciting to body and spirit.[4] We don't stand this, Hilton, I fancy. And now I must go to bed. It is late and very quiet. My mother is asleep. Two maids—the third has left and cannot be replaced—are asleep also. Percy comes to lunch to morrow, I dine with Leo on Monday, Thursday I go to stop with Mrs Borchgrevink in the Lakes.[5] And so our lives go on, the items in them so failing to coincide that at times we are afraid. This is a blunder though. Nothing is gained by coincidence. So good night, and good luck.

Love from

M organ .

ALS: Cambridge University Library, for Lord Kennet

[1] About 20 July EMF went with George Barger to a physiological congress in Stockholm. On 23 July he was in Copenhagen. On 13 August he went to Elsinore with a young man named Aage, whom he met selling papers, 'very gay & gentle, probably doesn't tell me the truth, but I don't tell it to him either.' EMF enjoyed the trip, although he and Barger had to 'thunder through Sweden in 3rd Class sleepers because all our money was gone' (to Ackerley [13 August 1926]. HRC).

[2] Perhaps the Mrs Schou mentioned in EMF's 'Locked Diary' (KCC), folio 60. Nelson touch: on 2 April 1801, Lord Nelson bombarded Copenhagen.

[3] I.e., Charles Mauron.

[4] The eight lectures delivered in Cambridge, January–March 1927, and published in October 1927 as *Aspects of the Novel*. For EMF on James, *The Ambassadors*, see *AN*, pp. 104–9, 145–6.

[5] His cousin Percy Whichelo, and Lionel Evelyn Oswald Charlton (1879–1956), called Leo. Charlton, an Air Commodore, was one of the first enthusiasts for military flying, as well as an early prophet of its dangerous consequences for the future. He was Air Attaché at the British Embassy, Washington, 1919–22, then Chief Staff Officer in the Iraq Command, 1923–4. He retired in 1928 after protesting air bombardments there. On EMF's Alexandria friend Aïda Borchgrevink, see Letter 155.

255 To W. J. H. Sprott

West Hackhurst, Abinger Hammer, Dorking
18 December 1926

Dear Mr Sprott

You will think me very funny, another letter so soon, but really life is too extraordinary—what do you think Agnes brought in with the tea *this* morning—Reading by Hugh Walpole. Mr Forster is as flabbergasted as myself though in a different way, as on opening 'Reading' it turns out to be dedicated to him.[1] I think there is nothing like a writer for giving another one a nice surprise, and one so on the spot too. You would love to see Mʳ Forster's face. It is in a series called 'These Diversions'—"Talking" by J. B. Priestley, "Dreaming" by De la Mare (Dreaming—odd again—) "Idling" by Robert Lynd, "Wandering" by Hilaire Belloc, ~~and~~ "Playgoing" by James Agate, and "Fucking" by ~~Sir William Marchant~~ Lady Gregory. But no more at present.

I. M.[2]

Yes. Very diverting.

As to wine, when you have drunk 2 doz bottles send them back in case—never mind about completing the third dozen. So glad you enjoyed it. Was the port good really? I want to get some, also red table wines, so all you can say is useful to me.

Please write again. I want to hear about Stan very much.[3] I am awfully sorry. What was it, and how long did he get?

I went to Weybridge—dully with mother yesterday to see a play, and secretly and amusingly about six weeks ago. My life is literary & idealistic since then. I hope the calm will not continue.

I don't know of a job for Bert—easily found doubtless. Very sad he's going. What arrangements are you making in his place? What's Charles [Lovett]'s job? And is Billy Peck cropped everywhere, or don't you know?

You must write again—your letter's all title pages.

Love from
Morgan.

Did you know that Mʳˢ Orlo Williams was once the wife of Sydney Waterlow?[4]

ALS: KCC

[1] Hugh Walpole, *Reading: An Essay: Being One of a Series of Essays edited by J. B. Priestley and entitled: These Diversions* (1926). The dedication in the English edition reads: 'For E. M. Forster / This Essay / with Admiration'; it was omitted from the American edition. The Walpole and Priestley essays are fact; the remainder are fictional.

[2] I.e., 'Isabella Moffat', a joke identity assumed by EMF in letters to Sprott.

[3] Stan, and others mentioned here: friends of Sprott.

[4] Orlando Cyprian (Orlo) Williams (1883–1967) became Clerk to the House of Commons in 1907 and retired in 1948; he wrote a number of books on the history of the House and some of its leading figures. In 1912 he married Alice Isabella Pollock, who was the first wife of Sydney Waterlow; cf. Letters 49, 79.

256   To Florence Barger

West Hackhurst, Abinger Hammer, Dorking
26 December 1926

Dearest Florence,

I must send you a little line, though you will have heard bits of me through George and through Nancy also. I did have such a marvellous concert with her. I shall never forget it, and there is scarcely anyone whom I could so like to have been with. We had the Debussy Quartet, which I haven't cared for hitherto, and the Franck Quintet which I suspect of being the greatest human achievement during my lifetime. It and I were both born in the same year (1879).[1]

A good deal of excitement, one way and another, has occurred. T. E. Lawrence did me proud, devoted a whole day to catching hold of me before his departure to India, and gave me a gorgeous copy of the private edition of 'The Seven Pillars of Wisdom', with practically all the illustrations.[2] I look forward to your reading it when you can [care] to do so. It is *a very great work*. I am certain. One wants to settle down to it comfortably. I hoped I should get some sort of copy, but that he should do me so regally was a very great pleasure and surprise. He has given me 'A Cape Cod Fire Lighter' also, hearing I was troubled with damp wood. I used to think him incapable of affection, but have changed my opinion, and think he has some for me. To be with him, or read him, is a great experience, as he has the power of making one feel one could do all he has done. I don't know whether this is a sign of genius, certainly few people possess it.

Frank Vicary writes constantly. Yes, we did have a very happy time together here. We have just ate [sic] a goose of his for Christmas. He's again been ill—kidney congestion—and his tiresome wife is always ill because she can't face the dentist. I am afraid that this last may become a real cloud on their life.

Edward Carpeth [Carpenter] and Co. are remarkably fit. I called there last week.

Things here are fairly good. Wireless a great success. I fear though that Ruth's state of health is worse than Mother reckons. All this bromide must be telling on her, and her leg is most obstinate in healing. She is always ill and Agnes generally cross, and I much wish that Mother would have considered Mrs Mackie: we do very much want fresh blood.[3] But that's out of the question. Practically no visitors come here to stop unless they ask to do so: when they ask it is all right, and mother makes no difficulty. The house is very cumbersome and it is a bore putting so much money into it and getting so little opportunity of entertaining in return. However, they are all getting old, and I mustn't fuss, and I have a real mental retreat in my London rooms, though my body occupies them seldom. Hashim is there now.[4] He was down for the day on Tuesday.

My lectures feel stale, and much will depend on my mood at the time of delivery. They are full of epigrams, with images, and all that, but I've not the least notion whether they'll come alive, or will help people to appreciate moods. 'Flecker's Magic' by Norman Matson has made a good deal of impression on me. The author sent me it. I know nothing about him—American.[5]

I have also received from Hugh Walpole a copy of his dish-water essay, entitled 'Reading' which he dedicates to me without bothering to ask my permission: didn't even bother to send me a copy until, in answer to a line of flighty apology, I asked for one.[6]

Well this is all about myself, but I know dearest Florence that's what you want. When do you come south?

Will mention all your affairs another time.

Your loving
Morgan.

Was re-reading Mohamed's letters today—the later ones. They have more affection and depth than those he wrote earlier, and gave me a good deal of comfort. I knew I minimised his worries at the end of his life but didn't realise how clearly he saw this too. Also I loved his references to you, dearest Florence.[7]

TTr supplied by Mollie Barger

[1] This was Claude Debussy's only completed string quartet (Op. 10, 1893). The César Franck quintet (1878–9) was first performed in 1880.

[2] The handsome 'Subscriber's Text' edition; May Buckingham inherited EMF's copy. Lawrence left for India in December 1926. He wrote to EMF (11 January 1927. KCC): 'India is considerably beyond the world, & in this depot [Karachi] they seem to read no papers. Bless them. / I'd like to think that that book is a good one—but, Lord, the bad writing & fumbled situation in it: and the sense of strain. You write as if it was no athletic feat at all.'

[3] Ruth: Ruth Goldsmith, the Forsters' cook, and Agnes Dowland, the housemaid.

[4] Hashim Ali: Masood's relative.

[5] See *Aspects of the Novel*, pp. 78–81. Norman Matson (1893–1965), American novelist and journalist of Norwegian descent, wrote short stories for popular American magazines and worked for the London *Daily Express* and for *L'Humanité* in Paris. *Flecker's Magic* (1926), his first novel, is about a Minnesota youth studying art in Paris.

[6] Walpole wrote (10 October 1924. KCC): 'I owe you so much for helping me years ago. Do you remember that it was to you that I sent the manuscript of my first novel? I thought then that I was going to be a whacking great novelist. However—I hope eternally... / As for yourself your books are the best thing in modern fiction to me, now that Conrad is dead.' Cf. Letter 71.

[7] About Florence, EMF later wrote to Sprott (8 August 1929. KCC): 'My relation to her is queer. I told her all about myself up to 1921—i.e. the year Mohammed died, and she has made something sacred and permanent for herself out of this, which fresh confidences would disturb.'

257   To Virginia Woolf

The Union Society, Cambridge
5 June 1927

Dear Virginia,

I don't arrange my thoughts about your book easily and am not sure that it invites arrangement.[1] I should like to come and see you and talk some time if I may. It is awfully sad, very beautiful both in

Harry Daley.   E. M. ('Francis') Bennett.

A boatrace day party at J.R. Ackerley's c. 1929. Left to
right: 2 Anwar Masood (?), 3 Tom Wichelo, 4 Mrs Roger Ackerley,
5 Leo Charlton, 7 Akbar Masood (?) standing, 10 J.R. Ackerley, 11 EME

(non-radiant) colour and shape, it stirs me much more to questions of whether and why than anything else you have written. The uneasiness of life seems to well up between all the words, the excitement of life on the other hand to be observed, stated. This I believe to be right: excitement would dry up those little winds. I must now read it again—am inclined to think it your best work (my mother by the way is sure it is—she took to it immensely). Thank you again for giving it me.

I am up here taking my part in the Life of the College, and, after so many years peaceful cadging, not enjoying it very much. Such a dirty place, always washing one's hands, and bad complicated food.

Morgan

ALS: Berg

[1] Virginia Woolf, *To the Lighthouse* (1927).

258   To Robert Graves

West Hackhurst, Abinger Hammer, Dorking
12 June 1927

This letter contains
No insults no threats
No chilblains
No jets
of acid.
It's placid.
It simply do come
From the partially dumb
Partially deaf
E.M.F.

Your poems are very nice—that on Philately
    contains truths long crying for *expression*.[1]
Since you say you want money and I have no great
    feeling for splendid editions, shall I return
You the copy of Welchman's Hose you gave me? It's
    a lovely book, probably valuable, and the Clipped
Stater, which I like most in it, and no doubt the
    others I liked, are reprinted in the collected edition.[2]

ALS: Southern Illinois University-Carbondale

[1] Graves, 'Philatelist Royal', in his *Poems 1928–1930*, pp. 9–11.
[2] Graves, 'The Clipped Stater', in his *Welchman's Hose*, pp. 40–5. Stater: a Persian gold coin or Daric paid to Alexander, who survives here as a common soldier.

259 To Virginia Woolf

Leyland [Lancashire]. 28 June 1927

This by return of post in haste. *I don't believe my method's wrong*! The trouble is I can't work it: through simple lack of the coordinating power that Ibsen had. My novels will be either almost-successes or failures:—probably in its future almost-successes, because experience enables one to substitute cleverness for force with increasing verisimilitude.[1] Would like to see you before France and will ring up if I can.

Sky solid ink, roads pimpled with rain. How will your train fare? I forget where it anchors.

With love and thanks
M

ALS: Berg

[1] EMF is replying to a draft of Virginia Woolf's article, 'The Novels of E. M. Forster', *The Atlantic Monthly*, 140 (1927), 642–8.

260 To Leonard Woolf

West Hackhurst, Abinger Hammer, Dorking
9 August 1927

Dear Leonard,

Thank you for your letter. I hope particularly that Virginia's article may appear in the 19th, for the reason that the most horrible acquaintance I have has informed me that he proposes to write about me there, and this will stop him. Be sure that she does not spoil the article by softening down or omitting anything; there is no individual phrase that I 'mind' in the least.[1]

Looking forward to the 10th of Sept.

Morgan

ALS: Sussex University

[1] Presumably the periodical *The Nineteenth Century and After*.

261 To T. E. Lawrence

West Hackhurst, Abinger Hammer, Dorking
9 August 1927

Dear T.E.S[haw].

I am very pleased to get your letters. Yes, we will not write about Posh any more unless there is practical reason. I keep in touch. You shall have a photograph of the picture when it's done—and you shall have the picture too the moment you are in a condition to be sold or given anything, but I know not when such a condition will arise.[1]

Thanks for the information about Mahmas, which rather puts your collator to shame. I had not as a matter of fact 'done' that section of the books yet. I don't know why I forgot Mahmas though. I remember everything about Awad.[2]

Your news interests me. I believe that reading, thinking, sitting in an aerodrome, are all right for you, and that suddenly you will find the world endurable. I wish I could give you my pelt, but if indeed I have one it cannot of course be given. I am sending you, in case you are still out for me, the proofs of my lectures (uncorrected). It is a spare copy—I do not want it back—and reads like a saucerful of last week's grape nuts. As for the short story, it is closely woven and distinguished, but it will not ever be published, as it belongs to the same class as the story which made you laugh. Do you remember, too, a novel I mentioned to you? I offered you the reading of it when you were in England, but you did not seem keen, I did not understand why.[3] These are items which you must have in your mind if you want to sum me up. Virginia Woolf, deprived of the items, has just made the attempt.[4] I will send you her article when it gets published. I suppose I am elusive and difficult, but there are one or two people (and you're one of them) to whom I'd like to be clear. I haven't any secrets from you—that is to say there's no question you asked which I wouldn't answer. But this again is not what you want, not what you want, alas.   Don't bother about reconciling the statements in my books with my conduct at the tea table. See whether you can reconcile the statements with each other, and you will find that you cannot, alas that you cannot. And even Virginia Woolf has discovered this.   If ever I ~~write~~ & publish a book again, a real one, it will be dedicated to you. Do not bother to refuse permission. I am bringing out some old short stories next spring. I like them. They will not however be dedicated to any one.[5]

Yours
E.M.F.

ALS: KCC

[1] Lawrence and EMF were trying to help 'Posh' Palmer after his discharge from the army. An Augustus John portrait drawing of him (present owner unknown) was to be sold and the proceeds paid to Palmer in instalments. EMF's letters to Palmer: HRC.

[2] Mahmas and Awad: members of Lawrence's Arabian bodyguard. EMF was trying to collate the 'Oxford' and 'Cranwell' editions of *Seven Pillars*, for a superior third version. Lawrence wrote to EMF (21 July 1927. KCC): 'Mahmas makes an unheroic entry and exit on page 468 [i.e. 486] of the Seven Pillars. Afterwards he came back to me, . . . He is, I fancy, the only one of my bodyguard, besides the two chief men, to have kept his right name throughout. I altered nearly all the Arab names, so that no one should be given away by the book.'

[3] Lectures: *Aspects of the Novel*. Short story: 'Doctor Woolacott'. 'Story . . . laugh': 'The Life to Come'. Novel: *Maurice*.

⁴ On Virginia Woolf's article, see Letter 259.
⁵ This was *The Eternal Moment and Other Stories*, published in March 1928. Nevertheless, they were addressed 'To T. E. in the Absence of anything else.' EMF wrote to Lawrence (15 October 1927. KCC): 'Do I think, ask the publishers, that they are *quite* as good as the Celestial Omnibus volume? I do not. I shall read them over in proof, and if I wish to and if you have not stopped me I may put To T. E. before them. . . . they seem all that I am likely to have to give you and I should like to give you something.'

262 To Robert Graves

West Hackhurst, Abinger Hammer, Dorking
26 September 1927

Dear Graves,
    I was very glad to get your letter this morning—the telephone message didn't reach me, or I would have rung you up. I can stand you in your setting though you tell me you cannot stand me in mine, and I am willing to come to your house again. We must fix something up later on. Are you quite sure you're a mountain and not a mouse? I'm quite sure I'm not Mohammed.

Yours ever
EMForster

ALS: Southern Illinois University-Carbondale

263 To T. E. Lawrence

King's [College].   17 November 1927

Dear T. E.
    Yes I know Doctor Woolacott is the best thing I've done and also unlike anyone else's work.¹ I am very glad it got you, I hope you will write again and at length. I want to know, among other things, when you first guessed the oncomer was a spook. Not until the cupboard, or before?
    The story makes me happy. It gives bodily ecstacy outside time and place. I shall never be able to give it again, but once is something.
    Odd that in my daily life I should be so timid and ingratiating and consequently so subject to pain. Your letter helps me a lot. I have gone through the story today in my mind, with the knowledge you have read it, and this ~~comforts me strengthens~~ hardens (got it!) me.
    I believe, as you know, that you are a "greater genius than myself" to use the dreary phrase, and put this in here to explain my attitude to you, and the things I say. Not for any other reason. Don't contradict me—only wastes time. Write again about Doctor Woolacott.² From your friend:—

Edward Morgan Forster

ALS: KCC

[1] EMF probably wrote 'Dr. Woolacott' (*LTC*, pp. 113–27) earlier in 1927. Lawrence had written: 'It's the most powerful thing I ever read. Nearly made me ill: and I haven't yet summoned up the courage to read it again. Some day I'll write you properly about it. A great privilege, it is, to get a thing like that. / Virginia [Woolf] obviously hadn't seen it: or she wouldn't have put so much piffle in her note on you. Which note also holds some very good stuff. I liked it: but she has only met the public side of you, apparently. Or else she doesn't know the difference between skin & bone. / . . . And the odd, extraordinary thing is that you go about talking quite carefully to us ordinary people. How on earth. . . . .' (Letter to EMF, 27 October 1927. KCC.)

[2] Lawrence sent a long analysis of the story (21 December 1927. ALS, KCC, TTr, Northwestern University Library). EMF replied in kind: see Letter 265.

264   To Alice Clara Forster

The Reform Club [London]
Monday [16 January 1928]

Dearest—I feel rather incoherent and sore so am stopping till tomorrow—minced turkey and poached egg is on the menu further to persuade me. Perhaps I may be down for lunch, but shall only want soup or bovril and egg. I went on straight to the Abbey—rather tiring but got a very good position, close to the procession and burial place. Mrs Hardy was so heavily veiled she could scarcely see to walk, I think. She was with Cockerill [*sic*] —Barrie put a few flowers by the grave for her. It was very wonderful standing close to such great people for so long—Ramsay MacDonald was by far the finest looking of them, and Baldwin the least fine—a bad face, I thought, which I hadn't at all expected, and he bore himself without dignity. Galsworthy & Barrie looked nice, Kipling, dumped between R. Mac. and B. Shaw, did not seem to appreciate his position.[1]

Hashim has been in—we had tea together.

Love from <u>Pop</u>

ALS: KCC

[1] Hardy died on 11 January 1928. His heart was buried at Stinsford after cremation on 14 January, and his ashes were buried at Westminster Abbey on the 16th. Sir Sydney Carlyle Cockerell (1867–1962) entered the world of literature and the arts when he became secretary to William Morris's Kelmscott Press, 1889–92; a partner in the Doves Press, 1900–4; then Director of the Fitzwilliam Museum, 1908–37. He was noted for his managing ways with friends' affairs and with art works that he coveted for the Museum. He had known Hardy since 1911 and was co-executor with Mrs Hardy. He took charge at the Abbey and also proceeded to sort Hardy's papers. Open strife between him and Mrs Hardy began on the very day of the funeral, in disagreement about a memorial; see Wilfrid Blunt, *Cockerell*, pp. 212–23; Robert Gittings, *The Older Hardy*, pp. 211–14.

265 To T. E. Lawrence

West Hackhurst, Abinger Hammer, Dorking
15 March 1928

Dear T. E.

Your letter of Feb. 16th is with me.[1] You seem nearly always ill, sometimes very ill, and I can still go for weeks with no more physical discomfort than slight tirednesses. This makes a gulf between us. You may remember what I feel like, but I can't guess what you feel like, except that it is necessarily lonely. <I imagine there is no communion between sufferers, each must go his own way, and it is only the un-pained who have anything like a common consciousness> I don't want to take your sufferings on myself— we both of us know too much for such a wish to be uttered—but I often wish I could help you in any other way.

No one will ever write to me as you wrote about <u>Doctor Woolacott.</u> It is the experience of a life time to get such praise and I don't think of it as praise. I mean never to send you anything of mine again (unless you should ask me to do so). What you have written has the effect of something absolute on me. Other people don't think the story good. One criticism is that I am too much involved and agitated, another that it is too laboured, too much in the form of notes. Many of the subtleties and illogicalities were felt not to come off. But I believe with you that it is the best thing I have done and that it hasn't been done before. I enclose some notes which I made on the reception of your previous letter. They may not interest you, but they are of no interest to anyone else.

I meant to write an ordinary letter but it does not seem possible. I will do so shortly.

E. M. F.

Doctor Woolacott Corrections arising out of T. E.'s letter.

I   ~~Convalescence......~~ ~~*67*~~ .

II   (Clothes) "Presently a visitor drifted in, a young man in good though rather provincial clothes, with a cap in his hand and...&[ct]
      —I think this is as near right as I shall ever get——~~Associating with that kind~~ is living with fellows like that.——~~Deliberately charming~~: all the sentence in which these words are goes from beginning to end: strength gained for image, though time-beat of narrative suffers.——not ~~alone.~~ . ~~louder than his own~~ omitted with great advantage——And by the way I have changed the visitor's previous remark from "Or even not talking" into "Saturday's my free afternoon, lucky". And perhaps Cl[esant]'s 'Yes' just before should be "What—what shall we say?"

With Bob Buckingham.

Left to right: Robin
Buckingham, May Buckingham,
EMF, Margaret French, Bob
Buckingham, London 1949.

I'll do him in yet   ~~ ~ ~~ .
Double edged sword, poison cloud, his broad shoulders sticking, all
    returned unused.
III   ~~Fatal, fatal~~   ~ ~ .
        Ring omitted: but 'something sharp' must ~~remain~~ remain

ALS: KCC

[1] Lawrence had written (16 February 1928. KCC): 'Your long letter replying to my Dr. W. impertinences came: I have been through it inch by inch with the text: and see now, much better, what were the difficulties you fought, in writing the story. What I thought were blemishes were put in to catch my eye, where they weren't the inevitable scars of creation. Truth is, I'm not of the class fit to read your writing: and that's a hard thing to say, for I read as carefully as anyone I know.'

266   To A. E. Housman

West Hackhurst, Abinger Hammer, Dorking
28 March 1928

Dear Professor Housman,
    The publishers are sending you a volume of short stories. They are not at all good but the second of them happens to be as near as I shall ever get to 'Hell Gate', and that is why they are coming to you.[1] I don't know whether there is such a thing as impersonal affection, but the words best express the feeling I have had towards you, through your poems, for the last thirty years, and I ask you to pardon this expression of it.
    No occasion to acknowledge this or book. I am occasionally in Trinity, and may happen to have the pleasure of meeting you then—Yours sincerely—EMForster

ALS: Bryn Mawr College, Seymour Adelman Collection

[1] Short stories: *The Eternal Moment* (1928), the second of which is 'The Point of It' (pp. 87-125). In Housman's *Last Poems* (1922), 'Hell Gate' is No. 31. Housman's response to this was so 'absolutely hateful', that EMF destroyed the letter 'after one rapid perusal'. He later discovered that Housman was revenging himself upon him for not dining often enough in Trinity College while Clark Lecturer. (EMF's Housman Memoir, MS: KCC). Cf. Letters 225, 332.

267   To G. Herbert Thring[1]

West Hackhurst, Abinger Hammer, Dorking
9 October 1928

Dear Mr Thring,
    Thank you for your very kind letter, informing me that I have been nominated to membership of the Council. The invitation is most gratifying, and under ordinary circumstances I should have accepted with pleasure.
    I do not however feel that I can well accept in view of your previous letter to me, namely that of September 21st, in which you

convey to me Lord Gorrell's decision as to the policy to be pursued by the Society in regard to THE WELL OF LONELINESS.[2] I can readily understand that the Committee, after carefully discussing the matter, (and, as you and I agreed, it is a difficult matter) might decide that it was impolitic to take any action as regards the censorship in connection with this particular book. That is a comprehensible attitude. But that the matter should be taboo, that it should be actually impossible to raise it for discussion either before the Committee or in the pages of THE AUTHOR, means that those who control the policy of the Society take a view of its responsibilities which I cannot share.[3]

Will you therefore please convey to the Committee my great appreciation of the honour that has been offered to me, and also inform them of the ground of my refusal?

Yours sincerely,
EMForster

TLS: The Society of Authors Film Archive

[1] George Herbert Thring (1859–1941), Secretary of The Society of Authors, 1892–1930.
[2] *The Well of Loneliness* (1928), novel about lesbians by Radclyffe Hall (Marguerite Antonia Radclyffe-Hall [1880–1943]), was ruled obscene by the Home Secretary, the notoriously puritanical Sir William Joynson-Hicks, 1st Viscount Brentford (1865–1932), generally known as 'Jix'. The Society of Authors, whose Chairman from 1928 to 1935 was Robert Gorrell Barnes, 3rd Baron Gorell (1884–1963), was deciding whether the book had enough literary merit to warrant its defence. EMF, who had campaigned vigorously in its favour, promised reluctantly to appear in court on its behalf. He wrote to Walpole (27 October 1928. HRC): 'Now this wretched case comes on, and I have promised to give evidence as to the decency of the tedious Well, if it's considered imperative. Duty appears to call—an unusual effort on her part—and I am responding, though with a heavy heart; I am certain to drop some awful brick.'
[3] *The Author*: journal of the Society, published since 1890.

268   To Hugh Walpole

In a train   31 October 1928

Dear Hugh Walpole,

So glad of your letter and that you don't think my refusal unreasonable. No, I don't for a moment think that the S[ociety] of A[uthors] could be compelled to discuss the 'Well' or other censored books, but I think it *ought*——when there has been regrettable publicity as at the present—to discuss them.[1] Part of its job. And, thinking this, I prefer to remain a private member of the Society: which has done and I am sure will continue to do good work as regards authors' agreements, copyright difficulties &c.

I think it very good of you to give evidence in this lamentable case. It is harder for you than for me, not only your much greater reputation but you're in full creative-mood whereas I'm turning out nothing. And it's hard even for me, and the knowledge you feel we've got to is a great consolation to me and will cause me to sleep better this evening than I did last night. Your welcome letter caught me just as I was leaving Edinburgh.

Yours ever
EMForster

ALS: HRC

[1] *The Well of Loneliness* case, brought against Jonathan Cape, its publisher, became a test of the 1857 Obscene Publications Act. EMF wrote to T. E. Lawrence: 'The big people (Shaw genuinely too big) declined to offer their evidence. Upright, nervy, and foolish, and 39 in number, we sat huddled together in Bow Street last Friday, rather disliking one another, and wondering whether this can be war. The magistrate was very polite. He said he did not think that we could help him. Counsel for the defence then waxed confident, and described us as the most distinguished set of witnesses who had ever been gathered in any court, and during his speech an enormous coal-black negro entered and tried to sit down beside him' (paragraph omitted from letter of 12 November 1928, in *Letters to T. E. Lawrence*, pp. 70–1 (TTr, KCC). The evidence of the distinguished thirty-nine was finally ruled inadmissible. An appeal on 14 December was denied. The author made things difficult for her supporters by insisting that they come out unequivocally for the book, not only as not obscene, but as a masterpiece, and at this many of them balked. Literary biographies and memoirs of the period abound with accounts of this episode, but see *EMF*, II, 153–5; [Forster] 'The New Censorship', *The Nation and The Athenaeum*, 43 (1928), 696; Forster and Virginia Woolf, 'The New Censorship' (letter), *ibid.*, 726; Virginia Woolf, *Letters*, III, 520, 525–6, 529–30, 555–6, 563; Lovat Dickson, *Radclyffe Hall at the Well of Loneliness*, pp. 156–71.

269 To Alice Clara Forster

In train—leaving Kimberley
29 July 1929

Dearest—I will attempt a line in this jolty train and post on reaching J'burg. Then I am sure to catch mail, though I shall have to post before further news of dearest. It is 9.30 P. M. I have washed some diamond dust out of my hair and neck, and lie in bed, not very tired though day has been strenuous. We arrived 9.0. A. M. and were the guests of the diamond-mine people all day.[1] I can't think why they did it. It was most impressive to see the whole countryside turned upside down for the sake of diamonds, barbed wire everywhere, black convicts working, police, rubbish heaps like mountains, holes in the ground 3000 feet deep; one of them, the Kimberley mine proper, is the biggest hole in the world—acres wide, and narrowing, pit after pit, the lowest pit being full of water. They have stopped working it, as the edges keep falling in. It is the most imbecile industry in the world, I suppose. We saw all the processes except actually getting out the soil. The most interesting is the last, where the grit is washed by water down a sort of sloping bagatelle board, smeared with vaseline. The diamonds, and nothing else, stick in the grease. We had a large blow out of a lunch at a hotel, wine, speeches, that old ruffian Cecil Rhodes was praised, altogether a most vulgar and interesting day.[2] I don't think I shall now ever give you or any body a diamond bracelet. The mines are in great difficulties now, not because they find too few stones, but because they find too many and prices would fall unless they held up their stocks.

Well, feeling very wise I will now go to sleep. After the mines, rather to please some other people, I joined in a car to a prehistoric site on the Modder River, and was rewarded by a very beautiful evening with spring-bok skipping close to the road and an attentive owl following the car. The country all seemed burnt, even the stones. Lovely donkeys—I counted 20, in pairs, harnessed to a cart.

Rand Club, Johannesburg.   29 July 1929

Dearest

Safely arrived and am writing in this notorious haunt of millionaires and swindlers to say that the mail from England will reach me at the University tomorrow only just before the mail for England leaves. So I shall leave this open for a very brief line on your news.

Host and hostess—with a number on their car to match my own (180) met me this morning.[3] All splendidly organised. He is a financier or newspaper controller or something, but I am only here till Sat. and have engagements with Canon Parker &^{ct} so I hope it'll all go easily.[4] Very hospitable, like everyone. Has made me a member of the Club—lives some miles out and is now about to pick me up in his car. We dine tomorrow with Mrs S. G. Millin, a South African novelist—she seems to me good, though I hadn't heard of her. Do read her *God's Stepchildren* if you can—it is about the poor coloured people whom I found so distressing at Cape Town.[5] The other lady of local note, Miss Fairbridge, is a sort of Mrs Cran—who by the way has written about S. A. too.[6]

Talk all around about whisky and horses, antlers all around on the walls.

––––––––––

[S. S.] Balmoral Castle mail just in—have peeped with love at your beloved letter.

This must go. All well. —Darling.

ALS: KCC

[1] The group were guests of the De Beers Diamond Company.

[2] The speech praising Rhodes was by Sir Thomas Henry Holland (1868–1947), who held a wide array of metallurgical and mining appointments. In 1929 he was President of the British Association, Vice-President of the Royal Society, and Rector of the Imperial College of Science and Technology.

[3] His host and hostess were a Mr and Mrs MacLeod. 'My own': members of the group were assigned numbers.

[4] Canon William Hasell Parker (18??–1935) was on the ship from England. He was Vicar, 1881–1935, of All Saints, Cockermouth (Cumbria).

[5] Mrs Sarah Gertrude (Liebson) Millin (1889–1968) was one of the most prolific South African writers of that era. Her novel *God's Stepchildren* (1924) deals with the problems of mixed marriages.

[6] Dorothea Fairbridge (1862–1931) wrote books on South African life and travel. Mrs George Cran (Marian Dudley Cran) (1879–1942) wrote improving books whose titles featured the word 'garden'.

270   To Robert Bridges

West Hackhurst, Abinger Hammer, Dorking
1 February 1930

Dear Bridges,

I have been reading in and thinking about The Testament of Beauty a good deal during the last month, indeed I must have read the whole of it more than twice, though not consecutively.[1] My thoughts about it are as unimportant as they must be about any philosophic work, but I wanted to let you know of my pleasure. The metre eases me, flies me along, I find no trouble here, nor with the spelling, and then I get such varied lovelinesses: often a definite phrase—e.g. the one which names the final resting place of the Divine Comedy; but sometimes a beauty on which I can't put and don't want to put my finger—something that is diffused through the depths of an argument—like light through water, and that doubtless implies one of the greater triumphs of the poetic art.—I move pretty blindly through all these countries, but know when I am in them.

A good deal more is in my mind, mainly about Christianity, but I won't attempt to get it down. Christ (*as revealed in the Gospels*) has never been loved by me, and this seems to part me not merely from the orthodox but from great companies of the unorthodox, amongst whom I should number yourself. Christ restated, with the name withdrawn and the gestures and accent altered, would ~~touch one in a very~~ seem different ~~way~~, and perhaps it is this restatement that I feel every now and then in your poem, and that moves me so much, especially at the end, where you speak of the soul returning the body's loving: although you don't restate openly.

However, that's enough. I am really only writing to thank you. When I'm next in Oxford, I look forward to calling on you. Will you thank Mrs Bridges very much for her letter, please.[2]

———

All is well here, except with our Lord Farrer's elms, which, with misplaced humility, have been bowing themselves down to the ground of our garden, or spanning Hackhurst Lane. I am engaged, for the moment, in moving into a small flat I've taken in town.[3]

With all kind remembrances to Mrs Bridges and yourself,

Yours ever
EMForster

ALS: Bodleian Library, for Lord Bridges

[1] Robert Bridges, *The Testament of Beauty: A Poem in Four Books* (1929). EMF had for some years felt an affinity with Bridges' views; cf. Letter 163.

[2] Mrs Bridges' letter does not survive.

[3] EMF was moving at this time from 27 Brunswick Square, which he had leased in 1925, to 26 Brunswick Square, which remained his London base till October 1939.

271   To David Cecil

King's College, Cambridge
2 March 1930

Dear Cecil,

I have only just read your Cowper, and this is to tell you how good I think it, and how perfectly written.[1] I can't add how much I've enjoyed it, for the reason that I share too much of C., including his dread of January, to feel comfortable while reading about him. Educated people have a few more straws to cling to in the 20th cent. than in the 18th—there is just that to say; fears about one's individual destiny are on the wane, and in my own case have yielded to fears of the next war, and to the certainty that if it ever starts, there will be no war after next. And then there is what one vaguely calls 'Freud'—not a very solid straw, not a freshly-smelling one, yet it would have supported Cowper in certain ways when he stumbled on the brink of his pit, and helped him to cause less agony to those who loved him. That last tragedy is, of course, one which only writers like yourself can bring out; it is entirely beyond the power of cynics; and it is the belief that you value what I do in human relationships that has made me venture to write to you. Also (which is very sympathetic) you seem to believe in it without hope of a reward.

Much else could be said, and has been said by good critics. It's an awfully amusing biography, it's thoroughly in its period—all that and plenty more. But I won't keep on and on.

Yours sincerely
EMForster

ALS: Recipient

[1] Cecil, *The Stricken Deer; or The Life of Cowper* (1929), biography of the English poet William Cowper (1731–1800), whose life was blighted by obsessive fear of eternal damnation. His first complete nervous collapse occurred after his father's death in 1756, when he spent eighteen months in an asylum, and they recurred at intervals thereafter. Cecil wrote to PNF (15 October 1979. PNF): 'I need not say how excited I was to get it [EMF's letter] & all the more because [I] barely knew him—I had met him once, I think at Garsington with the Morrells.' See Letters 220, 221.

272   To Frieda Richtofen Lawrence

King's College, Cambridge
4 March 1930

I have had such a shock over D.H.L.[1] He was always in my heart, and I think too of the books he would still have written.

I have been thinking about you too, and wondering how you are, and what you will do. It's difficult to write, and please don't answer this. I wish I could help you.

EMForster

ALS: Bancroft Library, University of California, Berkeley

[1] D. H. Lawrence died at Vence, France, on 2 March 1930. Frieda replied ([n. d.] KCC): 'Lawrence died so splendidly—Inch by inch he fought & life with him never lost its glamour, not right to the end, when he asked for morphine & died without pain or struggle—He looked unconquered & fulfilled when he was dead, all the suffering smoothed out—If England ever produced a perfect rose, he was it, thorns & perfume & splendour—He has left me his love without a grudge, we had our grudges out; & from that other side, that I did not know, before his death, he gives me his strength & his love for life—Don't feel sorry for me, it would be wrong, I am so rich, what woman has had what I have had? & now I have my grief—It's other people I pity, I can tell you, who never knew the glamour & wonder of things—'

273   To Charles Mauron

West Hackhurst, Abinger Hammer, Dorking
6 April 1930

My dear Charles,

I have been meaning to write to you for a long time, and was very pleased to hear, though now that I do write back I am in foolishly bad spirits. The fact that I don't create, or get idler, is depressing me, even to the point of making me self-conscious and disinclining me to see certain people. *You* will never [be] among those people, and somehow I feel it easier to mention these things to you than to almost anyone. I can trust you neither to despise me nor to become yourself sympathetically depressed; the one or the other of these fears generally keeps me silent—the latter generally, for contempt is quite a bearable discomfort. Well, I don't know what to do with my existence, my memory's worse, my vitality probably less, and yet I am feeling perfectly well—unless the sense that I couldn't face anything except what I actually do face is a sign of morbidity. There is no doubt that work would put every thing right, but what work? I think that you are right and that to rag the saints is the most obvious, but it is so difficult to start and to wake myself from my tiring dream. I never felt work was a duty—indeed, the less one adds to civilisation the longer perhaps it will take to topple over. But not to feel intact, not to [be] able to expose oneself to certain contacts because of self-consciousness—that really is an aweful nuisance, and

I spend a good deal of time now with people who are (vaguely speaking) my inferiors, and to whom I can very easily be kind.

However, I mustn't presume upon your insensitiveness too far! We English are unfortunately circumstanced I think, as soon as we run off the rails; something which must be the Puritan conscience begins to complain in us and to say that an accident's a disaster.

As regard[s] my coming out to you, I haven't any plans. What about the end of May or some time in June? I have lost my engagement book (losing everything is part of my present bother), so don't know when Whitsun is, which we might do well to avoid. It will be a great pleasure to come—I always feel so happy with you and Marie, and I hope from your letter that she is better, but won't write about that today, only about myself. I am now 51, and perhaps the fact that I'm awfully young in some ways makes difficulties that wouldn't come to people who bow themselves down all of a piece.

With love and thanks for your letter and for a great deal more from

Morgan

TLS: Alice Mauron

274   To Ottoline Morrell

West Hackhurst, Abinger Hammer, Dorking
17 April 1930

Dear Ottoline,

How kind of you to write. I did see Frieda, and the old formulae, which used to ~~seem~~ be so agitating, sounded rather pathetic in the lounge of the Kingsley Hotel.[1] Like you, I have been reading the poems and novels a good deal lately; indeed I broadcast on them last night. And do you observe what a ball you have set rolling through the columns of the Nation? You will scarcely have an old friend left. Clive now enters, I hear, but I haven't seen his letter yet.[2]

Yes, I should like to come and see you so much. I will call or ring you up when next I am in town. I suppose a secretary has long since been found for your brother.

Yours very sincerely
EMForster

ALS: HRC

[1] The Kingsley Temperance Hotel in Bloomsbury Way was a favourite of EMF and his mother. On this meeting with Frieda Lawrence, see EMF, II, 164–5.

[2] See O[ttoline] M[orrell], 'D. H. Lawrence, 1885–1930: By One of His Friends', The Nation and The Athenaeum, 46 (1930), 859–60. She wrote simply and appreciatively about her meeting with Lawrence in 1915, and about his reactions to the war and its effects on him. EMF referred to him as 'the greatest imaginative novelist of our generation' (ibid., p. 888), which brought contentious replies from T. S. Eliot and Clive Bell (N&A, 47 [1930], 11, 76–7), and

replies from EMF (*ibid.*, pp. 45, 109). See also EMF's broadcast on 16 April, 'D. H. Lawrence', *The Listener*, 3 (1930), 753–4.

275 To Charles Mauron

West Hackhurst, Abinger Hammer, Dorking
5 June 1930

My dear Charles,

You will think that your letter killed me, whereas it actually gave me life, and why in that case I did not at once write to you and say so is one of the mysteries of life. I knew it would be a kind letter, I didn't know it would be such a helpful one, and since then I have been feeling less low, and, though not going to the lengths of reading Aristophanes, more inclined to strike out in new directions. Or—better still—I have been struck out into new directions for Clive Bell and T. S. Eliot have suddenly attacked me in the Nation. 'You could have knocked me down', or rather could have if I hadn't received your letter. I will send you the Nation correspondance—it isn't here to hand. I conducted it superbly, according to my own opinion.[1]

About our next meeting—I think it is that that has really extended my silence, for I have been hoping to suggest a date, and a little web of engagements kept dancing before me. What are your plans, and those of Marie, during July? I want to be in Paris at the beginning of August, and I thought that, if it suited you, I could come down to you for a little first, but this may interrupt other arrangements, I mean it may not fit in with Marie's holidays. Let me know. I ought to have written long before. I know this.

I shall want, among other things, to talk over a course of lectures I am to give at Cambridge on 'The Creator as Critic'—at least that is its present title.[2] They have asked me to lecture for the Tripos on some subject connected with criticism, and I suggested 'Criticism of the Novel' in the first place, which was hailed with rapture. Then, in view of your letter and my own higher or newer star, I wrote again, and said 'No. I withdraw. Another course about the Novel would bore me,' and received in answer some rather sadly compliments, saying that I was a very distinguished person, and they were pleased to get me in any case. Poor things, they know the course will not be good, they say in muffled tones that it is a 'major subject', and they are right. But why should I not read Dryden for the first time? Or allude, when I have learnt to pronounce his name, to Corneille and to Tasso? My notion, you see, is to select some writers who have also done criticism. This means that nearly all literature lies open to me, but I shall pay particular attention to writers who have got into the soup—have either written a book and then said afterwards what books are, or else have said what books are, and then write a book. This surely should provide some seasonable fun. And inconsistency trying to disguise itself as development provides the rarest flavour of all.

This letter shall go. It is about myself from first to last, and the last is, is your 'de Segonzac' book out yet? I have been expected [*sic*] to hear of it, but have not.[3]

With affection and gratitude and with love for you both from

Morgan

TLS: Alice Mauron

[1] The correspondence about D. H. Lawrence: Letter 274.
[2] A course of eight lectures at the Arts School in the 1931 Lent Term. The title was first listed in the *Cambridge University Reporter* for 1 October 1930 (p. 82) as 'The Creative Artist as Critic'; in the *Reporter* for 19 December it became 'The Creator as Critic'. Surviving (probably partial) material (KCC) has four titles in EMF's autograph or typescript: 'Creation and Criticism', 'Self Defense', 'Selfcriticism & Selfextension', 'Criticism of Life'.
[3] Mauron admired the French painter André Dunoyer de Segonzac (1884–1974). This is perhaps an allusion to Mauron's *Poèmes en prose* (1930), with an illustration by Segonzac.

276   To Unidentified Recipient

c/o Messrs Arnold, 41 Maddox St.
Bond St. [London] W.
13 August 1930

Dear Madam
    Thank you for your kind letter. I am glad that you enjoyed my book, but hope that you will not pay much attention either to it or to any other work of literary criticism.[1] When one is actually writing novels—as you tell me you are—I think it is most important that one should trust one's own inclination, instincts, and tastes, and should not go to other writers to find out what a novel is or ought to be. Books like mine or Mr Richards' or Mr Lubbock's are all very well for students or examinees, but, seriously, I think they may do more harm than good to those who are actually engaged in creative work.[2] If 20th century values do not appeal to you, you ought certainly to ignore them.

No, I don't think I would draw any definite line between 'story' & plot: the first seems to me to range events in their time-sequence, the second to stress causality.

Wishing you good luck in your forthcoming book.

I am yours faithfully
EMForster.

ALS: Columbia University

[1] My book: *Aspects of the Novel*.
[2] I. A. Richards (1893–1979), distinguished member of the English Faculty at Cambridge,

and Professor of English at Harvard from 1944. His *Principles of Literary Criticism* (1924) became a standard text. On Percy Lubbock, see Letter 41; EMF undoubtedly refers to his *The Craft of Fiction*.

277   To Siegfried Sassoon

West Hackhurst, Abinger Hammer, Dorking
12 December 1930

My dear Siegfried,

When you are inclined, please send me a line about Stephen.[1] I have not heard of him for some little time, and I have thought of him during these fogs.

I hoped you would have been lunching with Mrs Hardy last Tuesday, but when it was over I was glad you had not come; *she* was all right and so, you say, am I; but Yeats Brown, a harmful goose, and J. C. Squire, a harmless one, quacked Fascism at each other across us. Squire really is *dreadful*—I do not dislike him at all. Mrs Squire also sat.[2]

Now if you had come too either something awful would have happened, and made Mrs Hardy sorry, or else by means of your what d'ye call it you would have led Yeats Brown to express his better side and thus left me ignorant of his real nature. For I fancy I shall prove right over Harmful Goose. Dear me, one doesn't like many people. I like Mrs Hardy. I like you.

Just back from 3 rather exhausting days. Do you ever have your mother staying with you in your flat? Mine loves being in mine, and fidgets from start to finish, with the result that towards finish she got rheumatism in her leg—would wash up, make beds, although I had arranged for a char. It is very curious, and curiously tiring. Every moment some defect is noted, or improvement suggested, in the realms of brushable or breakable objects; dressers are seen to squeak, linoleum to cockle, the scullery blind cord drips into the sink, the looking glass in the bath room hangs too high, don't open that tongue, the bread'll do but not the milk, I tell you who *ought* to be asked, that's Agnes Hill, oh and poor Rosie, and if you *could* bear to have Percy and Dutchie they would never cease talking about it.[3]

No more, apparently, does

Morgan

His Monkey Wife by John Collier has been amusing me, but it might repel you. Dunno.[4]

ALS: George Sassoon

[1] Sassoon's friend, the Hon. Stephen J. N. Tennant (1906–   ), artist and aesthete.

[2] Francis Charles Claypon Yeats-Brown (1886–1944), soldier and author, went to India with the Cavalry in 1906 and during the First World War was in the 5th Irish Lancers, the experience that produced his best-known book, *Lives of a Bengal Lancer* (1930). He was

Assistant Editor of *The Spectator*, 1926–8. Sir John Collings Squire (1884–1958) was on the staff of *The New Statesman*, 1913–18, and editor of *The London Mercury*, 1919–34.

[3] Agnes Hill had been paid companion to Laura Forster. Rosie: his aunt Rosalie Alford. Percy and Dutchie: his cousin Percy Whichelo and his wife Clare.

[4] John Collier, *His Monkey Wife; or Married to A Chimp* (1930).

THE PUBLIC SCENE,
1931–8

By the 1930s Forster, now convinced that he would write no more novels, felt the urge to exert himself more on the public scene. He became a popular broadcaster, and for a time in 1934 he wrote a regular column in *Time and Tide*, commenting on affairs of the day. In the same year he was appointed President of the newly-founded National Council for Civil Liberties and threw himself energetically into the Council's current campaign against the Government's Sedition Bill. His self-appointed role was that of a liberal humanist, ready to keep communications open with communists in the cause of liberty and anti-fascism, and as such he was chosen to lead the British delegation to the communist-oriented International Congress of Writers in Paris in June 1935.

After Lowes Dickinson's death in 1932, Forster wrote a biography of him at the invitation of Dickinson's family. In 1935 he published *Abinger Harvest*, a successful selection from his own articles and reviews. He was also much in demand as a reviewer, especially in *The Listener*, of which J. R. Ackerley was now literary editor. Soon after T. E. Lawrence's death in 1935, Forster began work on an authorised edition of Lawrence's letters, but—having recently had to pay substantial compensation for an inadvertent libel in *Abinger Harvest*—he insisted on full protection against libel damages and withdrew when this was not forthcoming.

As writer and moralist Forster had become an influence on a new generation of novelists that included William Plomer and Christopher Isherwood, both of whom become his close friends, and also of left-wing poets such as Auden and Day-Lewis. They excepted him from their hatred of the 'old men' whom they blamed for the 1914–18 war and other evils and, as the decade continued, they came to regard him as a kind of secular saint and 'anti-heroic hero'.

In 1932 his friend Bob Buckingham married May Hockey, a nurse, and after some sharp initial jealousies a strong friendship sprang up between Forster and May. In 1937, both Masood and the Maharaja of Dewas died; Forster himself survived a dangerous prostate operation in 1935–6.

278   To Alice Clara Forster

The Reform Club [London].   1 January 1931

Dearest—A Happy New Year to you again and thank the maids for
the nice card. I feel wan but cheerful. Last night I walked out to view
the crowds, and thought *shall* I just see if the Hydaris would like to
see the New Year in. I called, with the greatest success.[1] They had
wanted to go but felt it too difficult. We rang up cars—none to be
had, and Lady H. then announced that if I thought fit she would go
in a bus. There were *ten* of us—another huge family joined—and
mercifully a bus stopped just outside the Hotel, and we all found
places, went past Trafalgar Square, and got to Ludgate Circus just at
12.0, where the bus ended. I discountenanced my dusky and
bejewelled flock from proceeding on foot to St Paul's, so we stood
for a little in the Circus, Sir Akbar bought an enormous balloon, the
youths and maidens rattles, we achieved another bus back to
Piccadilly Circus, and heard the New Year rung in from the top.
People in the crowd much interested. "And do the ladies talk
English? How wonderful." From Piccadilly we all walked back to
the Hotel. I wasn't back till 1.0, and barely up in time to meet the
boys. They were very nice, but went on to their friends and I shall
not see them till this evening at the B.B.C.

Well this isn't all. Hardly had I seen them off before Lady H. and
a niece drove up in their car. Lady H. had remembered my birthday,
and gave me a lovely bouquet of flowers a *gigantic* basket of fruit,
including a pineapple, and surreptitiously slipped an envelope into
my hand at parting, with a murmur that I must accept it, she wished
it was not so little. I heard something chink and thought it was silver.
I opened the envelope————*seven pounds* (two in gold). I feel
quite staggered. If she wasn't Indian I shouldn't like to take it, as it is
I am delighted to do so. I am now going there to tea!

I send the boys to the Circus tomorrow—their choice.[2] I am
getting off. I get so bored with worried animals—and we all go to a
cinema of their choice Sat. afternoon & dine with Sir Amin.[3]

No time for more.

Much love—Percy writes very nicely, but it has been a tiresome
affair.

Pop's love.

Thanks for pen. The diary was an old one.

ALS: KCC

[1] On the Hydaris, see Letter 212.
[2] Apparently, Anwar and Akbar Masood.
[3] Sir Amin Jung (1863–19??) was Sir Ahmed Hussain, knighted in 1922. 'Amin Jung' was
one part of a Hyderabad honorary title.

279   To Charles Mauron
West Hackhurst, Abinger Hammer, Dorking
7 February 1931

My dear Charles,
I felt you were floating too, when I walked by your side for a little in London. We are rather alike I do think—two dried but not discoloured leaves—curiously unattached although I possess a leasehold house and you a wife. (Children make the difference, probably. I expect the real barriers are between those who have and haven't them.) But I float differently in regard to you and to Roger. I think I did tell you once—I am much fonder of you than of him, in fact very fond of you, and you mustn't ever let your views of me and his coincide, or ever suppose I'm likely to float out of your life. I ~~expect~~ respect and revere Roger, he's a great man and a saint too, he amuses and charms me, but that's not the same, and I think that when he complains of my elusiveness he a little deceives himself; for at the bottom of his heart he wants to have seen me rather than to see me—I can't bring him any ideas or news that he hasn't already.[1]
I am here for a weekend, returning to Cambridge tomorrow. It isn't bad there, in fact much better than I expected, my room's warm, I've got a nice lecture-theatre, and as soon as I begin to speak feel what I'm saying is a success.[2] Is it *true*, however? Murmurs of 'no' from the knowing. But who cares? Not the undergraduates. Not I. Hitherto I have delivered myself on

1   Creation and Criticism
    (sleep)   (awake)
2   Self Defence
    (Dryden—Corneille—Tasso)
3 ⎰Self Criticism
   ⎪(Henry James)
   ⎱Self Extension
    (Henry James, James Joyce)
and have to do
4   Criticism of Life
    (Matthew Arnold, Tolstoy)
5   Dryden, Johnson
6   Coleridge

Boileau also ran, but not very far. When I thought of what I wanted to say about him, I thought of you on that bridge, and when I thought of what you said, I thought of Marie.[3] So Boileau's progress was frog-like, and at every third hop he was back in my lap. The lectures have only to last 50 minutes—a mercy, for except about Henry James I never have enough to say. It is a nuisance—as you and I have likewise agreed—to have so little to say, to feel, and to think. The three items are all present, and admirable in quality, but ~~unduly~~ very small, so that one's public appearances ~~are~~ grow precarious. At the end of mine I am now regularly visited by a violent cough which rushes me out of the theatre toboggan fashion and tips me into an arm chair in the combination room at Kings. It is my usual throat cough, but unusually welcome.

My mother has taken my flat while I'm away, and stops with her sister there. It's not exactly restful, letting to ladies of 70, and what with that and cousins being stricken dead in their beds at Brighton, much time has been wasted.[4] I seem to have read a good deal, though, and life, whatever life may be, is all right.

I have heard from Stock, and lost his address, but shall get it from Virginia at the end of the week. Am delighted to be translated if it's by you, and shall send him a Howards End—he suggests that and A Room with a View, but I thought H. E. for a start.[5]

Is Gaudier-Brzeska any good as an artist? Have just read his queer little life. He was mothered by an elderly Polish lady who died mad.[6]

With love from

Morgan

re monys (i) glad about the fr. 300—will pick them up when I come. (ii) will try to make independent terms with Stock if he nibbles, you shall do the same, and we will pool and divide the results as usual.

ALS: Alice Mauron

[1] On Roger Fry and the Maurons, see Letter 252.
[2] On these Cambridge lectures, see Letter 275.
[3] Allusion to Marie Mauron.
[4] Sister: Rosalie Alford. Cousins: cousin singular, Herbert Whichelo (1874–1931).
[5] Stock: a French publisher. Charles Mauron's translation of *A Room With a View* (*Avec vue sur l'Arno*) was published by Robert Laffont in 1947 and his translations of *Howards End* (*Le legs de Mrs. Wilcox*), *The Longest Journey* (*Le plus long des voyages*) and *Where Angels Fear to Tread* (*Monteriano*) were published by Plon in 1950, 1952 and 1954 respectively.
[6] Henri Gaudier-Brzeska, (1891–1915), French sculptor, settled in London in 1911 with Sophie Brzeska, a Polish woman some twenty years his senior, and added her name to his own. He was a founder-member of the London Group in 1913, and in 1914 he joined Wyndham Lewis's Vorticist movement. He died on the Western Front after a quixotic enlistment following arrest for avoidance of French military service. EMF wrote of him as having 'the queerest little life imaginable. . . . queer and little because it was so short . . . .' See EMF, 'An Artist's Life', *The Spectator*, 146 (1931), 669, review of H. S. Ede, *A Life of Gaudier-Brzeska* (limited edition, 1930) published also as *Savage Messiah* (1931; new edition, 1971).

280   To Hermon Ould

King's College, Cambridge
12 February 1931

Dear Mr Ould,

In common with other members of Brooke's old college, I have received the enclosed, the matter and the manner of which I regard as equally deplorable.[1]

I regret that I must terminate my connection with the P.E.N. I had no conception that it would promote such a scheme.

Yours sincerely
EMForster

ALS: HRC (P.E.N. papers)

[1] Hermon Ould (1886–1951), dramatist, poet, critic, and translator, was General Secretary, International P.E.N. Club, from 1926. He had sent EMF a travel brochure on a cruise to Skyros, connected with the unveiling of the monument to Rupert Brooke, organised by the P.E.N.; see *EMF*, II, 173. Ould, somewhat puzzled, replied that he had 'refused categorically to do propaganda on behalf of the cruise, but it seemed part of my duty . . . to distribute the pamphlets . . . I am afraid the Committee of the P.E.N. would be quite bewildered by your letter . . .' (13 February 1931. HRC: P.E.N.).

281   To Hermon Ould

King's College, Cambridge
17 February 1931

Dear Mr Ould,
    I am sorry not to have written more clearly. You are quite right in thinking that I did not disapprove of the Memorial scheme—indeed I sent a small subscription to it, if my memory is correct. My letter referred to the cruise. I gather that, like myself, you deplore it, and I think you are right in refusing to do propaganda on its behalf: it appears to be a purely commercial undertaking, aggravated by every circumstance of bad taste. But I cannot reconcile this refusal with the fact that envelopes have been sent out, bearing the PEN stamp and containing a brochure which emphasises the PEN's connection with the cruise, and invites applications from Great Britain to be sent to your address.
    I desire to withdraw from the PEN on the ground that it should not have undertaken propaganda for the cruise, and has in fact undertaken it. Will you please lay this before your committee.[1]

Yours sincerely
EMForster

ALS: HRC (P.E.N. papers)

[1] Ould replied (18 February 1931. HRC: P.E.N.) repeating that although he disliked the cruise publicity in P.E.N.'s name, 'the whole thing is so small a side issue to the real purpose of the P.E.N., but I cannot really feel, as you do, that the undertaking is "aggravated by every circumstance of bad taste".' This ended the exchange, and friendly relations were resumed.

282   To T. S. Eliot

King's College, Cambridge
28 February 1931

Dear Eliot,

I don't know whether I ought to be troubling you with this, or de la Mare, or the firm generally, but perhaps you will be so kind as to hand it on to the appropriate department. It's about an MS by a friend of mine, Charlton, which has I believe been submitted via J. C. Squire, and is being not unfavourably considered.[1]

Charlton understands, though, that he may be advised to alter his narrative from 3rd person to 1st. He is against doing this, and as I am against him doing it I said I'd venture to write on the matter, and try to put my opinion.

It seems to me that the 3rd person, like the numerous photographs, is an integral part of the scheme, and that if it was altered the writer's peculiar dryness and detachment would disappear, and we should just be left with another addition to the With Rod & Gun through the Empire series. I don't know that Charlton's good on himself—I don't know who is—but he is certainly out to be impartial, and that a man of action should be so out, and should not hide his head in the nearest loyalty, struck me as most remarkable; and I did think that he was well inspired, under these circumstances, not to admit 'I', with its implications of zest. 'He' may seem clumsy, and may hold up the rush of action, but it does the work which has to be done here, in my judgment.

I hope you, and the firm generally, won't mind me writing like this—not my business, I know, but I should be so pleased if he managed to get the MS. taken by F. & F., and so sorry if there happened to be a hitch over this particular point.

Yours sincerely
E. M. Forster

ALS: Houghton Library

[1] Richard de la Mare (1901–   ), son of the poet Walter de la Mare, had been with Faber and Faber since 1925, and was its Chairman, 1960–71. *Charlton* (1931), which Leo Charlton felt was 'too sincere and revealing for the crudity of "I"', kept its third-person narrator; see also *More Charlton*, p. 108.

283   To Forrest Reid

West Hackhurst, Abinger Hammer, Dorking
17 March 1931

My dear F. R.

I have delayed writing to you because I was wanting to fix, approximately, the date of a visit to Dublin, and then to ask you your plans, in the hope that I might spend a few days with you either before the visit or after. I was so very happy when I stayed with you the other time. It now looks as if I could be in Ireland about May 10th. What happens to you about then? I fear I can't stop long, either at Dublin or Belfast, as I have been away so much from home, and have furthermore to be at Aberdeen on April Fool's Day, in order to receive an hon[or]ary degree in Law.

I read *Saturday Night at the Greyhound*, much liked the character of Tom, and thought the whole book promising, that is to say on the verge of real tragedy.[1] It didn't quite succeed, I think, because some of the characters were stagey—Fred Flack was a barber's block and Ruth emptily bizarre. If she had been simplified and presented as a decent ordinary lady, the situation would have been strengthened, but she was spoiled by the writer's class-consciousness. He felt bound to make her petulant and perverse, so that one doubts whether she would have saved the household even if the police hadn't raided. D. H. Lawrence failed with his 'Ladies' in much the same way.[2] (Not that the parallel between him & Simpson can be pressed further).

I should think the unpublished book, where he can be always himself, must be splendid. I wonder whether you would be able to persuade him to allow me to read it some day. The Woolfs read it and praised it highly to me a couple of years ago: he actually submitted it to them for publication—they were very sorry they couldn't take it. They also spoke of the third MS which they think better, and less popular, than *S. N.*—They are sure to publish it now that *S.N.*—— has succeeded.[3]

I am just down from Cambridge, which was cold and ruinously expensive. My lectures felt rather unreal. I didn't mind enough about the various literary problems under review, and I couldn't make myself mind. Bob Buckingham (that policeman) came up for a Sunday, which was very nice.[4] I have got to know him much better, as you may imagine, since the day when you were driven out into the street (and I shall never forget, dear F. R. the *way* you went out—the kindness and the affection of it can't be described, but remain, with so much else of you, in my heart)

This Saturday I go to the boat race at Joe's. I really think he has broken with Albert at last. He even tried to leave Hammersmith, but this alas has fallen through. I was particularly anxious he should leave on account of Harry; the bad impression H. made on you in my flat has been justified, and I wish Joe would clear out of the district.[5]

I hope that sacred love didn't quite absorb profane in Uncle Stephen.[6] I wish you hadn't had to omit some poacher passages.

With love from
E. M. F.

ALS: Stephen Gilbert

[1] This novel by John Hampson Simpson (1901–55), who wrote as 'John Hampson', was published by Hogarth Press (1931), reprinted by Penguin (1937), and was dedicated to Reid. Simpson was the son of a failed Birmingham theatrical producer. His mother, a physical training instructor, made him feel a weakling, and at the age of sixteen he ran away from home and for some years lived a hand-to-mouth existence, with a brief period in jail for book-thieving. About 1925 he joined a family named Wilson, at their house 'Four Ashes' near Birmingham, as nurse to their mentally retarded son. The arrangement prospered, and Simpson soon came to be regarded as a son of the house. He began to write, and in 1931, through William Plomer's influence with the Woolfs, his novel was published and achieved great success. Forster came to know him in 1932 and became a regular correspondent and a frequent visitor to 'Four Ashes'. The Wilsons were very hospitable to refugees from Nazi Europe, and Simpson, although homosexual, married the Austrian actress Teresa Ghiese in order to give her a passport. In the 1930s he became a leader of a little 'Birmingham Group' of novelists. Simpson's own later novels, however, were progressively less successful. In his last years he followed an esoteric religious cult. Simpson was tiny and odd-looking, with a cowlick and a Hapsburg chin, but he was a generous and masterful encourager of other self-taught writers. In Forster's view he was a saint-like character. On Simpson and the Wilsons, see Walter Allen, *As I Walked Down New Grub Street*, pp. 55–71.

[2] That is, women characters of high social station.

[3] The Woolfs admired, but felt unable to publish, Simpson's novel on a homosexual theme. The third manuscript is unidentified.

[4] Robert Joseph Buckingham (1904–75) was born in Somers Town, London, of very poor parents. On leaving school he moved from one ill-paid job to another, helping to support his brothers and sisters on his tiny earnings, until in the mid-1920s he joined the police and was posted to the same Hammersmith Section House as EMF's policeman friend Harry Daley. EMF met Buckingham in 1930 at a boat-race party at J. R. Ackerley's flat and developed an ardent friendship with him, which was not interrupted by Buckingham's marriage in 1932 to May Hockey, and indeed remained his chief affection for the rest of his life. Bob and May's only child was named Robert Morgan. Bob Buckingham was physically large and good-looking, genial and a good talker. He was keen on many kinds of sport, especially rowing, and was continually taking up, and dropping, new interests. In the Second World War he abandoned his erstwhile pacifism and volunteered for the Air Force but was rejected because of defective eyesight. In 1951 he became a probation officer in Coventry.

[5] Albert: sailor friend of Ackerley. See Ackerley, *My Father and Myself*, pp. 126–31. Harry: Harry Daley. See p. 69 above; and *EMF*, II, 141–3.

[6] Reid, *Uncle Stephen* (1931), reprinted in 1946.

284   To W. J. H. Sprott

West Hackhurst, Abinger Hammer, Dorking
16 July 1931

Dearest Sebastian.

As for the flat, do come for the 22nd as well as the 23rd. If I want to sleep there myself on the 23rd, will be there be room [*sic*], or does Les come?[1] I have got muddled. (Don't on any account put him off.) And if the flat should be wanted at 12.0. midday on the 24th (not by me!) is it possible to you to leave it empty by that time? I am coming up on the 23rd to lunch with Dobrée, and if flat's full shall either proceed to Cambridge or sleep at Joe's—no difficulty in either.[2]

What think you of Maisie her letter as apart from her handwriting?[3] Like you, I am not much worried over the thing except by it's being there, which one resents, and it is annoying to think that I have enhanced him in her eyes. Such a thing to get to know a writer! On the other hand this sort of thing is inevitable for him, and I got to know him just when, and only because, he had broken off an engagement. So the class of events one calls Fate have worked more for me than against. I'm quite sure that his feeling for me is something he has never had before. It's a spiritual feeling which has extended to my physique—pardon, cher maitre, such nomenclature; I desire to convey that it's something he calls MORGAN he's got hold of, so that my lack of youth and presence, which in other relationships might hinder or depress me, are here no disadvantage, in fact the reverse. He must be made to see that there can't be a menage à trois, which I think is his dream, and, for the moment, possibly hers too; but he should easily see this when told.

Yes, the flat in the rain must have been dreary, but what price Gwen Lally at Tewkesbury?[4] Here I lay happily in bed, or read, or finished Voltaire, or talked pleasantly with my mother. I enclose the £20; judging by the paper this morning you and I can be the only people left who have any money. If there is not the general crash, I shall send you some more at Christmas. If there is, I suppose we may all be much where we are.

Oh the Bells, the Woolves—or rather Virginia, for I do like Leonard! Oh how I do agree, and if to become anti-Bloomsbury were not to become Bloomsbury, how I would become it! But to turn one's backside to them is the only course—they will never have the grace to penetrate it, their inquisitiveness never had any spunk, that is why one loathes it so. Turned well away from them, let one read their books, which are *very* good, and look at their mural designs, which may be good too, and that is the end. I am sorry at what you say about Lytton, and surprised—I thought his curiosity was of the pardonable type, and that he was getting both solid and charming. What was it you mean? Ottoline I like better, now that you do, and I look forward to seeing her, which I certainly usen't to, but I 'don't altogether trust her'—helpful phrase. It's excellent news that the Bells &ct are ravaged by fear; now that's the sort of thing I should never have thought of![5]

Had a lot more to say, but can't remember, so had better stop. I believe, since I began to write, that Les does come on the 23rd, so I definitely won't come for the night, though I may see you during the day.

Much pleased with my own Voltaire article.[6]

Love to your mother. Love to Velda.[7]

Love to you
M.

TLS: KCC

[1] Les: friend of Sprott.

[2] Bonamy Dobrée (1891–1974), editor and biographer; Professor of English Literature at Leeds University, 1936–55, noted for his studies on the eighteenth century.

³ I.e. May Hockey: she and Bob Buckingham were married on 31 August 1932; see *EMF*, II, 168–9.

⁴ Miss Gwen Lally, OBE (died 1963) was a lady of pronounced personality who described herself as 'Pageant Master, Play Producer, Lecturer'. She directed Tewkesbury's 'great historical pageant' presented during the week of 11 July; it was rained out on 14 July.

⁵ Some undated autograph notes by EMF (Cavafy papers: Savidis. Photocopies: KCC) are replies to an interviewer on the subject of English literature: 'There are very few literary and artistic ~~movements~~ *groups* in England and this distinguishes ~~us~~ it, both for good and evil, from other countries. Writers tend to work in isolation, and only to come together when their liberties are menaced . . . The only definite group I can think of is *"Bloomsbury"*, which consists of a number of people of intellectual integrity, high critical ability, independent incomes, and emancipated outlook. Their enemies call them "high brow" and "superior", and accuse them of sterility. But they have already produced Lytton Strachey, J. M. Keynes, Virginia Woolf (that most talented and poetic novelist), Roger Fry (our chief art-critic), Arthur Waley (the great Japanese scholar and translator)—not to mention writers of the younger generation such as David Garnett. "Bloomsbury" by no means represents all English literature. It is sophisticated and self conscious, and often lacks spontaneity and warmth. But it is certainly a creative force and the literary histories of the future will probably estimate it highly.' Clive Bell (1881–1964) was married to Virginia Woolf's sister Vanessa.

⁶ Forster, 'Incongruities: Weighing Fire' and 'Incongruities: Voltaire's Slugs', *New York Herald Tribune*, 23 and 30 August 1931, Section 11, pp. 1, 4. See Kirkpatrick, p. 129.

⁷ Velda Mary Sprott (1906–   ), Sprott's sister.

285   To George Thomson[1]

West Hackhurst, Abinger Hammer, Dorking
1 August 1931

Dear George,

I like what Keats says about pain because he is young, but if he was my age I should disagree with it, I think.[2] I think the doctrine that pain's an opportunity for the spirit *hardens* more readily than any other doctrine I know, it gets glib and educational and gets used by people who have forgotten what pain is. When I'm told by clergymen, for instance, that war, and war alone, brings out what's deepest in human nature, my feeling is that I'd rather human nature was permanently impoverished than have another war—indeed I feel that always, and perhaps that is one of the few differences between yourself and me. Pain can be distilled by memory into a sort of happiness—I know—but there's also direct happiness and I want a very high place for that. It's vulgarised because people think it can be ordered like something from a shop, or subscribed to like a club, but if it's conceived of as a chance for which one hopes to be ready it seems to me desirable, and to justify human existence.

Pain is good, I'd say, when it's incidental to Love. In 'I give up my life for my friend' it is my friend, not my death, that matters. And sometimes I needn't give up my life for him, I can live for him, and with him, and the power of the spirit is then equally manifested, I should think.

Pain can be so overwhelming that it has tempted people in all ages to look for some inherent value in it[.]

I was in Cambridge myself last week. I can hardly think of Alister as a human being at all, I forget he is in the room and am quite surprised when his mouth opens and he puts a piece of cake in. Richard Braithwaite strikes me as all alive, but I never take any noise he makes seriously. Knowing that I can't meet such Cambridge people on their own ground of philosophy, brainishness, and all that, and knowing that you can, I feel of course very pleased when you disagree with them. Perhaps healthful runnels descend from them, as from a glacier, but it must be trying to live up there, and I wonder how they mutually manage it.[3]

We had a first-class college meeting. Hugh clowned deliberately and with complete success on the subject of the route to the new library-loft. 'You will then go out through the window, which will thus become a door' was one phrase, and 'since access to the W.C. would allow people to take away the books, special keys must be provided' was another. Then there was a 'turn' over the picture of an ecclesiastic, which were we to buy, and Boris Ord who never says anything, saw an opportunity of saying something, and suggested that, before we decided, it ought to be cleaned. 'In the opinion of the expert it has already been *over*cleaned, it has been *damaged* by cleaning, it would otherwise have cost us *more*' came mildly from Milner. But B. O. emptily persisted: yes, yes, the robe, the book, the face, yes, but the background, the coat of arms, no contrast. '*Over*cleaned, all *over*cleaned, *all* overcleaned' said chanted Milner in extreme weariness, until we bought the hygienic object for £75.——But perhaps the best of all was Maynard's indignation when he was accused by Sheppard of not telling a lie. A whole career seemed epitomised in his disclaimer.[4]

I expect I should like Galway and anyway I want to come, but we mustn't expect to find anything like Watermill there, or anything like it. I shan't feel quite easy until you are installed *as Professor*, and if I were you I would pretend to be unable to find a house until that has occurred.[5] But I am rather suspicious. I do like to be paid—America promises to pay me £200, the Spectator £30, the Woolves £25, the B.B.C. £20, Desmond [MacCarthy] £20, and perhaps all the cheques, even the last named, will reach me, but I shall feel more restful when they do. It is nice getting all this money, as I have been losing investments like everyone else in the last few months. Now I shall be rich again, as I have not been for a long time, and I am not again making the mistake of investing, or even of letting it lie in the Bank. I shall bury it to be disinterred as wanted, and if anyone should find it first, he won't rob me nearly as much as Lord Kylsant has, and I can think it was Jimmy Dunn, or someone else who ought to dig up money.[6]

On Wednesday I go to the flat (which is at present occupied by Sidney Meredith) and Anwar and Akbar [Masood] come for a week.[7] There is a vermilion telephone opposite, so I may not go much to the bakers—the one I like, who takes his holiday in Zurich, is not often there, and the girl has got immensely older, and is indeed a new girl. Then (i.e. it's after the 13th of August), I go to France sometime—my doctor friend caught dysentery at Aleppo and has stuck in Buda Pesth, so I shall not go to Holland with her in her car.[8] I may take Bob for a few days to France—I want to, but his operation has still not come off. Really it's awful the way the working classes are chivvied and teased: three sacks fell out of a crane on to his brother, who is a porter, bruised him to a jelly and ruined his clothes. The R[ailwa]y co. admitted liability and paid the doctor, but when it came to the clothes said 'Oh no we can't pay for them too.' If Ted brought the case into court, he's bound to win it, but he's equally bound to lose his job, of which the Co. is well aware—well aware that he's aware, I mean, and that it's more worth his while to buy a new suit and hate in silence.

My mother is well, but has given water on the knee to my aunt through making her help to clear out the garden-room——three days' work, at the end of which every bally little box was put back again, so that the garden room is as impassible as formerly. Mother did it when the maids are on holiday, so that they wouldn't interfere. We live largely on fresh fruit (currants, logan berries &[ct]) which are just wet with water and put with sugar in a pie dish overnight. Did you know about this? It is much nicer than stewed fruit and means no cooking.

Currants remind me of birds: have you yet found out whether those hooded crows which I thought I saw in masses from the tram were an illusion or not? I could have sworn I saw heaps of hooded crows. Here the excitement has been a greater spotted woodpecker feeding its child close to the house. They came daily.

I will end now, but will write again before long, and hope that you will do the same. Please give my love to Moya. I am very sorry that she should have had to suffer so much.

Yours affectionately
Morgan.

The other night the moon rose very interestingly behind a distant tree. First it looked like Queen Victoria, then like a heart, then like a shamrock, and I thought you would think "the moon is gradually improving."

ALS: Recipient

[1] George Derwent Thomson (1903–82) received a BA degree from King's in 1926, was Fellow and Assistant Lecturer in Classics there until 1931, when he took a position at Galway University. He returned briefly to King's, then became Professor of Classics at Birmingham University in 1937.
[2] See the journal letter to the George Keats family: 'Do you not see how necessary a World

of Pains and troubles is to school an Intelligence and make it a soul?' (*The Letters of John Keats*, ed. Hyder E. Rollins, II, 102–3).

[3] Alister George Watson (1908–82), mathematician. Richard Bevan Braithwaite (1900–), at that time University Lecturer in Moral Science; see Letter 100.

[4] Hugh George Edmund Durnford (1886–1965), Bursar of King's, 1919–35. Bernhard (Boris) Ord (1897–1961), Organist of King's College and Organist to the University, 1929–58; University Lecturer in Music, 1936–58; and Conductor of the Cambridge Musical Society. The Rev. Eric Milner-White (1884–1963), Fellow and Dean of King's from 1918; a somewhat high-church cleric. On Keynes and Sheppard, see Letter 48.

[5] EMF was intermediary between Thomson and King's, with the result that he did not take the Dublin post. Watermill: home of Moya Llewelyn Davies (1895–1943), at Raheny, not far from Dublin.

[6] Jimmy Dunn: Irish ne'er-do-well whom Thomson met on a train. Kylsant: in 1928, Owen Cosby Phillips, 1st Baron Kylsant of Carmarthen (1863–1937), landowner and shipping magnate, was tried on charges of misrepresenting stock of the Royal Mail Steam Packet Company. He went to prison in 1931. See also Letter 340 below.

[7] Sydney: daughter of Hugh and Christabel Meredith, one of their first set of twins, born 1908.

[8] Dr Anna Petronella van Heerden (1887–1975), EMF's South African hostess in 1929. They planned a Continental trip for August 1931.

286   To William Plomer[1]

West Hackhurst, Abinger Hammer, Dorking
24 September 1931

Dear Plomer,

Thank you very much for Sadleo; I have enjoyed it, and specially appreciated the shape of the end (which I visualise as   ╲╱   :—far more touching and true to my mind than   ╲╮   , which is most people's notion of a tragic ending. Nothing, really, is sadder or more final than a 'reconciliation'. I have ~~just~~ lately read 'Le grand Meaulnes', and found myself thinking of it sometimes, for it also moves in the region where happiness is lost because it is feared.[2]

I have to go away now, for about a fortnight. I hope that we shall meet when I get back. Again thanking you:

Yours sincerely
EMForster.

Sorry to have written the title of your book wrong: I started with it wrong in my head.   I'd like to talk more about it when we meet, if you'd care to

ALS: Durham University

[1] William Charles Franklyn Plomer (1903–73), novelist and poet, grew up partly in Africa, where his father was in the colonial service, and partly in England. After school days at Rugby, he farmed in Africa and for a time ran a trading station in Zululand. His first novel, *Turbott Wolfe*, published by the Hogarth Press in 1926, dealt with black-white relations and created a considerable stir in South Africa. On the strength of its success he joined Roy Campbell in launching the literary magazine *Voorslag*; then, in 1927, he went on impulse to live for two years in Japan. His novel *Sado* (1931) describes East–West conflicts and contrasts, and evokes his life there. In 1929 he settled in London, living by his pen and as a publisher's reader. EMF came to know him in 1931 and through him met several other young writers, among them Christopher Isherwood. Plomer was witty, ironic, and somewhat secretive, with

a collector's passion for oddities. In his autobiographical volume *At Home* (1958) he gives an amusing picture of EMF, pp. 107–11.

² Alain-Fournier (pseudonym of Henri-Alban Fournier [1886–1914]), *Le grand Meaulnes* (1913), translated as *The Wanderer* (1929) and as *The Lost Domain* (1959): novel of the conflicts of dream and reality, and of the impossibility of preserving a youthful ideal.

287   To Virginia Woolf

West Hackhurst, Abinger Hammer, Dorking
12 November 1931

Dear Virginia,

I have only just had your letter. I am so sorry that I can't get up to dine tomorrow, and I should have liked to meet [John] Simpson, too.

I expect I shall write to you again when I have re read The Waves, I have been looking in it and talking about it, at Cambridge.¹ It's difficult to express oneself about a work which one feels to be so very important, but I've the sort of excitement over it which comes from believing that one's encountered a classic. We shall see—or rather the next fifty years will, when you and I won't see any longer. For the moment, I'm very glad that the book is making a good trial trip.²

With love from
Morgan

I.F.S.—Irish Free State. On all George Thomson's envelopes anyhow, tell Leonard, and thank Leonard for his letter.

ALS: Berg

¹ Virginia Woolf, *The Waves*, published 8 October 1931.
² She copied 'Morgan's unsolicited letter' into her diary for 16 November: 'I daresay that gives me more substantial pleasure than any letter I've had about the book. Yes, I think it does, coming from Morgan' (*Diary*, IV, 52). Cf. her letter of 8 November 1931 to Hugh Walpole, in her *Letters*, IV, 402.

288   To W. J. H. Sprott

West Hackhurst, Abinger Hammer, Dorking
4 December 1931

Dearest Sebastian,

You are warmly invited to lunch here on the 14ᵗʰ, but now do you want to come? For I don't think I want to come up to town that night, since I must be up for the night of the 15ᵗʰ. What *I want* then is for you to lunch here on the 14ᵗʰ (or tea, if it suited your routes better), and to lunch with me in town on the 15ᵗʰ.

Will you do what I want?

Nay, I have been greatly tossed by the Waives, and you will be delighted to hear that I was *repelled* by the emotion emanating from Percival, told Leonard so, and he told Virginia.[1] But moderate your content. With this repulsion mingles the conviction that the book will be a classic, and while you will pertly pipe up 'Well why not?' the gap isn't, for a *person* of *culture*, so easy to skip. For there is emotion, and I was interested to learn that Vanessa too was overcome by it, though in a favourable sense. The position is that I have got to being bored by Virginia's superciliousness and maliciousness, which she has often ~~used to wound~~ wounded me with in the past, and with this boredom comes a more detached view of her work. A new book of hers ~~is~~ affects me like a newly discovered manuscript. One unrolls the papyrus—yes! this time a masterpiece. This too I have told her. I don't know what she makes of the gap.

Your remark about her hatred interests and cheers me, and perhaps it is true.

Love from **me**organ.

I put in cheque for £10, which I mentioned for December, and I will write again on the subject of money in the New Year, when I shall know better how I stand. Mother sold her furniture well—£115 when they expected £80—and is selling the house for £1750—probably worth £2000, but what a blessing to have found a purchaser.[2]

ALS: KCC

[1] Percival: character in Virginia Woolf's *The Waves*.
[2] Furniture and house in Plymouth, sold after death of EMF's great-aunt Eliza Fowler.

289 To Brian Walter Fagan[1]

West Hackhurst, Abinger Hammer, Dorking
22 July 1932

Dear Fagan,

Thank you; but of what use are pinpricks to one who has been permanently spavined in Roumania?[2] No one had ever heard I wrote novels, and when I mentioned it I was warned in a friendly undertone to keep silent. 'On ne fait pas des romans ici… en effet, on les fait mais…. Cher monsieur, vous n'êtes pas par hazard professeur?' So I said I was Professor of English Literature at Cambridge, counting on Q never coming so far. If he does he will have a thin time.[3]

Yours sincerely,
EMForster

¹ Brian Walter Fagan (1893–1971) was Director of Edward Arnold & Company; he retired in 1960. He was President of the Publishers' Association, 1945–7.

² EMF is reacting to a letter (15 July 1932) from Miss E. I. Page, who had enjoyed *Howards End* but was puzzled about the author, who was apparently 'not very well known'. EMF went to Rumania on 3 June 1932 and returned home on 23 June. He was the guest of an old Weybridge friend, Sir Alex Randall (1892–1977), First Secretary at the British Embassy in Bucharest, 1930–3.

³ Sir Arthur Thomas Quiller-Couch (1863–1944), known by his *nom-de-plume* 'Q', man of letters and King Edward VII Professor of English Literature at Cambridge since 1912, was knighted in 1910 for his services to literature and to the study of English literature.

290   To W. J. H. Sprott

[26 Brunswick Square, London]
4 October 1932

Dearest Jack

I find it difficult to write, but now that your major troubles are better I can try.¹ I think I ought to write, but it hurts me, it seems like blaming my lover and beloved. I went to tea with him at the S[ection] H[ouse] ~~to day~~ yesterday and shall again to ~~morrow~~ day—he is working for his sergeants exam. I can hardly ever see him. Dear Jack, it is as I feared, only worse—the woman is domineering sly and *knowing* and at present she seems to have got him down.* I have also a physiological trouble of which you do not know. When I cannot "get what I want" I have tempers like collar-burning Charles, these came on last night, they are canny & calculating & non-suicidal and I hate them, and even if Bob gets the woman under control when his seed comes out of her next year—shall I be in a state to profit? Is there any remedy for these? I do not want to go to a doctor. Perhaps I behave like this because of my week end at Cambridge in Goldie's rooms—but that seemed just sadness, which one always bears, it is the addition to sadness that's unmanageable. I know you will write back what you can. Thank you about Jim to whom I have written suitably. If he should turn up I might be glad. I don't want to come to Notts nor to lend this flat to any one at present, though if you came here alone I should be glad to see you. We needn't worry over Les much I believe—he will soon resolve into his natural constituents. I am so glad about Ted. Probably May will want to retain her cornet too some time, still she doesn't see that yet.—Joe is just fetching me to lunch, then I meet mother and take her to Putney. I am alone here till Friday, when she comes for two nights, home Sunday, up here Monday for a broadcast (on Goldie).—Looked in at Roger [Fry]'s last night. Gerald [Heard] there, wanting news of you.²

M's love

* I don't mean he has "refused" or is likely to.

ALS: KCC

¹ EMF wrote this letter during the period of adjustment to Bob Buckingham's marriage. To Sprott's suggestion that he go abroad, he replied ([6 October 1932] KCC): 'But how can I? bound by contract to the B.B.C. to the end of the year and by written (though not contractual) promise to continue till about March? Perhaps I could get off the latter, and perhaps this is a reason why you should mention the whole thing to Joe [Ackerley] when he comes. Bob asked me if I'd told him (of the marriage), but I felt it easier to go on without ~~understanding and~~ his understanding and sympathy, or most people's.' What had really 'wrecked' him, he wrote, was the time consumed by Bob's examinations for promotion. EMF would go abroad only 'because I can't stand it, not because I fear being a difficulty to him. He's protective and likes difficulties—I think.' For another part of this letter, see *EMF*, II, 182.
² Gerald (Henry Fitz Gerald) Heard (1889–1971), a Cambridge graduate, worked in the cooperative movement in Ireland and in England, as secretary to Horace Plunkett. Heard then became an author, lecturer, and broadcaster on religious and scientific subjects, and an influential authority on the techniques of meditation. Among his many books is *Pain, Sex and Time* (1939).

291 To Florence Barger

West Hackhurst, Abinger Hammer, Dorking
9 February 1933

Dearest Florence,

I went to the Kenya debate yesterday, and thought I should like to write you a line while it is fresh in my mind. A pretty gloomy scene, I needn't say. Donner, the conservative opener, was a fair-haired child, and Lunn (Socialist) who moved the amendment made the mistake of saying that he welcomed *any* opportunity of destroying the government. This allowed later speakers to suggest that he was using native wrongs as a cat's paw. He was a decent fellow, but did not do any good. What I carry away, though, is that Cunliffe-Lister is one of the shiftiest and evillest people I've been in the same room with for a long time. I will try to find out more about him from the Hilton Youngs. One would not trust him for one second as a tradesman or a friend, and one is asked to trust him as a politician. He is very clever in the Mephistophelian style, and insolent when he dared. Hamilton—who was excellent—he had to treat with respect. The best speech was by Wedgwood; he made an excellent point, and very quietly, over the prohibition to natives in Kenya (though not in Tanganikya!) to own land. I left before the blackamoor in the Gallery ~~protested~~ made a demonstration and had to be turned out. I'm so glad he misbehaved. You will have seen the government carries their motion, and any reference to the virtues of the settlers was greeted with great applause.¹

But I must stop and get on with Goldie's book, which I find more interesting and occupying than I expected. I have just been for two days to the Ashbees, going through the material there.² Also in interviewing Miss Stawell, who was less trying than I feared.³—It would be very kind of you to send that book to Bob, and to say if you will that you look forward to making his wife's acquaintance, as this will please him. I don't know about sending the Odyssey too—he is ready for it on [*sic*] some moods, but one doesn't know how often they prevail against the excitements of housekeeping and the arrival (in due course) of a child.

Mother has had a return of her eye trouble, but not bad, and she remains in fair spirits. I have just been writing an introduction to the book written by that Irish Civic Guardsman (George Thomson's friend). It is a lovely piece of work—the book I mean, but my introduction isn't bad either![4]

Do get hold of William Plomer's little book on Rhodes—it's very sympathetic.[5]

With love, and hoping soon to hear all your news:

M.

TLS: KCC

[1] On 8 February both Houses debated native rights in connection with a gold strike in Kenyan native reserves in 1931. The Colonial administration planned to take native land for 'development' without resettling those dispossessed. This violated a 1930 Native Rights Ordinance. The Government held that the land taken was 'negligible'—that developing the mines would do more for the natives than the lost land could do. In the Commons, the Government carried its measure, 208 votes to 57. Sir Patrick William Donner (1904–   ), MP for West Islington, was also Honorary Secretary of the India Defence League. William Lunn (1872–1942), Labour MP, had been a child miner in Yorkshire; he was Parliamentary Under-Secretary of State for the Dominions Office, 1927–31. Sir Philip Cunliffe-Lister, later 1st Earl of Swinton (1884–1972), was Secretary of State for the Colonies, 1931–5. Sir Robert Hamilton (1867–1944) voted against the Government; he was Parliamentary Under-Secretary of State for the Colonial Office, 1931–4. Colonel the Rt. Hon. Josiah Clement Wedgwood (1872–1943) was Vice-Chairman of the Labour Party, 1921–4, and had been a Resident Magistrate in the Transvaal, 1902–4. On the debate and vote, see *Hansard*, 8 February 1933, cols. 187–262.

[2] For his biography of Dickinson. He had been visiting Charles Robert Ashbee (1863–1942), architectural designer and critic, writer on town planning. See *GLD*, pp. 29, 138–9.

[3] Florence Melian Stawell (1869–1936), Australian-born classicist who entered Newnham College in 1889 and was a classical don there for a year before resigning on grounds of ill health. She settled in London and continued literary work, which included collaboration with G. L. Dickinson on *Goethe & Faust, An Interpretation* (1928).

[4] This was Maurice O'Sullivan (1904–50), whose memoir *Twenty Years A-Growing* (1933) was translated from the original Irish by Moya Llewelyn Davies and George Thomson, with Introductory Note (pp. v–vi) by EMF. It describes life on Great Blasket Island, off the Kerry coast, where O'Sullivan grew up.

[5] In his *Cecil Rhodes* (1933), Plomer gives Rhodes credit, where he can, for courage and enterprise, without hiding his arrogance or drive for power.

292   To Alice Clara Forster

Dunquin[1] [Co. Kerry, Ireland]
Sunday   [9 April 1933]

Dearest—There seems a chance of this reaching England before I do as the other young man—a pleasant student from Trinity,

Dublin—is going into Ballyferriter. The postman who calls here does so so as to miss the post. We have just been to Mass—200 squashed in a dense crowd in the chapel just close by—the address means 'village of the chapel'. Now we sit in the kitchen with food looming, and then we go to the cove to say goodbye to the Islanders, six boat-loads of whom have come in for the service, and also to look for some sea weed, sometimes obtainable at low tide, which is good for tuffet! Tuffet is a difficulty for me.

The people here are certainly very charming—no self conscious-ness. The weather, since we returned, has been colder & greyer than before, so I am glad the expedition is behind us safely. My tooth collapsed yesterday as I expected, but I get on pretty well and think I shall be able to survive until after Easter—it is a nuisance, as I wanted to be at home & work and now I shall have to hang about after David's pleasure.[2]

I will let you know my plans on Wednesday when I have got to the flat.

All cooking over peat here—it is a new house but arranged in the old fashion. The bread is beautiful—done in a sort of cauldron which hangs over the fire from a hook and also wears a hat of hot peat on its lid. The meat, cooked in a similar fashion, is not bad, except that it contains such enormous quantities of kag mag. We leave mountains on the plate, which the dog, the puppy, & the cat devour. The family consists of Mrs Casey, known as 'Kate the Princess' because her father was called 'King' in the island, her enormous wild looking husband, husband's mother, usually crouched on a settle in a shawl, and a gay girl helper, also stray labourers.[3] It is unexpectedly clean, and the life often reminds me of India. Country very bare and wild—no trees, but plenty of primroses and violets on the turf walls. Hope I have not caught a flea at

[Page or pages missing here.]

It was like a football scrum getting in and out—every one shoving and laughing. I knelt behind George and so had something to haul myself up by—we were all on the floor and some people rolled over. The priest and the policeman went off afterwards in a car.[4] I have become 'chatty' with Maurice O'Sullivan's elder brother, known as the 'Tailor'. I like him better than Maurice himself. Several of them speak English when alone with me but are too shy to venture before one another. It is one of the few Irish speaking districts in Kerry, and they are accustomed to visitors who come to study the language, not only from Dublin & England but from all over Europe.

I think our serving of food is now at hand, so will stop.

Pop's love

ALS: KCC

¹ EMF and George Thomson visited Dingle and the Blasket Islands, stayed for a few days in Dunquin, then went over with the Post to Great Blasket. O'Sullivan was not with them; he could not get leave from his job in the mainland police. See EMF's 'Maurice O'Sullivan', *The Listener*, 44 (1950), 59. EMF is apparently mistaken or confused there about the first meeting with him, for he suggests that they met *after* this first visit to the island.

² David: David Thompson, EMF's dentist.

³ The Irish playwright John Millington Synge (1871–1909), who visited the Blaskets about 1908, explains that the Postman, called 'The King' because of his regal bearing, acted as official spokesman to wrecked sailors and other visitors. Synge stayed in his home, and EMF and Thomson seem to have spent a night or two in the cottage next door. Kate—'The Princess'—married and moved to Dunquin, and EMF is writing from her house. Cf. Synge, *In Wicklow, West Kerry and Connemara*, pp. 83–107.

⁴ This must refer to the Mass mentioned above.

293   To John Collier¹

West Hackhurst, Abinger Hammer, Dorking
[Early Summer 1933]

Dear Collier,

I wanted to read *Tom's a cold* again before writing to you about it, but I have lent it and it won't come back.² I enjoyed it enormously and now wish I had said so at once. It gave an England just over the edge of the one I know and love, so that I got a dizzy feeling at moments which was aesthetically new. Leaving aside the question of how good you are—you're certainly the most *original* writer going, in my opinion, and when I read you my ordinary critical apparatus is ~~no good~~ no use to me. I feel, for instance, that you have condemned civilisation without regret, without zest, and without conceiving any alternative verdict as possible. This ought to make you remote from me, and yet, when I read you, your landscape is all around me. I face most writers—unless I turn my back on them!—but Tom's a cold, even more completely than His Monkey Wife, is an enveloper.

It's a great satisfaction to me to know that you admire my work.

I have meant to write on other grounds: to thank you for my pleasant visit and to enquire after Mʳˢ Collier and the success of her treatment at Thring—I do hope all went well.

Thank you very much indeed for giving me the book. I may write to you again after re-reading.

Yours ever
EMForster

ALS: University of Iowa

¹ EMF and the novelist John Collier (1901–80) began corresponding in 1930, after EMF read *His Monkey Wife*; see Letter 277; *EMF*, II, 167.

² Collier's novel, *Tom's a-cold* (1933), depicts Britain in 1995, reverted to primitive, anarchic tribal society as a result of wars and invasions.

294   To Robert J. Buckingham

Flat.   [26 Brunswick Square, London W.C.]
Sunday [early June 1933]

My ever dear Bob,

If Tuesday is possible I shall wire that morning, but I have not much hope, and silence means you are not to come.

Yes—there will be our holiday, I know, but the happiest hours of my life will always be the short hours we can spend together in the flat. Damn King Kong![1] Talking to you alone every now and then about the little things that happen to me—that's what *I* like and we haven't had a talk for such a time. If we don't meet Tuesday, I expect to be up in town about Wednesday June 7th. Let me know whether you can meet me about then, also the dates of your sporting events. I am awfully glad you are doing a bit of exercise.

I forgot to give you the chain, which I snapped the other day. I should be so grateful if you would take it back to the shop where you bought it and get it mended. I don't like to take it any where else in case it is spoiled.

The Hydaris gave us practically the same things for lunch which we had last night—with the addition of a prawn curry from which we are only just recovering. I enclose some cardomum for May to try, but they are not as good as at the restaurant.

Hope all is well, including [Hashim?] Ali. I nearly dropped in at tea time this afternoon but wasn't sure it would be convenient. (Not that I could have eaten anything without being sick.) I walked on Clapham Common instead and found the house where I used to stop with my great-aunt when I was a little boy. She was born in 1798![2] It seems incredible. Here is your baby, who is in a little way mine, because he bears my name, and he is born in 1933: one hundred and thirty five years later, and I have lived to see them both.

Love,
Morgan.

Anwar [Masood] just in—rather gloomy. Indigestion I think.

ALS: May Buckingham

[1] The 1933 film, opened in London on 17 April.
[2] I.e., Marianne Thornton. The house was Battersea Rise. See EMF's *Marianne Thornton*, pp. 15–20.

295   To Christopher Isherwood[1]

West Hackhurst, Abinger Hammer, Dorking
16 July 1933

Dear Isherwood

I am so very pleased to get your letter and reply at once. I did reply at once to your postcard too, as you will see from the enclosed, but you will also see why it was never finished. And perhaps this letter will be as dull. Yet I have a feeling to the contrary and will at all events not wait until tomorrow to make sure.

Do I know Greece well? I should hope so. I was there in 1903 and have not been there since. I got tuned up by a modern Greek who stole another archaeologist's coat before we landed and said I had given it to him. For I was an archaeologist in 1903, just as I was a surgeon from 1915–19 in Egypt, and a physiologist in 1924 at Stockholm and an ethnologist for 1927 in Africa.[2] What remains, however, to our present purpose is a remark made to the surgeon by Cavafy, who was himself an official in the Third Irrigation Circle and a great poet. Cavafy said "Never forget about the Greeks that we are bankrupt. That is the difference between us and ancient Greeks, and, my dear Forster, between us and yourselves. Pray, my dear Forster, that you—you English with your capacity for adventure—never lose your capital, otherwise you will resemble us, restless, shifty, liars ..." Which is an answer of a sort to your question. And I think that both the cruelty and the exaltation of cunning could be parallelled in the 5th century B. C.

My own questions are of a different type and vary in vulgarity from "Who are you with?" to "Where does the money come from to build a house?" You need not answer any of them when you write but I do hope you will write. I am still in England and still unable to decide whether she is good or evil, but at the moment of writing occupied in loving her and in wondering how you could have left the zinnias and the gooseberries, which I have just gathered, for your goats and their flesh. The bother of talking and of moving increases as I get older, so I would rather talk English to Bob even though my mother does think his voice common, and be driven round the western counties by him in a car, advancing to be sure into Wales, but retreating from it on the grounds that it was un-homey, and that the Welsh did not wash. We were away for a fortnight, and how, life being like this, any of these questions ever will be decided I can't see. I mean I look back in your case on a constant alternation of emotions about England, Europe, and anti-Europe. I wish I felt that 'old experience might attain to something like prophetic strain.'[3] Then one could know whether to live here or abroad in time.

Of the people you met that day at Esher, our hosts are much as usual, Joe Ackerley is back from a holiday in France, and Dawkins is taking one in Greece at the beginning of August.[4] I don't know whether you wish him to be given your address. I shall give it him if you say, but not otherwise. Bob I have mentioned and also myself. I have just been to Cambridge but find it rather queer. I can't tell you how glad I am you liked my book.[5] Yes, if the pendulum keeps swinging in its present direction it might get published in time. But the more one meets decent & sensible people, of whom there are now a good few, the more does one forget the millions of beasts and idiots who still prowl in the darkness, ready to gibber and devour. I think I had a truer view of civilisation thirty years ago, when I regarded myself as hiding a fatal secret. Though I am of course much more civilised myself now than I was then, and so are we all, those good few of us who count.—What do you mean by 'impure books'? I daresay I agree, but don't just know what you mean.

I expect to be here or in my flat till the end of the year. Now do please write. I will send you Twenty Years a growing tomorrow.[6]

Yours ever
E M Forster

ALS: Recipient

[1] Christopher Isherwood (1904–   ) and EMF met in September 1932, introduced by Plomer after EMF read and liked Isherwood's novel *The Memorial* (1932). Isherwood had been influenced by EMF since 1926.

[2] Archaeologist: his 1903 cruise with Nathaniel Wedd; see Letter 39. Physiologist: actually in 1926, when he went with George Barger to the Physiologists' Congress (Letter 254). Ethnologist: actually, 1929, the British Association tour of South Africa (Letter 269).

[3] Compare Milton, 'Il Penseroso', lines 173–4.

[4] Esher: home of Leo Charlton and his friend Tom Wichelo. Richard MacGillivray Dawkins (1871–1955), Bywater and Sotheby Professor of Byzantine and Modern Greek Language and Literature at Oxford, 1920–39.

[5] I.e. *Maurice*. For Isherwood's opinion, see his *Christopher and His Kind*, pp. 99–100.

[6] Maurice O'Sullivan's book: see Letter 291.

296   To Siegfried Sassoon

West Hackhurst, Abinger Hammer, Dorking
6 November 1933

Dear Siegfried,

Since the announcement is in the Times this morning I would like to send you a line of affection and good wishes, and (in a sense) of farewell.[1] You have been an unseen companion to me for many years now, and I am sorrier than ever to have missed you when I called in the summer.

I know nothing of the circumstances, so I will not write more, except just to say that my own circumstances have been happy for the last four or five years, in spite of occasional darkness. I am glad to have lived so long.

With good wishes for your happiness from

Morgan.

ALS: George Sassoon

[1] Announcement of Sassoon's engagement to Hester Gatty.

297   To Christopher Isherwood

The Woolf's, Rodmell [Sussex]
7 April 1934

Dear Isherwood,

I was very glad to hear from you and learn that you are both in the same boat. It all sounds nice. Grand Canary will be warm if dear, and I wish I was in Mr Abercrombie's pyjamas.[1] Here the cold is incessant and I am irritated at being left so much "to myself" in the various short visits I have been paying. First there was a preparatory school in Dorsetshire for Easter where my host was either fomenting the toes of the little boys, or at Church, or thinking about Rudolf Steiner while he put all the wrong letters into the wrong envelopes and had to write them all again.[2] Then, near Salisbury, was Stephen Tennant, sick and unable to be in the room with his guest for more than 20 minutes twice a day, and covering his eyes with a bandage when he drove to town, in case the scenery made him giddy.[3] And here, with less excuse, I think, are the W's, who read, Leonard the Observer, and Virginia the Sunday Times, and then retired to literary shanties to write till lunch.—At least L. has just come out, but I, piqued, continue my letter to you, and he, not displeased, cuts the dead wood out of a Buddleia with a small rusty saw. No doubt I am exacting or deficient in resources, but I am fed up with these two-day visits where I am left to myself. It's a bit of sham modernity like the silent greeting. When *I* entertain—but I get out of that by never being able to entertain. When *you* entertain—but you can get round that by suggesting I 'join' you somewhere sometime. That's quite different, and possibly always better. Hospitality, where art thou? Gone down the general drain, perhaps, with freehold estates and pairs of bags.

But Viertel—after what you say I really shall invite him to the Reform Club.[4] The fact that he praised my eyes is very reassuring, because one's eyes are always with one, they do not vary from day to day like the complexion or the intelligence. Let him gaze his fill. I shall certainly like to see him again and to thank him—which will probably be a mistake—for a most remarkable and enjoyable evening. I have often thought about it and described it to other people without interesting them. It *is* a milieu—so energetic friendly & horrible. I can't believe everything isn't going to crash when such a waggon gets so many stars hitched behind. Every film I ever see will now appear incredibly good, also I shall suppose that it has allowed ~~some~~ people like you & Heintz to escape for a bit into the sun.

Virginia has now come out, aprony from some article or passage, and has suggested a photograph should be taken of me. L. thinks it a good idea, and continues to saw the buddleia. It is 5 minutes to one—no, one, the bell rings, and I must jolly well lock this letter up during lunch, or it'll get read. I know these particular ethics. This evening we go to a meeting of the Memoir Club, at Maynard Keynes, and if this letter were read there, and aloud by me, it might be the star turn.[5]

12 April 1934

Memoir Club and much else over. I am back at home, quarrelling with my ground landlord through our respective solicitors.[6] He lives 100 yards away from me, but before we can exchange a reply there is

$$\left.\begin{array}{l}\text{letter from self to sol} \\ \text{letter from self's sol to his} \\ \text{letter from his sol to him} \\ \text{letter from him to his sol} \\ \text{letter from his sol to mine} \\ \text{letter from my sol to me}\end{array}\right\}\ \text{one week, with luck}$$

17 April 1934

Still waiting for the reply, and think I shall go to the South of France. Bob is ill, or rather laid up, and I can only see him in his own home. I must send this letter at once, or it will never go. Please write and tell me the colour of Mr Abercrombie's pyjamas. I do hope you will have a good time. Please give my regards to Heintz.

Yours
E M Forster

My blow for British freedom is struck on Thursday.[7]

ALS: Recipient

[1] Isherwood was travelling with his German friend Heinz, who had been refused entry into England when he arrived there on 4 January 1934. They left Holland for the Canary Islands on 4 April. See Isherwood, *Christopher and His Kind*, pp. 122–5; Finney, *Christopher Isherwood*, pp. 104–5. Mr Abercrombie's pyjamas: speculation about a fellow-passenger of Isherwood, on the S.S. *Zeelandia*.

[2] Rudolf Steiner (1861–1925), Austrian philospher; formulator of anthroposophy, which posits a spiritual world accessible to man's latent faculties.

[3] Stephen Tennant: see Letter 277.

[4] In 1933–4 Isherwood and Margaret Kennedy (1896–1967) wrote the script for the film *Little Friend* (1934), directed by the Viennese-born Berthold Viertel (1885–1953). Dr Bergmann, in Isherwood's novel, *Prater Violet* (1945) is modelled on him; see Finney, *Christopher Isherwood*, pp. 103–5. EMF visited the *Little Friend* set and was impressed at that time by the strangeness of the film-making process. The film was based on the novel by Ernest Lothar, *Kleine Freundin* (1931), translated in 1933 by Willa and Edwin Muir.

[5] Reading other people's letters was a Bloomsbury habit. On EMF and the Memoir Club, see *EMF*, II, 66.

[6] Landlord: Lord Farrer.

[7] This occasion is unidentified.

298   To Leonard Woolf

West Hackhurst, Abinger Hammer, Dorking
24 May 1934

Dear Leonard,

I am, once more, asking your advice. Having at last realised that Imperial Chemicals make poison gas I have sold out my holding. A sum of £138 has resulted and I want to devote all or part of it to anti-war work: Mrs Zangwill appeals for a salary for Miss Allen, secretary for Women's Peace Crusade—is this a good object or do you know of a better?[1] Then there is the Council for Civil Liberties of which I did become president, but this is less on the spot.[2]

I am writing in Time & Tide this month, and would like to refer to my own action, if I could find an effective formula which will induce other people to overhaul their investments.[3]

Yours ever
Morgan

I go to B[runswick] Sq[uare] on Saturday. I am just back from France.

ALS: Berg

[1] This was Edith Ayrton Zangwill (1870–1945), wife of the novelist and Zionist Israel Zangwill (1864–1926). She was very active in the Women's Peace Crusade, in a family tradition that included her mother, one of the earliest British women doctors, and her stepmother, a physicist. Miss Allen: Elizabeth Acland Allen (d. 1969), a noted peace campaigner and Secretary to the National Council for Civil Liberties, 1942–60.
[2] EMF became President of the N.C.C.L., on 22 February 1934.
[3] Forster, 'Notes on the Way', Time and Tide, 15 (1934), 695–6: 'I will wash my hands in innocency and so will I go to thine altar? Impossible. There's nowhere to wash.' This provoked 'Investment for Peace—or War', (ibid., pp. 761–2), an editorial opinion that EMF's action was less simple than it appeared.

299   To Christopher Isherwood

West Hackhurst, Abinger Hammer, Dorking
9 August 1934

Dear Isherwood,

I was very glad to get your letter and feel that there is a sort of alliance between us. Let me know when you get to England—you may even be there already. Some of your news was good. I do hope that Heintz will have no further trouble with the customs.[1] Yes—let's hope that if there's a crash we shall all behave well, but I do not even know yet what 'well' will be. It is all so inconceivable. I work up into a fuss about it for a little, and then calm down, write the Book of the Abinger Pageant, go in a char à banc to Oxford with eighteen policemen on Bank Holiday, prepare to entertain Mrs Myslakowska, who tried to seduce me in Cracow two years ago in order to get rid of her husband, and is now in England.[2] Then I get fussed, and contribute Notes on Passing Events to the newspapers, which you would easily follow if I sent them to you, or go on a deputation to the Attorney General in connection with the Sedition Bill.[3] I think it is sensible and suitable, this alternation between fuss and calm, and I gather you are practicing it yourself. It is the right conduct for our time—better than all calm, and far far better than all fuss. But if the war started, I don't know what would be right. The very meaning of words would change, and 'war' be the most meaningless of them all.

I meant to write you a letter full of news, as you might like some, but it all boils down to my having a certain amount of trouble at home, and very little elsewhere. Next week I shall go to town to see Bob. The week after he will stop with me at my flat. The day after that (Aug 22nd) I go to Falmouth and pay a visit to the Hilton Youngs. I have known H. Y. a great many years and am fond of him, and I get on with her. Her son, Peter Scott, is rather an enigma, a toad without a jewel perhaps, though a pleasant toad. He paints pictures of geese, pictures of geese, pictures of geese, pictures of geese, and no sooner has Sir Philip Sassoon or Mr Amery opened them than he has painted still more pictures of geese. He has also written a short story about a crane, which is rather on my mind, as I have lost it. However that is surely enough about Peter Scott.[4] I expect to be quite comfortable down there, but not to stop very long. I would rather like to start some more writing for one thing. I am very glad to have done that Lowes Dickinson book.[5]

We will talk about January when you return. Have you been reading any thing to speak of? I am just finishing Anna Karenina, which I never got through before. I do not think it is very good—except for the balancing of the two couples, which is certainly marvellous. Any other writer would have had to tether them into their position with a few strings, but Tolstoy leaves them to float naturally in his air. I can't think of any other novelist, dramatist, &ct. who could do this. It's neither a plan, nor is it a happy chance. It's something for which there's no word in criticism. I didn't even know Tolstoy could do it—I don't remember anything of the type in War & Peace—and in this respect A. K. has been a great pleasure. But the characters are not really masterpieces, Anna has been much overpraised and Kitty's nothing at all. And what's still more disappointing and surprising to me the sense of family groups—so overwhelming in W. & P. and so desirable here— never gets conveyed. Perhaps all the characters ought to have been introduced as children.

However, that's enough for Anna. She has taken even more room than Pete Scott's geese geese geese, and I don't know whether you've read her or want to.

What I did mean to say, when I asked you whether you were

reading, was to ask you whether you were writing. I was looking forward to your novel so much.[6] However if you can't get it done it can't be helped. I don't suppose it matters. It's much better not to write under the tyranny of time. "This, this have I achieved before civilisation crashes"? No, no.—I feel advancing at this point to some Grand Pronouncement. However it will not come. I must knock off and write a line to Bob, who is at this moment—which is midnight—driving about a mystery car with a wireless set inside it to detect "crime."

Please give kind greetings to Heintz if you are with him. I shall send this to Wm. Plomer. He may know your whereabouts.

Yours ever
E M Forster.

ALS: Recipient

[1] Heinz . . . customs: see Letter 297.
[2] Forster, *The Pageant of Abinger* (1934), presented 14 and 18 July in aid of the Parish Church Preservation Fund; see *EMF*, II, 197–9. Mrs Myslakowska was a Polish translator, and EMF's visit to her prompted the idea of her translating his work; in fact she published a translation of *A Passage to India* (*W Słońcu Indy*, 1938).
[3] Forster, 'Notes on the Way', in *Time and Tide*; see Kirkpatrick, pp. 133, 135, 139. 'Sedition Bill': the Incitement to Disaffection Bill, aimed at Communist literature and making it an offence to own or to distribute literature 'liable to seduce soldiers or sailors from their duty or allegiance'. Sir Thomas Inskip (1876–1947) was Attorney General, 1928–9 and 1932–6.
[4] Peter Scott (1909–   ), author, artist, naturalist; son of the Antarctic explorer Robert Scott and Lady Kathleen Scott (1878–1947); she married Hilton Young in 1922. Peter Scott was knighted in 1973 for services to wildlife preservation. His autobiography opens thus: 'All animals have interested me, and birds more than others, but wild geese have an almost mystical importance' (*The Eye of the Wind*, p. 3). Sir Philip Sassoon (1888–1939), politician and connoisseur, Secretary of State for Air, 1924–9 and 1931–7. Mr Amery: probably Leopold Stennett Amery (1873–1955), Secretary of State for the Colonies, 1924–9; for Dominion Affairs, 1925–9; for India and for Burma, 1940–5.
[5] That is, EMF's *Goldsworthy Lowes Dickinson*, published in 1934.
[6] Isherwood was writing the novel that became *Mr. Norris Changes Trains*.

300 To William Plomer

West Hackhurst, Abinger Hammer, Dorking
28 September 1934

Dear William,

I have just written a line to your mother. I am so glad that I should be any satisfaction to her.

I hope you are feeling better and will lie down if you aren't. Doctors are so dreary.

I want to know the developments in Regent's Park, if there were any. I had meant to send a message. (Was rather taken.) I went back to the flat to get a cooler shirt, and returned to find that my mother had had a visit from Mr R. Alford and his daughter Anne, whom I was glad to miss, and was feeling important and cheerful.[1]

My feet seem screwed off—the heat. I must go to bed. I expect to be up on Thursday. Perhaps we can meet about my articles.

Mr J. D. Beresford—will I speak on peace at Brighton—Mr Tetton—will I read a paper to the Nash Society, at Cambridge—Miss Hilda Browning—will I take the chair while Mrs Amabel Williams Ellis reports on Literature at Moscow—Mr John Macmillan, his story—Leo Charlton, his lectures—Stephen [Spender] his poem—Professor Otto of Marburg a[m] L[ahn]—can I give him details of the festival of Gokul Ashtami which I describe in a Passage to India and do I think it is a vegetation myth.[2] (Yes—I think you are right, though I forget what it was you said.)

I don't believe Quen[n]ell's really on the spot.[3] Perhaps I'm not either and am a bit old fashioned as regards form. What seems to [be] not satisfactory in the book is a thing which I find wrong in A Passage to India. I tried to show that India is an unexplainable muddle by introducing an unexplained muddle—Miss Quested's experience in the cave. When asked what happened there, *I don't know*. And you, ~~hoping~~ expecting to show the untidiness of London, have left your book untidy.—Some fallacy, not a serious one, has seduced us both, some confusion between the dish and the dinner.

I'm all for these London books of yours. They seem to me about a real town.[4]

Love from
Morgan

Sat[urday]
This morning, Mr John Macmillan why haven't I written about his story—Leo why haven't I written about the lectures, James Hanley will I 'introduce' Passion before Death in a new edition, and your Phoebe Fenwick Gaye herself, will I write a send off to a new sort of Time & Tide.[5] My instant reaction is to meet you again in Regent's Park, but alas I cannot

More love from
Morgan

ALS: Durham University

[1] Robert Alford was the stepson of EMF's aunt Rosalie Whichelo. In 1936 Anne Stella Alford married Sir Richard Thomas Dyke Acland, 15th Baronet (1906–   ) MP.

[2] John Davys Beresford (1873–1947), a then-famous author of quiet, reflective novels. Mr Tetton and the Nash Society: unidentified. Hilda Browning, author of *Women under Fascism and Communism* (1934). Amabel Williams-Ellis (1894–84), left-wing writer, daughter of *Spectator* editor John St Loe Strachey (1860–1927). John Macmillan (untraced). Leo Charlton's 1935 lectures at Trinity College, Cambridge, were published as *War from the Air: Past, Present, Future*; see his *More Charlton*, pp. 111–15. Stephen Spender, *Poems* (1934). Professor Otto: probably Rudolf Otto (1869–1937), evangelical theologian; Professor at Marburg University from 1917. On Gokul Ashtami, see *PI*, pp. 274–81.

[3] See Peter Quennell, 'New Novels', *The New Statesman*, 8 (1934), 397. Reviewing

Plomer's *The Invaders* (1934), he complains that 'a shade of ambiguity seems to cloud the narrative'.

⁴ Plomer's 'London books': both *The Invaders* and *The Case Is Altered* (1932) are about English provincials in London.

⁵ The 1935 edition of James Hanley's *A Passion before Death* (1930) has no Preface by EMF. Hanley (1901–   ) came from a Dublin working-class family. Years at sea, 1914–24, provided material for several novels, including *Boy* (1931), which brought on a major challenge to censorship regulations. Phoebe Fenwick Gaye (1905–19   ) wrote a biography of John Gay (1938).

301   To Alan Patrick Herbert[1]

West Hackhurst, Abinger Hammer, Dorking
10 October 1934

Dear A. P. Herbert,

The Council for Civil Liberties, of which you are so good as to be a vice-president, is in great need of funds—particularly in connection with the meeting to be held in the Central Hall on October the 18ᵗʰ.

I have suggested to our secretary that I should write to you and ask whether you could send him a contribution. I have no doubt that you have many calls on you, but I think that the moment is an important one, and that the need is urgent. I have sent £50 myself.

Yours sincerely,
EMForster

Personal

Since drafting the above I have received your letter, and since last I wrote I have come to much the same conclusion as your own. No, I doubt the pledge working.[2] And I agree that some of the opposition to the Bill has been a bit factitious and unwise.

I hope though that you will find time to go into the Bill a little, since you have cared to join our list of vice presidents, and will decide how best it may be opposed. An article from you in some paper would be of the greatest help at this point, and freshen up the whole campaign. This Council is too much in the hands of left wing doctrinaires, and I have been doing ~~all~~ what I can to induce people of independent outlook, such as yourself, to take a part.

EMF

Please give my kind remembrances to Mʳˢ Herbert.

TLS, ALS: Victor J. Rosen

¹ Sir Alan Patrick Herbert (1890–1971), author of light verse, novels, plays, and witty essays; and a reformer of the divorce laws.

² EMF wrote this letter during the controversy surrounding preparations for the mass meeting called by the National Council for Civil Liberties, for 18 October at the Central Hall, Westminster, to protest the Sedition Bill. EMF objected to the 'pledge' that committed members to protest by distributing at Aldershot army camp the so-called 'seditious' speeches

of the then Prime Minister, Ramsay MacDonald, made during the First World War and the General Strike of 1926. EMF wrote to Ronald Kidd (6 October 1934. Hull): 'I now write about my own position. . . . to many people the pledge will appeal as an opportunity for demonstrating against the government, or for idealistic action; to me it appears as a gamble of whose soundness I remain unconvinced.' The meeting was held as scheduled. EMF spoke but was unhappy with press treatment of it and said so in 'Still the Sedition Bill!' *Time and Tide*, 15 (1934), 1340.

302 To Sir Thomas Inskip

[N. p.]   27 October 1934

The Rt. Hon. The Attorney-General   Rejected draft[1]
The House of Commons, S.W.1

Dear Sir Thomas,
I think it exceedingly kind of you to have written to me as you have, when acknowledging the receipt of our Resolution in the Central Hall. When you received our deputation on July 30th, I tried to express on its behalf our appreciation of your consideration and courtesy, and I was glad to have the opportunity of saying this again on Oct 18th in a more informal way and before an audience of some thousands. I wish I could feel any assurance that if the Bill becomes law, it will be administered in the spirit in which it has been expounded. I feel that my own objections are as deeply rooted as ever. I earnestly hope that the Government will withdraw the Bill for it is alienating people in all sections of society and of the most varying intellectual equipment.
Again thanking you very sincerely for your kind letter.

Yours very truly,
[E. M. Forster]

TLU/cc, signature in another hand. Hull University: N.C.C.L. Papers

[1] This draft letter is typical of the courteous but firm tone that EMF, as President of the National Council for Civil Liberties, maintained toward Sir Thomas Inskip, Attorney-General, on the subject of the Incitement to Disaffection Bill, or 'Sedition Bill'. At a mass meeting on 23 May 1934 the Council had called for its withdrawal, and this was embodied in a letter of 6 June addressed to him. Sir Thomas replied (8 June) that the list of the Council's Vice-Presidents made it unlikely that it would pay attention to anything he might say on the subject, and the Council responded (30 June) with a clause-by-clause analysis of the Bill. Ronald Kidd, in an article, 'The Incitement to Disaffection Bill' (*The Spectator*, 153 [1934], 17) charged him with misrepresenting the Bill, then pressed him for a reply (11 July), which, when forthcoming (13 July), was that further correspondence was pointless; moreover (19 July) a deputation was useless unless Kidd withdrew his charges. Sir Thomas told him (24 July) that he stood by his statements but would consent to see a deputation on 30 July if its members would refrain from making statements like those in Kidd's article. A delegation representing the Council and the Trades Union Congress duly called on Sir Thomas, but mutual irritation continued, largely because of another Kidd article, 'The Progress of the Sedition Bill' (*The Labour Monthly*, 16 [1934], 613–20). EMF found himself in an awkward position. After rewriting the letter of which the above is a draft, he wrote to Kidd (12 November): 'I have written to Inskip as I promised, and hope his reply won't make my resignation a necessity.' The Bill, much watered down, became law in November, but this first major effort gave the Council national credit as an effective organisation. (All letters cited and

quoted above, with much additional material, are in the N.C.C.L. Papers in the Brynmor Jones Library at the University of Hull.)

To George Thomson in Ireland, EMF wrote (20 October 1934. Recipient): 'I spoke last Thursday for over 20 minutes to about 2000 people in the Central Hall Westminster, yes *and did it very well* but for all the good it is I might just as well have addressed the gnats in Glenmalure. . . . The wireless and the press scarcely noticed us, they want opposition stifled. It is very disheartening and a little scaring. The Bp. of Birmingham, J. B. Priestley, and a legal expert all very good—enthusiasm—and then silence.' Ernest William Barnes (1874–1953) was Bishop of Birmingham, 1924–53.

303   To Peter Burra

West Hackhurst, Abinger Hammer, Dorking
29 November 1934

Dear Sir,

I wish to thank you for your article in this month's Nineteenth Century.[1] I don't feel able to discuss whether what you have written is true, still less whether it is deserved, but nothing that I have read about myself has ever given me more pleasure; more than that, I feel that you have brought me great help at the moment when I am needing it. Thank you very much indeed. I was particularly glad that you should have seen the intended importance of Stephen Wonham, and your remark that the prose heightened before his entrance lifts me up too.[2]

Yours truly
EMForster

The closing sentence of A Room with a View was intended I think to connect with Miss Bartlett, though it might well have the connection you suggest.[3]

I have been looking at my books lately, partly on account of your article. I think A Passage to India stands, but the fissures in the others are considerable. I wish one didn't date so, though it is hopeless to try and avoid datability while writing

ALS: Helen Moody

[1] Peter Burra (1909–37), literary and music critic, died in an airplane crash almost above his own cottage at Bucklesbury, Berkshire. His article, 'The Novels of E. M. Forster' (*The Nineteenth Century and After*, 116 [1934], 581–94) attracted EMF's attention. He wrote to Plomer (21 November [1934]. Durham): Naturally I liked the 19th cent. article, also it moved me to think of "real goods" and may have some effect on me in the future. It made me think, in this connection, of the work of younger writers whom I admire, as well as of my own. Burra must have a very unusual critical equipment—he seems to go right through all externals and recall us to our true business.' The essay was reprinted in the Everyman's Library edition of *Passage* (1942), pp. xi–xxviii.

[2] Burra wrote (p. xxiii): 'When he [Stephen Wonham, in *LJ*] makes his first appearance, a third of the way through the book, the writing is lifted up like music to herald his approach.'

[3] EMF intended the words 'a love more mysterious than this,' in the penultimate sentence of *RWV*, to refer to the half-conscious encouragement that Miss Bartlett, despite appearances, had given to the love between George and Lucy. Burra seems to connect it (p. xxiv) with their posterity: i.e. love of children.

304   To Christopher Isherwood

West Hackhurst, Abinger Hammer, Dorking
16 January 1935

Dear Isherwood,

Dʳ Norman Haire has tittered to William [Plomer] that if my novels were analysed they would reveal a pretty mess, and that the works of H. Walpole and S. Maugham would be even prettier.[1] So I thought I would set to myself, and began last night in a lockable book.[2] There are things in my earlier stuff which are obvious enough to me now, though less so when I wrote them—e.g. the rescue of Eustace by Gennaro in the Story of a Panic, and Gino's savaging of Philip in ~~a Room with a View~~ Where Angels..., and there is one curious episode: the sacrificial burning of a number of short stories in 1922 in order that a Passage to India might get finished. So I thought I would put all this down, but soon got tired and am unlocking myself to you instead. I wish you were in England for several reasons. For one thing we always agreed to spend January together—do you remember—and it's already half gone. For another thing I would very much have liked your advice over the council for Civil Liberties. Can I work with people like Claude Cockburn or not?[3] You could have told me. I can't be a communist because I can't apply my mind to communism. There may be other reasons: you could have told me. And oh my god tomorrow evening we are to consider what my committee calls a 'Charter', and to specify what blessings in the way of free speech free thought and free assemblage we propose to confer not only on Great Britain but on North Ireland, India, and West Africa.[4] Substitute 'f' for 'ch' is my own thought, but even thus amended the charter will not carry far, for it has no guts behind it. We have no money, or if we have immediately spend it. The evening after that will be better—a play by Virginia called 'Freshwater' (or 'an evening at the bay'), and the evening after that will be best, for Bob comes.[5]

Dʳ Norman Haire, about whom William has already made numerous puns, leads one a circuitous course I must say. To start again at my own writings, I am trying to put together a volume of reprints.[6] There is plenty of stuff and much of it quite good in patches, but slight terrors steal over me. It's been so ineffective, when one considers the course of affairs, and it's so imperfect when compared with real writing.

I was very pleased to hear from you. I 'owed' you a letter as a matter of fact, and had it been written at the proper time should have told you how much I liked Little Friend. It was wonderfully little spoilt. I went three times.[7] I wish that Len would act again. I hardly ever see anyone whom I care to look at on the films. My other news would have been that, last November, I went for a day to the Saar. It was more like some one else's expedition than my own, but a great success. Thence I proceeded for a week to St Rémy de Provence, where I often go. This was a great success, too, but sunshine and calm instead of fog and romance.[8]

Well it is 1.0. A. M. and I seem to have written nothing at all. Day after day goes by in a muddle. We had curried eggs for supper, I have read half a letter of Horace Walpole's, M[rs] O'Brien and Miss Pollak think M[rs] Morgan is going to be married, the wireless is less good for regional, Sir Akbar Hydari writes on gold-speckled paper which was used for ancient Moghul documents. What is one to do with all that? I will go to bed. I am at last getting a few dreams again about lovely landscapes and trying to remain very quiet when I wake up so that I may remember them.

Please give my remembrances to Paul Kryger and my regards to Heintz.[9] I do hope you will both get to England some time soon. I don't suppose I shall get to Denmark unless I can do so with or without Bob—i.e. during his holidays, which again I have not much chance of spending with him. With love.

E. M. Forster.

17 January 1935
    The Danes, always thoughtful, have decided this morning to translate A Passage to India and I am signing the contract. Or was it that you gingered them? They are Berlingske Forlag, 34 Pielstraede, Copenhagen K.[10]

TLS: Recipient

[1] Norman Haire (1892–1952), writer on sexual behaviour and birth-control, and operator of birth-control clinics.
[2] EMF's 'locked diary' (KCC).
[3] Claud Cockburn (1904–81), left-wing journalist, correspondent for *The Times* in New York and Washington, 1929–32; for *The Daily Worker*, 1935–46.
[4] Nothing specific in N.C.C.L. records (Hull) seems to be a record of this meeting. There *is* a file (1/11) on a civil rights case in Ireland, on which the Council decided to leave action to an independent Irish civil rights organisation, if such a group should be forthcoming.
[5] Virginia Woolf's brief comedy about the Julia Cameron circle on the Isle of Wight was begun in 1923, then rewritten for performance in Vanessa Bell's studio on 18 January 1935. See *Freshwater: A Comedy*, ed. Lucio P. Ruotolo (1976).
[6] That is, *Abinger Harvest* (1936).
[7] On *Little Friend*, see Letter 297.
[8] He visited the Maurons, 30 November – 6 December 1934, after several days in Germany.
[9] Paul Kryger was a Danish friend of Stephen Spender.
[10] Berlingske Forlag published *Indiske Dage* in 1935; see Kirkpatrick, p. 162.

305 To Peter Burra

West Hackhurst, Abinger Hammer, Dorking
13 February 1935

Dear Sir,
    I was pleased to get your letter and had meant to answer it

before. I have been looking at some of my novels, and particularly at the Longest Journey. I am amazed and exasperated at the way in which I *insisted* on doing things wrong there. It wasn't incompetence; it was a perversity the origins of which I can no longer trace. But for this, it would have been my best piece of work, I am sure. (Howards End I lose patience with—a Passage to India is certainly the best). The L. J. has never stopped working in my mind, it is the only book which has ever given back something to the places from which I took it.

I thought Montgomery Belgion silly, and I did not take your article as a counterblast to his, nor think of him while I read you.[1]

Perhaps we shall meet some time in London, but I am diffident of meeting a critic whose work has touched me as much as yours has. Criticism as a rule is occupied with praise or blame. I am going to get a book on Virginia Woolf which I believe you have written, and I should be very glad if you would send me a list of any other publications.[2] I do not keep up with things regularly, indeed it was only through the advice of a friend that I got hold of the number of the 19th Century which has meant so much to me.[3]

Yours faithfully
EMForster.

ALS: Helen Moody

[1] Montgomery Belgion (1892–1973), critic and historian, argues that EMF's stress on the all-importance of instinct, combined with his undisputed talent, leads to 'mockery and sneering' that represent 'diabolical' values: see 'The Diabolism of Mr. E. M. Forster', *The Criterion*, 14 (1934), 54–73.

[2] The book on Virginia Woolf was apparently never published. Burra's other publications include *Baroque and Gothic Sentimentalism, An Essay* (1931), *Van Gogh* (1934), and *Wordsworth* (1936).

[3] The friend: William Plomer. The number: i.e. containing Peter Burra's article (Letter 303).

306 To Charles Mauron

West Hackhurst, Abinger Hammer, Dorking
31 May 1935

My dear Charles

Just a line of love and thanks. I am afraid that the other English delegates, who are appalling, have cast half an eye-glass on the Recamier [Hotel] too; do you know of any alternative?—I am in touch with Aldous Huxley: he seems to be the only bright spot.[1]

T. E. Lawrence was buried the day I should have gone to stop with him, upsetting this sort of thing. I won't write about him, am annoyed with every one who does, and feel distinguished and rather miserable. We shall all calm down, and if he had lived and lived into trouble there is no doubt that the Fascists would have tried to use him as a mascot. I shouldn't have said until this month that I was very fond of him, now it seems to me that I have been. I had a queer interview with his brother yesterday.[2]

Much love. Will write again.

Morgan.

ALS: Alice Mauron

[1] This was a five-day International Congress of Writers, planned by a group of Communist writers, foremost of whom was André Malraux; it opened in Paris on 21 June 1935. Besides EMF and Aldous Huxley (1894–1963), the English delegation included John Strachey (1901–63); Amabel Williams-Ellis, his sister; and Ralph Winston Fox (1900–37), English Communist and author of books on Genghis Khan and Lenin. Charles Mauron was to join EMF in Paris as his translator.

[2] Lawrence was buried on 21 May. The interview was with Professor Arnold Walter Lawrence (1900–   ), Laurence Professor of Classical Archaeology at Cambridge, 1944–51.

307 To Alice Clara Forster

[Paris]   Saturday [22 June 1935]

Dearest I feel very much doing my duty and it is quite as tiring as I expected. What a world and what a whirl! We had 3 hours of conference last night, 3 this afternoon, and as much as I can stand this evening, and so on till Tuesday night. I can understand scarcely anything which is said, since a microphone distorts it all and the French speak so quickly and the other nationalities so badly. I did pretty well myself considering—I don't think I was heard well because I was too tall for the microphone. Charles hit it better, his translation was very good, and he followed me paragraph by paragraph. The audience was enormous—4,000—and gave me good applause, no doubt poor things because they were fresh. There were not so many this afternoon when Aldous Huxley made a very good speech.[1] We all say much the same thing, though some of us say we are communists and others that we aren't. The microphone is a curse—you can't raise your voice or throw it about, or the thing blasts, and if you drop your voice the thing gives out. However that is enough about oratory. I called on Akbar yesterday—about 10 minute walk—he was out but came this morning.[2] I took him and Charles to have lemonade at the Café de la Paix, close to the Opera, which I knew A. would like as it is smart, and then to a cheap restaurant. The weather *was* appalling—stuffy and grey—but it was nice today, we are close to the river, indeed I have a view of it out of the window.

Yesterday Gide and Malraux took us out to dinner—no question of dress clothes, and it is far too hot to wear the Dorking blues.[3] Tomorrow we lunch with Jean Richard Bloch—he was in London some years ago and I was aimiable. I like him personally much better than the other French writers I meet, and his wife is charming too.[4] We shall just eat quietly in their flat. Charles seems happy and

With Lily Forster at West Hackhurst.

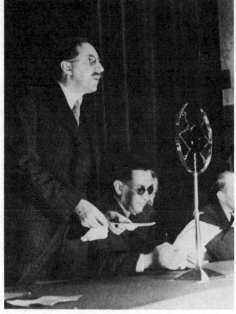

EMF (Charles Mauron seated beside
him) addressing the International
Congress of Writers in Paris, 1935.

doesn't get as tired as I do. My feet feel nearly off. I shall be glad when it is over and never do it again, but it has been interesting meeting these droves of outlandish people. C. has been most useful. Poor man, he had a letter from Marie this morning and lost it in the street before it was read. There is a lovely picture exhibition on (Italian art) which we shall visit as soon as strength and opportunity offer. Also I want to go to the Cluny—we are close to it.

Charles back—Marie's letter found.

Here is Siegfried—is it not a queer affair. A. W. Lawrence did tell me about it.[5] I must get off the bed, dress and limp forth for food. I will let you know plans when I know them—we are of course here till Wednesday. C. has said nothing yet as to my coming south.

Much love from
Pop.

ALS: KCC

[1] The ostensible occasion of the Congress, as explained by its leading organiser André Malraux, was that the Soviet Union, often accused of stifling culture, wanted a public opportunity for its writers to expound their ideas. (It was also an opportunity to exploit the prestige of Malraux's friend André Gide, a recent convert to Communism.) There were strong delegations not only from Russia but from France and from among central-European anti-Fascist writers. EMF spoke early on the first day, on 'Liberty in England'. He said that English freedom was race-bound and class-bound; nevertheless he believed in liberty and thought that the English version might have something to offer to the world. As regards politics, the audience would have guessed that he was not a fascist and might have guessed, rightly, that he was not a Communist either—though perhaps he might have been one if he had been a younger and braver man. Communism did many things which were evil, but he knew that it intended good. For Britain the main danger was not from fascism so much as from what he called 'Fabio-fascism': dictatorship working away quietly behind constitutional forms. His speech, much of which was inaudible, was received without enthusiasm by the mainly Communist audience. The five-day Congress, which was interspersed with scuffles with the Surrealists and with Trotskyites, left a trail of recrimination. Aldous Huxley wrote to Gide to complain of the endless Communist demagoguery, and Gide himself complained to the Russian ambassador in France about the attitude of the Russian delegation over the case of the novelist Victor Serge (1890–1947), arrested by the GPU in 1933 for alleged Trotskyite activities. See Sybille Bedford, *Aldous Huxley: A Biography*, II, 303–4; Maria Van Rysselberghe, *Les Cahiers de la petite Dame. Notes pour l'histoire authentique d'André Gide, 1929–37*, V, 440; Jean Lacouture, *André Malraux*, trans. A. Sheridan, pp. 189–90.

[2] Akbar Masood: his presence in Paris is unexplained.

[3] This dinner ended on a sour note; see *EMF*, II, 195–6. Dorking blues: probably a suit purchased in Dorking.

[4] Jean Richard Bloch (1884–1947), French Communist historian, novelist, journalist; co-Director of the paper *Ce Soir* in 1937. In 1934, at the First Congress of Soviet Writers, in Moscow, he was reprimanded for excessive individualism; nevertheless, he was in Russia as a radio and news journalist, 1941–5, after which he returned to Paris and to *Ce Soir*.

[5] Perhaps an event connected with Sassoon: unexplained.

308 To J. B. Priestley

West Hackhurst, Abinger Hammer, Dorking
12 July 1935

Dear Priestley,

I well understand your doubts, and more or less express them in

an article in the New Statesman. But I think that writers of the
'liberal' type should give this new Association a trial.[1] I shall clear
out of it myself if it gets too left wing, so will Huxley, and this the
promotors know. I've never taken the P.E.N. very seriously since it
organised that beano to the grave of Rupert Brooke, and (if Wells'
Barcelona speech was reported to me correctly) it proposes to
concentrate on social intercourse in the future.[2] Which is a very
good thing, but which does leave an opening for something else.

My speech is to come out in the London Mercury—more or less
the sort of remarks which you have heard me make before.[3]

Yours sincerely,
EMForster

TLS: HRC

[1] Forster, 'International Congress of Writers', *The New Statesman and Nation*, n. s. 10
(1935), 9. To James Hanley he wrote (12 July 1935. Liverpool Record Office): 'The congress
itself seemed to me a moderate success, and worth holding, but it's no use overpraising it, or
pretending that great difficulties don't lie ahead. Mrs [Amabel] Williams Ellis is asking you to
join the committee, I believe; I do hope you'll join, as does Aldous Huxley. It's so important
that people whose main interests are not political should take part. Otherwise the thing will
degenerate into a communist stunt.' International Association of Writers: EMF's connection
with it remained minimal.

[2] On the 'Brooke beano', see Letters 280, 281. Barcelona speech: Wells, as President of the
International Federation of the P.E.N., spoke at the 13th International Congress, Barcelona,
20–25 May. He said that he intended to resign because it left him too little time for other
activities, and also because in recent years the P.E.N. had had to choose between political
commitment and becoming 'an international Club which confined its function to the
organising of dinners and excursions'. He saw liberty threatened more from the Left than
from the Right. The speech aroused 'a considerable amount of discussion'. See *P.E.N. News*, 7
(1935), 3–6.

[3] Forster, 'Liberty in England <An Address Delivered at the Congrès International des
Ecrivains at Paris on June 21st>', *The London Mercury*, 32 (1935), 327–31; reprinted, *AH*, pp.
62–8.

309   To May Buckingham

[26 Brunswick Square, London W. C. 1]
as from: West Hackhurst, Abinger Hammer,
Dorking.   10 August 1935

Dear May,
R. told me your disappointing report. I know that you were more
or less anticipating it, but it is very depressing all the same. I won't
go on about it, for you wouldn't wish me to. You know what all
your friends feel.[1]

I hope that the changes of scene during his holiday will benefit R.
We have just worked out a programme—Holland (or Belgium) till
about the 29th, then a day or two with the Wilsons (i.e. with John),
and then a day or two in North Wales.[2] But the whole thing can be
altered at any moment if it is thought better to do so, ~~whatever~~
without any inconvenience to myself.—He seems all right and was

gay with Anwar this morning, so in *that* way you needn't worry.[3]

I haven't cared so very much either for Proud Man or Rebel Passion. I think they are written by nice people, and speculate in an interesting way, but they aren't what I call imaginative and in neither case do the central characters come alive. I do want in a book *either* accurate information (which of course neither of these novels set out to give) *or* what I call artistic achievement. This is rather a vague phrase—it's meant to include good character drawing, exciting narrative (P. M. was rather thrilling over the man who murdered little girls but not elsewhere), and a witty or poetical outlook. Huxley's Brave New World is often disgusting, but it is witty and vivid, the scenes bite in, but in these books they don't.[4] I wonder whether you've read Bunyan's Pilgrim's Progress since school days: the outlook is absurdly narrow minded, but there the vision of the world is to me imaginative and exciting in just the way Rebel Passion isn't—with its pedestrian trot of the Monk & the Child up and down the centuries!

Of the two books I thought P. M. the more original, R. P. the pleasanter in its outlook.

I am writing in the flat actually. Jack Sprott arrives tomorrow— for six weeks! (that is to say he will be here when I don't want it for any other purpose. He is doing a special course on Vocational Training at some institute of Psychology. He is awfully good at his work, but doesn't get recognition because he doesn't or can't produce a book on it. I hope this specialised study will get him some recognition at Nottingham).—Robert & I think he must jolly well lend us his car when we want it, since I've lent the flat. We haven't found out yet what he thinks.

Joe is off on holiday to Malta.

Well I'll stop this rambling. Don't trouble to reply though letters are always very welcome.

With love,
Morgan

ALS: Recipient

[1] May Buckingham was ill with tuberculosis.

[2] EMF and Bob Buckingham made this trip to Holland; see *EMF*, II, 209–10. The Wilsons were the Birmingham friends of John Simpson; see Letter 283.

[3] Masood's son Anwar was apparently staying in EMF's flat, and he and his brother Akbar were frequently under EMF's care while at school in England.

[4] This letter is typical of a number of those in which EMF made an obvious effort to educate the Buckinghams and to introduce them to new concepts and ideas about the arts and literature, an effort that they appreciated both then and later. *Proud Man* (1934) is by Constantine Murray (pseudonym); *The Rebel Passion* (1929), by Katherine (Kay) Burdekin. *Brave New World: A Novel* was published in 1932.

310   To William Plomer

Max Gate, Dorchester.   20 August 1935

Dear William

My train reaches Waterloo tomorrow (Wednesday) at 12.49. I wonder whether there is any hope of your meeting it and lunching. Do if you possibly can—shall look out for you. I go home that evening, up on Friday, and to Amsterdam Saturday.

This paper is called 'Hardy Bond,' and has a picture of the Birthplace on the block. In my bedroom is a photograph of T. H. and first wife on a breakwater, a photograph of T. H. and Edemund Goose on a garden seat, an etching of T. H. by Strang and a very funny Max of the Prince of Wales, his bowler flying off his head as he rushes forward to T. H. crying 'Mayn't I call you Tom?'[1] Eileen is not very well and the cook gives trouble by always supplying an extra course to each meal.[2] "I must again apologise for the dreary length of this meal—it would be more bearable if we were a larger party." I arrived yesterday and unluckily coincided with Dr Marie Stopes who had called for a presentation copy of 'The Well Beloved' and scarcely had she gone when there was a second misfortune—breakfast spoons with the tea cups.[3] This evening the Matron of the Cottage Hospital comes to dine. It is to be hoped nothing will go wrong.

Yesterday morning I spent at the excavations at Maiden Castle with my cousin, and yesterday afternoon ditto, hearing him try a case of rape.[4] It was very odd and moving—absolutely unlike what one reads. The prisoner, a nice looking young labourer with a fixed smile, when asked what he had to say to each bit of evidence bobbed up with 'nothing at arl, sur' and plumped down. He signed a deposition agreeing to every thing except that he said he hadn't come off. However the doctor said he had. He'll be tried now at the assizes, but my cousin who seems sensible & humane, is sure he is dotty and has ordered a medical examination. The girl was a young housemaid—they had never seen each [other] before. She was smoking as she walked across the down—probably this set him going. She seems to have struggled up to a certain point, and then let him do it. What a pity he couldn't have put it somewhere else!

Well I will conclude now, stunned by the twitter of eight budgerigars: "unluckily the most intelligent of them flew away". I hope to see you or failing that to get your news. Achille has written again—for 100 francs.[5] He has been attacked 'en pleine ville' and robbed of all his savings. I don't know but have sent £1.

Love from
Morgan

Just off to the *Museum*.[6]

ALS: Durham University

1 EMF is visiting Mrs Hardy. For a photograph of Hardy and Edmund Gosse at Max Gate in 1927, see Michael Millgate, *Thomas Hardy: A Biography*, following p. 528. William Strang's etching is frontispiece to Volume 1, Mellstock Edition, Wessex Novels (1919–20). Max Beerbohm's untitled drawing (1923) commemorating the Prince's visit to Max Gate on 20 July 1923 is owned by the Dorset County Council, Dorchester.
2 Eileen: perhaps a nickname for Florence Hardy; see Letter 349.
3 Dr Marie Stopes (1880–1958), botanist and founder of Britain's first birth-control clinic, lived at Norbury Park, near Dorking, and owned the Old Lighthouse on Portland Bill, Dorset, which figures in Hardy's novel, *The Well-Beloved* (1897).
4 The magistrate was Ernest Ruthven Sykes (1868–1954), Justice of the Peace in Dorset, 1911–49; Chairman, Dorset Quarter Sessions Court, 1934–46; President of the Dorset Natural History and Archaeological Society, 1942–5. His stepson describes him as having a 'most admirable character, . . . never loud and always fair'.
5 Achille Morgenroth: a French sailor whom EMF had met in Toulon in 1929.
6 Probably the Dorset County Museum.

311   To Robert J. Buckingham

[44 Clifton Gardens, Maida Vale, London[1]]
Tuesday   [17 December 1935]

Dear Bob,

Operation at 9.0. A. M. tomorrow.[2] Correct Telephone Number for *enquiries* is Welbeck 4662. I think you got given the surgeon's number.

This is written in Joe's hole. I go in in about ½ an hour. I feel gay and calm, but have an open mind as to whether I shall get through or not[.] I don't say this to anyone else, but I love you too much to say anything but the truth. I don't feel afraid of anything and it is your love that has made me be like this. I hope to come back to you and everything and be as before, and I will try my best to do so. If I should go under or come out as an unattractive invalid, it can't be helped. Some things in my case are against me—e.g. the distended bladder may have [been] worrying the kidneys. On the other hand I'm young for the thing and blood pressure is all right.

Love
Morgan.

ALS: May Buckingham

1 Ackerley's address.
2 This was the first part of a two-stage prostate operation; the second took place in February 1936.

312 To Forrest Reid

West Hackhurst, Abinger Hammer, Dorking
17 January 1936

My dear F. R.

Thanks for your affectionate letter. My latest news is as above. I have been sent down here to get fit for the second part of the operation—it's not to be for a month at earliest. I feel all right, but my blood-test is unfavourable.

I don't see that you can possibly bring Following Darkness up to date.[1] It's grotesque. If there are faults, they are as much a part of the book as its merits. Tell the publishers to stick in an aeroplane and be done.—I expect I shall enjoy your early Tom, though of course what I do want and shan't get is a full-length poacher.[2]—I expect you know that Peter Burra, who wrote about me so greatly to my pleasure, is now writing about you.[3] Oh, and by the way, I am reprinting in my miscellany-volume that little article about you which I did in the Nation years ago.[4]

I miss Bob here dreadfully—he came to see me almost every day in the Nursing Home for a month and did countless jobs. I do feel very grateful to his wife for making it easy for him. Joe came constantly too; my mother & aunt occupied my flat.

I am very glad to hear such good news of Stephen's health and work. Do write again when you find time, and excuse inadequate replies.—John Simpson comes for the day next Tuesday. I saw H[ugh] Meredith once or twice.

Love from
E. M.

ALS: Stephen Gilbert

[1] Reid's 1912 novel: see Letter 97. Reid rewrote it as Peter Waring (1937).
[2] Reid, Young Tom, or Very Mixed Company (1941).
[3] Burra's article was never published. EMF had written to Burra about it on 6 January 1937 (H. Moody): 'I agree it isn't altogether successful, but there's material in it for something as condensed and as echoing as your creation out ot me. / Would you let F. R. himself read it, if he wishes to do so? / I agreed with most of your judgments and must have another try at Brian Westby which most ot his admirers like so much [novel by Reid (1934)].'
[4] Forster, 'The World of Forrest Reid', The Nation, 27 (1920), 47–8; reprinted as 'Forrest Reid', AH, pp. 77–83.

313 To Leonard Woolf

[N. p.]   27 March 1936

Dear Leonard,

I was scared at realising that emigration is being talked of; however one must come out of one's anaesthetic sometimes. Various things which cannot be removed from England hold me to it, so that I could never emigrate myself, but if I was married or had children to be saved I should think of it, certainly.

It is so odd, to be nursed through a dangerous illness with so much kindness and sense, in order to return to a civilisation which has neither kindness nor sense. For the moment I want to throw up everything, For Intellectual Liberty included, but shall keep quiet until I've found my feet.[1]—This, in the strictly physical sense, will occur 'towards the end of next week' the doctor says, if all goes well; so I am hoping for a run of good luck for a change and to come with you Thursday.

I do wish Virginia's novel was finished.[2] I suppose it is impossible that she should allow you or anyone else to take the typescript out of her hands for the final revise. A strange suggestion, but the situation is strange, and since she is so detached about her ~~illness~~ health she might just conceivably consider it.

With love to her and to yourself.

M.

ALS: Sussex University

[1] For Intellectual Liberty: a British society of anti-Fascist intellectuals. See Virginia Woolf, *Letters*, VI, 99.
[2] Virginia Woolf, *The Years* (1937), which was causing her much depression.

314   To Leonard Woolf

West Hackhurst, Abinger Hammer, Dorking
24 May 1936

Dear Leonard,

For several reasons this is a difficult period for people of our generation and I don't find it easy to write letters. I hear that you and Virginia are still in the country. Is this so and have you given up your idea of a tour? I should very much like a line about her health.

As for mine, I feel and look all right but am under treatment for bladder-infection which I understand is a not unusual aftermath. I have swallowed mandelic acid and nauseous cachets for a fortnight, and am now told that I am much better and may knock off in a few days. Much more tiresome are my feet which have 'dropped' owing to being so long in bed, and I can't walk in any reasonable sense of the word. I believe massage will get this better, and start it this week—when by the way I reenter public life in the form of a cocktail party which Intellectual Liberty is offering to some journalists. One could scarcely hope for a more symbolic episode. I should like to see it staged in a revue—with Imperial Chemicals Ltd functioning in full activity on the backcloth.

Meanwhile my Alexandria Guide *is* being reprinted. The local archaeological society there has taken it up, and a fussy and polite but seemingly competent American judge called Jasper G. Brinton writes me endlessly. The president of the society was unluckily an

Italian, and dead against le Forster, since a guide by an Italian already exists. The strife was transferred to the Municipal Council, where after a heated debate the Anglo Saxons and their allies were completely victorious, and the Municipality voted no less than £200 to the expenses. Nor did Judge Jasper G. B. rest there. Going on to the newly established le tourisme bureau, he received from the Bey in charge a promise of £100 more. The local Whitehead Morris is in ecstacy. All is perfect, and knowing my Alexandria I await the next move: the vetoing of the project in Cairo.[1]

Here is this all-English stuff of T. E.'s, letters to and from, filling an immense Canterbury and overflowing down the piano. The trustees have been very decent with me so far, and I like the brother. If I *had* the freedom they ask me to have I might produce a gem. For example from Lord Trenchard: "I am still a little sad and tired. I sometimes think people do not realise that I do not want to use the Air Force for killing only: the fact of an Air Force being about should in time ensure that we may not continually go on the war-path with as many casualties as we did in the past."[2] Then a sex-rave from Robert Graves abusing Virginia and myself for the niceties between the sheets which we *should* observe if we went to bed together. Another rave from Ezra Pound. <All this private of course>

I shall be in London for the first week in June I think. Please let me know your plans if you have any.

With love to Virginia and yourself.

Morgan.

ALS: Sussex University

[1] This was the 1938 (2nd) edition of *Alexandria: A History and A Guide*; cf. Letters 190, 200. Jasper Yeates Brinton (1878–1973) was a Philadelphia-born lawyer and writer on international law. He became Justice in the Court of Appeals in the Mixed Courts of Egypt. His enthusiasm for EMF's book was directly responsible for the new edition. He urged the Société Royale d'Archéologie d'Alexandrie, of which he was the President, to take up the project, and he found a group of friends who largely rewrote the 'Guide' section of the book. He also enlisted the support of agencies such as the Ministry of Commerce and Industry and the Office of Tourism. EMF wrote to him (5 February 1936. John Brinton): 'As far as I am concerned, I should be delighted if the distinguished society of which you are President should republish my *Alexandria*: it is a book for which I have always had an affection, for the writing of it helped me through some difficult days, and I should like to see it in print.'

[2] Hugh Montagu Trenchard, 1st Viscount Trenchard (1873–1956) entered the Army in 1893 and was Chief of Air Staff, 1918–29; Principal Air ADC to the King, 1921–5; and Commissioner of the (London) Metropolitan Police, 1931–5.

315   To Cecil Day-Lewis[1]

West Hackhurst, Abinger Hammer, Dorking
6 June 1936

Dear Day Lewis,

Many thanks for your letter; also the proposer has written to me and kindly given details.—As an old fashioned liberal if anything, I'm in my usual dilemma, and don't like the idea of imposing an anti-fascist test on a non-political organisation. And this, it seems to me, is what would happen if the Society of Authors was affiliated to the T[rades] U[nion] C[ongress]. I expect my ideas want overhauling and I ought to face the fact that in 1936 every organisation must be political and that it's one's job to affiliate, in the right direction.[2]

I've used the Society myself mainly as a means of screwing more money out of publishers. I have also prodded it a little towards maintaining our rights of self-expression—it has been much better over this since Kilham Roberts became secretary. I think Gorell's awful. I had a most unsatisfactory correspondence with him over the Well of Loneliness affair.[3]

Don't trouble to answer this: if we don't meet on the 24th I hope we'll meet elsewhere. I've been laid up and don't get about much yet.

Yours
EMForster.

ALS: Jill (Balcon) Day-Lewis

[1] Cecil Day-Lewis (1906–72), poet and writer of detective stories (pseudonym, Nicholas Blake); Professor of Poetry at Oxford, 1951–5; Poet Laureate from 1968, succeeding John Masefield. In the 1930s he followed Auden in linking poetry and left-wing politics. The 1940s, however, found Day-Lewis withdrawn from political activity, living in the country, and translating Virgil's *Georgics* (1940), with a Foreword (pp. 9–11) that contains the lines: 'Where are the war poets? the fools inquire / We were the prophets of a changeable morning / Who hoped for much but saw the clouds forewarning: . . . .'

[2] Day-Lewis seconded a proposal at The Society of Authors on 24 June 1936, that it revise its rules so that it could join the TUC. He also suggested that writers should form a popular front to combat the increasing danger of Fascism. This was rejected, but Day-Lewis published an article, 'The Association of Writers' (*The Author*, 49 [1938], 55–7), which he signed as Chairman of the International Association of Writers for the Defence of Culture; it provoked a spate of letters (*ibid.*, pp. 105–6, 134–5).

[3] Ronald Gorell Barnes, 3rd Baron Gorell, see Letter 267. EMF forwarded this correspondence to Hugh Walpole.

316   To Arnold Walter Lawrence

West Hackhurst, Abinger Hammer, Dorking
16 June 1936

Dear Lawrence,

I enclose Mrs Fontana: sorry.[1]

I think I had better write you a comparatively formal note, which can be shown to the other trustees if necessary.[2] I understand from you that, while still wanting the book to be mainly letters, they are keener on additional matter than they were, and would indeed welcome something which tended to be a biography, and was anyhow a 'book'. I sympathise with this, but fear that now I've gone into the material, I see no book there. Here are my reasons.

In the first place I can't treat his parentage and origins properly, and it hampers any biography to make such a lame start. In the second place I can say little about his personal emotions—he kept them quiet and those who could probably tell me something about them will also remain silent. All very natural and creditable, but it further diminishes the chance of producing a coherent and interesting book about him. Then—a third loss—all the main drama goes too, for the great moment of his life has already been handled by himself and by two excellent biographers.[3]

I'm driven then to the conclusion that a selection from the letters, with explanations by myself and any other remarks ~~about him~~ which occur to me, is the only line. If I tried to do a book on him of the Lowes Dickinson type I am sure it would be bad. (The L. D. is good within its limits, because in that case I had all the material which makes a biography good.)[4] Perhaps my unseasonable illness leaves me less inventive—it certainly leaves me less mobile. If I thought any one would do the job better than I can, I'd give it up, and if the trustees believe they could find a better workman than myself, they needn't hesitate to tell me. My present feeling is that things are as good as they can be expected to be, but that the trustees must not hope for an outcome of the 'Life and Letters' type.—I'd like to take this opportunity of thanking them for the consideration with which they are treating me.

I will write to Colonel Dawnay. I should also like to talk my difficulties over with Wilson of Bumpus.[5]

Yours ever,
EMForster.

TLS: Recipient

[1] Mrs Winifred Fontana (1880–19) was the wife of R. A. Fontana, British Consul at Aleppo. For her recollections of Lawrence, see *T. E. Lawrence by His Friends*, ed. A. W. Lawrence, pp. 81–5.

[2] Professor A. W. Lawrence had asked EMF to edit T. E. Lawrence's letters. He sought advice from Denys Kilham Roberts (1903–76), Secretary of The Society of Authors, 1935–63.

'They don't want a "Life", but suggest that, besides any necessary commentary, I should try to convey some picture of the man. The length of the book is at my discretion; they expect me to take from a year to two years over it.' He wondered whether he ought to ask for advances and for expenses of typist and a secretary if needed. He concluded: 'In fairness to the trustees, I must point out that M𝑟 A. W. Lawrence has already done a substantial amount of work himself; he has collected several hundreds letters, and sent them to me typed—usually in duplicate. My main work will be one of selection, arrangement, and comment, though there will be a certain amount of further letters to collect, and a certain amount of interviewing to do' (8 April 1936. S. of A. Film Archive). A later problem was that of indemnity against libel charges, a point on which EMF was already sensitive because of the libel suit over republication of his essay, 'A Flood in the Office', in *Abinger Harvest*; see Letter 201. This led him to give up the Lawrence project.

[3] Robert Graves, *Lawrence and the Arabs* (1927); in America, *Lawrence and the Arabian Adventure* (1928). Basil Henry Liddell Hart, '*T. E. Lawrence': In Arabia and After* (1934).

[4] I.e., EMF's biography of Dickinson, for which he drew on GLD's frank MS 'Recollections', since published (*Autobiography*, ed. Sir Dennis Proctor, 1973).

[5] Alan Geoffrey Charles Dawnay (1888–1938) joined the Coldstream Guards in 1909 and progressed by 1930 to General Staff Officer 1st Grade at the War Office. He was Controller of the BBC Programme Division, 1933–5. He had been one of T. E. Lawrence's closest friends and associates. John Gideon Wilson (1876–1963), noted London bookseller, manager of Bumpus's Oxford Street shop, London.

317   To Alice Clara Forster

Flat [26 Brunswick Square, London W.C. 1]
Sunday [4 October 1936]

Dearest—got up this morning to find your letter &𝑐𝑡. Have just had lunch at Deborah's—now an Indian comes, then Bob B unless this Fascist trouble stops him, and tomorrow I have dentist and then a man called Robinson (work), possibly followed by Harold [Barger?], as you may see.[1] So sorry about Tuesday. I had tried to shift Aldous [Huxley] to Monday, as please explain to M𝑟𝑠 Mawe.

I stopped two nights in Oxford, as they were not going to their cottage this week end after all. Affectionate messages from Arthur & Margaret, and a gift to you from the latter of some *celeriac*—delicious I thought it.[2] An enormous party of cousins and children there last night—about 20 in all.

You will have seen about the function in the Times. I don't like the plaque at all—so hatchet-faced. There is a picture of it in Saturday's no. A large audience, mostly drawn by curiosity. I had an inferior ticket but placed myself well—at 11.30 a miscellaneous procession came up the staircase having unveiled the plaque en route—vice-chancellor of the university and other dignitaries—trumpeters from the R.A.F., Winston Churchill, the Mayor—who is a lady—preceded by her mace, and Kennington with a black cockatoo of hair sticking up, but otherwise very tidy—M𝑟𝑠 K. told me afterward that they had both taken a long time getting him ready. W. C. very good—an old man's voice but K says that is because his false teeth are a failure.[3] Then we had a superior lunch party at All Souls of 14. Lovely wine, rather too strong, food rather scanty. I had a few words with my host—Lionel Curtis, didn't like him, and a few words with Colonel Dawnay, civil as usual.[4] Met and liked Colonel Newcombe and his French wife.[5] She said to me "M[rs] Lawrence *lovs* me so much that I may kiss her *here here* with my rouged lips and leave spots on her face and still she doesn't mind." I wasn't introduced to W. C.—no doubt could have been if I had tried, but no advantage to me. I sat between the rival candidates for Parliament—Lindermann and Sir Arthur Salter, who was a friend of Goldie's.[6] Winston was aimiable, especially after his whisky and we listened to some of his talk. Meanwhile a lot of wives, who had not been invited to the lunch, had gathered in the courtyards of the college and were strolling about there. I joined M[rs] Kennington & M[rs] Newcombe, and the wife of the Warden showed us the magnificent library. It's a remarkable college.

Must now get ready for the Indian. Hope he won't tire me! All ready for tea, thanks to M[rs] F[raser].[7]

Pop's love. Love to M[rs]Mawe

M[rs] K. enquired after the pussies.

ALS: KCC

[1] Deborah, Indian, Robinson: unidentified. Harold: apparently a letter from Harold Barger, enclosed. Bob Buckingham was no doubt on call because of activities of Oswald Mosley's British Union of Fascists. On 4 October it held meetings and intended to march in the East End of London. At the last minute the Home Office prohibited the march, but a counter-demonstration brought on police intervention.

[2] On Arthur Gillett, see Letter 62.

[3] On 3 October a plaque to T. E. Lawrence, by the painter and sculptor Eric Kennington (1888–1960), one of the illustrators of *Seven Pillars of Wisdom*, was unveiled at the Oxford High School, which Lawrence had attended. For the plaque and for Churchill's speech see *The Times*, 3 October, p. 16; and 'Lawrence of Arabia . . . The Versatility of Genius', 5 October, pp. 13–14.

[4] Lionel George Curtis (1872–1955), barrister, served in the South African War and in the Colonial Government of the Transvaal, and as Adviser on Irish Affairs in the Colonial Office, 1921–4; an influential imperial propagandist.

[5] Colonel Stewart Francis Newcombe (1878–1956) took a lively interest in Arab affairs; served in the South African War, 1899–1900; in Egypt, 1901–11; and was Army Chief Engineer for Malta, 1922–32.

[6] Frederic Alexander Lindermann, 1st Viscount Cherwell (1886–1957) was Professor of Experimental Philosophy at Oxford. He was Churchill's confidential scientific adviser during the Second World War. Sir Arthur Salter (1881–1975), created 1st Baron Salter in 1953, was Gladstone Professor of Political Theory and Institutions, Oxford, 1934–44; MP for Oxford University, 1937–50. Goldie: G. L. Dickinson.

[7] Mrs Fraser looked after his flat.

318   To Stephen Spender[1]

West Hackhurst, Abinger Hammer, Dorking
10 January 1937

Dear Stephen,

I suspect you've got that rather interesting and tiresome man (Robert Bridges) wrong.[2] I used to think him not so much noble as naughty, and was very fond of him, and remember how when the war ended he was the first person with any reputation to risk who said we'd better not be vindictive.[3] He was class bound and all that, and oh dear how he lowered his voice before articulating the word 'passion', still he saw science was important—which was more than George Meredith and the rest of them could see—and managed to get broadcasting into The Testament of Beauty, which is a creditable scoop for so old a man.[4] Events moved too quickly for him, yes: now they move far quicker, and if in twenty years there is such a thing as an old man, *he'll* be infinitely more on the shelf.

That Greek vase is still here. I feel I ought to give it back now that you've 'set up house.' However I shan't, and shall wish you all happiness without it.

Morgan

Haven't your address in my head.

ALS: Bancroft Library, University of California, Berkeley

[1] Stephen Spender (1909–   ), poet and critic, was co-editor of *Horizon: A Review of Literature and Art*, 1939–41, and of *Encounter*, 1953–67.
[2] Edward J. Thompson (1886–1946), a genuine (non-official) Old India Hand, recalled a Bridges opinion of EMF: 'Bridges once remarked to me, of E. M. Forster, that of all men living he had the most brilliantly photographic mind. . . . When Bridges pointed this out, I remembered incidents, vignettes in *A Passage to India*, pictures of things I had never seen consciously, though I spent far longer in India than Forster did—things which at once I recognized when the novelist introduced them, so that I had to exclaim, "Yes, that's true! I have seen it, though I did not *know* I had seen it!"' (*Robert Bridges, 1844–1930*, p. 89.) Spender's comment does not survive.
[3] On 18 October 1920 (p. 8) *The Times* published ' "Reconciliation": Oxford Letter to German Intellectuals', an appeal from an Oxford group, of impressive credentials, for renewed ties with their German and Austrian counterparts. In a leading article (p. 13), 'An Ill-Judged Appeal', *The Times* declared that 'the great majority of Oxford men will share our regret at the singularly ill-advised and inopportune appeal, ...' Bridges wrote an eloquent defence; see 'The Poet Laureate on Reconciliation', *The Times*, 27 October 1920, pp. 13–14.
[4] In Bridges's *The Testament of Beauty*, I, lines 722–36: 'Science comforting man's animal poverty / . . . above her globe-spread net / of speeded intercourse hath outrun all magic, / and disclosing the secrecy of the reticent air / hath woven a seamless web of invisible strands / spiriting the dumb inane with the quick matter of life: . . . .'

319   To Christopher Isherwood

West Hackhurst, Abinger Hammer, Dorking
27 February 1937

Dear Christopher,

I will put down some impressions in case they are useful towards alterations in the acting version.[1]

Act I—splendid. My only query was M^rs R's circumambulation, the discussion about the two sons, and the slinking away of Levantine James: "but this will come clear later on."

Act II—kept me more critical. The *monk*—not good nor good to look at. Presages are not interesting in themselves, and Ransom's, which is interesting, comes out well enough in his ensuing talk with the Abbot. John S[impson?] and I felt the monk could be cut.

The *Abbott*—the finest scene in the whole play. Quite marvellous. Then troubles gather, for which the meagre scenery isn't wholly responsible. The elimination of Lamp made me wonder "How will they get rid of the other two?" Ian's was good— jealousy does carry one along. David's too slow. Then Ransom— falling into the audience almost, realistic, panting: "I will kill the demon"—it wouldn't live in that theatrical bleakness, nor would M^rs R's rocking chair. I'm sure the changes here are all for the worse; the summit ought to seethe with visions as soon as R. goes wampy; and why not? You couldn't, even with expensive settings, carry out this losing of comrades in the course of a long crawl, unless you thickened the summit climax with reminiscences. James *must* be put back—besides, the preparation with him in Act I is left hanging in the air. And I should have thought the Abbot back too.

Then we thought the farce of the final scene quite wrong. The villainy is much more telling if the villains are left to speak it with dignity. To show them up by making them squabble and giving them ridiculous flags is a great mistake, and I don't think it was made in the text. When they've intoned their faiths, I'd have the Announcer: "Dance music will now follow— —" and curtain to a strain from those amazing singers.

The A's—v. good. Their dash off to Hove shouldn't have been cut. The other two tragedies I saw in the play were the temptation to exercise power, good too, and the mother-business which doesn't work out as it should dramatically.

How good the music is—and the acting. Play didn't seem the least long, and if you remove the monk there should be time to restore some essentials.

Veiled figure, not demon, Mother on ice-throne, not rocking chair. The rocking chair is the sounder, but it won't come across. It's a moment when you *must* sacrifice psychological propriety to poetry.

Will be up Thursday and will ring you.

With love,
Morgan.

ALS: Recipient

[1] *The Ascent of F.6* by Wystan Hugh Auden (1907–73) and Isherwood, opened at the Mercury Theatre, London, on 26 February 1937. Rupert Doone (1904–66), of the Group Theatre, directed. Music was by Benjamin Britten (1913–76), then supporting himself in London by writing incidental theatre music. The 'amazing singers': Britten's incidental songs were performed by a trio. EMF's comments follow the action of that performance. The published text (1936) has some variations. Cf. EMF's review, 'Chormopuloda', *The Listener*, 16/2 (1936), Supp. vii; reprinted as 'The Ascent of F6', *TCD*, pp. 257–9.

320   To Christopher Isherwood

West Hackhurst, Abinger Hammer, Dorking
2 March 1937

Dear Christopher,
    Could you have tea with me on Thursday at 4.30.? I would come up and go straight to my flat and meet you. I dine out at 8.0.—Or I could go to the Club.—
    Yes, I see the Visions would tear holes in that stage.[1] So does a rocking-chair. You want something easy for the spectator, and the easiest is mother in white on ice-throne. I am annoyed that the success of the play has been risked by such narrow circumstances. I shall not feel happy until it has been transferred.
    The final scene (microphone) is excellent, and there is a grand addition (Lady Isabel's) to the text. My only complaint is that it was all guyed and consequently rogered. I wouldn't end with mother's paw-paw.—Her acting wasn't up to the standard by the way.[2]
    Dukes must have wanted to keep the party to those concerned in the play, so I'm glad we didn't stay on.[3]
    Hoping you can manage Thursday:

With love from Morgan

ALS: Recipient

[1] Continues discussion of *The Ascent of F.6.*
[2] Dorothy Holmes-Gore (1896–1977) played the Mother.
[3] Ashley Dukes (1885–1959), dramatist and critic, and proprietor of the Mercury Theatre, which he opened in 1933 in an unused London hall. Its prestige was securely established in 1935 with Dukes's triumphant production of T. S. Eliot's *Murder in the Cathedral.*

321   To Frank Arthur Swinnerton

Reform Club [London] S.W.
2 April 1937

Dear Swinnerton,
    Thanks for your letter. I note that you hold to your anecdote and to your interpretation thereof.[1]
    Lynd writes: "The story is, of course, untrue." He has no recollection of my remark, and suggests that, if I made it, I must have meant 'Why should Lynd care to join this club?' The suggestion is plausible, and perhaps may commend itself to you. He emphasises that, if the incident had occurred as you describe it, it would certainly have remained in his mind as unique in his experiences of hosts, and he cannot imagine "from what deaf man" you picked it up.
    I certainly *was* wounded at the idea that I might have wounded

Lynd, and that is why I troubled to take this matter up. Otherwise I should have ignored it. He happens to mention that he has seldom met you during the last twenty years, and that is precisely my own case.

Yours sincerely
EMForster

ALS: University of Arkansas

[1] Frank Arthur Swinnerton (1884–1982), novelist and critic, is best known for his surveys of literary history, beginning with *The Georgian Literary Scene* (1935). Robert Lynd (1879–1949), essayist and journalist, wrote regularly for *The New Statesman* as 'Y.Y.' On the incident referred to here, see *Swinnerton: An Autobiography*, p. 293. A member of EMF's London club allegedly remarked that Lynd, EMF's guest, should also be a member, to which EMF replied, according to Swinnerton, 'Why?' EMF had written to Swinnerton (12 March 1937. Arkansas): 'I have just read about E. M. Forster in *Swinnerton*, and feel moved to say that if *Forster* should ever be written there would be no account in it of Frank Swinnerton, for the reason that, as I understand knowledge, you and I do not know one another.' Swinnerton's letter does not survive, nor does Lynd's.

322   To Christopher Isherwood

West Hackhurst, Abinger Hammer, Dorking
30 April 1937

Dear Christopher—thank you for the cheque, £5 in repayment for 500 francs. I never tire of helping people in such ways as these. I was also glad to get your letter, though how are you? I don't suppose you are very well, what an endless run round. When we meet I have much to ask—partly about the inadequacy of Mr Norris.[1]

Now there is Peter Burra, killed while flying, and I keep thinking about death. The worst thing in it is that people seem different as soon as it has happened, and one will seem different oneself. The word 'loss' is inadequate. I have lost my fountain pen, but it does not alter.

No doubt every thing in human beings is changing all the time; and so, under the surface, is one's feelings for them——indeed here there are two factors for self's human too. O see Proust! But it's so difficult to remember the change is going on, especially when one establishes what are called 'permanent' relationships in daily life. Death turns the dead person into something worse than nothing— something ~~extraordinary~~ *deflecting*—where all one's affection for him or criticism of him becomes false. The most satisfactory dead are those who have published books.

With best love to Heinz and to you. I am hoping for news about the Mexican passport.[2]

Bob will be spending the weekend of the 8th–10th with me—I suppose in the flat.

Morgan.

ALS: Recipient

¹ EMF replies to an Isherwood letter of 27 April 1937 (KCC). Gerald Hamilton (1889–1970), born Gerald Frank Hamilton Souter, and Isherwood both wrote ambiguous statements about his being the model for Mr Norris, in Isherwood's *Mr. Norris Changes Trains* (1935), with its picture of Berlin life during Germany's descent into Nazism; see Hamilton, *Mr. Norris and I: An Autobiographical Sketch*, and a Prologue by Isherwood, pp. 9–12. However, Hamilton's account of his life and exploits offers more than a suggestion of Isherwood's source for that character.

² Isherwood had persuaded his mother to pay £1,000 to Hamilton's lawyers for Mexican nationality for Heinz—a fruitless and Mr Norris-like project.

323   To Edmund Blunden

West Hackhurst, Abinger Hammer, Dorking
1 May 1937

Dear Edmund Blunden,

I wasn't at Oxford and was never at Göttingen, so that I have no right to comment on your letter in today's Times, but I know you won't resent my writing a line to you.¹

It's true that the general public here knows nothing of the working of German Universities. But it *does* know something about the Germans who have not been allowed to stop in them, and have been driven out not merely because they are Jews or Communists, but because they are—well, people like ourselves, the sort of people who wrote for the *Nation*. I used to hear about the work of the—"Academic Assistance Committee" I think it was called, which used to provide for exiled students and teachers, and had much to do, and I hear more particularly about the persecution of scientists and the deterioration of German science from George Barger, who is Professor of Chemistry at Edinburgh, and no politician or very reluctantly one.

You fear that Oxford's abstention may be political. I expect it is and don't see how it could help being, and her acceptance would have been political also. Germany has chosen to make every relationship political, and no non-political relationship with her appears to be possible.

I didn't fight in the war and so haven't that special generosity towards Germans which all decent people who fought with them seem to have. At the same time, I have usually liked them, thought the Versailles treaty monstrous, and hoped for the success of Weimar. So I don't write in any hostility. But their present conception of a University is so ~~different from~~ repugnant to ours that I'm glad that (with the exception of Durham) we've refused Göttingen's invitation.

I wish you had said a bit more about conditions there. I wonder what there was in your lectures which (you imply) *might* not have been received by your audiences in a generous & sympathetic manner, but was in fact so received. I wonder what freedom you *took*, in other words. And then your phrase "the highest purposes of study." I felt that in the circumstances you might have ~~expounded~~ defined this. To my mind "the highest purposes" include the dispassionate reading of history and the <dispassionate> examination of racial origins.

This letter's longer than I intended. Do please excuse it. I hope that you are well and enjoying your work. I hear of you sometimes through Siegfried [Sassoon], but have not had the good fortune to meet you for a long time.

With good wishes, and apologies;

Yours sincerely
EMForster

I think it's good that individuals should go to Germany & get into touch with individual Germans. It's these corporate actions which seem to me doubtful.

ALS: HRC

¹ Edmund Charles Blunden (1896–1974), poet, critic, biographer; joined the staff of *The Athenaeum* after the First World War, and the *TLS* in 1943; Fellow and Tutor, Merton College, Oxford, from 1931; Professor of Poetry, 1966–8. Blunden criticised Oxford's decision to send no delegate to Göttingen's bicentenary celebrations: 'If the reasons . . . are in the nature of political disapproval, surely they are themselves political; they smack of coercion rather than freedom of opinion.' Blunden, lecturing at Göttingen, had found it 'a great and spirited university going about its work in a normal temper. The vision of a reconstructed Germany constitutes no barrier there, for all I could perceive, between the teacher or student and the highest purposes of study' ('The Göttingen Celebrations', *The Times*, 1 May 1937, p. 12). On Blunden's political attitudes during the 1930s see Thomas Mallon, *Edmund Blunden*, pp. 68–9.

324   To Christopher Isherwood

West Hackhurst, Abinger Hammer, Dorking
4 July 1937

Dear Christopher,

I think the date is the 7ᵗʰ; please send my love and Bob's also as soon as it is possible to do so.

Meanwhile I hope you will not find it too dreary in England. I have found it drearier myself since you have been here.—Of course you know what I mean, as they invariably add in England.

I will come up on Tuesday, will bring 2 or 3 of those stories with me, and will ring you up. I hope that your foot is better.

I have written a very emotional poem, and cannot make out whether it is good or not. The title is:

Landor at Sea
I strove with none for none was worth my strife;
Reason I loved, and, next to reason, doubt;
I warmed both hands before the fire of life
And put it out.[1]

——————— : ———————

I have also been considering what has been most satisfactory in my own life, and ruling out Bob on the ground that he is not in a cheap edition I have come to the conclusion that it is the *Passage to India*. It's amazing luck that one's best book should be the widest read one, and the one most likely to do good, as well. When writing the *Passage* I thought it a failure, and it was only owing to Leonard that I was encouraged to finish it, but ever since publication I have felt satisfied, and find very little in it that nauseates or irritates me.

So I shall ring up—probably about 5.0 on Tuesday, or perhaps you might then ring the flat. Bob will be with me and we might meet you later if all are free.

With best love,
Morgan.

ALS: Recipient

[1] Parody of Walter Savage Landor, 'I strove with none, for none was worth my strife' (*Complete Works*, ed. T. Earle Welby, XV, 226); it appeared in *The New Statesman and Nation*, n. s. 16 (1938), 219, signed E.M.F.

325   To Alice Clara Forster

Hotel de Londres, 3 Rue Bonaparte, Paris[1]
23 July 1937

Dearest—Will write you a line before I go off. An unexpected wire from Joe says that he will arrive this afternoon for a weekend. I cannot think that, with Nancy so ill, he will actually manage it, but shall 'cut' the last meeting to meet his train on the chance. I have found it interesting, but the French difficult to follow, and the English translation, which is supposed to be given after each speech, most inadequate. (English and French are the two official languages of the League). I have spoken twice, once on the subject of state-interference with writers: and the other time—yesterday—I made a polite and quite clever attack on the Fascists, to which they, cleverer still, made no reply. Gilbert Murray seems pleased with me, and nominated me to serve on a subcommittee, but I managed to get off and to get Thornton Wilder put on it instead—the American who wrote the Bridge of San Luis Rey.[2] It will all end in nothing of course—except that the French, who are always working for their own ends, will try to utilise any resolution in order to get something for themselves out of the French Gov^t.—Murray and I are the only English here, but several speak English well.

Charles Marie and I had dinner yesterday and will lunch today. They behave cheerfully but Julian Bell's death will be a terrible loss to them. I have written to Virginia—I did not feel I could write to poor Vanessa. No one mentions Clive, but no doubt he will be upset too.[3]

I must close now and go. Best love to Rosie. Got your line this morning.

M.

ALS: KCC

[1] EMF is attending a session, 20–24 July 1937, of the League of Nations' Institut International de Coopération Intellectuelle, 2nd Paris Entretien, 20–23 July, to which he was invited by Gilbert Murray (1866–1957), Regius Professor of Greek at Oxford, 1908–36; Chairman, League of Nations Union, 1928–40; member of the International Committee, 1928–40. EMF had replied (11 May 1937): 'I am not helpful on committees, owing to diffidence and to my slowness in seizing on points as they occur. I have also no great faith in the committee achieving practical results. On the other hand the ~~chief~~ first subject under discussion—the moral and material position of the author—is one which interests me a good deal.' Murray replied (14 May) that it was only an 'Entretien, or conversation, about the future of literature', and the French poet Paul Valéry 'always has interesting things to say, but as he whispers them confidentially into his moustache one does not get the full enjoyment out of them. The main weakness of the Entretiens is that the Latins do all the talking.' EMF urged (15 July) that the session consider 'the moral position of the writer in the immediate future', and his written text deals with 'the writer's moral position in the face of the growing claim of the state, ...' (These letters: Murray Papers, Bodleian.) When the session opened, EMF told the participants that he thought the writer's moral situation more crucial than even his material situation, and more difficult: he must express his personality, and at the same time he must aid the progress of civilisation. His position is complicated by the fact that his conception of civilisation so often fails to coincide with the official conception. EMF concluded: 'Thus I share the anxiety of our President, and like him I believe the days of literature, as we have loved and practised it, are perhaps numbered.' See Le Destin prochain des lettres, Bulletin No. 8 of the Institute for International Cooperation (1938), pp. 108–11, 234–7. See also, EMF's 'A Conversation', The Spectator, 159 (1937), 269–70.

[2] The American novelist and playwright Thornton Niven Wilder (1897–1975), author of the Pulitzer Prize-winning The Bridge of San Luis Rey (1927).

[3] On 20 July the Bells' son Julian (1908–37), drawn by the Civil War, was killed in Spain. EMF's letter to Virginia Woolf has not been found.

326 To William Plomer

[N. p.   17 November 1937][1]

I may be a back number, my dear William, but you must remember what I back upon. Nor is it a mere façade, for I have been invited to sit at Sir Frank Brown's own table, and then to contribute to the foundation of Rudyard Kipling scholarships and to the creation of plaques and windows both at Windsor and at Westward Ho![2] There is a vast committee, representing the whole of the

Unpopular Front and including Sir Hugh Walpole.[3] If I was richer and more cynical I would attend, though for a lady I should be hard put to it.

I also enclose a catalogue, which it is for you rather than for me to throw away, since there are various reproductions of handwriting in it.

I just am back from Paris, where I had an influenza cold, and did not find Leo the easiest of continental comrades. He too had an influenza-cold, and Tom had a third.[4] But intellectually and spiritually I enjoyed myself. The pictures were marvellous—I did not see them on my previous visit—and I saw and, also saw through, Giroudoux's [sic] Electre, which has drawn critical audiences for months. It is an uncalculated take, and very attractive.[5] Another evening we had Georges Dutuit [sic] to a meal.[6] He was appalled by us, as well he might be, and did not 'behave very well'. Leo, who was the host, reached sizzling point once or twice afterwards, and will perhaps detonate when he reaches Joe. We were expecting of course that G. D. would take us on somewhere, but he early struck the note of being no Parisian, and shook us off with some firmness to rejoin his friends at the Deux Magots.

All this time Nancy sat in a back-bedroom with her dog at Dover and Sandy, who had been bitten by it, with Miss Phillips & Miss Hughes.[7]

And now tell me whom *you* have been sitting with.

Morgan.

ALS: Durham University

[1] Date in Plomer's hand.

[2] The United Services College, Westward Ho!, Bideford, Devon, where Kipling was at school.

[3] Sir Frank (Herbert) Brown (1868–1959) journalist, and editor of various Indian papers; on *The Times of India* staff from 1902; Honorary Secretary, East India Association, 1927–54. EMF's letter is on the verso of the invitation to 'Mr. E. M. Forster & lady', for the dinner of The Rudyard Kipling Memorial Library and campaign to raise fifty scholarships for the Imperial Service College, Windsor. Churchill's toast to Kipling was reprinted (*The Times*, 18 November, p. 16) with resounding sub-headings such as 'Inspiration of India' and 'In Letters of Gold'.

[4] EMF's second visit to the Paris Exhibition, which finally closed on 28 November; see his 'The Last Parade', a report requested by John Lehmann for *New Writing*, 4 (1937), 1–5; reprinted, *TCD*, pp. 15–23. He was with Leo Charlton and Tom Wichelo.

[5] *Electre* (1937), by (Hippolyte–) Jean Giraudoux (1882–1944), French novelist, essayist, author of highly stylised plays on classical or Biblical subjects.

[6] Georges Duthuit (1891–19   ), French critic and friend of both Joe Ackerley and his sister, Nancy Ackerley West (1899–1979).

[7] Sandy is apparently a friend of Ackerley's sister Nancy, unidentified. Miss Phillips and Miss Hughes: landladies of Ackerley's Dover flat, called by him the 'Holy Ladies'.

327   To Leonard Woolf

West Hackhurst, Abinger Hammer
10 January 1938

Dear Leonard

I have just finished Rose's book. It is most considerate and tactful, gratifying, and in a sense intelligent, but tamely conceived and badly written, especially towards the close. Not a good book I am afraid. And as you say, no conclusion is reached. What very odd things people do! Perhaps it may seem fresher to others than it does to me; at all events the narratives won't be so familiar to them.

Will you be asking Arnold's to advertise in it? I don't know what publishers do in such a situation.[1]

I have been persuaded by Gerald Shove to talk to his Society at Cambridge next week end. I am not looking forward to it much.[2]

No word from the Penguins. But they are leading me to fill up some of my gaps—Scenes from Clerical Life, for instance; and am struggling now with Guy Mannering.[3]

Thought your clear thinking talk *very good*, so did any one else who has mentioned it to me.[4]

Love to Virginia.

Morgan

ALS: Sussex University

[1] Rose Macaulay, *The Writings of E. M. Forster* (1938). Hogarth Press published it in March, and EMF must have had a proof or an advance copy. See the review, 'The Work of E. M. Forster: Miss Macaulay's Appreciation', *TLS*, 19 March 1938, p. 185.

[2] Gerald Frank Shove (1887-1947), Fellow and Lecturer, King's College, and Reader in Economics, Cambridge University. His 'Peace Society' was the New Peace Movement, organised as a response to the Spanish Civil War, in hope of averting a general war. It attracted most of the Cambridge moderate leftists. Shove, its Chairman, had in 1934 founded the Lowes Dickinson Society for Kingsmen, 'to discuss impartially and, as far as possible without political bias, the problem of War'. (Minute book: KCC). EMF was almost certainly to address a meeting of the New Peace Movement, which brought in outside speakers.

[3] Penguins: probably a reference to the Penguin edition of Maurice O'Sullivan's *Twenty Years A-Growing*, published on 1 July 1938.

[4] Woolf, 'Clear Thinking', BBC talk broadcast on 14 December 1937. See 'Does Education Neutralise Thought?' *The Listener*, 18 (1937), 1366-8.

328   To John (Hampson) Simpson

West Hackhurst, Abinger Hammer, Dorking
24 January 1938

Dear John,

So glad that so far as the flat went the visit was a success. I thought Bill very nice.[1]

Have received Walter Allen's novel from his publisher, and cannot get on with it, which is inconvenient to me.[2] I found both the people and the situations so uninteresting and dreary. With the exception of Leslie Halward, no writer who knows the working classes seems to find in them the good temper and charm which I find in them during my superficial contacts.[3] It's all poverty, exasperation, disease, and attempts to free oneself: and this, untransfigured by poetry, makes difficult reading. I'm particularly sorry, as W. A. once wrote something about me which I appreciated very much. No doubt there's a lot in the book and I must have another try.

With affectionate greetings to all at Four Ashes.[4]

Morgan

ALS: KCC

[1] A. W. ('Bill') Dodd was a friend of Simpson. He wrote plays and stories. One of these latter, 'Before Auction', was published in *The London Mercury*, 38 (1938), 537–44.

[2] *Innocence Is Drowned* (1938) by Walter Ernest Allen (1911–   ), novelist, broadcaster, critic. Allen had previously published an article 'Homage to E. M. Forster', *Mermaid*, new series 6 (1935–6), 243–5.

[3] Leslie Halward (1906–76), formerly a die-sinker, plasterer, and tool-maker. In *Let Me Tell You* (1938), he describes how he became a writer and a member, with Simpson and Allen, of the 'Birmingham Group' of writers.

[4] The Wilson family's home.

329   To William Plomer

Wallington, Cambo, Morpeth
9 February 1938

Dear William,

Thank you for the poems. I like both of them extremely. I understand most of the second one—Joe, who of course understands all, has promised to explain it to the last drop[.] I do hope that you will write more and allow nothing, not even a novel, to intervene. I feel that you are much more a poet than any one else I know, and that a good deal of what we say or do must be irrelevant in your eyes, and indeed unnoticeable.[1] As for me, I am trying to construct a philosophy.[2]

I am supposed to be on the loose at the present moment, and behaving adventurously in purlieus and pubs, but of course the usual thing has occurred, and I am vegetating cosily under someone's wing. However, one doesn't often get the chance of staying with a socialistic and atheistical Lord Lieutenant. They must be very rare, any how pubs and purlieus are commoner than this house. Decorated by the frescoes of William Bell Scott, the Central Hall is at present occupied by ten very arm-pitty young women who are learning to do country dances. Opening out of it, is the Library, one of three very fine eighteenth cent. rooms, with Italian stucco

At Dover, 1937: above left: J. R. Ackerley with William Plomer;
above right, left to right: Bob Buckingham, EMF and J. R. Ackerley.

John Simpson ('John Hampson').

With Christopher Isherwood at Ostende, 1937.

ceilings. Here sit the L. L. and myself, he doing a patience, I writing with a cat on my knee, and several books belonging to the late Lord Macaulay lying negligently around me. Patricia, the daughter, is out farming if you can do so by night, Miss Bulmer the keen handsome secretary, is in Newcastle inciting the People's Theatre to perform Gorki.[3] I leave to morrow, much to my regret, and try to walk along the Roman Wall. I haven't enjoyed a country visit so much for a long time. We drive over the estate which is enormous and largely moorland, look into lime kilns, and talk about planting trees. All the people seem to be well off.

It will be very nice seeing you for a Wednesday night-or-so when it fits in with your arrangements. I get back some time next week. My mother is at present in the flat with Aunt Rosalie. They have enjoyed 100 men and a girl very much.[4]

With love, and looking forward to seeing you soon:

Morgan

ALS: Durham University

[1] For Plomer on himself as poet, see his *Autobiography*, pp. 381–4.
[2] He was writing 'Two Cheers for Democracy', *The Nation* (New York), 147 (1938), 65–8; reprinted as 'What I Believe'. See Kirkpatrick, pp. 59, 66–8, 138.
[3] C. P. Trevelyan, who succeeded his father as 3rd Baronet in 1924, was President, Board of Education, 1924 and 1929–31; and Lord Lieutenant for the County of Northumberland, 1930–49. On the Trevelyans and Wallington, given to the National Trust in 1941, see Raleigh Trevelyan, *A Pre-Raphaelite Circle* (1978). William Bell Scott (1811–90), poet and painter, was a Pre-Raphaelite hanger-on. Miss Edith Bulmer: a much-loved Wallington estate secretary.
[4] *100 Men and a Girl*, a saccharine 1937 film with Leopold Stokowski, the Philadelphia Orchestra, and Deanna Durbin.

330   To Christopher Isherwood

Fritton Hithe, Nr. Gt. Yarmouth[1]
28 August 1938

Dearest Christopher,

There was and perhaps somewhere is an Epilogue chapter to *Maurice* but everyone thought it a mistake.[2] Kitty, on an old-maidish weekend in Yorkshire, comes across them both as woodcutters. This seemed both too short and too long. Yes, Maurice chucked his office, and—though the tale is set pre-war— they went to the war I suppose. That would now make them, if alive, now about 50 each. I can only still see them together if they have passed a life of adventures together.—I have sometimes thought of Alec marrying.

The third section of the book was once much the weakest. I have worked on it cautiously as I gained new experience being very careful not to *make* it my experience. I was in 1914 ignorant in this way of class—it stimulated my imagination, that was all. About ten years later I met old Reg Palmer, (and about seventeen years later Bob) which gave me knowledge, and stuffed the form of Alex out in places suitable to his physique. But I tried to keep him as the dream which turned into the scare and then into the mate. I was always determined not to end sadly—as we were saying, it is not worth while.

Yes, Maurice is a good man I think and so a nice one.—I think, to run back in this letter, that part III should have been more gradual and longer, more social wrenchings shown or heard 'off'.

I wish it could be published, especially after getting your letter. But it isn't so much my mother now—it's Bob. Everyone connects him with me, and this Dover muddle showed me how careful I must be not to bring bother or harm his way.[3] My 'Life' if briefly and blazingly written, might be worth doing after my death, but that's ruled out too while he lives.

Your letter firmed me up a lot. It certainly is a comfort to know that my work is respected by someone whom I respect and am as fond of as you. It confirms my belief that life is not all nonsense and cruelty—the inversion of Victorian complacency—but has hard spots of sense and love bobbing about in it here and there. The people here, in this Hithe, seem grimly chaotic, just holding on to the wharves till they slip off, the news gets worse and worse, and they don't seem able to feel—still less are they able to *do*, none of us can do that. I warrant you, I silence them all at the breakfast table.

However, my visit is in no sense a failure. We bathe, go to Lowestoft Regatta, sit in the Lake-ward sloping garden. On Tuesday I go to c/o J. <Icelandic> Sprott, Magavelda, Blakeney, Norfolk, and to the flat for a night on Friday, where will ring you up.[4]

My mother much enjoyed your visit, she writes. I specifically liked the talk about China, or rather the Atlas. I think a good deal about the book. It's a major technical problem. Howsoever that's solved, the book will come easily, but unless the solution is the correct one, the book won't be good. And I cannot think what the correct solution is. Perhaps Wysten [sic] divinely distrait, will hit on it, but I am more disposed to rely on you.[5]

Well I must conclude, hoping that you will like this letter and your household its envelope. Coronets seen everywhere, on the little boats, on the bigger boats, on the bath towels. I cannot make it out. Host & hostess are out calling on some Colmans ('we're all mustered here'—) Weyland [sic] and his cousin—15 or 16, pleasant—have gone out in a pram, which is a little boat, to visit boys across the lake, and I have been walking round the estate with Lady K.'s slightly critical elder sister.[6]

With much love, & great gratitude from

M.

ALS: Recipient

[1] Home of the Hilton Youngs (Lord and Lady Kennet).
[2] The typescript of this Epilogue is at King's College.
[3] Ackerley's landladies had asked him to leave.
[4] 'Icelandic': unexplained.
[5] Isherwood and Auden had just returned from China and were writing *Journey to a War* (1939). The technical problem may have been that of gracefully combining Auden's poems and Isherwood's prose; see Finney, *Christopher Isherwood*, pp. 168–70.
[6] Colmans ... mustered: the Colman family, then and now leading manufacturers of mustard in Britain: Norwich was their business centre. Wayland Hilton Young (1923–   ), 2nd Baron Kennet of the Dene.

331   To Unidentified Recipient

Reform Club [London] S.W.
5 September 1938

Dear Madam,

Thank you for your letter and for telling me of your experiences. Yes—English guests (or rather some English guests) are indeed the difficulty in this country. In India there are *some* reasons for segregation: not really sound reasons, still they exist. In England they don't exist, yet there is a tendency in some quarters to introduce them, and to saddle us with race- and caste- troubles which do not belong to us at all.

About Hinduism, though, I don't quite follow you. In the first place, many Indians are not Hindus at all, but Moslems, Sikhs, Christians &[ct]. In the second place, many Hindus have abandoned their orthodoxy, and it does not seem fair that, when they come to England, they should be penalised because other Hindus remain orthodox. And in the third place, I don't think that a Hindu hotel manager (whether orthodox or not) would try to exclude non-Hindus from his hotel.——The gist of which is that Indians, whether Hindu or not, *have* a right to feel aggrieved at their exclusion from hotels in this country.

It is anyhow abominable that they should be excluded from the *large* hotels—and it was of these that D[r] Thompson & myself were particularly thinking when we entered this controversy.[1] The smaller establishments, like your own, naturally tend to select their guests more, since the guests will be thrown into more ~~intense~~ intimate contact with one another; I am very interested to hear of the lines upon which you are working, and wish you continued success.

Yours truly
EMForster.

ALS: Beinecke Library

[1] Edward J. Thompson wrote to *The New Statesman and Nation* about indignities to Indians at British hotels; see 'Indians in England', n. s. 16 (1938), 247–8. EMF responded with similar instances from his own experience (*ibid.*, pp. 311–12).

332   To Hilton Young

West Hackhurst, Abinger Hammer, Dorking
13 October 1938

Dear Hilton,

That story was written over twenty years ago when I was comparatively young, so you must not call me to account for it now.[1] I remember it was rather an experiment (as was the preceding one) and that I was trying to get a harder and—as you say—a crueller focus on life than is usual with me. It is a view of life (not an explanation unless one swallows the mysticism) and it does not tell us what to do—we are caught any way, whether we idle or work. It would give less pain if I had brought out the *affection* between the two young men rather than the fact that they were once young: this was done by Housman in his poem about Hell Gate, and it was also done on a stupendous scale and with a change of sex by Dante, when Beatrice guides him through the Divine Comedy in his middle age.[2]

Barring mysticism and the possibility of love explaining the universe—what are we to do where we are now? Like all our contemporaries I am vexed by decreasing powers and even by named diseases or diseaselets, and have to summon such defences as I can. The two best seem to be the old ones: courage and unpossessiveness. As long as one can exercise these, one can keep oneself so to speak from smelling unpleasingly. There is something very profound in that notion of dying in the odour of sanctity—it's an impossible ideal yet it's worth living towards it at our age.

Yours affectionately
Morgan.

ALS: Cambridge University Library, for Lord Kennet

[1] Probably 'The Point of It', *The English Review*, 9 (1911), 615–30; reprinted in *EMOS*, pp. 87–125.
[2] For EMF on this Housman poem, see Letter 266.

333   To Cecil Day-Lewis

West Hackhurst, Abinger Hammer, Dorking
30 October 1938

Dear Day Lewis,

I am so ashamed at not writing before. It was not "age's dim recalcitrance" for I liked the book and was proud to be connected with it.[1] But, like many more, I have been in a queer statis these past weeks, alternating between gloom and resolute cheerfulness, and in neither state is one an intelligent correspondent. I can see no way out of our dilemma. Either we yield to the Nazis and they subdue us. *Or* we stand up to them, come to resemble them in the process, and are subdued to them that way. Your poems, particularly the long one, offer the possibility of heroic action, and many will be satisfied by that; but not you nor I.[2] I fear that this letter, now I do send it is but a seedy one; but since I spoke up for Communism at Paris three years ago, I have disillusionments which don't altogether proceed from my own weakness.[3] Russia, perhaps through no fault of her own, seems to be going in the wrong direction; too much uniformity and *too* much bloodshed. Perhaps—and perhaps under another name—Communism will restart after the next European catastrophe and do better. Indeed a vision sometimes comes to me that it will start again and again, always more strongly, and in the end be too strong for the catastrophes. But that won't be in our time, nor perhaps in Europe's. If *that* is the way I think my own job is to fall out and die by the way side.—Have tried to put this in an article in the London Mercury which you may possibly see (September).[4]

I know you won't mind dedicating your work to someone who has less faith than yourself. Though it seems the wrong way round.

Technically, my opinions of poetry are valueless, but I thought the writing good. References to child very moving.[5] I tell myself I am glad I have none, but the future of such children I meet distresses me as if they were mine often, so not much is gained here.

Thank you again for the book, and please pardon a silence which was not due either to indifference or to inappreciation.

My London Phone number (not in book) is *Terminus 5804*. I mention this in case you are able to ring me up some time. I should so like to see you again.

Yours sincerely
EMForster.

ALS: Jill (Balcon) Day-Lewis

[1] Day-Lewis's *Overtures to Death* (1938) is dedicated to EMF. 'Age's dim recalcitrance': p. 33.

[2] Long poem: either the title poem, pp. 26–35, or 'The Nabara', pp. 41–52.

[3] That is, at the Communist-dominated International Congress of Writers in Paris, 21–25 June 1935. In fact, EMF expressed respect for Communists while disassociating himself from Communism's views; see Letter 307.

[4] See Forster, 'Credo' (a version of 'What I Believe'), *The London Mercury*, 38 (1938), 397–404.

[5] Perhaps a reference to the poem 'Passage from Childhood', in *Overtures to Death*, pp. 59–60.

THE DARK AGES RETURNED,
1939–46

Forster's attitude during the uneasy post-Munich days was that it was absurd, from then on, to pretend to measure up to events and that the best approach was 'an alternation of fuss and calm'. He paid a valedictory visit to Geneva in June 1939, with Charles Mauron, and, with the coming of war, resigned himself to an indefinite period of isolation. The idea of a return to the Dark Ages took hold of him, and he spent some months during 1943 studying the Fathers of the Church for possible illumination. Meanwhile he had, in fact, soon resumed various public activities. For several years during and immediately after the war he broadcast weekly or monthly to India about books, and as president of the National Council for Civil Liberties he led a successful campaign against the BBC's political blacklisting of performers.

Early in 1945 his mother, who was ninety, fell ill and died. Her parting was peaceful, and he reacted with grief but not with despair, and for some weeks he occupied himself in reducing their accumulation of papers and possessions. He had no clear plan for his life, and when the All-India P.E.N. invited him to speak at a conference of writers in Jaipur in 1945, he accepted eagerly. He was in India from October to December and was, naturally, lionised—to his regret, from one point of view, for it restricted his freedom of movement. However, he enjoyed happy reunions with old friends (and made some new ones) in Delhi, Calcutta, Hyderabad, and Bombay, and this unexpected expedition helped assuage his grief over his mother.

A dismaying surprise awaited him on his return. The ground-landlords of West Hackhurst, the Farrers, who had allowed the Forsters to remain there during Lily's lifetime, though the lease had run out some years earlier, now wanted the house for a member of their own family.

334   To Robert J. Buckingham

W[est] H[ackhurst].   21 April 1939

Dear Bob,
I expect I should like to see you about Thursday or Friday

morning next week—will write again. I suppose you haven't a leave, which would enable us to have a meal together. Isn't the weather lovely! I am slacking out of doors.

We had a curious meeting of the tenants over A.R.P. What things people say! I cannot think they mean them. The gentleman in the basement got in the most frightful state in case someone got into the shelter for which *he* paid, said there must be an air-warden at the entrance to examine tickets, otherwise he should use his fists. I got them in the end to agree to what I wanted, and have now written to the landlords.[1]

I didn't think you looking too well, I expect you want some roast-beef inside you. I enjoyed our morbid meal, and now we need not have another like it. I forgot to say, what you know, that if I am the one to be left I will do what I can to look after Robin & May. We none of us know what will happen, or how we shall behave. You must not worry too much over the mutilation-fear. It may not happen, and if it does it's not your fault—unlike going off one's chump, which one feels one ought to be able to help. I would hate to be loathed, but not to be pitied if pity means love. I went two years ago through a particularly humiliating and repellent illness, but I never felt ashamed or outcaste because of the goodness of my friends. Love does a good deal to cancel what seems unbearable. If it can't cancel it, I agree that death is the best alternative. One can't crawl about being despised.

Jack [Sprott], and God knows who else, is in the flat at the present moment, I don't know for how long. He comes down to lunch here on Sunday.

Am very interested in your oils, and was struck by the improvement made by breaking up the water in the big one. I think they are a bit hard and unromantic at present, but that you will soon learn the technique more suitable to your view of things. I mean, you aren't just on the "decorative" stunt which I find so boring. Your water-colours get at something more poetical than that, and so in time will your oils. I liked the leaves of the tree ever so, the bird less so: it was nicely done but showed no muscular force. This is the bother of painting from a model, of course.[2]

Nice message to you from [Francis] Bennett, saying he enjoyed seeing you.—Write to Moya when you find time.[3]

Love,
Morgan

ALS: May Buckingham

[1] This was apparently an Air Raid Precautions meeting of the tenants at 9 Arlington Park Mansions, EMF's Chiswick flat.

[2] Bob Buckingham had been making water-colour sketches that he used later for oil paintings. The 'big one' may have been called 'Morning Amsterdam', from the sketch done in 1935 while in Holland with EMF. The bird model was a stuffed woodpecker presented by a spinster aunt of May's, for whom it had great sentimental value; for the family, considerably

less. Bob thought of painting its portrait for the aunt but gave it up. (Both paintings owned by
May Buckingham.)
    [3] On Moya Llewelyn Davies, one of the translators of Maurice O'Sullivan's *Twenty Years
A-Growing*, see Letter 291.

335 To Denys Kilham Roberts

[N. p.] 20 May 1939[1]

I have just received your letter, and the draft, so add this line. If
you don't want to teach the Committee their business, I certainly
don't want to teach you and Miss Barber yours! I thought the
treatment of the points selected admirable, and have no comment to
make on it.[2]

I do suggest though that in your preamble you should point out,
as drily as possible, that an author's work has or may have an
aesthetic side. It would not be necessary to point this out to a
committee of Frenchmen, but an English committee is always
obtuse here. The assumption, hitherto, is that the author's outlook
is the same as the journalist's. No one (except perhaps Porter and
Birkett), realises that English literature is an important matter, not
to say a national asset, and that owing to the present working of the
libel laws the authors of to day have not as good chance of turning
out valuable work as had the authors of the past.[3]

For instance it was blith[e]ly suggested last Wednesday by
Oswald Cox (solicitor to the Daily Telegraph) that authors had
nothing to complain of, since they could always insure.[4] I objected
that, even if insurance was otherwise practicable, it would mean that
the MSS would have to be vetted by a lawyer, who would naturally
err on the side of caution, and insist on words, phrases, incidents,
being tamed and dulled; he would never have passed Bleak House,
e.g. There is an ~~attitude~~ idea,—which you could in your legal
capacity combat more effectively than myself, since I am afraid of
appearing self-interested and 'precious'—that an author ought to be
content if he can get published, and should not resent being
published in a mangled form. He is supposed to write in order to
make a living—which is roughly true of the journalist, but money is
generally only *one* of the author's objectives—vanity, the desire to
create, the belief that he has a 'message' also come in.

I write this very diffusely, but it may serve you as the material for
a few words. In the eyes of the Committee we are not an important
body, much less important than the journalists. But, such as we are,
we represent English literature, and I think it will do no harm if this
were tactfully indicated. Anyhow no one will say it if we don't.

The Publishers' memorandum, Christian proudly tells me, is now
complete, and extends to 10000 words![5] Our brevity will be a great
contrast. Other points, besides the two you discuss, will doubtless

come up in the interview. We are to have three weeks' repose, resuming our sessions on June 7, when I believe we are to hear some big press organisation. No important interest (with the exception of the B.B.C.) has got its memorandum ready yet.

Please let me know if there is anything which I can do. Porter did not want the memoranda 'handed out' to you in case other organisations complained of preferential treatment, but of course I can always show them to you, and let you know what is going on. Serjeant Sullivan did not cut much ice.[6]

EMF

TLS: The Society of Authors Film Archive

[1] This amplifies EMF's letter (19 May 1939. S. of A.) to Kilham Roberts, about the Society's evidence before the Committee on the Law of Defamation, appointed by the Lord Chancellor to consider that law 'and to report what changes in the existing law, practices and procedure relating to the matter are desirable'. Kilham Roberts told EMF (17 Feb. 1939. S. of A.) that he was asked to suggest 'two or three eminent authors whom I thought qualified, for various reasons', for the Committee being appointed to consider the present law. He suggested EMF, Hugh Walpole, and Ernest Raymond (1888–1974), author of the very popular *Tell England* (1922), and Somerset Maugham. The suit resulting from 'A Flood in the Office' (Letter 201) and the abandonment of the T. E. Lawrence project (Letter 313) gave EMF a personal interest in this issue. The Chairman was Lord Samuel Lowry Porter (1877–1956), Lord of Appeal, Supreme Court of North Ireland, 1938–54. Hearings began with BBC evidence given on 4 May 1939. Evidence came also from groups such as the Newspaper Proprietors' Association, the National Association of Wholesale Newsagents, the Publishers' Association, the Institute of Journalists, and the well-known barrister Richard Augustus Willes (1881–1966). EMF resigned from the Committee in 1948 because he found it too slow to act. (EMF's annotated copies of the confidential minutes of eleven days of the hearings, eight of these in June–July 1939, and several supplementary memoranda: KCC.)

[2] The Society of Authors gave evidence on 27 July 1939. In the letter above EMF writes about its Supplementary Memorandum (his copy: KCC). The Society states that it feels itself, by virtue of its past history, to be 'in a position to judge whether authors are at any time labouring under difficulties and whether and to what extent such difficulties may be removed or reduced by legislation or other means'. It addressed itself primarily to two points: first, 'the basis of liability in actions for libel and slander'—a point often difficult to establish because authors accused of libel are reluctant to disclose details connected with 'accidental choice of the name or circumstances of an existing person for one of the more disreputable characters in his story . . .': that is, inadvertent as distinguished from malicious slander; and second, 'speculative litigation', suits by persons 'whose primary object is the recovery of substantial damages rather than the restoration of their good names'. Mary Elizabeth Barber (1911–79) joined the staff of The Society of Authors in 1936 and was its General Secretary, 1963–71.

[3] William Norman Birkett, later Baron Birkett (1883–1962), barrister and author of books on criminal justice, cricket, books and reading, and the English countryside. He became King's Counsel in 1924; Judge of the King's Bench Division, High Court of Justice, 1941–50; and Lord Justice of Appeal, 1950–7.

[4] Oswald Cox (1868–1957), solicitor for the *Daily Telegraph* for more than twenty-five years.

[5] Bertram Christian (1870–1953), publisher; President of the Publishers' Association. Two hearings (7 and 8 June) were taken up by evidence from the Newspaper Proprietors' Association.

[6] Alexander Martin Sullivan (1871–1959) was an Irish barrister who began to practise also at the English bar in 1899. In 1920 he became 1st King's Serjeant, the last to hold the office. He continued to use the title by courtesy. An impressive courtroom figure, he was an authority on libel law.

336   To Robert J. Buckingham

as from W[est] H[ackhurst], but in
flat really   [26 Brunswick Square, London]
19 July 1939

Dear Bob,

I remembered what it was I wanted to ask you—to move the bureau a little further inland. However there wasn't time to do other things properly, let alone that.

If you call living a full life seeing me once a fortnight, I don't.

So please look ahead over the next few weeks, and don't get taken by surprise either by night-duty or by your own annual leave or by my visit to Stockholm at the beginning of September.[1] And in particular fix up when you can come for the night, which you have not done since our walking tour.

At this point my nose began to bleed, you will think from passion, but I drove my finger into it really. Perhaps from over eating, as I have been to lunch at the Ivy and dinner at the Club.—Norman Birkett. I thought he was going to ruin me on the a la carte menu, but as a matter of fact he didn't work out as expensive as you with the fixed dinner. Any how it was worth it from the point of view of literature as I poured my heart out to him afterwards on the subject of all the harm the *fear* of libel does to writers, as apart from the actual occasions on which they pay damages. He thinks he likes literature very much, so he does in the book-collector's sense, and I got my stuff across in a way I couldn't have in the committee. He (says he) is going to invite me for a week end—tennis, cricket, bowls, golf, a swimming bath and a Swedish wife all included. I shall hardly know where to turn.[2]

Florence came here yesterday in wretched form—Harold leaves for America tomorrow, and has made her build a shelter in the garden first. Joe [Ackerley] to supper, also rotten, William's news bad, in fact you and sometimes I seem the only cheerful people. Tomorrow I talk to Rumanian students, lunch with Sir Sydney Waterlow, who will complain to me of <no, libellous: tell you when I see you, ha ha!> and save civilisation at the Civil Liberties. An absolutely bloody day, still it keeps me feeling important. Was very pleased to see you win your little piss-pot.[3] That made me feel important too, and in a better way.

It is 2.0 A.M. and I must really go to bed instead of continuing to write what may be a very interesting letter, and which Robin after the next great war may be able to sell for a considerable sum. It (the war) is to start during the next few weeks (?)—the period which at the beginning of this letter I have bidden you consider. Truly we live in strange times, Bob, and the only thing which is really real in them is love.

Morgan

Can't find my gas mask anywhere[.] Thought it was in the cupboard here—you adjusted it one time.

ALS: May Buckingham

¹ He was to have attended a P.E.N. Congress in Stockholm but withdrew because of the war situation.
² This rather strenuous visit apparently never took place.
³ A rowing trophy.

337   To Hugh Walpole

West Hackhurst, Abinger Hammer, Dorking
4 August 1939

Dear Hugh,
    Many thanks for your letter. I am sorry you could not come along, but Kilham Roberts read out the letter you wrote him: it was most helpful in illustrating the case which he presented. The [Society of] Authors put up an excellent show, and several members of the Libel Committee praised it to me afterwards.¹
    So I feel grateful to you. Less grateful to you for your review of F. L. Lucas' *Journal* in the Daily Sketch! I understand anyone disagreeing with the book, and disagreeing violently with its politics, but to call it 'contemptible' seems to me quite extraordinary. Did you not think it a sincere book? And when you were playing that well-worn card of the ordinary man, did you realise that Lucas served with distinction in the last war and was badly wounded, that he has offered his services at the present juncture, and that incidentally he is not a Professor? You say that his book would have made you angry, had it been more important: well, your review angers me, whatever its importance. Do let me have a line about it, and if I have got you wrong please tell me where.²

Yours ever,
E. M. Forster

ALS: HRC

¹ Walpole's letter has not been found.
² Frank Laurence Lucas (1894–1967), poet and scholar; Fellow of King's College, from 1920, and Lecturer in the English Department; a Lieutenant in the 7th Royal West Kent Regiment and the Intelligence Corps. For Walpole's review of his *Journal under the Terror* (1939), an examination of British reactions to the September crisis of 1938, see 'This Book Is Contemptible in Spirit . . .', *Daily Sketch*, 24 July 1939, p. 10. Walpole called it 'symptomatic of a lot of hysterical feeling bred largely in intellectual England', and an explanation of 'why Professor Lucas has never yet got there'.

338   To Hilton Young

W[est] H[ackhurst]   17 November 1939

I am so very sorry dear Hilton that my little things in the New Statesman have distressed you. I find it difficult to answer your letter, because of the affection in it and of the affection which I feel.[1]

I feel that I am dissecting *not* humanity but the toils in which the human spirit and body have been caught. *That*, when I think it out consciously, is my answer; though when writing I merely went ahead because I was interested, which is what I usually do. I don't intend to change my outlook because of war, until war forces me to change it, as it at any moment may. I don't, because the ship is sinking, want to join in 'abide with me', though fine fellows, finer than myself, are singing it with voices which can already be heard.[2] The closing down of criticism, and the division of criticism into "responsible" and "illegitimate" are two of the things I am out against, and whose victory would in my judgment hasten the coming of darkness.

I got this morning a letter telling me that my deflation of M[rs] Miniver is "almost a form of national service." Which, I need not add, is rubbish. Yet it shows that what may discourage one reader may comfort another.

I believe in love. And I have said so in a pamphlet which, you told me, didn't say any thing in particular to you.[3]

We both believe in love.

———————————

As for *your* damned pamphlet: damned because lost while I was flitting from flat to flat: lost before read, which has much annoyed me.[4] However it will turn up, and then I will read it and probably write about it. I think it may clear up some of my muddles. Any how it is a part of the book about yourself which I have for a long time wanted you to do. Every now and then I come on pieces which I want to see fitted together. Some are public pieces—e.g. an article I once saw in the D[aily] T[elegraph] pointing out that expenditure upon armaments need not *in these days* lead to national bankruptcy: an extraordinarily interesting and depressing view. I want, too, to be told what correlation (if any) you make between your business and public activities and your notions about the universe. And so I go on and on. And when the pamphlet has turned up I shall go further. I only believe in democracy because I am afraid to believe in anything else: history giving me, I submit, good reasons for such fear.

When in London I sometimes go to the 1.o. concerts at the National Gallery. I suppose there is no chance of your coming with me.[5]

Morgan

ALS: Cambridge University Library, for Lord Kennet

¹ Forster, 'They Hold Their Tongues', and 'The Top Drawer But One', *The New Statesman and Nation*, n. s. 18 (1939), 453, 648. In the first, EMF writes that 'when Satire visits our madhouse,' war's absurdities will be presented as a ballet of the absurd, which 'will not end with an all-round laugh and a kindly apotheosis of the average man. It will have a touch of the rancid flatness which is a part of true satire—for Satire does not merely bite the victim, it lets down the reader too.' The second reviews *Mrs. Miniver* (1939), Jan Struther's novel about an idealised British housewife bravely enduring the war. EMF's opinion was that she had style, but not *Style*: 'She assumes . . . that she can create the atmosphere of Madame de Sevigné by behaving like Mrs. Carlyle.'
² Young is apparently thinking of the hymn sung on the sinking *Titanic* in 1912; that, however, was 'Nearer, my God, to Thee'. See EMF's response, in Letter 340.
³ Forster, *What I Believe* (1939); cf. Kirkpatrick, p. 59.
⁴ Pamphlet: *The Evidence You Shall Give* (privately printed 1939), about democracy, which Kennet circulated to a few friends.
⁵ EMF went often to the lunchtime concerts at the National Gallery, organised by pianist Myra Hess (1890–1965) from 10 October 1939 to 9 April 1946. See Marian C. McKenna, *Myra Hess: A Portrait*, pp. 120–94. EMF contributed 'From the Audience' (pp. 6–7) to a 1944 pamphlet issued by the Concerts Committee, *The National Gallery Concerts*.

339   To Richard Antony Rendall[1]

Reform Club, Pall Mall [London] S.W. 1
4 February 1940

Dear Rendall

It was very nice to hear from you. My impulse was to say no, as I have already done a freedom (in peace-time) debate, and though I took a good deal of trouble over it didn't think my performance at all good. I find it awfully difficult to simulate spontaneity.[2]

I would like to see you before deciding, though, if you think well.

Fee. Should want twenty guineas, and your contracts dep^t may turn this down.

What I feel about the war. I don't want to lose it. I don't expect Victory,* and I can't join in any 'build-a-new-world' stuff. Once in a lifetime one can swallow that, but not twice. On the other hand I feel that this is a writers' and artists' war more strongly than I did in 1914. The Kaiser might have let them carry on—Hitler wouldn't (Quotations from his speeches: from Lenin's too). And I can answer the question "Why should a creative artist want freedom of expression? He's not a politician?" Answer, psychological; if he moves in constant fear of censorship or internment, he can't function properly.

Conclusions My attitude's fairly consistent and patriotic rather than not, but negative and gray. What's positive and coloured in it, doesn't and can't come in, and it's probable that you and Hodson would do better with some one who shows blood externally like J. B. Priestley—whose attitude I much admire.

Will you on the above kindly send me a line to 9, Arlington Park

Mansions, Chiswick, W. 4, and let me know whether I should come and see you on *Wednesday morning*?

Yours ever

EMForster

* with big V!

ALS: BBC Written Archives

[1] Richard Antony Rendall (1907–57) joined the BBC as announcer in 1928 and by 1940 had moved through various departments to become Director of Empire Services; then Acting Controller, Overseas Services, in 1944; and Controller, Talks Division, 1945–50. For his view of the scope and duties of the Overseas Service, see Asa Briggs, *The History of Broadcasting in the United Kingdom*, II, 186–7.

[2] On 1 February 1940, Rendall informed EMF that the Talks Section was planning to run a series called 'This Freedom', designed to 'analyse before the world some of the fundamental liberties which this country believes to be worth fighting for'. The interviewer would be Henry Vincent Hodson (1906–   ), writer on economics and Director of the Empire Publicity Division, Ministry of Information (1939–41); later Editor of *The Sunday Times*. EMF was asked to discuss the freedom of the artist, and Rendall added: 'The purpose of the series is propagandist but we are anxious that this should not exclude but rather encourage the expression of "differences of opinion".'

EMF wrote a script but added that he doubted himself the right man for the job, and on 3 March he wrote to Ormond Wilson (1907–   ), Assistant Staff Contributor to Overseas News, that he had reservations about the libel laws, the laws relating to blasphemy and to obscenity, and the 'colour-prejudice encountered by my fellow-writers from India in this country'. Wilson replied (4 March) that the script lacked a positive note: could EMF perhaps stress (1) England's relatively few legal restrictions on freedom of speech and action, (2) her variety of outlets for artists and writers, (3) the interest in diversity of ideas, and (4) 'a long and stable tradition that the writer and artist should be allowed to say what he likes.' EMF replied (6 March) that he might work in (3) and (4), but what he really wanted to say was that England enjoyed more of such freedoms than did the Empire, and particularly India. The discussion was broadcast on 11 March. Wilson wrote (12 March) that although the series was not intended as propaganda, 'yours was an excellent propaganda talk just because you were, and sounded, so completely genuine; but it was excellent, too, apart from this.' EMF was unwilling to let the propaganda point drop. On 12 March he wrote to Marjorie Wace (Mrs Ormond Wilson) (1904–44), who was Empire Talks Organiser, that Wilson (i.e. Rendall) *did* originally use that word. EMF added: 'Whether, when talks are propaganda, one ought to mention it is another question: anyhow we cut the word out of the final script.' Anyhow Miss Wace had the final word when she replied (13 March) that everything the BBC did in wartime was propaganda. (All letters: BBC.) EMF's previous 'freedom in peacetime debate' was 'Efficiency and Liberty—Great Britain: Discussion between E. M. Forster and Captain A. M. Ludovici, with Wilson Harris in the Chair'; it was broadcast on 4 March 1938. See *The Listener*, 19 (1938), 497–8, 530–1.

340   To Hilton Young

West Hackhurst, Abinger Hammer, Dorking
15 February 1940

Dear Hilton,

I must really try to string together the phrases that have been rolling about in my mind since I got your letter———especially as Kathleen suggested to me the other night that I might have thought it the wrong sort of letter, and had therefore not answered it.[1] (As if any letter you wrote me *could* be the wrong sort. Damn Kathleen.)

You sent me (i) an account of yourself (ii) a defence of yourself and of our society. (i) & (ii) tend to run into one another, as you say. I found the 'account' easier to follow because I could test it against myself. The 'defence' involves all sorts of experiences, both of men and of organisations, which I haven't got and alas never shall have.

In the 'account' I understood most of the reasons that induce you to make money. Indeed the only one that stumped me was that you should derive any amusement from beating money-grubbers at their own game. What would be my parallel in my own job? I suppose, to write like Dennis Wheatley, have even bigger sales, and be obliged to meet him socially.[2] In none of which do I find any attraction. The truth is, I think, that (i) is verging into (ii); you do believe that a society which ~~permits me~~ encourages money-making is good, and that good men should try to make money in it, and you have a faith (which I don't share) that the Youngs rather than the Kylsants will come to the top. Your other motives I follow pretty well, and some of them I even imitate: I too want to be comfortable when I'm old, and to keep up my little family tradition—though I am faced here by (ii) again: I don't believe that the present fabric of society is going to survive. I love my books as dearly as you can love yours, but it is typical of us that whereas you should stick in armorial bookplates I should only write in mine 'E. M. Forster, at West Hackhurst.' I don't feel *of* any where. I wish I did. It is not that I am déraciné. It is that the soil is being washed away.

I'll come back to the soil in a minute. I mustn't forget the main question in my previous letter, which was Why don't you do philosophy? You reply in effect 'Because I shouldn't do it well.' Even if you didn't do it well, this doesn't seem much of an answer if philosophy fascinates and amuses you, and I think it does. You rightly point out that this amusement and the amusement of outdistancing money-grubbers are ~~different~~ irreconcilables, still they both occur in time, and the hours you give to the one you might give to the other. I suppose you feel you can serve, fulfil, nourish, yourself, better by making a large income————I use these words in a sort of 16th century Renaissance sense of course, and I felt while reading your letter that you belonged to that Renaissance, though you have added to it the modern turn which leads you to serve yourself through services rendered by you to the community.[3] Feeling thus, you will naturally go on making your income larger and larger. I ~~feel~~ believe this is the wrong choice. You and I agree that money is nothing. But don't you agree that the more money one handles and the more one handles money, the more difficult it is to regard it as nothing? The parts of Communism and of Christianity that interest me are *not* their boring equalitarianisms, but their attempts to cut out money. I do think money is dangerous, and I know more about its dangers than you suppose, for my great grandfather was quite a famous banker, and some of his canniness runs in my blood, and tempts me to prefer money to the things it buys.[4]

I believe the above ¶ was intended to send you back to your philosophy-books, but it has got a little mixed, and I will pass on to the soil. No—not just yet, for there is criticism. We disagree here violently. I cling to criticism, much as you cling to that still mistier abstraction, justice. I see that criticism must be restricted, all that; but to deny her terrifies me, and if the past is on my side here why should the present not be? Why should you think that *just now* dumb obedience is best? It might be if we were sure it wasn't the Kylsants who were giving the orders.

I must now go to bed.

16 February 1940

Next day, and not a very nice one.

I like Whig Dukes, also Tory ones, but how do you propose to provide them with retinues and demesnes? You can give them investments and ducal impulses, but you can't give them back the feudal system—a system which I often wish had lasted for ever. Here is my main criticism of your (ii). You will not realise that social relationships based upon the ownership or occupation of land are at an end. Industrialism, quick transport, all the things you know such a lot about and I nothing, have destroyed them. We have no hope of prolonging those past lovelinesses, though in my heart I shall always honour them. I don't honour what I call the Kylsant imitations (sorry to use this word so often, and it may be the wrong word) and, as a writer, I would rather be scruffy in a garden city than sit at a table below *their* salt. Aristocracy has to be planted in the soil, or it goes bad.

I think this works in all my phrases, though it scarcely covers all your points. I feel so much aware of my own inexperience, and the part of a whimsical decorator is the only one which I could play competently. I enjoy trying to measure myself against you, though.

You mentioned your writings, and declared I didn't think much of them. Twitted, I look up the Land & Sea to do again, and found I had all my old admiration for it. Your poems, it's true, I don't like much, but I do like your prose.[5]

Morgan

ALS: Cambridge University Library, for Lord Kennet

[1] Young's reply [n.d.] (TTr. supplied by Lord Kennet) to Letter 338 is worth quoting here since it provides the context for EMF's reply, and since both letters tell so much about the writers' attitudes: 'Your letter is full of prods. How do I relate what I think with what I do? That means for me, why, since I am interested in philosophy and religion, do I work at making a large income in the City? I often ask, and look for an answer, in a jungle of thoughts, in which I can distinguish only a few particular trees, such as these. *Fear.* I don't want to be

uncomfortable when old or sick. *Family affection.* I have a wife and child and want them to be comfortable and safe. *Tradition.* I was brought up in a certain setting, and it is a pleasure to me to be able to maintain it. I have the added stimulus that my family was failing to maintain it, and in youth I was aware of defeat in a struggle in which I am now successful. That brings me to *Self esteem.* I like to find I can do easily what others find it hard to do. It amuses me to do as well as the typical money-grubbers at their own game, although I am not a t.m.-g. *Circumstances.* I worked as a servant of the public, without wages, for 35 years, and was prepared to go on doing so, but the public said, as it were "Here are honours and dignities. Goodbye." I felt that there was a misunderstanding somewhere: but that was that. *Commonsense.* I think as a matter of fact that I had done about all I could in public life. What I which makes work of the sort useful. But why do I not spend my time on the activities characteristic of an elder statesman, and not on making thousands a year? ... It is *commonsense* for me to make a large income. The work I do is useful to the community. It is useful to the community that I should do it, because it can be sure that I shall do it honestly on the whole. It is the best work I can do.

'This brings me to this criticism business. Alternative to doing what I am doing, I might be criticising the rulers, in the Lords. But I am against criticism. In our race and society and time it is the besetting sin. It threatens the existence of our liberty and all else we love. Lack of self control, to hold our tongues and stifle our complaints and control our individual choices, for a common good, is our curse. I feel a better man, shutting up when I feel outraged, than I should being ever so constructively and legitimately critical, or destructively and illegitimately. . . . .

'When I ask myself "why do this city-work when you might be thinking about religion and philosophy?" I know that the answer is "that it is a false alternative. I should not be thinking about them." My mind is not capable of continuous application to speculative thought. . . . My work, which I do quite easily as far as mental effort goes, gives me leisure enough to await their coming and enjoy them when they come. You will not quarrel with me Morgan, for refraining from the theoretical in favour of the practical life, for I do not think you have found anything congenial in the little I have written.

'I had a good hard try, in earlier days, at direct works of charity and mercy, and made up my mind not to. I could do, and have done, far more in service by using my wits in public life, tidying up on the large scale, than by going about being kind to individuals. . . . I dislike and reject equalitarian ideals and the starveling culture of the garden-suburb, which is all the culture they allow. The things best worth having can only be had in a stratified society. I believe in having Whig dukes, and should like to have been one myself.

'But what is all this coil about money (which I am making myself—the coil I mean) anyhow? It does not matter vitally to me having a large income. I should be the same person, as I hope and believe, without. . . . Christian ethic seems to me based on a fallacy, and I reject it. Altruism, self-denial, and service, are not ends in themselves. They are means subservient to the true end of my being, which is to be as much, both in quantity and quality of being, as I can. I am free to serve my own ends, remembering, as a condition, that to serve them I must in much serve others first.

'. . . Why not organise and stimulate without reward? Yes, I might. I have done so, by the way, for 35 years. But how many are willing to do so? What is the good of my agreeing to an arrangement which cannot possibly work in the world as a whole? I should do harm, by obscuring the economic bases of society. This has become more of an apologia than I meant it to be when I began. I meant only to describe a state of mind: but natural pugnacity has turned a description into a defence. . . .

'I was trying to free my mind from trimmings and fusses and spend more of the hours I have left in attending to more careful and absorbing thoughts when this horrid business began all over again for the second time, under circumstances so much more difficult than the first. So, you see, I *was* singing "Abide with me", when the war interrupted, and I on my side do not intend if I can help it to allow it wholly to divert me from singing, any more than you from singing.'

[2] Dennis Yeates Wheatley (1897–1977), writer of popular novels and mysteries.

[3] 'Belonged . . . Renaissance': cf. EMF's story, 'Arthur Snatchfold', *LTC*, p. 108. In it, the middle-aged hero puts on 'the Renaissance armour that suited him so well'.

[4] I.e. Henry Thornton (1760–1815).

[5] Young, *By Sea and Land*: see Letter 142; 'your poems': *A Muse at Sea; Verses* (1919).

341   To Denys Kilham Roberts

West Hackhurst, Abinger Hammer, Dorking
15 February 1940

Dear Mr Kilham Roberts

I am glad to hear of the symposium.[1] I will confine myself to point (5), on which I have a practical suggestion. The B.B.C. should be approached and asked to devote more time to books and in particular to reintroduce the fortnightly occasional weekly reviews of current literature which it offered supplied some years ago. I suggest that there should be two reviewers, one of the extrovert the other of the introvert type, and that they should be changed every three or six months. I know that the B.B.C. has objections to this will raise objections, and I know their nature, but I feel it might be persuaded to waive them, in view of the desperate situation of contemporary culture. It has already been sympathetic and reasonable about criticism of its musical programmes, and it has improved them.

The B.B.C. has in my judgement two jobs (i) to give licence holders what they want, (ii)

I could enlarge on the above, but do not want to take up your room. My idea is that the Director General should be immediately approached, and asked if he will consent to receive a deputation of authors. Publishers and literary agents should not take part in the deputation, though I realise that their [word illegible and deleted] their situation is likewise grave.

Yours sincerely
EMForster

ALS: The Society of Authors Film Archive

[1] See Letter 346.

342   To Robert J. Buckingham

[N. p.]   28 February 1940

Dear Bob,

By Jove I'll try a little hitting back, and will take a piece of Refugees paper for the purpose.[1] You scoffing at me because I'm not master in my own house and making out your own position is so different! Now look here—you never come and stop with me in the flat in these days, though *I* would have come up any day you named for the last 5 months. May has never suggested you should come (now has she?) and she has got you placed just where you don't like to suggest it, yourself, as being unfair on her. I am very fond indeed of May as you know, indeed I love her, and I do not blame her, but I do blame you for not standing up against feminine technique better than this. You have a leave a week, but week after week is never the right week.—This may seem a silly fuss to make considering we are just as fond of one another whether you come to stop or not, but I'm not all that spiritual and unselfish, whatever you are, and I don't intend those visits of nine or ten years' standing to come to an end for want of a little arranging.

Have written to Ted and asked him to send to the flat his times of work during March.[2] Then when I see you we will fix up the first date for a meal that suits all five after this week. Will see you Goldhawk Road Stn. 11.0. Saturday, and let's hope it won't rain. If it does, we'll have to fall back on a nice lunch and a play in town. Have asked Frank Vicary to come for a night on Sunday.[3] It will be very kind of you to ring the gas-people—they say it will be 2 or 3 days and I should be very glad if they would clear out this week. No point in ringing them in the flat as the telephone is under a dust-sheet.

Love,
Morgan

ALS: May Buckingham

[1] Written on paper of the Dorking and District Refugee Committee.
[2] Edward William Buckingham (1909–68), Bob's brother.
[3] On Frank Vicary, see Letter 156.

343   To Robert J. Buckingham

W[est] H[ackhurst].   29 May 1940

Dear Bob, what a lovely day we spent together. I don't think I have ever been happier with you, the weather, the rowing, the flowers, all made it into a sort of poetry. Siegfried's poem 'Everyone suddenly burst out singing' came into my mind at Kew, and I felt the trees &[ct] were all taking flight into a better place and taking us with them. I don't often feel like that at my age, but you probably understand since you appreciated the curiousness and the timelessness of time in Priestley's play.[1] I haven't lived as much as I might have in that country, indeed it isn't easy to get there except in the company of someone whom one loves. It is so easy to go on inside a little case of wisecracks and sneers and being slightly tough lest one gets hurt. What a thing to have someone whom you're fond of and can trust! Even that sad and lovely film we saw in the evening seemed to belong—compassion and enjoyment are joined up together somehow, though one doesn't feel them both at the same time. It must be grand to have the eye that *sees* things, like yourself: i.e. colours, shapes of clouds, &[ct]. As soon as I look I start to think—though I am better at that since knowing you, it is one of the things you've shown me.

_____

Mrs Mawe is stopping on indefinitely, which means that Wolfgang's visit is off unless he cares to go to that flat and be partly alone, which I don't suppose he will. I have written him.²

Florence seemed in trouble over the phone, over some Dutch relative who had been interned. I could not make out. I hope you'll ring her some time.

I am to do the pamphlet, as now the B.B.C. (i.e. Malcolm) want me to broadcast regularly to India.³ I may also be doing Local Defence! funny if I was in the field before you. I don't expect it will have to come to anything, as I cannot fire a gun. Bone and the rabbit-cartridges are to go out tonight.⁴

Stephen Spender did not bore me at lunch, for the reason that he was in Devonshire—'Horizon' is to be shifted.⁵

If I can get up next week, can you see me any morning, or are some dates impossible. Mention let me know soon, and also (which goes without saying) let me know whenever it is possible for you to stay.

Forrest Reid's new vol. of biography, 'Private Road' is one of the best things he's ever done.⁶ I'm just enchanted by it, also it's very witty and well written. It really ought to have got into the first paragraph of this letter, for it's a sort of poetry too.

Love
Morgan

ALS: May Buckingham

¹ Sassoon, 'Everyone Sang', in his *Collected Poems*, p. 124. J. B. Priestley, *I Have Been Here Before*, first produced at the Royalty Theatre, London, on 22 September 1937; published in 1938. It draws on Petr Dem'yanovich Ouspensky's *A New Model of the Universe* (1931).
² On Lily Forster's old friend Cecilia Mawe, see Letter 17. Wolfgang: probably Simpson's refugee friend Wolfgang von Einsiedel; see Letter 344.
³ Forster, *Nordic Twilight*. Macmillan War Pamphlets No. 3, published 10 September 1940.
⁴ Bone, the gardener, was on duty with a rabbit-gun.
⁵ That is, the magazine's editorial offices were being evacuated from London. Stephen Spender was co-editor, 1940–1 of *Horizon*, which commenced publication in January 1940 and continued until 1950.
⁶ Published in 1940.

344   To John (Hampson) Simpson

W[est] H[ackhurst].   3 July 1940

My dear John,

I have had your distressing letter. I am very glad that W[olfgang] felt such friendship towards me—it is the only thing that steadies us all in these times. Please let me know as soon as you hear from him.¹

I'm afraid trouble is shifting in this direction now. We are in the line of defence for London, the downs are to be entrenched, and the district is suddenly unsafe. My fear—I have had it for some time—is that we shall be ordered to evacuate this house. I don't think my mother would survive it, but have to plan as if she would, and select two or three avenues for retreat in case, when the time comes, one of them is free. London itself may be possible, everything is so topsy turvy, and I hope next week to provision my flat. Then there is your part—Dorridge—it would be a comfort to be near friends, and such friends. Is the district full at present?

We should only ~~be moved if~~ move under compulsion. I would much rather be blown up in my own house, and be done.[2]

I am well, and planning to go this week end with Bob to Stephen Tennant's mansion near Salisbury. It should be pleasant, if the world holds. I don't worry too much—one has a sort of bounce to one, don't you find. The worst moment is when one wakes up in the morning, and suddenly remembers.

I am tearing up papers and fill the wastepaper basket nightly, mostly with old letters. I don't know what to do with my unpublished stories, of which there are an untidy bunch. They are mostly frivolous, many would be repelled by them, and I don't really know whether they are any good.

My papers, if you ever had to look for them, are for the moment in the cupboard in the sitting room, by the fireplace. I don't expect you will have to look after them—Sprott is first on the list of those who have promised to act as ex[ecut]ors, and you will only be bothered if he won't or can't.

Well I must knock off, dear John, and go to bed. Love to all. Keep going—though I can't really say why.

Morgan

Have just heard that our friend Richard Wiener has been interned too—I had hoped that, being a Jew, he would escape, and there is his poor wife left alone.[3]

ALS: KCC

[1] Wolfgang von Einsiedel (1903–67) was a refugee who had guyed Hitler in print, was framed by a faked diary, and escaped from Germany while still on bail. He was helped by John Simpson and his generous Birmingham friends, the Wilsons. Wolfgang was interned in Canada and upon release broadcast anti-Nazi propaganda.

[2] On 31 January 1941 EMF wrote to Isherwood: 'I am certainly more cushiony and courageous than I was, but more irritable and with fears of hysteria. I don't expect to behave well when the trouble starts, shall be offended and maybe go mad, running slowly in large circles with my head down is the way I see myself—I think I once told you.' Trouble did eventually shift in their directions, and he wrote to Isherwood on 6 June 1944: 'The windows keep shaking, my poor mother calls down for assurance (she is very good over this hateful rubbish) and I call up that it is guns. Probably it is. But Christopher how disgusting, how difficult not to grumble in a war's 5th year, how impossible for me to create a book. I wonder whether you, by sheer will power, will succeed, as you intend to do.' (Both letters, Isherwood Collection.)

[3] Richard Wiener was an Austrian Jewish refugee on whose behalf EMF appeared before a tribunal, but to no avail.

345   To Naomi Mitchison[1]

West Hackhurst, Abinger Hammer, Surrey
27 July 1940

Dear Naomi,

I was distressed to get your letter and hear your bad (personal) news. I think there are times when it is almost impossible to bear up against a private knock. I have had the good luck not to have one since the war started. I expect Naomi you will soon recover, though you ~~say~~ feel for the moment you can't, and will again believe in what it is natural to you to believe in. No one can do more, or otherwise, and ~~though~~ those who care for personal relationships will continue to care for them, although the persons themselves are now ravelled-out entities rather than solids, and are obliged to wave at one another instead of making satisfying contacts. Well I wave at you! Perhaps the staircase is going up really, I don't know, can't know. All I can do is to "behave well" on it, with the full knowledge that my behaviour cannot alter the course of events. My rules for my own good conduct are a little strange, and may divert you. They were in my mind when your letter arrived:—

> Obey orders
> Ignore advice
> Do not advise
> Help your neighbours
> Be interested
> Don't listen in.

These are not precepts for the future, but they do summarise what has been most suitable in my own behaviour during the last ten months.

No, I don't hear from Gerald [Heard] now or from any of them. I think they ought to write to us, but I believe that they find us all so unhappy and so odd that they are scared. I shall write again to them, and pull their leg a bit——I fancy they all stand upon one.[2]

I look forward to hearing from you again, with the news that your health is better and you feel more up to going on. For go on we must, carrying forward our scraps of the past into the future a bit, though we don't know whether the future can use them.

Yours
EMForster

ALS: National Library of Scotland

[1] Naomi Margaret Mitchison (1897–   ), author of books in a variety of genres: novels and 'documentary novels', travel books, fantasies and children's books, autobiography.

[2] Christopher Isherwood, Gerald Heard, Aldous Huxley, and W. H. Auden had gone to the United States and were to settle there, thus incurring adverse comments at home. An epigram signed W.R.M., 'To Certain Intellectuals Safe in America', appeared in *The Spectator*, 164 (1940), 833. EMF wrote to suggest that there ought to be 'a close time for snarling at absent intellectuals'; see 'These "Lost Leaders"', *The Spectator*, 165 (1940), 12.

346   To Christopher V. Salmon[1]

West Hackhurst, Abinger Hammer, Dorking
17 August 1940

Dear Mr Salmon

Thank you for your letter. I should have enjoyed meeting you, and I think the suggested series would have been very suitable if the B.B.C.s attitude to literature had been different.[2] But what has *it* done of recent years to bring the public into relation with writers either dead or alive? What attempt has it made to treat our national heritage in letters seriously? With its miserable record, I don't think it's in a position to invite authors to chat!

I won't bother you with data and suggestions. For one thing it isn't of course your fault (please be so kind as to read this letter as an impersonal one), and for another thing one of your colleagues was so good as to see me at the beginning of the year and discuss the whole problem—without any results.

I am sure that individual officials, and probably individual directors too, think English literature a valuable national asset. And they control an organisation which is exempted from the financial anxieties which vex the ordinary publisher, and which can address the public, on one wave length alone, for over a hundred hours a week. They have convictions and they have power, and my God look at their performance.

If the performances had been different, it would have been fun to discuss who could be compèred at the microphone and how. As it is, I feel it too wry a jest.

Yours sincerely
EMForster.

I hope I've made it plain that the B.B.C.s neglect of *contemporary* literature is only part of my case against it—though since the present will one day become the past it is an important part.

ALS: BBC Written Archives

---

[1] Christopher Verney Salmon (1901–60) joined the BBC in 1934; a producer who, after the Munich crisis, organised a notable series 'Everyman and the Crisis', which was broadcast in 1938. See *The Listener*, 20 (1939), 832–4, 899–900, 954–5, 1009–10, 1074, 1125, 1188–9, 1253.

[2] Salmon wrote to EMF (15 August 1940) asking him to join an Autumn series in which writers would 'answer questions about their work' and be asked to 'discuss generally the influence of language and the relation of the writer to his public'. The above is EMF's reply. After receiving it, Salmon wrote (20 August) regretting his disinclination to help. Some unfinished business is a part of this acid exchange with Salmon. On 3 May 1940 EMF had written to Sir George Reginald Barnes (1904–60), who had been in the BBC Talks Department since 1935 and in 1941 would become Director of Talks. EMF suggested that Barnes meet with Kilham Roberts and others from The Society of Authors, to discuss the possibility of more air time for books and writers. They had met on 17 May, but little had resulted. (All letters: BBC.)

347   To Christopher V. Salmon

West Hackhurst, Abinger Hammer, Dorking
22 August 1940

Dear M⁻ Salmon,

Thank you for your letter. I am sorry that the Authors' Society postponed sending in their suggestions, and that the B.B.C. on receiving them postponed the proposed conference. As for myself, I feel that I have done the very little which an individual can hope to do. Were I more influential, I would go upstairs and enquire why there is not a different policy in higher quarters. But I have no qualifications for doing this. I do not even know on which door to knock. I can only discuss things with Barnes and yourself, and put it to you that *nil* minutes for books in a week (that is what happened one week) does not seem quite right.[1]

This Witness Box course is pretty trivial, don't you think, and no amount of advice, good or bad, could make it otherwise. It's books, not writers, that matter. I'm all for triviality if it occurs in a scheme which also admits seriousness, but can't get any fun out of it when it stands alone.[2]

However I mustn't bother you with another long letter, and I hope to have the pleasure of meeting you sometime.

Yours sincerely
EMForster.

ALS: BBC Written Archives

[1] In January 1941 George Barnes and EMF again discussed comparative air time. Barnes, who classed news and informative talks with literature, calculated (22 January) that of 119 hours, six were given to literature and eighteen to serious music in the same week: 'Literary Broadcasts' from 12 January to 18 January amounted to 355 minutes. The postponed meeting took place on 12 March. EMF, speaking for the Society, said that the amount of time allotted 'to Letters, and in particular to contemporary Letters, was small when compared with the time allotted to the Corporation's total programme output. . . . the Corporation had a duty towards good literature . . . similar to its obligation towards religious broadcasts and serious musical broadcasts.' Some improvements did in fact eventually follow. (Letter and summary of discussion: BBC.)

[2] 'The Writer in the Witness Box' was an interview series conducted by Desmond Hawkins (1908–   ), novelist, critic, editor, and radio producer. It was designed to discuss the art of the professional writer and his relation to his public. See 'The Writer in the Witness Box', *The Listener*, 24 (1940), 474.

348   To Forrest Reid

West Hackhurst, Abinger Hammer, Dorking
30 September 1940

My dear F. R.

Your letter of the 25ᵗʰ reached me on the 28ᵗʰ, and to day I get your line acknowledging the receipt of my pamphlet.[1] I had better signalise this Anglo-Irish rapprochement by replying at once. I got up to London for a few hours on Friday. It is a depressing sight, but so far only one pane of glass in my flat is damaged and Bob is undamaged completely. How Knox can enjoy the situation passes me, but I suppose if your head is under the water or being hit by a glove it doesn't notice anything outside it.[2] M[rs] Barger's house has been wrecked by a bomb and so has Joe's mother's—no one injured.[3] It is exactly like school-life. Every one except me is a goose and forgets what school was.

I go on with Beethoven at moments, and copy out a sample page of my notes. The square brackets refer to bars. I do it with Tovey's numbered edition, and as you are unlikely to have a copy of it I'm afraid my notes can't be intelligible.[4] I'm keen on a vision of Beethoven reached through playing him as well as listening to him, and based upon details. Your crow on a tower is exactly what I want, but out of what is the tower built? Unfortunately so much of him I can't play, and though I had begun to buy the more difficult sonatas for my gramophone they are immured in town. Even once on a record helps. The last movement of the "Hammerclavier", which I used to think so harsh and senseless, is revealing itself as a gigantic beauty, tearing down veil after veil away from the night as it gathers strength—However if I go on like this the Censor will think I am using a code.

I wish you could send me the sifting of your tales of youth when it is finished. I suppose you know a novel called 'Le Grand Meaulnes' whose author I forget, and whom you might by the way tell me of? Though it isn't exactly a tale of youth.—I am now reading "La vie intime de Voltaire" by Perez and Maugras.[5] I got it out of the London Library by chance, it is delightful. Mostly about his days at Ferney, when he was famous happy and very tiresome, with a passion for acting. I went to Ferney with my beloved and lost Charles Mauron, when we were in Switzerland last year.[6] It is your sort of park—I mean the sort one can't quite get into but somehow does—and squeezed against its railings we saw the church he built with the inscription

/   DEO EREXIT   \

/   VOLTAIRE   \

on its pediment. For he believed in proportion.

Well dear F. R. I must not chatter more. Poor Meredith is most tiresome. My mother, who was most interested in the story, agrees with you that Prosser ought to have gone out. However it would be difficult for any one as hospitable as he is to do so. I think M. is a tease, and also incapable of realising the limits within which his charm will, and outside which it won't, work.[7]

Love as always from your

E. M.

Beethoven   Op. 90   <u>Sonata in E. Minor</u>

<u>First Movement</u>

[1-81] a single gigantic gesture, although there are pauses in it and changes of theme. Lyric emotion until [65] when there is a good little growl, repeated in [71], which *might* introduce a fiercer mood. It doesn't, the gesture dies, the hand falls in peace. Though the actual sounds are less delicious than the 1st movement of Op. 101, the general effect is sweeter because the flow isn't interrupted or in spurts. I find lovely the continuation: the bars [82-84] echoing [79-81]; minims echoing crochets [*sic*]; I feel sure they belong to what comes after, not to what has gone, though I don't know how to prove this. The original motive returns in [84] but pricked with quavers; it becomes a little scholarly & harsh, and I don't enjoy myself so much until [108], when it has done its stuff and the first motive (or rather the second theme in it; [8] originally) comes in at [108], and itself turns very scholarly in the base [*sic*]. Movement almost in the front rank. So exciting and touching that I am always surprised to get to the end. One of the many Beethoven pieces that couldn't be any other piece.

<u>Second Movement</u>

Alas, you are boring. Such a gay rich tune—one would prophecy [*sic*] up to [24] that you *must* be a success. Suspension of judgment then starts: expectation of something gayer, richer, overwhelmingly so. This never comes, and I always find you too long, though you are not much longer than the first movement, which always seems too short. Goldie——the last time I saw him listening to music, in Gerald Heard's flat, felt the same.

This general judgment must be modified in particulars—e.g. how gracious is the new theme at [60]. But Beethoven has been too trustful of his opening tune—the trustfulness which is so tedious in Schubert. Years ago, at M[rs] Hope Wedgwood's at Idlerocks, the same criticism was brought against the 1st movement of the Moonlight, but undeservedly, because *there* the tune has dignity and can naturally meander, *there* it can bear the whole burden of the movement by itself.

ALS: Stephen Gilbert

[1] Forster, *Nordic Twilight*.
[2] Sir Samuel Knox Cunningham (1909–76), Reid's friend, later well known as an Ulster Protestant politician.

³ Florence Barger lived with the Forsters until May 1942, when she found another home in London.
⁴ Square brackets: here rendered as boxes. Cf. Donald Francis Tovey, *A Companion to Beethoven's Pianoforte Sonatas (Complete Analyses)* (1931). EMF began a manuscript note book (KCC) in which he planned to annotate all the piano sonatas, and which he directed on 28 September 1939 should be sent to Mauron, who suggested the scheme, in case of his own death. He did not succeed in writing on all the sonatas. However, after reading 'The Problem of Evil and Suffering in Beethoven's Pianoforte Sonatas', by E.H.W. Meyerstein (*Music Review*, 5 [1944], 96), EMF wrote to him (24 November 1944. HRC): 'They are well worth recording, these subjective reactions,. . . As to the 1ˢᵗ movement of the Apassionata I'm disposed to think everyone is wrong except myself, ...'
⁵ On Alain-Fournier's *Le grand Meaulnes*, cf. Letter 286. Lucien Perey and Gaston Maugras, *La Vie intime de Voltaire aux Délices et à Ferney 1754–1778* (1885).
⁶ On EMF's visit to Ferney, 'a farewell to civilised enjoyments', in 1939, see *TC*, pp. 355–8; and *EMF*, II, 233.
⁷ This apparently alludes to some social contretemps of H. O. Meredith, involving J. Stanley Prosser, a Belfast friend of Reid; see Brian Taylor, *The Green Avenue*, pp. 89, 189.

349   To William Plomer

W[est] H[ackhurst]   16 October 1940

Dear William,
I will write on someone else's paper too, and Lord Carlow's, come[?] It is the ends of a tale by Holbrooke Jackson's [*sic*] which he (C) printed as a Christmas present for his friends. I have found no use, either anal or ocular, for the middle, but the ends ~~papers~~ will do to write on, especially as the patines of fine gold do not seem to drag the ink.¹ My three ladies are below, trying to listen to César Franck, and a bomber is overhead, on its way to all I love in London.² I write in a mood of military and aerial depression: the navy I leave to you, but it seems to me that the Germans have got our defences beat generally, and in particular have worked out a device for destroying our fighters.
But my depression is strictly limited, and as above defined.
What you say about self pity is most interesting.³ Why has no one worked it out? I have always assumed it is bad, but since your letter arrived have felt grave misgivings. It is certainly no worse than picking one's nose if it isn't seen, and it may be much better: the gain in comfort and (in Verlaine's case) creative power, may more than justify the malaise caused to the onlookers. For self-pity, per se, is not an appetising spectacle. Don't you agree here? And I'm not sure that it is connected with pity for others, which I agree with you in approving[.]
I think the subject is connected with another one: namely the attempt to arouse and retain the interest of other people in oneself and one's goings on—a black art which most of us practice. It has often seemed to me that a judicious mixture of good and bad fortune is important. If you are always having illnesses, like Frank Vicary, or that friend of Joe's who broke first the one and then the other leg, you ~~must~~ may bore people (it was this that your mother,—though I

didn't know her—appeared to realise so ~~clearly~~ finely). But if you have an operation and then not another until it is forgotten, you will score, and score more than if you kept health. Self pity may be valuable here. A little spasm of it, though not in itself appetising to the beholder, may cause him salutary surprise.

I'm much more in a moral treatise than is suitable for me, and rather wandering way from your more interesting point—i.e. is self-pity as wretched as it [is] supposed to be. I can't get clear here, because my states of mind get muddled up, when I try to consider them, with the states of mind which I think they produce in others. Because Bob dislikes self-pity I have tried to cure myself of it: I want him to keep fond of me. He may be quite wrong in his attitude. In fact I will have it out with him on Friday.

I hope to come up then—not much of a hope. I have managed my tip and runs so far: "once too often, once too often ...". says the wagging forefinger, vulgar as only Fate's can be. "Count no man happy until he be dead." That is another remark of Fate's and uttered, as it would be, through Herodotus.[4] Of course death is probably going to be frightening and painful. But it will only make the tiniest modification in the sum of one's life. For that reason I wish all my friends were as old as I am. Not for other reasons, God no.

Hughie Waterston left last week, our farewell was much friendlier than I expected.[5] We are going to miss one another. The fields are deserted, but I do not mind this in this too-full world, and I like the rain which drummed so hard this afternoon upon my umbrella that the internal combustion engines around me were inaudible. The longing for a world which is silent or only disturbed by 'natural' sounds haunts one, and for you dear William it must be unattainable in your driven life. I still get it occasionally. Where you gain just a little perhaps is in contacts with odd people at this odd time. The asceticism is dreary, though I hope the words "not so badly fixed really" do bear some tangible meaning. John Simpson's visit went by all too quick. It was very good of him to come. They keep hearing from Wolfgang but W. has so far had nothing from them, although they write, wire, post packages, &ct.[6] Our treatment of the refugees and the speech of Duff Cooper when Italy entered the war are the two national vilenesses which I can't forget.[7]

Well well I ramble on, and, since I began to do so, Mrs Mawe's internal combustion engine has been heard at the W. C. and she has gone to bed, and Florence Barger has finished a fawn coloured linen bag for her daughter and she has gone to bed, and my mother, still dispensing advice, has gone, and Agnes has gone, not sorry to be unable to attend her sister's funeral, and the cat has gone and found the other cat which had already gone sleeping on the kitchen table in the dark, and I alone watch, and write a very long letter as my letters go. Perhaps I am influenced by Voltaire, about whom I am reading. "La Vie Intime de V. aux Délices et à Ferney" is a readable book: (by Perez & Maugras:) I picked it up by chance.[8] How Voltaire went on and on! How I do approve him in many ways. Indeed I find nothing *repellent* in him. But I can't imagine being alone with him with any pleasure.

You don't mention Ted. He is still safe down in Somerset I hope. What a shave Murdo seems to have had—I am so glad he is all right.[9]

There are some very nice letters from Mrs Hardy in the Cockerell book which Joe has sent me. I do not know what the relations between them were, Siegfried said that, in his capacity of executor to Hardy, he [Cockerell] pinched her behind. Anyhow:

We had a very quiet Christmas, we two, alone with Wessie, our only diversing being that T. H. *would* give Wessie goose and plum pudding and the result was what might have been expected. . . . . He saw a ghost in Stinsford Churchyard on Christmas Eve and his sister Kate says it must have been their grandfather upon whose grave T. H. had just placed a sprig of holly—the first time he had ever done so. The ghost said: "A green Christmas."—T. H. replied, "I like a green Christmas." Then the ghost went into the church, and, being full of curiosity, T. followed to see who this strange man in 18th century dress might be—and found no one. That is quite true—a real Christmas ghost story.

With love from
<Eileen>[10]

ALU: Durham University

[1] Lionel Arthur Henry Seymour Dawson-Damer, 6th Earl of Portarlington, Baron Dawson, and Viscount Carlow (1883–1959), owned a private press, the Corvinus Press, London. Holbrook Jackson, *The Story of Don Vincente* (1939), sixty copies printed. 'Patines . . . gold'; Shakespeare, *The Merchant of Venice*, V, i, 62–3.

[2] His mother, Cecilia Mawe, and Florence Barger.

[3] Plomer's letter does not survive.

[4] Herodotus, in his *Histories* (I, 32), attributes the remark to Solon.

[5] Hugh Waterston was the son of Scottish neighbours at Hackhurst Farm and had recently moved to a farm in Kent.

[6] On Wolfgang von Einsiedel, see Letter 344.

[7] Duff Cooper, 'Enter Second Murderer', *The Listener*, 23 (1940), 1111–12; a broadcast 10 June 1940, on Mussolini's entrance into the war, in which he sneered at the Italian national character. The Rt. Hon. Alfred Duff Cooper, 1st Viscount Norwich (1890–1954), was diplomat, author, and MP; Minister of Information, 1940–2; Ambassador to France, 1944–7.

[8] On *La Vie intime*, cf. Letter 348.

[9] Ted, Murdo: friends of Plomer, unidentified.

[10] See *Friends of a Lifetime; Letters to Sydney Carlyle Cockerell*, ed. Viola Meynell, pp. 305–6, where this letter (27 December 1919) is *not* signed 'Eileen'. Hardy's biographer, Robert Gittings, does not mention bottom-pinching but does state that Cockerell embittered Florence Hardy's last years; see Gittings, *The Older Hardy*, pp. 279–84.

350   To John Lehmann[1]

West Hackhurst, Abinger Hammer, Dorking
21 December 1940

Dear John,

Many thanks for your Penguin.[2] The publisher had already sent me one, and I was about to write to you and say how good I thought it. It struck me as a real clearing up of the matter for the benefit of some future chronicler of the decade, or indeed for yourself if you take on that job some time, and you are well qualified to do this. And it also helped to clear up *me*, and I now see better than last week where I stand in relation to all this left-wing stuff. I'm very glad the relation isn't a remote one, and I thank you very much for what you say about me.[3]—My difficulty with working class writers is that they don't make the working class come alive—Leslie Halward is an exception, but as you imply he is not very important. They give *me* information and they give their comrades gratification, but that's all; gloom, indignation, aspiration in plenty, and plenty of stains on the tablecloth and coal-dust in the mine—but no living beings to experience them. Consequently I find a lot of what you have (very rightly) published dull. Or put it another way: I find that we middle-class do demand that people in fiction should seem to be alive, and I realise too that this demand may not be as important as I think, and that there may be a fiction I am not conditioned to appreciate, in which Ted at the table, Ed in the mine, and Bert at the works need not be differentiated. But I can't look at them in that way myself, and the working class people I know don't seem so to look at them either though their judgements are different from mine because it is more important to them than to me whether a man has money or not.

What's so good—among other things—is the way you relate the literature to the heaving political background. In connection with this, Christopher's *The Lost* stands out as it didn't before.[4] Something lost for us, I fear, no one'll ever mirror the whole flux now—it's splashed too much of the mirrors. A certain awareness (nice word, yes) is possible, though, and you help one to exercise it.

Many small points occur to me. Auden & Wm. Plomer are the poets I like best, and I particularly like what Auden wrote in the China book, which I think you don't mention.[5]—Ce Soir was run by J. R. Bloch, thought [*sic*][6]—Don't Marx & Engels like Balzac because he gives them so much material appropriate to a decaying society?[7]—A section needed on the Conference spirit?—the only sort of literary life which these new little international authors had access to. I wish I had been to more conferences. They were very strange things.[8]

You'll make me read some new people—particularly Gibbon

Tom Coley, on a motor trip with
EMF and William Roerick from
Paris to the Lascaux Caves and back.

With William Roerick at King's,
Cambridge.

Left to right: EMF with George Tooker and Paul Cadmus in Provincetown, Mass., 1947.

whose letter was splendid. Also John Lepper, who wrote very kindly to me once. And must not ignore Edmund Wilson any more.[9]

I have further complicated, or simplified, my life by spraining an ankle during one of my rare visits to London. I do hope I shall get up again soon, I expect so, and I shall much like to see you.

Yours ever
EMForster

ALS: HRC

[1] John Frederick Lehmann (1907–   ), author, critic, and publisher; founder-editor, *New Writing*, 1936–8, and *Orpheus*, 1948–9; partner and general manager, Hogarth Press, 1938–46; Managing Director, John Lehmann Ltd., to 1952; editor, *London Magazine*, 1954–61.

[2] *New Writing in Europe*, ed. Lehmann (1940).

[3] 'The style that Forster perfected, is simplicity of construction and easy flow, . . . was one of the chief reasons for his popularity with the younger writers. But even more important, I am inclined to think, has been the central idea behind his art: the idea of reconciliation' (*ibid.*, pp. 21–2).

[4] 'The Lost': Isherwood's intended title of a larger novel that would have incorporated his German novels.

[5] China book: Auden and Isherwood's *Journey to a War*.

[6] On Bloch and *Ce Soir*, see Letter 307.

[7] See S. S. Prawer, *Karl Marx and World Literature*, pp. 118–19: 'Despite the difference between their political attitudes, Marx revelled in Balzac, often quoted him and seriously planned to write a book about him.' See also *Marx & Engels on Literature and Art*, ed. Lee Baxendall and Stefan Morawski, which quotes (p. 116) a draft letter of 1888 by Engels on Balzac, 'whom I consider a far greater master of realism than all the Zolas passés, presents, et à venir, . . .' EMF wrote (*CB*, p. 116): 'Surprised at M[arx]'s humanity culture and sensitiveness.'

[8] Conferences: i.e. gatherings of writers like the 1935 Congress in Paris.

[9] Lewis Grassic Gibbon: pseudonym of James Leslie Mitchell (1901–35), Scots vernacular novelist, author of the trilogy *A Scots Quair* (1946); his letter, in *New Writing in Europe*, pp. 131–2. John Lepper: friend of Lehmann and, for a time, his secretary. Edmund Wilson (1895–1972), American critic and novelist; editor, *The New Republic*, 1926–31.

351   To Cecil Day-Lewis

West Hackhurst, Abinger Hammer, Dorking
14 February 1941

Dear Day Lewis

Your Poems in War Time seemed to me the best you have done—though I am very unstable over poetry. They were about things I could focus: particularly the Watching Post and the Stand To.[1] Those insensitive abstractions—even the Freedom I goad myself to write about occasionally—seem so dim beside the attempt of yourself and your neighbours to prevent strangers whom you don't want from coming down on the top of you. It's a dim battle for the most part: ignorant armies clashing by night, I suspect.[2] The bad news so frightening, the good news enough to make any decent person sick, and yet no possibility of recommending peace. In the dimness it is only the rag-tag fighters who stand out clear.

I ask myself (vide your first poem) whether I am at all to blame for this.[3] It's *logical* to conclude I am especially as I am, even now, a mass of soft options. But I find it so difficult to *feel* that I am, and perhaps the feeling entails the recognition of an active principle of evil, against which one ought to have been more watchful.

Well let's hope something acceptable will come along—not that Better England which can only last ten minutes, but the better world which will make our lanes and fields again habitable. It won't come in my day—and selfishly I don't want it to, for I do cling increasingly, as older people must, to Culture: and I ~~can bear seeing~~ prefer to see Culture swept away by what's bad rather than by what's good. (Haven't put this too clearly, and a bit paradoxically but you see what I mean—I shirk burying my own dead much as I decline to forget my lost friends or to cease mourning France.)—To what extent can one chuck past loyalties, and remain capable of loyalty to anything? It's a question that bothers me. I wonder whether you've considered it.—Well thank you anyhow for your Christmas poems, which as you see make me think, or anyhow run on. I like 'It would be strange' too.[4]

Yours ever with all good wishes. EMForster

ALS: Jill (Balcon) Day-Lewis

[1] In Day-Lewis, *Poems in Wartime*: 'The Watching Post' and 'The Stand-To', pp. 10, 13-14.
[2] Matthew Arnold, 'Dover Beach' (1867): 'And we are here as on a darkling plain / Swept with confused alarms of struggle and flight, / Where ignorant armies clash by night.'
[3] 'The Dead', *Poems in Wartime*, p. 7.
[4] 'It Would Be Strange', *ibid.*, p. 11.

352   To Frederick (Wolff) Oglivie[1]

Reform Club, Pall Mall [London] S.W. 1
17 March 1941

Dear M[r] Oglivie,

I am extremely sorry to trouble you with this letter, but I feel with D[r] Vaughan Williams over the victimisation of private opinions by the B.B.C. and I am therefore most reluctantly cancelling two forthcoming broadcasts which I was to have given.[2] I am writing to the officials concerned with them (M[r] Bullett and Sir Malcolm Darling) to express my deep regret.[3]

If in the future the 'ban' should be lifted, and the B.B.C. should again desire me to speak, I should be most happy to do so.

I have of course read with care what M[r] Duff Cooper said in the House, and regret that I did not find it reassuring.[4]

Yours truly
E. M. Forster

I may perhaps add that I am neither a Communist nor a Pacifist, and that I believe in going on with the war.[5]

ALS: BBC Written Archives

[1] Frederick Oglivie (1893–1949) was Director-General of the BBC 1938–42. He had been Professor of Political Economy at the University of Edinburgh, 1926–34; and President and Vice-Chancellor, Queen's University, Belfast, 1934–8. He succeeded Sir John Reith (later Lord Reith) (1889–1971) as Controller of the BBC.

[2] In September 1939 the BBC was trying to cope with the confusion about its role, as related to that of a Ministry of Information, in imminent or actual war. By December 1940, necessary supervision of news content had expanded to include activities of persons whose opinions, whether or not heard on the air, were critical of Government policy. Opposition quickly came from groups like the National Council for Civil Liberties and from liberal journals. The role of the N.C.C.L. is documented in its file labelled 'B.B.C. Victimisation' (Hull). The Council adhered to its formal statement, adopted on 5 June 1940, that certain wartime restrictions are necessary and reasonable. However, 'the essence of democracy consists in the actions of all authorities being guided by a balanced and well-informed public opinion.' The Press must be 'free to explain and deal fearlessly with all issues.' The case that particularly brought BBC bans to the Council's attention was that of Sir Hugh Roberton (1874–1952), founder of the Glasgow Orpheus Choir and its conductor, 1906–51. Other names then came to light, among them three distinguished churchmen: George Fielden MacLeod (1895–), founder and leader of the Iona Community, 1938–67; Canon Charles Earle Raven (1885–1964), Master of Christ's College from 1939; and the Rev. Donald Oliver Soper (1903–), Methodist minister and Superintendent, 1936–78, of the West London Mission, Kingsway Hall. The bans were aimed particularly at those who had attended and/or subscribed to the 'People's Convention', launched in London on 12 January, at a Communist-sponsored rally advocating separate peace proposals and a home government more representative of the working people.

[3] On 19 March EMF sent Darling an 'official note': 'Since this letter may perhaps be seen by others as well as yourself, I should add that I am not a member of the People's Convention, nor a Communist, nor a Pacifist, and that I believe in the prosecution of the war.' He cancelled a broadcast on Masood, a talk on Indian writers, and the famous talk on George Crabbe (see Letter 368). Also, on 18 March, Oglivie wrote to EMF and sent a BBC policy statement of 13 March: the sole criterion for banning an individual from the air was '"public agitation against the national war effort" (the phrase which you use in your letter, "the victimisation of private opinions").' Both letters: BBC Written Archives. Gerald Bullett (1893–1958), miscellaneous writer, was in the BBC Talks Department (African Service), 1940–3.

[4] On 12 March 1941, Duff Cooper, as Minister of Information, answered questions in the House of Commons on B.B.C. policy. It was, he said, 'not to invite to the microphone persons who have taken part in public agitation against the war effort'. He supported this policy. Artists' private opinions were no business of the BBC, but those who took up extra-arts agitation must not expect 'to be given the great privilege—it is a privilege and not a right—of being employed by the B.B.C.' (*Hansard*, 12 March 1941, col. 1269).

[5] Also on 17 March, EMF was a principal speaker at an N.C.C.L. public meeting in the Conway Hall, where he insisted that the banned broadcasters were not making a fuss about freedom of speech at the microphone, but away from it, in which case any illegal act was a matter for the courts. He announced that he had cancelled his broadcasts and that Ralph Vaughan Williams had withdrawn permission for performance of one of his works. (Records of this meeting: Hull.)

353   To Zulfikar Bokhari[1]

West Hackhurst, Abinger Hammer, Dorking
23 March 1941

Dear Mʳ Bokhari

I am so glad that we are going on with your idea of a talk or talks on Indian Writers. I am free any Monday after the middle of April, but am unluckily unable to make any plans just yet.

I have, with Vaughan Williams and some other artists, declined to broadcast while there is any ~~thing like an 'opinion test~~' attempt to victimise artists on account of their private opinions. I have seen ~~him~~ V. W. this morning about Mʳ Churchill's statement, and we agree that we must examine its wording carefully.[2] We haven't, either, yet received any replies from the Director General to the letters we wrote him a few days ago.

When this matter is fixed up I will write to you again, and if all goes well—and I hope it will—I much look forward to working for you.

With all good wishes

Yours sincerely
EMForster

ALS: BBC Written Archives

[1] Zulfikar A. C. Bokhari had been seconded to Darling from All-India Radio. He later became Director General of Radio Pakistan. See Letter 356.

[2] On 20 March Churchill stated, ambiguously, in the House of Commons that the BBC had 'reconsidered the cases of those artistes who attended the People's Convention, and have decided that they shall not be debarred from giving performances in the broadcast in the normal way as opportunity arises. It is no part of His Majesty's government to accord the special facilities of the microphone to persons whose words and actions are calculated to hamper the nation in its struggle for life. But the connection between this and musical and dramatic performances of all kinds, or the relationship of such performances to political acts and opinions, are not apparent or worth while establishing.' When asked whether a man who exercises his right to be a conscientious objector would be allowed to broadcast, Churchill used his wit to evade the issue. No, he said, musicians should not be penalised, but 'we shall have to retain a certain amount of power in the selection of the music. Very spirited renderings of "Deutschland Über Alles" would hardly be permissible.' *The Times* reported 'cheers' and 'laughter' and 'Prime Minister against "Man-Hunting"' (21 March 1941, p. 2). Darling, replying on 22 March to EMF's letter of 19 March cancelling the Masood broadcast, wrote that he was not surprised and appreciated EMF's motives, but hoped that he would reconsider in view of Churchill's statement in the House (BBC).

354   To Leonard Woolf

Fletton Tower, Peterborough[1]
3 April 1941

Dear Leonard,

I have just seen the Times feel a bit trembly and unable to think of anyone but myself, I will write again to you.[2] As I daresay you know she had invited me to come and I had suggested doing so ~~Later~~ later in this month. I am just going to Cambridge, dear Leonard, it will seem empty and strange, I can't write any more now, only send my deepest love and sadness. Leslie Humphry came over that very day, and we talked a great deal about Virginia, he will be desolated like so many of all generations.[3]

Morgan

ALS: University of Sussex

[1] EMF was delivering a lecture to a local literary society, on Indian novelists.
[2] Virginia Woolf had been missing since 28 March. On 3 April *The Times* stated that she must be presumed drowned in the River Ouse and published her obituary (pp. 4, 7).
[3] Leslie Humphreys (1917–49): he and Virginia Woolf's niece, Judith Stephen, rented a cottage in Rodmell for a time and used to visit the Woolfs almost daily.

355 To Frederick (Wolff) Oglivie

West Hackhurst, Abinger Hammer, Dorking
21 April 1941

Dear Oglivie,

I should have answered your kind letter before, but the situation kept changing (in my judgement for the better) and I thought I would wait until it stabilized.[1]

The mishandling of the 'People's Convention' was of course soon rectified, but while it was in progress I think that the phrase 'victimisation of private opinion' fairly described it, and a good many of us were anxious that no opportunity for such victimisation should recur. We did not feel that the P[rime] M[inister]'s speech offered sufficient guarantee. Its tone was reassuring, but its phrasing was vague. It left great latitude for interpretation, particularly in its references to artists, &[ct], and I wished, and still wish, that the Corporation could have issued a statement, announcing what interpretation it proposed to apply.

However this may not have been possible, and any how the next best thing has happened: namely the appointment of excellent additional governors. In view of this, I feel that the situation is satisfactory, and I am writing to ~~various~~ Malcolm Darling and other officials on the staff, to inform them that I shall be very happy to resume broadcasting if desired to do so.[2] (If the former situation recurred, I should of course have to renew my protest—little as that individual protest is worth.)

Yours sincerely
EMForster.

ALS: BBC Written Archives

[1] That is, Oglivie's letter of 18 March; see Letter 352. On 6 April 1941 (BBC) EMF wrote to Salmon: 'I should like to work for you very much. July will be best, for at present my relations with the Corporation are unresolved. I hoped they might clear last week so that I could suggest April, but they haven't (it's over that "ban" business—Vaughan Williams, Rose Macaulay and myself are acting together).'

[2] On 5 September 1939 the BBC Board of Governors was reduced from seven members to two, in order to tighten its link to the Ministry of Information. This was viewed with alarm by many who worried about freedom of opinion in broadcasting, and in April 1941 the Board was reconstituted with seven members. See Asa Briggs, *The History of Broadcasting in the United Kingdom*, III, 336–40. EMF's cancelled talks were now rescheduled, the Masood talk for 13 May, Crabbe for 17 May, and a third cancellation, the talk on Indian writers that had been promised to Bokhari.

356   To Malcolm Darling

W[est] H[ackhurst]   19 July 1941

Dearest Malcolm,

I feel a good deal concerned and enraged at the way ~~the B.B.C.~~ they are treating you, and am convinced that you ought to resign now—or anyhow threaten resignation if your requirements are not instantly met, and, if they are not met, carry out your threat. It is not dignified that, after a large career like yours, you should be tied up and worried by all this indoors nonsense. They hauled you out of India to give you powers which you weren't keen on having and now they won't allow you to use them. I know that you would have resigned before, but for your staff; your desire to protect them has surely been carried far enough.[1]

I wish I could talk it over with you. You would be all right financially if you resigned, wouldn't you? Or would you be obliged to take another paid job? Is the expense of April's illness, which is bound to be considerable, a factor which has to be considered?[2]

I note your times this week in London. I am up for a night this Monday (the 21st) myself, and a second visit may be difficult, especially as my uncle who was on a visit here was taken ill suddenly and I had to take him off in an ambulance to Guildford Hospital.[3] Please let me know when next you come up to town. I am so upset by the affair. It would never have developed if there had been a proper attitude in high quarters.

It is odd but two or three days ago I was thinking of the Cave on Devi very vividly and longing to be in there for a moment away from all this welter of canniness and compromise. I don't remember the place particularly clearly, but you mentioned it to me, and no doubt that brought it back. I think that many other people have similar longings, and that what passes for religion over here does nothing to assuage them.

I keep well and so does my mother, though worried by my uncle's illness—He was here, by the way, when you stayed at Abinger Hatch Hotel, and surprised me by enquiring, with appreciation and solicitude, about Jimmy. I had forgotten entirely that you had met.

It is just possible I could get up to see you this coming week. Not likely, but it is worth your detailing your programme I think, if not too much bother to you.

I don't feel inclined to do that broadcast at present—or indeed any except the two I have contracted for. I must try and find that Cave on Devi first. I have an idea it doesn't really look like a cave at all.

                                        Your affectionate   Morgan

ALS: HRC

[1] The BBC had set up a new Hindustani Service, begun on 11 May 1940. The Viceroy, who selected Darling as its Editor, also selected as Sub-Editor Lionel Fielden (1896–1974), who joined the BBC in 1927. Relations between Darling, on the one hand, and, on the other, Fielden and his assistant Zulfikar Bokhari, broke down almost at once. Fielden, whom EMF had supported in his early days with All-India Radio, resigned in August 1941 and left the BBC in November; for his account of his Indian radio career, see his *The Natural Bent*, pp. 149–216. Darling resigned in December 1943. Bokhari remained until 1946, although on 2 August 1940 he had written a memorandum, 'Indian Programmes', addressed to the Editor of the Indian Section (i.e. Darling) and asking whether 'the whole question boils down to . . . whether the BBC can trust the Indian, whether it is myself, or anybody else' (BBC). EMF's sympathies appear here to remain with Darling, but on 7 August 1940 (HRC) he wrote to him: 'If I were Oglivie, I would sack you both and appoint an Indian . . . .'
[2] April Darling (1921–   ), Malcolm's daughter.
[3] This was EMF's uncle Philip Whichelo.

357 W. J. H. Sprott

Dorking and District Refugee Committee
20 September 1941

Dearest Jack

Have you read Gerald's Call to Prayer?[1] I would rather like you to so that I may hear what you say. Of course it only provokes snorts from the patriotic and squeals from the refined. I have just been writing to him, on this stolen paper, and have told him he has made me glad that I have never yielded to my praying-instinct, since nothing is so perilous as mis-prayer, and nothing so easy. I have been active myself too lately—i.e. spiritually active—at the much-too-much laughed at P.E.N. Club, which held its 17th International Congress last week, and people from about 30 nations were at it, so come. Wells quarrelled with Madariaga, Herr Neumann with M. Jules Romains (absent), the Czechs with the Norwegians, on the subject of Atlantic civilisation, the Poles with Mr Priestley because he mentioned Russia, Alfred Kerr with Erika Mann, the Americans with no one, and had no occasion to, for Mr Cordell Hull had reserved rooms for them at the Savoy. Rose Macaulay lost another MS., Nancy Cunard drank in the slips, Rebecca West as always knew best. I made two contacts in the PEN. sense—Hsiao Chien of whom I shall see more, and Arthur Koestler, more doubtful, but he was sympathetic and sensitive.[2] The air was so bright with the sharpening of private knives and the donning of local armour, that by the time I made my speech, on the New Disorder, books had been happily forgotten, and I caused a painful shock by referring to them.[3] I said that the only order in existence, except (query?) the mystic order, was the aesthetic order, and I hoped for a social and political mess which would be more favourable to creative writers than is the present mess. 'Art for Art's Sake?' shouted I, in loud scornful tones, so that all felt no doubt as to the answer. But the answer when it came was 'I should just think so.' I broadcast to India, too, I sit on platforms to commemorate Tagore.[4] Indeed, if this letter was preserved, it would prove that there was much intellectual activity in England at this supreme crisis. Written out of another selection of facts, it would prove that England was intellectually inert, or grovellingly sensual. What material we do bequeath to the historians!

At this point, I must go and, an England which quietly went on at its normal life, let the chickens out, but when I have done this I will address you further.

I do, and I am glad that in an England so morally lawless more should not have been stolen from you. How very mysterious, and how upset poor Charles must have been? I want news of him. I never sent a coat, because the coat I had thought off [sic] had disappeared, either on to Bone or on to a Boggart, no one was sure.[5] But now I fear he is in some sort of uniform. I want too to hear more about your agriculture. Did anything come of it? It sounded heavy and tantalizing going.

Here I have had another row with the Farrers, and this time they have got the best of it, owing to an initial mistake by myself.[6] [Sentence deleted. Eds.]

All is well here otherwise and your visit often spoken of with pleasure. And I am largely dressed in your presents and shaven by them. Is there—and please note the connection—any hope of your coming south again?

I knew Ketton-Cremer's brother—that is to say we spent an afternoon with him once—so felt I ought to write a line of sadness about him. But they are difficult, these lines.[7]

Florence Barger is still here, to our joy. This afternoon we call on those moderate applicants for the Dunmow Flitch, M^r & Mrs Pethick-Lawrence.[8] Tomorrow I have Civil Liberties, Aunt Rosalie, & wine, and Wednesday I may be going to stay with Desmond & Molly M[acCarthy].

M's love, dear Jack, and to Charles

ALS: KCC

[1] Gerald Heard, *The Creed of Christ: An Interpretation of the Lord's Prayer* (1941).
[2] Salvador de Madariaga (1886–1978), Spanish diplomat, publicist, and poet and literary critic; entered the League of Nations Secretariat in 1921; lived in exile in England, 1936–76, when he returned to Spain. Jules Romains (i.e. Louis-Henri-Jean Farigoule) (1885–1972), French novelist, poet, and dramatist, lived in the United States from 1940 until the end of the

war. Robert Neumann (1897–1975), novelist, Secretary to the Austrian P.E.N., was living in London; on 15 July 1941 he spoke at a P.E.N. luncheon where he described Austria as a 'modest country', skilled in the technique of 'living without security'. Alfred Kerr (1867–1948), German theatre critic and historian, known for his advocacy of freedom for theatres, emigrated to London in 1933, then returned to Germany after the war. Erika Mann (1905–69), daughter of Thomas Mann; author of children's books and essays, and editor of her father's letters; in 1935 a marriage to W. H. Auden made possible her emigration to the United States in 1936. Nancy Cunard (1896–1965), art collector, and proprietor of the Hours Press. Rebecca West (i.e. Cicely Isabel Fairfield [1892–1983]), novelist, critic, and documentary journalist, took her pen name from the heroine of Ibsen's *Rosmersholm*. Hsiao Ch'ien (1911–) was at King's College from 1942 to 1944, when he started a Chinese news agency in London. He left for Shanghai in March 1946; in 1980 he was reported alive and well. Arthur Koestler (1905–83), Hungarian-born journalist, novelist and foreign correspondent, author of anti-Communist works, was in the British Pioneer Corps, 1941–2.

³ Forster, 'The New Disorder', in *Horizon*, 4 (1941), 379–84; see also Kirkpatrick, p. 143.

⁴ Rabindranath Tagore died on 7 August 1941; see 'In Memory of Tagore', *The Times*, 1 October 1941, p. 7. Among the speakers were Edward J. Thompson and William Rothenstein.

⁵ Charles: Sprott's friend is Charles Lovett. Bone: the Forsters' gardener.

⁶ This was a second row over the field, with its diagonal path, which EMF rented from the Farrers.

⁷ Robert Wyndham Ketton-Cremer (1906–69), literary scholar and Norfolk historian, lived at Felbrigg, on the northern coast of Norfolk. His brother, Richard Thomas Ketton-Cremer (1909–41), who joined the RAF Volunteer Reserve, died during the German assault on Crete.

⁸ The Dunmow Flitch was a side of bacon given annually, in a tradition dating from the twelfth century, at Dunmow in Essex, to the couple who could swear that for the year past they never wished they had not married. Frederick William Pethick-Lawrence, 1st Baron Pethick-Lawrence of Peaslake (1871–1961), liberal newspaper published and ardent feminist, as was Lady Pethick-Lawrence, who died in 1954.

358   To Arthur Koestler

West Hackhurst, Abinger Hammer, Dorking
28 September 1941

Dear Mʳ Koestler,

I hope that you will have time to see me when you are next on leave: I can usually get up to London at a few days' notice.

I got an early read of Scum of the Earth, for Cape kindly sent me a copy.¹ It is strange to read, and to know all the time that one may soon have to face such conditions oneself—in my case without much courage, and certainly with no resourcefulness; but if they do come along I think this particular reading will help me. Your book fills up the gap between peace-mentality and war-mentality, which I find so dizzying to look into, and does suggest that we ~~are~~ remain the same people, and have the right to be discriminating in our judgements and gay in our spirits, if we can. It is the crushing of the human spirit *from within* which is so terrible; active participation by the individual in what the bureaux and the camps are doing from outside. I'd like to avoid that, and though I am a good deal older than you[,] hope that I may succeed in doing so.

I am glad to see the book is getting good notices, and hope it will sell well. I haven't read darkness at noon—shall do so this week.²

I wonder what one ought to think about Jules Romains.[3] I see he can't remain President, but don't like the idea of an anti-Vichy test in a literary organisation.—Here again, I haven't had to face Vichy-conditions yet.—

With all good wishes, and hoping for the pleasure of another meeting:

Yours sincerely
EMForster.

ALS: Estate of Arthur Koestler

[1] *Scum of the Earth* (1941), Koestler's account of his internment in France and escape to England in 1939.

[2] *Darkness at Noon* (1941), Koestler's novel about the arrest and interrogations of a Russian political prisoner. After reading it, EMF wrote to Koestler (9 December 1941): 'I liked Darkness at Noon—that is to say it duly gripped and held me. My only criticism is that the second interview—with Gletkin I think his name was—had too long a central section: the beginning and the end were all right.—Rubashov's Diary was the most damning indictment of Stalinism I have seen but I suppose an exaggeration, for the Russians couldn't have fought as they have if they had so little to fight for.' Rubashov's second interrogation is by Ivanov; the long, third interrogation by Gletkin.

[3] I.e., Romains as President of the International P.E.N. Club.

359   To Arthur Koestler

West Hackhurst, Abinger Hammer, Dorking
9 October 1941

Dear M[r] Koestler,

That is good news—I mean about your leave. It would have been nice to see you here, but it is rather out of the way, and perhaps town may be better. Let me know your exact dates when you know them. Or, to be exact myself, would you care to come to feed at the Reform Club, 104 Pall Mall S. W. 1. on Monday the 20th itself at 6.30. P. M.? I can easily manage other places and dates if this doesn't suit you.

I am pleased and touched that you should have been writing about my work. Generally speaking, I am ignored on "the Continent", and this has been a disapointment to me, the only serious disappointment in my literary career I think. Also what you say about the camouflaging of the cave is most interesting to me, and I don't think any one here has said it. It *might* be a new technique, but I am more inclined to ascribe it to our National Jokiness; the defect—for I think it is one—which causes our soldiers to be so humoursome in the trenches and dodge the Evil Moment with a grin.—Poor chaps, we'll[?] let them dodge even if "foreigners" do find them uncanny. But a writer isn't under equal compulsion.—I wonder whether you have studied English nonchalance systematically. I think there is much to be found out about it, and perhaps the next few months will help in its dissection. We ourselves have invested too heavily in it to be detached.

I hope that your hand is now better.

With all good wishes, and looking forward to seeing you:

Yours sincerely
EMForster.

ALS: Estate of Arthur Koestler

360   To Robert J. Buckingham

W[est] H[ackhurst].   18 January 1942

Dear Bob,

I can't see you now before Friday or Saturday, and think Saturday would be the better. Please let me know which. I shall only come for the day on Wednesday now. Tuesday Aunt Rosalie arrives, and Thursday is mother's birthday.

Have heard from Ted. He is not enjoying the snow but Shirley is. All seems well. I have told him how to find the Cooling Gallery, and sent him a catalogue.[1]

I wish we talked seriously more often, but probably it only comes when it has to come.

I liked what you said about "Blessed are the Meek."

Part of the trouble of finding out what Christ said meant is that the Gospels translate his words from the Aramaic he spoke into a poor and unusual Greek—e.g. in 'Give us this day our *daily* bread' the 'daily' is a word not found elsewhere, which entitles old Gerald to say it means the Eucharist.[2] The word for 'Meek' is quite common, it is true, and always in that sense of 'gentle, mild.' Still Christ *may*, in Aramaic, have blessed those who realise their own smallness in the universe, and promised them the inheritance of this particular spot in it as a reward. I hope he did, it would accord with what's best in the scientific spirit anyhow, and as for the Meek he does them quite well enough in some of the other Beatitudes.

Mother's cold is much better and Florence's a little so. I have been writing letters the whole morning.

Let me know as soon as possible whether Fri. or Sat.

Love
M.

Thought May might like the enclosed.[3]

ALS: May Buckingham

[1] Ted: Edward Buckingham, Bob's brother; Shirley (1936–   ), Edward's daughter. The Cooling Gallery, at 93 New Bond Street, held monthly exhibitions by artists engaged as firemen, air raid wardens, and the like. Bob exhibited a painting of ARP War Auxiliaries stationed at Chiswick House.

² Gerald Heard (*The Creed of Christ*, pp. 98–101) translates 'daily bread' as ' "bread of the coming day," it cannot apply to physical food.'
³ Not traced.

361   To Max Beerbohm

West Hackhurst, Abinger Hammer,
Dorking, Surrey [Early March (?) 1942]

Dear Sir Max Beerbohm,
I have perused with pleasure the account of Zuleika's alleged visit to Cambridge, but regret you should have lent credence to it. I told you *years and years ago* what happened to her, and you have never listened to me: she was shunted into a siding at Bletchley.¹
This letter, though an extremely important one, requires no reply. With every good wish to Lady Beerbohm and to yourself.

Yours sincerely
(Signed) E. M. Forster

TTr: Cecil Transcripts, Merton College Library

¹ The caricaturist, essayist, and broadcaster Sir Max Beerbohm (1872–1956) and his wife returned to England from their home in Italy during the war and settled at Abinger Common. Sir Sydney Castle Roberts (1887–1966), Secretary of Cambridge University Press, 1922–48, Master of Pembroke College, 1948–58, and Vice-Chancellor of the University, 1949–51, wrote *Zuleika in Cambridge* (1941). It is a sequel to Max's *Zuleika Dobson* (1911), in which a conjuress lures the Oxford men to watery deaths in the Isis. She has no similar success at Cambridge, whose men were apparently of sterner stuff. Max wrote to Roberts (4 October 1941): 'I had often wondered what happened when Zuleika went on to Cambridge. And now I *know*, beyond any shadow of a doubt. . . . Very often a jeu d'esprit flags in the middle, and crumbles all away at the end. Yours is good *all through*.' However, Max declined to allow Roberts to quote his comments in the body of the book: 'I should much prefer them to appear somewhere on the "jacket" of the book, nowhere else' (18 October 1941). (Both letters, Nan Hooper.)

362   To Max Beerbohm

West Hackhurst, Abinger Hammer,
Dorking, Surrey
12 March 1942

My dear Max Beerbohm,
Oh but 'wrong again' is not a scientific exclamation. To you, after a fortnight's reflection, I would rather say that, with every appearance of objectivity and with some slight inclination towards it, you have fallen into the symmetric fallacy nevertheless. You do not know what that is? You have read your Ruskin merely?¹ Very well. The symmetric fallacy is that which leads a person to be unable to conceive of Oxford without Cambridge, and to send Zuleika, at all costs, from one to the other. Ah! Life is not so balanced as that.

Look into your truer self, and I feel convinced that you will agree.

Yours [?]
(Signed) E. M. Forster

I was aware, being a student, of Maeterlinck's relict. But she left a little baby behind her, and Melisande of Bletchley would never have stooped to that.[2]

TTr: Cecil Transcripts, Merton College Library

[1] No doubt a reference to Ruskin's phrase, the 'pathetic fallacy'.

[2] In Maeterlinck's play *Pelléas et Mélisande* (1892), the dying Mélisande gives birth to a daughter.

363 To Robert J. Buckingham

9 A[rlington] P[ark]
M[ansions, Chiswick]
Sat. [20 February 1943]

Dear Bob,

I forgot to say yesterday that as next Tuesday is a Tuesday I shall have to catch the 12.45. from Waterloo to the soldiers.[1] So don't be too late.

I felt a bit sad at some of the things you said yesterday, not that you meant to make me sad, but you made me think of my limitations whereas generally you make me forget them. I believe that you are right—that particular experiences which I can't ever have *might* make the two people who share it feel that they are in touch with the universe through each other. What a pity all (normal) people don't get it. I started thinking after you left of Dr Marie Stopes. What a heap of good that woman must have done by spreading the technique of happiness. The world owes her more than it realise[s].

I have been washing up steadily, and have come to the conclusion that you are rather a reckless cooker as regards dirtying spoons. I did enjoy the food and the champagne (though not the red wine) and woke this morning without a headache for the first time for a week. Now I must see what awaits me at West Hackhurst. "Don't worry too much in advance" must be my motto, indeed it's the best motto for every one in this age of break-up.

I find myself awfully indifferent to my own death, but easily upset when people I love are threatened: I suppose most people, shits excepted, feel like this.

Love,
Morgan.

ALS: May Buckingham

[1] EMF gave weekly talks to soldiers, in a camp near Abinger.

364   To William Plomer

W[est] H[ackhurst]   21 March 1943

My dear William,

I could dine with you on Friday the 26th, or if that does not suit you, on Thursday the 25th. Your letter gave me pleasure and comfort. Most of the people whose opinion I respect like that pamphlet—with the exception of Koestler, who condemns it as a 'short cut': from what, across what, to what, I'm not clear. And I like it myself.[1]

I have been rereading the letters of my loved and lost Charles Mauron, and have been getting terribly sad, yet fortified against this England within whose suety walls we are all immured, and wherein we communicate dimly I think—except for the special occasions when we go to bed with one another, occasions which only arise for a few special people. Otherwise what a fortress of boredom and edification—lashed at by what a sea of blood! Charles is now drowning some where in that sea. He includes his wife, St Remy, and all Europe for me: "continental culture" as the newspaper articles used to call it. Now one is supposed either to say "French collapse—deplorable" or "France will rise again"—and I find both remarks nauseating and false.

This is connected, I don't see very clearly how, with your kind letter and ~~your~~ our faith in aristocracy. I have myself to face a world which is tragic without becoming tragic myself. That is *my* job. Charles' letters are full of oblique hints: "Méfiez vous mon cher Morgan, vous avez trop de respect pour les hommes et les relations humains [*sic*]: aimez les, s'il vous plait ainsi, mais ne les respectez pas—le respect est triste et pesant. Lisez un peu d'Aristophane chaque soir...."[2]

I had three days holiday with Hugh Waterston (Oundle) and Jack Sprott (Notts), and could have done with three weeks. H. drove me all over Northamptonshire, a county I have not visited: the valley of the Welland is charming. Here now is Surrey again and its Ladies: my mother—better—Dr Marie Stopes full of foolish beans,—a lady unknown with whom I had to take a three mile walk when we were both stranded by a bus, &ct. You on the other hand have been to Sussex, and on Ash Wednesday, so tells me Joe.

I do hope we shall meet this week.

Morgan.

ALS: Durham University

[1] See *Writers in Freedom: A Symposium based on the XVII International Congress of the P.E.N. Club*, ed. H[ermon] Ould (1941), EMF's speech (pp. 74–7) shared this topic with that of Hsiao Ch'ien, who thought his was 'irrelevant to the theme of the Congress' and was therefore not to be included in the Symposium. However, Ould included extracts (pp. 77–8) from a letter written a few days after the Congress.

365   To William Plomer

W[est] H[ackhurst]
Sunday [April 1943]

Dearest William,

Hope to be free to come to the Wednesday meal this week. Would you send me a line to the flat saying when and where, and I will turn up if I possibly can.

I got Ebenezer Jones out of the Library[.] The Naked Thinker is curious and the poem to Kate's Stomacher curiouser and curiouser.¹ There is certainly room for an anthology of people saying what they didn't mean to. Mʳˢ Hannah More and Mʳˢ Gaskell could both contribute to it. So perhaps could Mʳ A. J. Munby, whom I have at last run down ('Dorothy', 1880; 'Verses old and new', 1865; 'Vestigia retrorsum', 1891). He liked them rough, and I think my aunt said that he was a civil servant.²

We had a very good meeting of the Memoir Club last week. Virginia's, Lytton's, and Roger's rumps were brilliant [several words inked out and illegible], and made me realise how much is past and passing and how, for understandable reasons, no civilisation or attempt at civilisation has succeeded Bloomsbury, and how much of my own time I waste with second rate people to whom I haven't even any obligation to be kind.³ So fired was I by the papers, and so back-fired it may be by the success of your Double Lives, that I took up my own pen yesterday and started recording the whole business of the Farrers and this house.⁴ The start is exactly 100 years ago, when my aunt saw another little girl's gold hair; and here is a theme.⁵ I am writing as quickly as Trollope and as badly as Balzac, but the sensation is novel. Do not mention this to any one. I am not mentioning it to any one else.

Jack Sprott brought me news of Joe, whom I haven't succeeded in seeing. Shall be up Tuesday to Friday I think.

Will like to hear about Frank Herman.

With love from

Morgan

ALS: Durham University

¹ In Jones, *Studies of Sensation and Event: Poems*, 'The Naked Thinker', pp. 1–10; 'The Gem of Coquettes', which serenades 'Kate's stomacher', pp. 73–5. 'Curiouser and curiouser': Lewis Carroll's Alice, as she grows from very small to very tall.

² Arthur Joseph Munby (1828–1910), barrister and poet, and a founder of the Working Men's College, London; observer and champion of women servants and manual workers. He married a domestic worker, Hannah Culwick (1833–1909); on their unusual but happy

marriage, see Derek Hudson, *Munby: Man of Two Worlds* (1972). Munby's *Dorothy: A Country Story, in Elegaic Verse* was published anonymously (1880).

[3] EMF joined the Bloomsbury group's Memoir Club in 1920; see Virginia Woolf, *Diary*, II, 77. Twice he resigned or threatened to resign, once because two of the younger members of the Strachey clan were added without his being consulted, and once because the club was bored by his paper about his family (i.e. 'West Hackhurst').

[4] Plomer, *Double Lives: An Autobiography*, incorporated in his *Autobiography* (1975). EMF had begun to write 'West Hackhurst: A Surrey Ramble'.

[5] The gold-haired girl was Katherine Euphemia Wedgwood: see Letter 1.

366   To Christopher Isherwood

West Hackhurst, Abinger Hammer, Dorking
14 December 1943

Dearest Christopher

You do send me good things—Bill Roehrich, and now I get a delicious food parcel: most welcome butter, and other delicacies.[1] The dried bananas are new to me, and we shall have some for Christmas. You have sent me a letter also. But I will begin with Bill, who completely bears out your note about him, and speaks of you with affection such as goes straight to my heart. I have only seen him twice so far: we lunched and he took me to his show and Stephen took us to tea at the Ritz afterwards, and the next morning we went about to book shops. I like him immensely, we have written to each other since, and all being well shall meet in London. At present they are on tour, and as he will be in Birmingham for Christmas I have put him in touch with John Simpson. He has such good observation too; few people would have overheard one lady saying to another in the Ritz "We still manage to wash the cow all over every day."

I wonder if a p. c. reached you, or will reach you; it was signed by Bob, May, Leo, Tom, William, Joe and self in my flat, and took you our love. "If that door would only open and Christopher come in!" said Bob, but it was a good party otherwise, and the biggest I have ever given—Margery Wilson, John Simpson's idiot's sister was there too.[2] I had made an effort and asked Leo up for two nights from Dover, and he made a greater effort and accepted, and Joe invited Tom. Leo & Tom also managed to get over here to lunch with my mother. They were fairly well and very nice.

The friend I miss even more than you is Charles Mauron, for the reason that he is working out, in his blindness and the darkness of France, some connection between mysticism and aesthetics with the help of Chinese philosophy: I should be able to absorb this, I think, better than I could absorb the connection *you* are working out with the help of India, between mysticism and conduct.[3] (Heavens what a sentence! quite Geraldean in its elaboration and misleadingness.[4] It makes me say, incidentally, that I like Charles better than you, which I don't, and that I absorb connections, which I can't.)

Returning to you, thank you very much dear Christopher for the account you give of your ritual. That I do follow, for I know that the universe is a queer place and that ritual is a way and perhaps the best way of acknowledging this. What I don't follow is your belief that when you are in trouble, as you soon may be like all of us, God will help you. You may be right of course, but I can't imagine the belief. It is too far beyond my powers, and I can't connect it with ritual.[5]

I still dispose my time between here and London, and make new acquaintances still, mostly of foreign nationality. I keep pretty well—staler and older, but managing to blame both these defects on to the war. Bob looks older too. I shall get a Christmas meal off their goose I hope. Robin is learning to play chess. With love as ever from

Morgan.

ALS: Recipient

[1] Isherwood's letter of 27 July 1943 introducing the American actor William Roerick (1912–   ) is the recto of EMF's letter to R. J. Buckingham, postmarked November 1943 (Buckingham). Roerick was touring in Irving Berlin's 1942 hit musical, *This Is The Army*.
[2] This card, dated 20 October, was received. Margery Wilson (19??–67) was the daughter of Simpson's Birmingham friends.
[3] See Mauron, *L'Homme triple* (1947) and EMF's review. 'Charles Mauron and L'Homme Triple', *Adam International Review*, 17 (1947), 17–18.
[4] Geraldean: reminiscent of Gerald Heard.
[5] Isherwood in California was following the lead of Huxley and Heard in embracing Eastern religions, and Vedanta in particular, into which Isherwood was led by the California guru, Swami Prabhavananda; he describes this in *My Guru and His Disciple* (1980) and his ritual in his letter of 21 June [1943]; the context for EMF's comments on 'God helping' are in that letter and in letters of 27 November [1943] and 22 January [1944]. (Isherwood letters: KCC.)

367   To Christopher Isherwood

West Hackhurst, Abinger Hammer, Dorking
28 February 1944

Dearest Christopher

Yours of 22–1–44 has been with me some little time and merits an answer. Your previous letter of 27–?–43 took a much longer time to come. Which brings me to Mr Norris. I had not heard of his conversion to Catholicism, but Tony Hyndman, into whom I ran in a tube, said that he was violently anti-Semite. This, and other rumours, has caused me not to see Mr N., though I am false to myself in not doing so. I ought to examine his depths for myself, since I got amusement out of his shallows in the continental days. Occasionally, when I have been where perhaps I shouldn't, I have been conscious of him through the reek.[1]

Bill Roehrich has gone missed by many, and particularly by me, for he has gone out of his way to be serious and sweet. It is long since

I have felt so close to such a young person. I don't know how much the 'well known writer' in me is important to him. Legitimately important in so far as he has been trying to make me write. He got down here for an afternoon and all loved him, and the day before he left we spent ten hours together trailing about London and the Churchill Club and got so thoroughly worn out that we could only grin at one another and say so. I have written at his introduction to Tommy Ryan. The other boy, with whom Tommy was, is killed or missing. As for Martinez, I have been hoping to hear from him, for Paul Cadmus also told him to look me up.[2] But no one has any news of him, and perhaps he may not be in this country.

You will have read of the renewed raids. All whom you know are safe, so far as I know. Bob had his usual heroic gruesome time, and has been very grave since, and has changed....come nearer to your point of view over this and to mine. No further satisfaction in smashing civilians in Germany. We are all feeling pretty serious minded. My flat shook, and the windows and doors of his flew about. I hope America will never have anything as bad, and I hope Poland &[ct] hope that we shall never suffer as they have. It is a ladder of misery, in which each rung is tempted to keep to itself, ignore the rung below it, criticise the rung above.

Yes, I'm aware of something in myself at times which isn't myself, and which Stephen wanders toward in his poem.[3] I don't like to call it God nor do I think it wisely so called, for the reason that the word 'God' has kept such bad company and hypnotises its users in wrong directions. I even queried your saying that it was infinitely *greater* than oneself; *different*, yes, but one hasn't the apparatus for measuring size.

I returned from London the day before yesterday with one of my pleurisy threats, and since then have mostly been sitting, quite well really, in the drawing room with my mother, and getting muddled and fidgetty. And I'm not content with my remarks on God. When the weather improves, and I can be alone, I will write about him again. Do you like Blake? Do you give good marks to generosity, tenderness? In what set of values are we to believe if generosity and tenderness are to colour our conduct?

Yes, William's autobiography is splendid.[4] I have written a long thing for me (40,000 words or so) about this house, and it's amusing in parts, but dispirited and scrappy, and any how couldn't be published because it criticises the living. I wrote partly as a social document, partly to read to the Memoir Society.[5]

Much love and Bob will be sending his. He is altering deeply but you would like him. I wish he would paint or even read, but know by analogy that he can't go further than gadgetting.

Morgan.

Two lovely food parcels, let me repeat, reached me from you at Christmas.

ALS: Recipient

[1] Mr Norris: that is, Gerald Hamilton. On his conversion to Catholicism, see his *Mr. Norris and I*, pp. 28–9. Tony Hyndman: T. A. R. Hyndman, a friend of Stephen Spender. (Isherwood's letters: KCC.) The second letter is that of 27 November 1943.

[2] Tommy Ryan: a friend of Roerick. Martinez: José Martinez (Berlanga) (1917–   ), dancer and teacher of ballet, and a friend of their friend Lincoln Kirstein (1907–   ), the New York ballet impresario. Isherwood had met Kirstein in New York. Paul Cadmus (1904–   ): American painter and etcher; a fan-letter to EMF began their acquaintance.

[3] Probably Spender's 'Explorations', in his *Collected Poems*, pp. 139–42.

[4] Plomer, *Double Lives*.

[5] That is, 'West Hackhurst'. Later EMF wrote to Isherwood ([1 May 1944.] Recipient): 'I did finish the memoir, rather against the grain, and the result is wry and peeved.'

368   To Benjamin Britten

West Hackhurst, Abinger Hammer, Dorking
12 December 1944

Dear Benjamin (I consider Dear Mr Forster of the nature of an anti-brick, especially when I have been meaning to write to you for some time). I was so glad to hear from you. I wish I could write about Crabbe, but recent public news, culminating in Greece, has got me down, and all I feel able to do is to limp through existing commitments. I dare not undertake new ones. And anyhow I could not have got the article ready by the beginning of February, as Crozier wants, for I should have had to reopen myself to the subject, or it to me, and do much reading and re-reading. I am very sorry for this. I do like opera, and am looking forward to yours. Will you explain to Crozier and thank him for his letter very much. I had no idea that I had turned you to Crabbe.[1] I feel very happy about it. Did you know that I had written an introduction to his son's life of him?[2] This is more detailed than the radio talk and I could send you a copy if you like (In the World's Classics).

I was going to tell you that I had got those damned records at last. Thus was my letter to have begun. The records of the Michelangelo Sonnets, and I was wondering whether you could refer me to the edition you used, or, kinder still, could perhaps lend me a copy of the National Gallery programme if you had one.[3] I have lost mine. And the edition I have taken out of the London Library is a cultured whirlpool in which so far I have only found the Sun and the Moon revolving.

I am companionable privately, at least I think so, and should much like to see you again, as soon after Christmas as you can manage it. I should like to meet Montagu Slater, too.[4] I get up to London about once a week.

Eric Fletcher.

EMF in his rooms at King's, Cambridge.

I must knock off now. I have rather neglected Christopher lately, and have had a gentle reminder from his quaint brother Richard.[5] I hope that you keep well, also Peter Pears, to whom kindly remember me.

I have another London address in my book, but will alter it to this one. My own number when I am up is CHI[swick] 2407 (not in Directory), but when writing it is better to write here.

All good wishes.

Yours   Morgan Forster.

ALS: Britten Estate

[1] Britten had returned to England in April 1942, after three years spent in Canada and the United States, his return inspired, in part, by EMF's article, 'George Crabbe: The Poet and the Man', first broadcast on the BBC Overseas Service; see *The Listener*, 25 (1941), 769–70. Crabbe (1754–1832) was born at Aldeburgh, on the Suffolk coast not far from Lowestoft, Britten's birthplace. EMF's evocation of Crabbe's and Britten's native ground, and of Crabbe's 1810 poem, *The Borough*, was decisive in turning Britten to the poem as a source for his opera *Peter Grimes* (Op. 33, 1945). Eric Crozier, Britten's producer, wanted EMF to write something on Crabbe, for *Benjamin Britten: Peter Grimes, the Sadler's Wells Opera Book No. 3* (1945). Crozier (1914–   ) had been Play Producer for BBC television, 1936–9, and in 1944 was producing operas at Sadler's Wells. He was Britten's producer, 1945–51; co-founder with Britten of The English Opera Group, 1947, and of the Aldeburgh Festival 1948; and librettist for Britten's operas *Albert Herring* (1947), *The Little Sweep* in *Let's Make an Opera* (1949), and the cantata *St. Nicholas* (1948).

[2] See EMF's Introduction (pp. [vii]–xix) to *The Life of George Crabbe, by His Son* (1932).

[3] Britten, *Seven Sonnets of Michelangelo* (Op. 22, 1940), written for his friend and collaborator, the tenor Peter Pears (1910–   ); performed on 22 October 1942 at one of Myra Hess's National Gallery concerts; first recorded and released in 1942. The sonnets are set from the Italian text. For the programme translation by Elizabeth Mayer and Peter Pears, see *Benjamin Britten*, comp. Donald Mitchell and John Evans, Plate 161.

[4] (Charles) Montagu Slater (1902–56), novelist, librettist of *Peter Grimes*.

[5] Isherwood's younger brother, Richard Graham Isherwood (1911–   ). The war and distance had widened the gulf between Christopher and friends in England. EMF wrote to Britten (c. 1945. Britten Estate) that 'scarcely any of his former friends over here seem able to think of Christopher as a human being whom one has loved and therefore loves. They turn all niggling and pedantic—they can't ever have thought of him as "Christopher". I remember all this prim ungenerosity in the other war too, and am depressed at the ignorance and feebleness of the heart.'

369   To Robert Buckingham

W[est] H[ackhurst]
Tuesday [postmark 13 March 1945]

Dear Bob,

You may have gathered from the p. s. on my last envelope that mother is dead.[1] Peacefully, while I was spooning her some lunch on Sunday, and the famous death-rattle wasn't too bad. I said 'Can you hear me?' and she nodded. I think there was something deeper between us than I knew, for the shock is worse than I expected. I can't explain—or could explain all too well, being a writer—but it has to do with the greatness of love and one's own smallness. I have had that feeling sometimes—only happily—when with you.

Florence has been very kind, and now Aunt Rosie's here in her place. Tomorrow the funeral—Percy coming, the other's prevented.[2] I can't look forward beyond that. Let me know your plans. If Agnes can be left alone for a day, or night, I am free now.—She has been splendid, helpful, thoughtful, moved, yet never pretending that she and mother liked one another. Love to you, also to May and Robin. You must expect to find me a bit altered. Let us meet soon. Mother is in the coffin now—the village people we know brought it up. Willie King's going up to the churchyard tomorrow, the rector's doing a graveside service, since there's fortunately no church.[3] I am eating and sleeping very fairly well—had a tiring morning registering the death at Dorking. Office only open from 9.0 to 10.0.

Civil Liberties definitely off, so it is not impossible I may see you rowing on the 24th, let us hope in your glory.

M's love

ALS: May Buckingham

[1] She died on 11 March. Just a year earlier EMF and Bob Buckingham had confirmed a wartime pact. 'Things are so serious that I want to remind you that my promise holds. If you should be killed, I will look after May and Robin, and see Robin through his education. If it should be the other way about, and I get wiped out, there won't be much for you to do for me, since it is unlikely that my mother will outlive me many months. Still she may need some little practical help, and you will give this I know' (EMF to Buckingham, [March] 1944. Buckingham).
[2] His cousin Percy Whichelo; 'the other' is unidentified.
[3] Willie King, the local builder. The nearest church was at Abinger Hatch.

370   To Val Henry Gielgud

West Hackhurst, Abinger Hammer, Dorking
16 March 1945

Dear M[r] Gielgud,

Thank you for your letter of March 10th. An outsider cannot, of course, appreciate where responsibility lies, but I hope that my protest may ensure more consideration from your department for my fellow authors in the future.[1]

What puzzles me, though, is not the official slip-up but the aesthetic obtuseness. It seems so strange that educated people should handle a writer's work without constructively wanting to communicate with him, in case he could help them. Why did none of you *want* to do this?

Yours sincerely
EMForster

ALS: BBC Written Archives

¹ EMF had written (25 February 1945) to Howard Rose (1882–1978), BBC producer, to protest lack of notification of performance of an adaptation by Alec Macdonald of the story, 'The Eternal Moment', on 26 February. EMF first learned of it from the *Radio Times*. Rose replied (27 February) that no discourtesy was intended; the adapter had apparently failed to get in touch with EMF. Gielgud (1900–), BBC Dramatic Director since 1929, was thus Rose's superior. (Both letters: BBC.)

371   To William Plomer

W[est] H[ackhurst]
Sunday [15 April 1945]¹

Dearest William

Tuesday is Sitwell day, and I had hoped we might both be in attendance, but a distant crackle, as of summer lightning, warns me against pleurisy, and I may not be in London to that extent.² I should be disappointed if they had to excuse me. I have been reading Osbert's autobiography, and greatly envy his energy and his willingness to control the course of events, also admire his geniality and excellent values. What he does not see though, and what is tragic, is that people who *claim* to lead, automatically disqualify themselves from leadership as soon as they stray from the solid rut and become interested in intangibles. The techniques of the ballroom, hunting field, feudal estate won't work any more. You get Sir George dictating to painters. You get his children identifying criticism with disloyalty. They could have influenced so much deeper if they had imposed themselves less.³

I write in bed. Agnes waits on me. Tinka lies on the eiderdown with some fleas, but they are said to be the garden sort which hop back into his ears as soon as they tread strange surroundings.⁴ I shall get up soon. I forget when I last saw you—not since mother's death, I know. I have been tearing up endlessly. All the local channels of salvage have been blocked, and Bone now makes bonfires. The solicitors, as usual, are not starting off very speedily, and [it] is partly to see them that I want to come up Tuesday if I can.

Have now got up. Seem better. Have been tearing up hundreds of letters in which one woman writes to another about the ill health of a third. So, as man to man, I must apologise for having mentioned my own.

Love

M.

ALS: Durham University

¹ Date in Plomer's hand.
² Forster had probably been invited to one of Edith Sitwell's luncheon parties at the Sesame Club in London.
³ Sir Osbert Sitwell, 5th Baronet (1892–1969), elder son of the autocratic Sir George Reresby Sitwell, 4th Baronet (1860–1943); brother of Sir Sacheverell Sitwell, 6th Baronet (1897–   ) and of the highly baroque Dame Edith Sitwell (1887–1964), poet and critic. Osbert Sitwell's five-volume autobiography and family memoir is the chronicle of a vanished heritage. On Sir George and Sargent's famous portrait of the Sitwell family (1900), still owned by them; see *Left Hand, Right Hand*, I, 206–44.
⁴ Tinka: one of the two cats.

372   To Basil Wright

West Hackhurst, Abinger Hammer, Dorking
15 May 1945

Dear Mʳ Wright,

Many thanks for your sketch-map and helpful letter. I much enjoyed seeing the film, and meeting you and your colleagues. I don't much trust my own judgement over films—I am either hyper-sensitive or obtuse—but I felt sympathetic to the general idea, and admired the fine sensitive details.¹

My trouble (not shared by Miss [Rose] Macaulay) is that—quite contrary to the intention of the producers—the film comes out with a social slant and suggests that ~~the world~~ Britain ought to be kept right for this one class of baby and not got right for babies in general. True, Tim must be someone, and why shouldn't he be born in a rectory and have a lovely church baptism instead of being an industrialist baby at a registry office? But that does establish the slant, and I submit it hasn't been sufficiently corrected. Something could have been done, by shots of, or references to, other babies born in this country, so that he would have been more representative of them. More important this than reminding him he might have been born a Pole, &ᶜᵗ. He might have been (might also have been a Nazi—a painful possibility often forgotten when the fancy thus roams!), but he might equally have been born in a Liverpool slum, the heir to similar perils but to inferior opportunities.

My other objection rather marches with the above. The England he is introduced to is strenuous and enduring but (with one exception) never gloomy or cynical, and that is much too simple and smug a picture of wartime England. Any how it doesn't go with what I've seen and could endorse, though it goes with all the other films I've seen, and with most of what I've listened in to. The exception is the immensely important shot of the grumbling youth, but it went by too quickly, nor have I located it in your scenario. It reminded me of Macleish's 'Land of the Free'.² I have just been looking again through that sensitive and powerful work, and am sure that a dose of it wouldn't harm Tim.

I didn't like the Soviet Youth song at the end, and probably this will have to be scrapped for political reasons. Otherwise each item, as item, was delightful and moving. Please pass this letter on to Mr Slater if it should have been in fact addressed to him, and any way I should like to come round to the Ministry again and have a talk with him at his convenience.[3] I forgot to ask whether, if I did attempt the job, you wanted me to talk the commentary as well as to write it.

I liked Mr Jennings' speaking immensely, and don't really know why you call in any one else.

I am keeping the scenario, if I may, to show to Mrs Barger. It shall come back finally.

Thank you for a very interesting show.

Yours sincerely
EMForster

ALS: Recipient

[1] Basil Wright (1907–), producer and director of documentary films, in 1929 joined John Grierson (1898–1972) in Crown Film Unit, attached to the Ministry of Information. In 1945 EMF was shown the film, in a rough-edited state, of *A Diary for Timothy* (1944–5). He was asked to edit and refine it, and to write a commentary. This was eventually spoken by Michael Redgrave. The director was Harry Watt-Humphrey Jennings (1907–50), who had filmed *London Can Take It* (1940).
[2] Archibald MacLeish, *Land of the Free—USA* (1938), poem introducing a book of photographs of dispossessed Americans in the dust-bowl years.
[3] Montagu Slater was with the Ministry of Information during the war and worked closely with EMF on this film. See Letter 368, note 4.

373 To Robert J. Buckingham

as from W[est] H[ackhurst]
27 July 1945

It's YOU Bob, not the boat. When the boat is finished and put away you'll concentrate in the same way on something else, unless you decide to stop yourself. You have always cared more for things than people, and now this is rather running away with you, so much so that at present you do as little for other people as you can. My own faults lie in the opposite direction. I am too unselfish and soppy. So I suggest that from now onward we each try to occupy a more central position. This will do neither of us any harm.

Wednesday turns out to suit me if it is better for you—will you please drop a p.c. to West Hackhurst saying that this is O. K.—also confirming the time 6.0 was it? I will bring along food

I cut along to Foyle's and got the previous book in Robin's series for the sum of 9^d

Florence is probably coming tomorrow for the week end.

Looking forward to Wednesday.

Love,
Morgan.

ALS: May Buckingham

374   To William Plomer

(State Guest Ho[use]. Jaipur)
21 October 1945

Dearest William,

You will be pleased, as am I, that a letter from Bobby Lancaster has just arrived at the above address. It help[s] to put lunch with the Viceroy in its place, though that was pleasant too.[1] He (the non Viceroy) was reported to be practically illiterate, so here goes another mark for him, and for me too if you feel disposed. It doesn't look as if we shall meet, though there is a chance at Madras.

Everything goes satisfactorily, and I am well and happy. Two days of the conference are over, and, nearly dead with boom-quack sounds, I have asked to be excused from a moonlight party on the roof of a local metal magnate, and am actually alone. I have shaken hands with hundreds of people, and autographed the tinted notebooks of hundreds of students, all with charming faces when there was time to look up at them. There have been some fine speeches, but the Town Hall is huge and high, and the microphones disastrous—always too tall or too short for the Indians who approached them, and offering no help to such words as eequale or eckestacy. Joe's message was read with others, and I dare say heard. Richard Church's and Edith Sitwell's also. Sarojini Naidu is president, loveliest of toads and a really first rate speaker of the intimate casual type.[2] Great humanity and charm. Also on the platform are Nehru and Rad[h]akrishnan (Oxon) not getting on at all well, and Sir Ismail Mirza, Prime Minister of the State. He made a moving address—a lesson to our vulgar politicians by God—but I could not hear it, because that time I was on the platform too.[3] Now I plunge into the audience, pursued by my agitated body-guard, a colonel, and plumping between any two people, who protect me from him, at the same time opening their tinted books. Yes, I am a great success, and the Maharajah has shaken my hand. The trouble is of course that I don't *see* anything, don't get the Indian impressions I want. It's all so crowded and organised, and you drive 200 miles in the car of an Englishman, very kind, who never stops humming Schubert. Practically every one is in India who could be—Malcolm Darling, the Masood boys, Mulk from the Cow, and Ahmed Ali—the last two actually here, and due back at any moment from the metal[l]urgic roof.[4] There is heaps of food, and the subsistence level seems not to falter, even for the poor; great physical comfort except in the trains, and if they get too bad you seem to ring for an aeroplane.

Well I must stop this chatter. Keep it, as it may remind me, and I have no time to keep a diary properly. I write all about the Wavells

to Aunt Rosalie, who would love it if you asked to see the letter.
Hope all is well dear William. No letters from England so far.

Morgan's love

ALS: Durham University

¹ Bobby Lancaster was a young soldier friend of Plomer. Lord Wavell (1883–1950) was
Viceroy, 1943–7.
² EMF set out on 5 October 1945 for the All-India P.E.N. Conference in Jaipur; see *HD*,
pp. 241–81. Richard Church (1893–1972), English poet. Sarojini Naidu (1879–1949), poet and
stateswoman, born in Hyderabad, educated in London, then married to the head of the
Nizam's medical service. She turned to social reform and the feminist movement; joined the
liberal Congress wing and in 1925 was the first woman to preside at a Congress session;
imprisoned as a Gandhian; in 1947, became Governor of the United Provinces.
³ Sarpevalli Radhakrishnan (1888–1975), scholar, statesman, and philosopher; President of
India, 1962–7. Sir Ismail Mirza (1883–1959), of Persian descent, was born and educated in
Bangalore; became dewan to the Maharaja of Mysore in 1926 and was Prime Minister of
Jaipur, 1942–6. He was a far-sighted town planner, an early advocate of socialism as a solution
for a poor country, and of Hindu-Muslim communal accommodation. The report of the
conference, *All-India Writers' Conference, Proceedings, 1945*, refers to EMF's speech as
'Literature Between Two Wars' (pp. 206–7) but does not provide its text. In pamphlet form it
was called *The Development of English Prose between 1918 and 1939*; see Kirkpatrick, pp.
62–3.
⁴ Mulk Raj Anand (1905–   ), Indian English-language novelist. Ahmed Ali (1910–   ),
novelist, author of *Twilight in Delhi* (1940), now a resident of Karachi.

375   To Robert J. Buckingham

Lalgarh Palace, Bikanir [*sic*], Rajputana
24 October 1945

Dear Bob

The Maharajah's guests, we sit in the red sandstone court of his
modern palace, looking over the marble pavements. No one is in
sight except a man with sort of mop in the shape of a ball attached to
a long piece of string. Every now and then he throws it at the
architecture in the hope of disturbing a pigeon and persuading it to
perch and shit elsewhere. Pigeons are sacred. Not so other animals,
and the walls of the huge apartments sprout every kind of head,
complete stuffed leopards glare round the billiard table, crocodiles
crawl, animals destroy each other in bronze groups down the
corridors, and if you manage to open a book (it is extremely heavy
and takes two to pull it from its morocco case) you will find it
contains photographs of Kills.

We got here yesterday from Jaipur—the guests of the Prime
Minister we thought: I knew him slightly in England years back. But
when we arrived we were elevated to the Palace. It is extremely interesting and we see a good deal of His Highness, who is one of the leading Indian Princes, frank and easy to talk to, and good to his people
in a patriarchical way, I should think. Our tea-picnic yesterday was
interrupted by a dirty man, who wailed before us and finally pulled
his turban off, and produced a petition from it like a conjurer.

Last night we dined in the courtyard, about eleven of us at a round table. Very informal and delicious food. I got off with the Catholic Archbishop of Ajmere, who is here to visit his flock. We chattered French and seemed delighted with each other, but I did not mention the more dubious authors, such as Gide.[1] In the midst of the banquet the electric light failed for an instant, and a great square of stars showed over our heads. Between them and us, round the top of the building, runs a covered passage through whose lattices ladies were probably looking—there is even one commanding the interior of my bedroom, it is not for me to wonder why.—Said room is as large as 137, and you could probably throw in Mr Locke and Phyllis too.[2] Behind it are bath-room, dressing room, W. C., all stretching up equally to heaven. Rather dark, no soap, and either airless or else you are whirled round like a leaf by the electric fans. And the noble mirror is in a different apartment from the honourable washstand, which means a good deal of exercise while shaving.—I mention these trifles not out of complaint, but because they fit in with the life of Royalty as I have always imagined it.

Ould has recovered from the colitis which kept him in a Delhi hospital for several days. My own inside, though not perfect, is adequate. I am a bit over tired and over full with food, but who in England would not envy the latter complaint? I am afraid things are getting pretty awful. I have had no letters from any one so far, but expect them on my return to Delhi. I am a bit homesick for 'our' flat: and I think a good deal of my mother. I lunched with the Viceroy while in Delhi, and thought how proud she would have been. It was a very pleasant function. I have written all about it to Aunt Rosalie.

Well Bob darling I must not forget to tell you (i) that the Jaipur conference was a thundering success, several hundred people attending, speeches of a high order, and Indians from remote parts of the peninsula meeting for the first time and getting on (ii) Nice affectionate letter from Anwar [Masood], and I hope to see him soon. Much has happened. They are now 'in' with their mother, and have married cousins on her side. Amtul is reported to have married again, and to be well, as is her little daughter.[3] (iii) I am seeing a lot of Ahmed Ali (iv) I shall be stopping in Calcutta with Hashim.—I must end up now with much love to May and Robin. Paper at an end and we are driving out (I hope) to see some ancient monuments. The penalty of greatness is powerlessness, and I am seldom able to see or do what I want. It is quite impossible for any one 'high up' to get to grips with the realities of India. Still I have managed to see one or two things that will keep me thinking.—Love.—Morgan.

PLEASE Keep my LETTERS

ALS: May Buckingham

[1] This was Leandro Guide Le Floch (1866–1946), Bishop of Ajmere, 1939–46.
[2] 137: the Buckinghams' address, 137 Hartswood Road, Shepherd's Bush, London W12.
[3] Amtul: formerly Masood's second wife.

376   To Robert Trevelyan

Ajanta.   26 November 1945

Dear Bob—I am not actually at the above, but recently have been, and often thought of you and Goldie. It was my third try—very successful and grand. You came from Jalgaon, I suppose. I came from the other direction—Aurangabad. There is a new road down the Ghat, with magnificent views, and a branch to the entrance of the ravine where the caves are. I stayed two nights in Guest House, four miles off in the plain, and spent a whole day in the Caves with the charming little Curator. Unfortunately he kept the best till the last, for purposes of light, and I was a bit hurried and tired over Caves 1 and 2, the best of the set don't you think. The paintings are an eye opener—the fusion of seriousness with delight in the outside world (including its minor pleasures) is so close, and so comforting[.] So few battle scenes, so little sense of sin—though of course both of them had to be there a little. The curse today is that they are here so much. I wonder whether Yazdani's volumes on Caves 1 and 2 are in the L[ondon] L[ibrary]. The reproductions are much better than Lady Herringham's. The big Boddisatva comes out well.[1]

I have been meaning to write to Bessie. Please show her this letter and give her much love. Aunt Rosalie has told me of her affectionate enquiries, and I believe Bessie has seen my letters to her. I have been much on the move, and one change I notice in India, since my previous visit 25 years ago, is that I am older. But I am enjoying it very much, and except at Calcutta have felt well. Oh, but that reminds me. *Suhrawardy*.[2] I had bad luck. He was at Darjeeling until the last day of my visit and we only had a talk in the midst of a 'buffet dinner'. I liked him very much. I would have stayed on to see more of him but one has to book one's reserved bunk on the railways many days beforehand, and it is impossible to have pliant plans. Chanda I saw much more of. He seemed rather inclined to score off other Indians, and I did not care for him as much as for S., but he was very pleasant and amusing. Both send many messages to you both. C.'s less ebullient brother is Principal of Santiniketan, and we went over for a night to that Shrine. It was less shriney than I expected, indeed there were some sensible remarks about the Passed Master.[3] Much kindness, and my two companions (Muslims) were moved, as was I.[4] I am afraid that the place does not cut much ice now, except as through the elderly and the theosophic. The educational side of it is too casual.

What a dreadful place Calcutta is, and how glad I was after a lonely and adventurous journey of two days to arrive at Hyderabad and find no less than 5 old friends (with their 4 new sons) on the platform to meet me.[5] All was instantly luxury and health. Exhilerating [sic] climate, city much improved, and now one of the nicest in India. Bombay is improved too—and I actually write from Bombay. It is indeed delightful, a sort of Alexandria set in Plymouth Sound. I wonder where it was that we three landed in that boat, rowed by the more unsuccessful Apostles, 33 years ago. Do you remember our landing?[6] The drawback now, as then, is the climate. But I am staying on Malabar Hill, in the house of Madame Wadia who runs the Indian P.E.N. and is the real angel of our visit, and I am very comfortable.[7] Poor Ould has had wretched luck: two bouts in a Delhi Hospital, and much the invalid. He is now with a journalist, correcting an article for the Bombay Chronicle. I expect I shall have to be interviewed when they are done.[8]

As for my return (Bob and Bessie), we have asked for air-passage round about Christmas, but don't know what we shall get. I should be glad to avoid Christmas at home, don't think I should really help poor Agnes by my presence.

Have been interrupted by the journalist. Will conclude with love, and hopes that all is well

Morgan

ALS: TCC

[1] In 1912–13 EMF missed the Ajanta Caves in Hyderabad State, and again in 1921–2 because of a sprained elbow. Ajanta's Buddhist frescoes and sculpture were neglected from at least the twelfth century until 1818, when officers of the Madras Army happened upon them. Efforts to copy the fading frescoes began in 1849 and still continue; the Caves are now a tourist attraction protected by the Government of India. Ghulam Yazdani, Director of Archaeology for the Nizam of Hyderabad, prepared *Ajanta: The Colour and Monochrome Reproductions . . . Based on Photographs* (1930–55). Lady Christiana Herringham (1853–1929) first visited the caves in the winter of 1906–7; she returned in 1909–10 and 1910–11 with assistants, to produce a set of copies published as *Ajanta Frescoes* (1915). 'Big Boddisatva': in Cave I. EMF noted in his travel-journal (23 November 1945. *HD*, p. 268) that 'the paintings have fused sadness with interest in the outer world, and have helped me towards doing the same'.

[2] Hassan Shahid Suhrawardy (1893–1963), from a distinguished Bengali Muslim family, became Rani Bageswari Professor of Fine Arts at Calcutta University in 1945. He was prominent in the Muslim League and the government of pre-1947 Bengal. As an Oxford student, he became friendly with Bridges and with Trevelyan, who wrote an affectionate poem, 'To Shahid Suhrawardy' (*Collected Works*, I, 288–9). About 1916 Suhrawardy went to Russia but fled after the March Revolution of 1917 and wandered about Europe for some years before returning to India.

[3] Anil Kumar Chanda (1906–76) had been Tagore's secretary and in 1945 was Principal of Visva-Bharati University at Santiniketan. His brother Apurba K. Chanda (1892–1967) was Principal of Presidency College, Calcutta. They entertained EMF together at Santiniketan. 'Passed Master': Tagore.

[4] Probably the novelist, Ahmed Ali, and Masood's relation, Hashim Ali, who was related also to Ahmed Ali.

[5] Among them the Mirza brothers, Abu Saeed, Sajjad, and Ahmed.

[6] EMF, Trevelyan, and Dickinson landed at Bombay on 26 October 1912.

[7] Mrs Sophia Wadia (1901–   ) organised the All-India P.E.N. Centre in Bombay, founded and edited *The Indian P.E.N.*, and presided at the Jaipur Writers' Conference.

[8] Hermon Ould, who travelled with EMF, fell ill immediately upon arriving in India.

377   To William Plomer

W[est] H[ackhurst]   3 July 1946

Dearest William.—Kindly sidetracked by you a little perhaps, Joe certainly did put out a much too favourable report. I am so very sorry. I wonder whether Bob has seen you yet. I shall not be up till next week I am afraid. Then I shall ring to see whether a visit is possible. Aunt Rosie has just arrived. She is much distressed, so is Agnes.   I have been working, if that is the word, for two days getting ready for the Jumble Sale. It takes place in the School tomorrow evening, I don't know what in aid of. The Farrers are also having one at Abinger Hall, but my jumble sale will come first. Boxes have been prised open, to see whether they should go, and one of them is full of gold and jewels, including a locket, studded with pearls in the form of a cross and disclosing two unknown people inside who have been facing one another in the darkness all this time, the man concave, mutton chop whiskers, his wife convex.   Have just been reading an article on me by a Russell's Viper called Ranjee G. Shahani. I received him into my bosom at someone's Edward Thompson's request back in Brunswick Square, to coach him in English and Shakespeare. I corresponded with him and tried to meet his wants, I recommended him for a Civil Grant, he got it, I presided at his v. poor lecture before the East India Society, I recommended him for a second Civil Grant, but less enthusiastically, for he had got nowhere achieved nothing in all these years, and he was annoyed at my tepidity, didn't I think get the grant, and, years passing again, has published this article called *"Englishmen whom we admire."*[1] It is better than anything else he has done, starts in a tone of perplexity, doesn't like to hurt the feelings of a person so sensitive and kind, but the truth is the truth, and I am a most disappointing writer, also no one seems to know anything about me, I am feebly satirical, "Miss Forster", and drink nothing but tea. Katherine Mansfield could not endure my work, Virginia Woolf tried to through feelings of friendliness but the truth was again the truth, T. E. Lawrence had to recant, André Maurois placed me between Flaubert and Ibsen (!), I have many detractors, but the Englishman whom he admires may yet write an excellent novel, hopes Ranjee G. Shahani.—Article sent me in proof by Sir Frank Brown, to persuade me to lecture to the East Indian Society in my turn.[2] There is one o'clock striking, it happens night after night, and I had meant to say how nice I think John Arlott is.[3] I rather hate doing literature with him, and would like to have met him in surroundings where books came in as a surprise. I gave him your address, and hope that to do so was cricket.

Tomorrow has come, and I reflected, during a rather short night, how very tiresome it was for Kilvert and others concerned that you were unable to attend his celebrations. I know that you are sorry too, and that to have heard the Bp's sermon would have been much.[4]

It strikes me that I almost know where Amblecote is but not quite, and that sooner than hunt amongst paper pyramids for the precise address, I will send this to 29.   Best love from Morgan, and deep sympathy with so much vexation and pain.

ALS: Durham University

[1] Ranjee Gudarsing Shahani (1904–68), writer on East-West literary and cultural relations, known principally for his *Shakespeare Through Eastern Eyes* (1932). His article is fifth of ten, on 'Some British I Admire', *Asiatic Review*, n. s. 42 (1946), 270–3. Shahani's admirations, extremely eclectic, include also Disraeli, Gladstone, and T. S. Eliot, among others.

[2] EMF summarises Shahani here more accurately than Shahani documents *his* sources; the only one cited specifically is unverifiable in print, a 1929 conversation with André Maurois, who 'gave pride of place to Mr. Forster among the English novelists of the time, but added: "He is a cross between Flaubert and Ibsen!"' For the others, compare *The Letters of T. E. Lawrence*, ed. David Garnett, pp. 466, 467, 531; *The Journal of Katherine Mansfield*, ed. John Middleton Murry, pp. 120–1; Virginia Woolf, 'The Novels of E. M. Forster'. "Miss Forster" is Shahani's *mot*: 'Often a fancy strikes us that when it suits him Mr. Forster can become, just by mumbling a mystic formula, Miss Forster.' Shahani may have thought that he was evening an old score. EMF wrote to Edward Garnett (17 December 1928. Northwestern University) that he had done his best to get Shahani into Cambridge—hence the 'free coaching for his thesis'—but the University had turned him down.

[3] John Arlott (1914–   ), general writer for the *Manchester Guardian*, BBC producer, noted cricket commentator and authority on wines. See his 'Forster and Broadcasting', in *Aspects of E. M. Forster*, ed. Oliver Stallybrass, pp. 87–92.

[4] Plomer edited *Kilvert's Diary: Selections from the Diary of the Rev. Francis Kilvert* (1938–40). Kilvert (1840–79) was Curate of Clyro, Radnorshire; on the diaries and the Kilvert Society, founded in 1948, see Plomer, *Autobiography*, pp. 364–73. On 5 July 1946 there was a commemorative service for Kilvert, in his church, St Michael's at Clyro, with an address by the Rt. Rev. Edward William Williamson (1892–1953), Bishop of Swansea and Brecon.

378   To John Hampson Simpson

W[est] H[ackhurst].   4 October 1946

Dear John,

I didn't notice how ill you looked. Others did, so to them this wretched news will come as less of a surprise. I am certain you do want a rest. This letter, besides sympathy, asks you to accept the enclosed, and to use it at the worst on Doctors, Pissing Nursey [?] Homes, &[ct], but if things go better on better things.

Have been meaning to write to you before, but have been terribly driven—2 or 3 days a week at the H. ov L. [House of Lords], which keeps me from brooding too much on myself. There ~~was~~ is ~~one~~ some nice news though—the village party to me was wonderful, we all danced and played games and I was given a lovely little book with over 100 names in it. Bob has been kind. I am (today) back from a night at Cambridge, slept in my new rooms, and if I am to live that sort of life things couldn't be nicer, the delicacy and generosity of the young Wilkinsons touched me a lot, also there is a meditative garden which will ease me of my most poignant loss.[1]—Also visited Rooksnest (Howards End).

27 letters await me, so 'no more just now' as Aunt Rosalie says, which reminds me that I took her and Bone and a lot of stuff in a car to the flat

My future or rather final time table:

Oct 24th—move to Cambridge & return to W. H.

Oct 28th—sale in Dorking

Oct 30th—Agnes ~~goes~~ moves to Barnet

Nov. 1st Jumble Sale in house.

William [Plomer] and his Charles [Erdman] came here last week. Bob comes for a night on Sunday.

Morgan's love.

Mrs Barger back in good form from the New World, and excited at my selling her house for her. She will be here (if necessary) during the last days here.

[1] Lancelot Patrick Wilkinson (1907–   ), Fellow of King's and university lecturer in classics, and his wife Sydney, had offered him a bed-sitting-room in their house.

THE FINAL YEARS,
1947–70

During 1946 King's College bestowed an honorary fellowship on Forster, and, it becoming known that he was to be homeless, the governing body took the unusual step of offering him a room in college, and the Wilkinsons also offered accommodation. He accepted and moved to Cambridge in November 1946, regarding it as a temporary arrangement. In fact he remained there for the rest of his life.

Five months after this move he made his first visit to America, invited to take part in a Symposium on Music Criticism at Harvard University. It was an opportunity to visit various American friends, including Bill Roerick and Tom Coley, with whom he stayed on their Massachusetts farm, and, after delivering his Harvard address, he embarked on an extensive sight-seeing tour that included the Grand Canyon, California, Chicago, and Niagara Falls.

Life in King's, after a little while, began to suit him very well, and his next few years were unusually productive. In 1951 he published *Two Cheers for Democracy*; in 1953 an Indian memoir, *The Hill of Devi*; and in 1956 *Marianne Thornton*, the biography of his great-aunt and benefactor. To his excitement, Benjamin Britten invited him to collaborate on an opera and, in collaboration with Eric Crozier, he produced the libretto for *Billy Budd*, based on Herman Melville's tale and first performed in December 1951.

He was by now very famous, and, in his Cambridge rooms (furnished in close resemblance to the drawing-room at West Hackhurst) he was visited by many admirers. He also acquired a considerable circle of undergraduate friends. In November 1960 he appeared as one of the leading witnesses in the *Lady Chatterley* trial. The Queen made him a Companion of Honour in 1953 and awarded him the Order of Merit in 1969.

Bob Buckingham reached police retirement age in 1951 and began a new career as a probation officer. It entailed his moving to Coventry, and as Forster's health declined (in 1961 he had the first of a succession of mild heart attacks), the Buckinghams' house there became more and more a second home. There he was taken after suffering a stroke in his college rooms in his ninety-second year, and there he died, very serenely, four days later.

379   To J. R. Ackerley

c/o Harcourt Brace
383 Madison Avenue, New York City
31 May 1947

D. M. J. Let us try a muddled line on our knee—one of those travelogue lines I am afraid, all about what has just been passed. Noel's warm greetings. I parted with him yesterday afternoon, after a nine days' visit—should have liked to stay longer, but Marietta was feverously studying for her Doctorate in Zoology. Noel was also studying hard—Russian—but always willing to stop and do something else hard instead, such as driving me 200 miles, walking to the middle of the Golden Gate Bridge, or entertaining a bunch of professors. I always liked him but had no idea he was so considerate and so recklessly generous. A happy marriage may have helped. He has picked a very nice girl I should say.[1]

Our other recent link is Gerald and Christopher W. whose long distance voices asked after you on the phone.[2] Christopher I. is in New York and I should be seeing him some when I get back there ~~next week~~.[3] I am on my way from San Francisco to Chicago on the "Feather River Route". It passes the Feather River in the dark, and the view from the window is the Californian desert, mistaken by me for the Nevadan. We have been travelling through Cal. for 6 hours. I have had breakfast with a negro sergeant major from Japan, and have listened to the negro Pullman attendant ticking off a white G. I. for washing in too smart a lavatory. "Gee I'm surprised at you fellows." The G. I. hung his spotty head.

I enjoy the charm and friendliness of America. What a contrast to malnourished disgruntled England! One is never snubbed, and sometimes the contrary. I sat for half-an-hour in Arizona on a wall which a Mexican was cementing for his mother, and a correspondence has resulted. Do you remember a Canadian airman I contacted.[4] Very nice letter from him too, and I am nerving myself to dash from Chicago to see him and the Niagara Falls. I have only just found out that they are close together. At Chicago I am lecturing or rather reading aloud from my work.[5] No trouble and seems to satisfy people. Then to New York, which I meant to reach on June 1ˢᵗ but shall be a fortnight late. Paul Cadmus has lent me his flat. It is in deepest Greenwich village. Very sympathetic.

We seem to have reached Nevada after all, but the oranges cherries apricots and bananas with which Noel loaded me have not been taken away. Each state is afraid of infection from the neighbouring state, and sometimes exacts vegetable holocausts at the boundary.—Have repaired to the Observation Car for ink, and it will not function in my Presentation Parker 51 Pen, and my Parker 51 ink is checked in my grip for Chicago. Such is civilisation and its occasionalities here, and now dear Joe I should be glad to hear from you. Bob and Jack have been my only correspondents—oh and Cousin Percy, who has been 'behaving', and reports favourably of Rosie [Alford].—Look her up if ever you feel inspired.[6] 13 Dungarvan Avenue. Give my love to William [Plomer] and John Morris.[7] Much to yourself and I hope you are snatching a little sunshine. I meant to return July 10th, but may be obliged to extend my permit and come a bit later.

We are travelling across a flat unlimitless plain.

M's best love. Address as on envelope.

ALS: HRC

[1] EMF left for the United States on 10 May 1947, to address a Harvard University Symposium on Music, and to see American friends. His paper was 'On Criticism in the Arts, Especially Music', published and broadcast under various titles: see Kirkpatrick, p. 146. Noel Voge was a wartime acquaintance who had stopped by the Thames to chat with Bob Buckingham, who was repairing a boat. Voge expressed admiration for EMF's work, and Bob arranged an introduction. Noel Voge (1912–) was writing a dissertation on Slavic morphology, at the University of California at Berkeley; Marietta Voge (1918–84?), joined the faculty of the School of Medicine at the University of California at Los Angeles, a specialist in tropical diseases. D.M.J.: Dear My Joe.

[2] Gerald Heard and his friend Christopher Wood (1900–76), who had settled at Laguna, near Hollywood.

[3] I.e., Christopher Isherwood.

[4] This was Johnny Kennedy (19??–1956), a wartime acquaintance. EMF's journal (KCC) for 7 June 1947 describes Kennedy's home scene, in Thorold, Ontario.

[5] He read from his works at the University of Chicago.

[6] Perhaps an allusion to the quarrels at West Hackhurst when EMF's cousin Percy Whichelo and his wife stayed there during the war.

[7] See Letter 400.

380   To Robert J. Buckingham

The Quadrangle Club, Chicago
5 June 1947

Dear Bob,

Your letter of May 8th with razor stuff has only just reached me. What a difference between ordinary mail and air! I am glad to have them, though the cut-throat is still in fair condition. I feel quite proud of myself and even of you. You never give me any news—did you get the boat out? I am afraid things are pretty beastly for all, and now comes this absurd heat-wave on the top of the cold. Thank you for seeing to the picture—£2.10.0 won't be too much if the job's successful. Send the second picture if you are satisfied with the result, and the flat will be full of gleaming limbs. You will want extra money, since you have kindly paid the taxes, and I enclose cheque (Any how do please pay the taxes if you haven't—you said you were going to).[1]

I will let you know when I arrive as soon as I can. Please, what are the dates of your holiday? Answer this, as my mother used to say. I miss you badly.

Forget what I wrote last, but am sure it was recently. I loved my time with Noel [Voge]—he is grand, and my goodness what generosity and indifference to conventions! You made a good pick that afternoon. We visited his elder brother, a chemist, who is more thoughtful, and noble and disinterested. They had an awful time over the funeral of their mother, who is an atheist, and wanted her ashes scattered into the Pacific. A horrid account of the vested interests which compel you to buy an expensive coffin, and an expensive urn, and then try to take the urn away from you. Is it like that in England? Noel's mother must have been wonderful. As we drove through a little town he would say "Mother went into the canning factory here, time she was broke." I said "What did *you* do?"—for his age was then 9. "Oh the four of us were all right with my sister to look to us—she was 13. Mother put us in a room and came back in the evening." At other times she kept school in remote places with her children as pupils. He thinks she kept on living in order to see him come back from the war. I don't think her death has cut him up much. In characters of his type there is a sort of hardness, mixed up with the unselfishness and affectionateness.

I am just doing, in friendship's name, a slightly risky thing: going into Canada for two days to stay with Johnny Kennedy the Canadian air force chap, who lives close to the Niagara Falls. He is so anxious I should come. People think I will get back into the States all right, but I can't get a guarantee of reentry, and may have delay and expense. Don't be too surprised if I arrive in England by steerage from Halifax.

I had a lovely journey here from the west via Western Pacific—Noel's advice. It is the only railway which goes *through* the Rockies—we seemed to be going through them for 16 hours, and the final descent down their eastern precipice onto the Great Plains was really a gasper. I stopped one night in Salt Lake City, saw the Temple, Tabernacle, &^{ct}, all hideously plain but interesting. You will think me quite a tough traveller, but everything is so easy here, really less bother than getting from Cambridge to London, also I *can* do things for myself when there is no one to do them for me, but others shall do them for me whenever possible.

I leave little time to describe Chicago. I did my stuff here last night, to an enormous audience, and was well heard, thanks to a good mike. One is so at their mercy. My most amusing conquest is over a prominent business man connected with the University who gave a small dinner in my honour and called out "We like you. We like your work. How can we interest you to stay? How do you know so much about human beings—about M^r & Mrs Abbey's difficulties?"[2] I wish I knew a fraction of what you know. How do you do it?" The English department, whom he usually ignores, is delighted at this homage to literature, and assures me that I could stay on at my own price as an adviser on character—i.e. this bloke (who is very naive and charming but very far from a fool) would consult me when any one came along of whose intentions he was doubtful. It is a genuine effort on his part to utilise, in the interests of the University, what he takes to be a Divine Spark.

Talking of that sort of thing, let me tell you that I have refused $25000 from Fox Films for the movie rights of a Room with a View. Stimulated by my refusal, they offer more, and wanted to fly to Noel's in a Plane. Any doubts I might have had, were resolved by reading Christopher's Prater Violet.[3] Nothing would have survived of the original except my name, and if I had tried to control the production I should have broken my heart at Hollywood, besides spending my life there.—By the way, English Films have an enormous boost in this country—all the young intellectuals talk about them as we do about the French. Huge excitement over Great Expectations.[4]

Still I don't mention Chicago. The University, where I am, has flown ten miles out with a shriek, and well it may, for the insecurity of life and property in the city is all that our newspapers tell us. Even here, the door of Professor Brown's flat has *five locks*. It is fantastic.[5] In Berkeley, the houses were left unlocked night and day. What a country of contrasts! The trouble here is the corrupt municipality and police.

I am getting some generalisations about America, which no doubt I shall forget. One is, the poorness in quality in the Civil Servants (except in the State Dept.=ls Foreign Office). The country is partly opposed to controls and rationing because it mistrusts the officials who would operate them.

Well I hope you are satisfied by now, Bob, at having a writer for a friend, and that, although a policeman, you will now take up a pen yourself. Just heard from Aunt Rosalie. Things don't go on too badly. All being well, I reach New York on the 9th, where Cadmus' flat is all ready for me. But I may get tangled up in Niagara.

I have a very nice suite here, but move down town this afternoon to stop with another Professor called Morton Dauen [*sic*] Zabel.[6] How do they *get* their names? He will take me to the theatre, also to the French pictures, which are very famous. Haven't got on—or off—with the negroes yet until the other day in the train. Two soldiers returning from Japan[.] Really charming, and having to do with literature is, in this country, an advantage; in England it arouses faint hostility or contempt. So I have added to my list of correspondents.

Chicago—is—oh well, a facade of skyscrapers facing a lake, and behind the facade every type of dubiousness.

Love to May and Robin. Hope all is well.

Love, Morgan

ALS: May Buckingham

[1] Bob Buckingham was apparently taking care of payments of taxes on EMF's Chiswick flat. The pictures were reproductions, gifts from Professor Zabel; see note 6 below, and Letter 381.

[2] The Abbeys were John Keats's guardians. See Forster, 'Mr. and Mrs. Abbey's Difficulties', *The London Mercury*, 6 (1922), 28–33; reprinted in *AH*, pp. 225–33. EMF (or someone else) may have mistaken for a 'businessman' Professor Napier Wilt (1896–1975), Chairman of the English Department at the University of Chicago, who probably gave this dinner at the Quadrangle Club.

[3] On Isherwood's novel, which deals with the making of a film, see Letter 297.

[4] David Lean's 1947 version of Dickens's novel.

[5] Edward Killoren Brown (1905–51), author of books on Canadian poetry, and on Matthew Arnold, Edith Wharton, Thomas Wolfe, and Willa Cather (completed by Leon Edel), became Professor of English at the University of Chicago in 1944.

[6] Morton Dauwen Zabel (1901–64), Professor of English at the University of Chicago.

381   To Robert J. Buckingham

K[ing's] C[ollege,] C[ambridge]
1 March 1948

Dear Bob,

Will be along Wednesday. The pictures have been framed, the Picasso looks well, but the frame of the Klee is too solemn—it wants jazzing up or anyhow colouring. I shall bring it along if I can, and maybe you will be so good as to be inspired.

Wonder how the train is getting on. Hope you won't sacrifice May too much to Robin, and chaw up her flower bed again. She has a life to lead too, and has to spend a good deal of it looking out of the back door. You love changing things, you know!

Have been reading my life of Goldie, and realise I am almost the age he was when he died.[1] I don't think myself nearly as old as I thought him. But I feel humble about my life and achievement when I compare them with his. He was not only noble and talented—he stuck things out and had such a capacity for work. He is seldom mentioned here.

Had much else to say, forget what, and must anyhow go to my supper with Patrick and Sydney.[2] I come up Wednesday. Have offered to spend Friday at Dover.—By the way a huge SIDE of bacon has now flown to me from the States.[3]

Everyone here is worried over events, and no wonder.—It is wretched for the boys. One I like, a miner called Eric Fletcher, is just bewildered between crocuses, home squalor, French literature, and the threat of war.[4] I am getting to know several of that sort—so much more to my taste than the finished Etonians or reserved Returned Warriors.

William [Plomer] and Charles are in Switzerland[.] Quelle fidélité!

Morgan's love.

ALS: May Buckingham

[1] Forster, *Goldsworthy Lowes Dickinson*. Dickinson died in 1932, three days short of his seventieth birthday.

[2] Patrick and Sydney Wilkinson: see Letter 378, note 1.

[3] American friends were generous with parcels to relieve Forster's shortages during the postwar rationing. One of these was Edith Oliver (1913–   ), theatrical reviewer and a staff member of *The New Yorker* since 1947.

[4] Eric Fletcher (1927–   ), son of a South Yorkshire miner, was educated at Doncaster Grammar School and at King's College. He specialises in adult and further education and in 1965 became Principal of the Barnet College of Further Education.

382 To Robert Trevelyan

The Reform Club [London]
7 April 1948

Dear Bob,

After all, I waited ¼ hour for the Green Line bus.[1] The clock inside the Hall must have been fast. I wish I could have seen more of you. I so appreciated your affection and helpfulness. It was the only pleasant spot in a rather odious day. I don't like the Dorking musicals.[2]

I have just read (for the first time) the Princess Casamassima.[3] It is much the most *exciting* James I have read. Towards the end he starts his cocooning and muffling, but the prison scene at the beginning is terrifying in its nakedness, and throughout there is an interest— unusual for him—in the social structure, and in different types of human beings and of dialects[:] Balzac no doubt; and I kept wishing he had developed into an English Balzac instead of a specialist in sensitiveness and a composer of patterns, who always tends to make his characters alike, and all of whose characters must be—at certain moments—"wonderful"

ALU, incomplete?: TCC

[1] A service operating between London and the Home Counties.
[2] A tradition begun with the first Leith Hill Music Festival in Dorking, in 1905.
[3] Published 1886.

383 To Peter Gamble[1]

King's College, Cambridge
14 May 1948

Dear Mr Gamble,

Thank you for your letter and for the *Forrest Reid*. I think he would have liked it—certainly it is a most delicate piece of work. He was fastidious and personal, so one never could be sure what he would like, it was part of his ~~personality~~ individuality, and of his charm. I enjoyed it very much myself, and I appreciated your references to me in it.

I must go back and read him again. In particular I must try the rewritten Peter Waring and Denis Bracknel. I liked Following Darkness so much that I find it difficult to tackle the revision.[2] (By the way was it, perhaps boot*leggers* that Katherine went off with? But I can't remember.)[3] I never understood his world as clearly as, perhaps, you do. There is a puritanism in him which unexpectedly condemns, and yet it is a world which is to be enjoyed and touched. Perhaps it *is* my home but he will have to ~~give more~~ make a few purgatorial passes over me before I am ready for it.

I feel proud at discovering him—though de la Mare was earlier in date.[4] He is a great treasure for a few people. (Some excellent critics, Virginia Woolf for instance, were not interested in him at all, and he had no interest outside his own range, no general curiosity about ~~life~~ civilisation.)

In your letter, which I have carelessly mislaid, I think you said you were not in touch with his friends. I think you should certainly show your 'appreciation' to them—e.g. to Bryson at Oxford.[5]

Again thanking you, and with all good wishes.

Yours sincerely
EMForster

The Coleridge reference (p. 2) isn't clear to me, and the Hardy paragraph should perhaps be recast.

P.S.   15 May 1948

Your letter has turned up just as I was about to post mine, so I add a few words. They are the more necessary, since I did not remember its contents accurately.

Peter Burra, who wrote about me in a way that pleased me, also wrote about Forrest Reid, but not in a way that pleased him; he found the essay too psycho-analytical, and it was, indeed, never published.

Thinking again about your 'appreciation' I do endorse what you say about the order of the 'Tom' Trilogy; it used to worry me—as the Oedipus-Antigone trilogy of Sophocles still worries me—because it was not published in chronological sequence.[6] I see now, with your assistance, that it is really an advance—backward through time towards reality.

This is an inadequate and scrappy note: I must read some of the books again. I am at present doing what he often chid me for not doing—reading some of the novels of Henry James.

I often wish that I could have done more for him than I did—praised him more, and better. Yet I saw him, on and off, for years. It is very natural that you should have this feeling of dissatisfaction too. I think it arises from the rareness of his quality. One had, and has, and should have, a feeling of one's own inadequacy.

EMF

ALS: HRC

[1] Peter Gamble: untraced, as his essay.
[2] On Reid's rewriting of *Following Darkness*, see his note in *Peter Waring*, the new version, p. 9.
[3] Katherine Dale rejects Peter Waring for the son of a wealthy boot-*maker*.
[4] Reid, while a Cambridge student, discovered the poetry of Walter de la Mare (1873–1956), and correspondence led to close friendship. Reid often stayed with de la Mare when in England. See Reid, *Walter de la Mare: A Critical Study* (1929); de la Mare, in an Introduction (pp. 9–16) to *Forrest Reid: A Portrait and a Study*, by Russell Burlingham, wrote that it had been 'an unbroken friendship of half my long lifetime; an inexhaustible patience (sadly needed); wise counsel; life-giving encouragement; a selfless sharing of all he cared for most'.
[5] John Norman Bryson (1896–1976), author of books on Matthew Arnold and Browning, was Lecturer at Balliol, Merton, and Oriel Colleges, Oxford, 1923–40; Fellow of Balliol, 1940–63; and Vincent Massey Fellow, 1949–61.
[6] Tom trilogy: Reid's novels, best read from *Young Tom* (1944), through *The Retreat* (1936) and *Uncle Stephen* (1931), although written in reverse order. Similarly, the *Antigone* of Sophocles, which deals with events later in date than those of *Oedipus Tyrannus* and *Oedipus at Colonus*, was written first, in 441BC.

384   To Christopher Isherwood

[N. p.] 25 June 1948

Dearest Christopher

Tennessee Williams got up too late to reach Cambridge. Vidal arrived and I wish hadn't, as I disliked him a lot. I hope anyhow he returned you Gerald's *Street Car*.[1] I am looking forward to seeing it on the stage, where its colour, violence, and seedfulness should be effective. I did not find the characters alive (my old whimper), but that is where actors and actresses are so useful. Alive themselves, often through no wish of their own, they are compelled to vivify the dramatist's ideas. I shouldn't have thought it was a good play—with the chief character an invalid who ought to have been looked after earlier. Still the stage is always surprising me into a good deal of pleasure. The poker scene might look lovely.

What I am really writing about though is *Maurice*. I should very much like a talk alone with you during the next week or so. I am ashamed at shirking publication but the objections are formidable. I am coming up on Tuesday for a night or probably two. Wednesday should be all right. If you wish to drop me a line here, do so. Otherwise I will ring you in London.

Lovely letter from Ben. Herring &[ct] comes to Cambridge at the end of the month.[2]

Love
Morgan

Left to right: Peter Pears, EMF, Benjamin Britten, Billy Burrell.

With Eric Crozier, c. 1950.

ALS: Recipient

[1] Tennessee Thomas Lanier Williams (1911–83), the American playwright and author of *A Streetcar Named Desire* (1947). EMF apparently borrowed a copy from Gerald Heard. Gore Vidal (1925–   ), American novelist and critic.

[2] Herring: Britten's comic opera *Albert Herring* (Op. 39, 1947) with libretto adapted by Eric Crozier from de Maupassant's story, 'Le rosier de Mme. Husson, see Letter 385. Albert, the mother-dominated son of the village grocery proprietress, is chosen King of the May on grounds of innocence, but gets drunk and disappears on a brief career of happy profligacy. For the libretto, see *The Operas of Benjamin Britten*, ed. David Herbert, pp. 135–66. After the Aldeburgh Festival, the English Opera Group took the opera on tour and performed in the Cambridge Arts Theatre. 'End of the month' refers to July, when EMF with Kenneth Harrison as co-host, gave the singers a party in their adjoining rooms on 30 July 1948. For Harrison, see Letter 397.

385 To Benjamin Britten

K[ing's] C[ollege] C[ambridge]
30 September 1948

Dearest Ben,

Much to write about but must concentrate on essentials (so called). Here is a map I took, here is a little book, here is a post card, look, and will you kindly fill in the name and post. I remember 'Knowles', but perhaps he was the builder.[1]

We had an interesting visit to Northants, not much time so did not call at the rectory. The Henry Moore is dignified and quiet and of a style suited to the Chapel, but the College will be hard to persuade.[2]

I have thought a good deal of our conversation about Christianity and some time we must talk again. I love the tenderness and pity and love, but they have a tendency to become interfering and weepy, which repels me and is I think bad. For instance even in St Matthew's, which ~~is~~ seemed all out to help, there was exposed a really shocking questionnaire for boys and girls, a sort of confessional. One of the questions was "Have you stolen anything? If so state what." Another: "Do you ever play any game which you would not like your mother to see?" (Answers to both questions ~~can be found in~~ supplied by Albert Herring!). What with this and what with the historical difficulties, I have to find my emotional explanation of the Universe, for of course I must find one, elsewhere.

Morgan's love, and to Peter [Pears] also.

ALS: Britten Estate

[1] This has some connection with Aldeburgh arrangements. The Knowles family were local builders, later estate agents.

[2] Henry Moore's *Madonna and Child* (1944) was a gift to St Matthew's Church, Northampton, from Canon J. Rowden Hussey (1865–1949), its vicar, 1893–1937, in thankfulness for his many years of service there. See Herbert Read, *Henry Moore: Sculpture*

and Drawing, frontispiece and pp. xvii–xxvi. EMF wrote to Eric Fletcher (22 October 1948: Recipient): 'The niches to be filled with statues are at the extreme east end of the chapel. The statues will have to be over 5 ft. high. I don't suppose the Henry Moore scheme will come to anything.' King's College had discussed commissioning a similar statue, but the proposal was abandoned.

386   To Eric Crozier

King's College, Cambridge
24 October 1948

Dear Eric,

I meant to answer your letter long ago, and now that I do write it is only in feeble acknowledgement. I was most interested in what you say, and particularly in your contrast between the tragic and the pathetic. Literature, &ct stirs me when it wakes me up to the greatness of the world. Galsworthy doesn't, Peter Grimes does, and therefore seems more than pathetic to me.[1]

Unluckily I have not got my mind on to a subject yet, which is the real feebleness of this letter. I must write to Ben also. My feeling is that you ought to start and do the thing—calling on me to look over your shoulder when you will. There seems to me good reason that Ben should not yet write again about the sea. I was attracted to Margaret Catchpole at first.[2]

Yours ever
EMF.

ALS: Britten Estate

[1] At meetings held between October and Christmas 1948, Crozier and EMF had begun to consider a possible next libretto for Britten. *Peter Grimes* dealt with the trial of the fisherman, Grimes, whose apprentices mysteriously died or disappeared at sea. That opera, begun in 1942, had its première on 7 June 1945 at Sadler's Wells, with Peter Pears in the title role.

[2] Richard Cobbold, *The History of Margaret Catchpole. A Suffolk Girl* (1845): about a servant girl fatally involved with a smuggler. Britten and Crozier had thought first of a social comedy set in an English country house. During one of their meetings EMF had said that 'comedy in any form has to be satirical or nostalgic' and that was why he wanted nothing to do with comedy. EMF, who at first was quite diffident about his ability to write a libretto, wanted grand opera: this was a change of direction for Britten and Crozier, who had set up the English Opera Group to produce small operas that the Group could do themselves. The new opera was commissioned for Covent Garden. (Information from Eric Crozier.)

387   To Benjamin Britten

King's College, Cambridge
20 December 1948

Dearest Ben

That is shattering news, the only good thing about it is the way you take it. A mercy the doctor lets you work.[1] I am so very sorry. Let me know when abouts in January you would like me to come and see you. I think Jan. 22ⁿᵈ is the only date I couldn't come so far. You and I and Eric ought certainly to meet and have a talk.[2]

Our original realism certainly wouldn't have worked. My idea was to start realistically, and then alter the ship and crew until they were what we wanted, and good and evil and eternal matters could shine through them. I believe this is safer than starting at the Mystery end—we keep human beings and the smell of tar. I like the idea of a chorus, shanties &ᶜᵗ, provided it is at the level of the half-informed Greek chorus, which was always making mistakes. The well-informed commentator, the person or personages outside time, would not here be suitable.

At least that is my first reaction, so I do not altogether agree with the three of you—formidable thought.[3] But the idea is all new to me, and I may change when I have thought more about it. I seem to have the fear of a lot of symbolic and inexpensive scenery, whereas I want grand opera mounted clearly and grandly; and I feel that a mystic Billy would not support more than two acts.

Melville, I believe, was often trying to do what I've tried to do. It is a difficult ~~thing~~ attempt, and even he has failed; the ordinary lovable (and hateable) human beings connected with immensities through the tricks of art. Billy *is* our Saviour, yet he is Billy, not Christ or Orion.[4] I believe that your music may effect the connections better than our words.

A little bird tells me that you would have been in my nest on the 1ˢᵗ. So I am sorrier than ever about your illness. However we shall be meeting soon. When I am with you, I should like, if I may, to ask over a nice King's boy for a meal—he is in the R.A.F. near Woodbridge.[5]

With love and please write again

Morgan

Is it duodenal?

Peter Bedford came to tea the other week—very easy and nice.[6]

ALS: Britten Estate

[1] This was one of Britten's periodic illnesses connected with tension of composition and production.

[2] Britten, Crozier, and EMF had now decided on Melville's *Billy Budd* as the source of libretto for the new opera.

[3] The three of you: Britten, Pears, and Crozier.

[4] Orion: on the importance of this constellation for EMF, see *EMF*, I, 162.

[5] This was Eric Fletcher.

[6] Peter Bedford (1931–   ), from a distinguished musical family, became Director of the Banff Festival.

388   To Eric Crozier

King's College, Cambridge
10 February 1949

Dear Eric,

I had two rapturous postcards from the travellers, but is there any news of their return?[1]

I should have very much liked a talk with Ben before tangling myself up too much with the U.S.A. If he, you, and Peter, were agreed to settle down to Billy Budd for the next three months or so, I should give up any thoughts of leaving England. That opera is much the most important bit of work which I see before me, and I would sacrifice much to it—certainly foreign travel.[2]

As far as I can see, it looks as if you and I will be joint-librettists, but the enterprise is still nebulous, and I think we shall do well not to define yet.[3] So far (which is not far) it has seemed to issue forth like a living being, without sponsors.

I seem fairly free for a visit to Portsmouth in the latter half of this month.[4]

Yours   E. M. Forster

ALS: Recipient

[1] Britten and Peter Pears were on holiday in Venice, then went on a concert tour.

[2] This was EMF's intended second trip to the United States, 19 May–14 June 1949. Bob Buckingham was to accompany him.

[3] EMF wrote to Britten ([February? 1949]): 'It looks to me that we [EMF and Crozier] shall be joint librettists, but we are agreed in leaving this open—Peter [Pears] ought also to be present whenever possible.' On 30 March he wrote again: 'Mainly, I *do* hope you will put pressure on B[oosey] & H[awkes, Britten's publisher] to countenance Eric's "Picture Post" article. We seem paralyzedly neurotic business men who won't reach conclusions. Personally I do very much want to be mentioned ~~about~~ in connection with Billy (who indeed wouldn't be) and I think this endless dribble of snippets undignified.' (Both letters, Britten Estate.) The article in question was Crozier's 'An Opera Team Sets to Work', *Picture Post*, 45 (1949), 29–31. A surviving draft of EMF's letter to its editor, Thomas Hopkinson (1905–) expresses appreciation for the publicity but goes on to 'correct a mistake in it, and also an omission. The caption to one of the illustrations describes Peter Pears as singing an aria out of the opera. Impossible. Not a single note of the music has been ~~composed~~ written. He was singing something else and That is the mistake. The omission is more serious. There is no adequate picture of Eric Crozier, who cooperated with me on the libretto, and without whom it would never have been written, and there is no mention of him in any caption' ([mid-October 1949]. Crozier).

[4] EMF and Crozier were going to see Nelson's flagship *Victory*.

389   To Lionel Trilling

King's College, Cambridge
16 April 1949

Dear Lionel Trilling

I have just been re-reading, and I am glad I did not do so before, the chapter in *The Middle of the Journey* about *Billy Budd*.[1] For I have some news for you. I have been writing, with Eric Crozier's help, a libretto on that subject for Benjamin Britten's next opera. It is practically finished in dramatic form, though the transformation of that into operatic form may take some time. How I would like to talk it over with you, and now possibly I may, for I hope to come to New York for a short time next month. It has been exciting work—the rescuing of Vere from his creator being no small problem. Claggart came easy—natural depravity, not evil, being the guide—and I have written him a monologue which though akin to Iago's in Verdi's, works out on different lines. And Billy himself caused much less trouble than I expected. *He* has a monologue at the end—or rather two: first the dreamy "Billy in the Darbies", followed by old Dansker bringing in not too obtrusively the eucharist of grog and biscuits which has been indicated—and then a heroic one about Fate; the black sea where he has caught sight of the far-gleaming sail that is not Fate.[2] (Melville's main note is Fate, but the note has an overtone to it.) The final scene—the hanging—is spectacle, with the hanging 'off' Then the lights fade, leaving Vere alone visible for an epilogue.—He was thus for a prologue too.—

I disagree, and no doubt was meant to disagree, with much of Maxim's article. But the stammer certainly is a difficulty: the 'devil's visiting card' no doubt, still the person on whom a card is left does differ in essence from the person who leaves them all over the ship, as Claggart did. (N. B. Why is it Vere's touch on Billy's shoulder that precipitates the blow?)

Our collaboration is being announced, so that is not a secret. But lots of the above details may be altered so they should not be passed round. No music has been written yet, though I worked under Britten's supervision. We settle down again at Aldeburgh in August.

You will gather that I have started ageing 70 in a way very interesting to myself. What an opera with all-male parts will be like, passes me; the only precedent, Le Jongleur de Notre Dame, is not encouraging.[3]

I come over to deliver an address at the American Academy—I am asked to talk for 25 minutes only, and it doesn't sound very congenial.[4] But it gives me the chance to keep my eye on America, which I am very glad to do, and to see my friends—I will write again.—Thank you for your letter, to which this musical monologue can scarcely pose as a reply.

Yours very sincerely
EMForster

ALS: Columbia University

[1] Lionel Trilling (1905-75), teacher and critic, was on the English faculty of Columbia University, 1931-75, and was George Edward Woodberry Professor, 1965-70, and University Professor of English, 1970-5. He and EMF met in New York in June 1947. Trilling's *E. M. Forster: A Study* (1943) initiated the mid-century revival of critical interest in

EMF's novels. In *The Middle of the Journey* (1947), Trilling's only novel, Gifford Maxim, who has left an unspecified Party, writes a review of a non-existent edition of *Billy Budd*, in which he discusses the nature of evil and the conflict between Spirit and Necessity (pp. 152–9, 174). The prototype for Maxim was the American ex-Communist, Whittaker Chambers; see Trilling's letter to his British publisher in Warburg, *All Authors Are Equal: The Publishing Life of Fredric Warburg 1936–1971*, pp. 125–6.
    ² EMF and Crozier drew upon the 1946 edition, with Introduction by William Plomer, pp. 7–10. The ballad, 'Billy in the Darbies', pp. 123–4.
    ³ Opera by Jules Massenet, written for the Monte Carlo Opera and first produced there in 1902, and in London in 1906. It is based on a medieval miracle play.
    ⁴ Forster, 'Art for Art's Sake', delivered at a combined meeting of the American Academy and the National Institute of Art and Letters; published in *Harper's Magazine*, 199 (1949), 31–4; see Kirkpatrick, p. 148.

390   To Frank Sargeson

King's College, Cambridge
12 November 1949

Dear Mʳ Sargeson,
   I have been reading *I saw in my Dream*, have indeed read most of it twice, and I felt I would like you to know how much your work interests me. Hence this letter. I suppose that the story *That Summer* is really more successful, but I find something extraordinarily haunting in this later novel, something which cannot be analysed or worked out logically, though no doubt the Freudians might have a shot at doing this.¹ The strong-room, Marge's W. C. and Cedric's cave are the same and not the same; they set the imagination, not the intellect, going; they cannot be patted into a symbol. I don't think many people will understand your book, and I don't understand ~~much of~~ a good deal of it myself. I wish we could meet and talk, but of that there is no chance.
   Of the isolated scenes, I find so vivid that of the uncles, and that of poor Mʳˢ Daley on Molly, and there is one passage (about Ranji and Cedric and the carving of their names) which I am going to copy out.
   With all good wishes—and with best wishes for Christmas, for this letter should reach you round about then:

Yours sincerely
EMForster.

ALS: Alexander Turnbull Library

   ¹ The novel *I Saw in My Dream* (1949) inspired this first letter to the New Zealand novelist Frank Sargeson (1903–82). The novella *That Summer*, first published in 1946, is in his *Collected Stories* (pp. 53–134), introduced by EMF (p. 5).

391   To Robert Trevelyan

4 Crabbe Street, Aldeburgh, Suffolk
(4 April 1950)

Dear Bob

How are you, with the better weather coming on? Fairly well, I hope. As for me, I have been having set-backs, the flesh being reluctant to heal at our age, but have been improving recently—thanks largely to a sensible local doctor—and have hopes of resuming normal life.[1] It is *most* comfortable here, and I go little walks and drives.

I am partly writing, though, to ask if you can help us over a passage in the Billy Budd libretto. Scene: Captain Vere's cabin, Ship is entering enemy waters. He is alone, reading, lays down book and says "Plutarch—the Greeks & the Romans—their troubles and ours are the same. May their virtues be ours and their heroism." And after a talk with his officers and a drink to the destruction of France he takes up his book (alone again) and ~~says~~ reads "At the battle of Salamis, the Athenians, with vastly inferior numbers...the Athenians..." lays book down, and listens to the men singing 'off' as the curtain falls.

The above sentences suit us, but I haven't been able to find anything like them in Plutarch, so they can't well stand. Do you know of any passage in the classics which a cultivated gentleman like Vere might be reading to himself in 1797, and might roughly illustrate the situation I've outlined? (Vere, you remember, is intellectual, conservative, patriotic, in touch with the common man in his own country, but averse to foreigners, particularly to the atheistical frogs whom he is about to fight.) Plutarch would have been just right. I suppose there is nothing in Herodotus...or Thucydides?—It's the general sentiment I'm hunting for, rather than a precise quotation. (He might, at a pinch, read a Greek Tragedian)[2]

I stay on here rather indefinitely—being of some use here, and not I hope much trouble. The opera goes well, and interests us both.—My love to Bessie. After leaving the Nursing Home, where she so kindly visited me, I stayed for a while at the Buckinghams, and then Ben Britten drove me, and May Buckingham, direct here by car. She has now gone back—I can look after myself all right now.

With love, and hoping for some news of yourself.

Morgan

If you can't solve our problem, I'll fix or fake something. Don't let it worry you too much

ALS: TCC

[1] He had had a second prostate operation in January.

[2] The libretto avoids direct quotation. Compare the two versions of the libretto in the Boosey & Hawkes editions: *Billy Budd: Opera in Four Acts* (1951), pp. 25, 28; and *Billy Budd: Opera in Two Acts* (1961), pp. 25, 27.

392   To Eric Fletcher

4 Crabbe Street, Aldeburgh, Suffolk
26 April 1950

Dear Eric,

Just a line of affection before I toddle off to bed. I am sorry in a way about Adelaide, quite thought you would land it, hope one of the other two jobs will mature.[1] I wish I could see you, but convalescence hasn't been as quick as I hoped, and I can't pay visits yet awhile or even establish myself at Cambridge. As soon as I am well enough to come and stay with you, I should very much like to do so. No hope, I suppose, of your coming out this way?

I was interested and repelled by the Ruskin book; Peter Quennell is a fish-like repellent observer, I think.[2] The danger of such studies is not that they give us psycho-analytic & physical details about authors—that's all right in itself—but that they deflect weak-minded readers from the created result. Not being all that weak-minded, I am not put off the Stones of Venice by being told that Ruskin tossed himself off, but some readers might be deflected or disgusted by the information and not read him in consequence, or read him wrongly.

It's all part of our old point: the secondary importance of criticism—so important, but so secondary. The critics—supported by a cowardly public which is too timid or too idle to make individual judgements—have got too big for their boots. It is still worse in America where, Ben [Britten] tells me, enormous photographs of critics who have praised a successful play are exhibited outside the theatre; the dramatist, the actors are not shown.

Hope Donald H. is going to write to me; hear rumours that Tom Wells will also. Frank Summers actually has. I enjoy letters from King's so much, and I enjoy your letters wherever they are posted.[3]

Am so sleepy, really must stop. My letter is getting to look like one of Robin Buckingham's—every 3rd word a mistake.

The Harewoods have been here for the weekend. *What* a nice chap he is—so gay, friendly, and straight.[4] I wish he hadn't shut himself up at King's, I expect that people whom we needn't mention tried to exploit him—while people like ourselves kept away. The week end before we had the Steins and Bob—also a great success.

With love, and please write again—Morgan

Nelson's portrait of me is to be exhibited in the R. A.—hung on the line[5]

ALS: Recipient

[1] Fletcher had applied for a lectureship in English at the University of Adelaide.

[2] Peter Quennell, *John Ruskin: The Portrait of a Prophet* (1949). Quennell (1905–   ), critic and biographer, edited *History Today*, 1951–79.

[3] Donald Noble Higginbottom (1925–   ) was a history scholar at King's and went to Yale under an arrangement financed by EMF. He entered the Foreign Office in 1953. Thomas Umfrey Wells (1927–   ), a New Zealander, was at King's, 1949–51. He became Headmaster of the Collegiate School, Wanganui, New Zealand, in 1960. Francis Summers (1919–   ) was at King's, 1949–52, studying social anthropology; he became an industrial training officer and, in 1964, a Lecturer at the Glasgow College of Building. Letters . . . posted: Fletcher had left the RAF in April and was living at home in South Yorkshire.

[4] George Henry Hubert Lascelles, 7th Earl of Harewood (1923–   ), was a Director of the Royal Opera House Covent Garden, 1951–3, and its Administrative Executive, 1953–60. Lady Harewood, later Mrs Jeremy Thorpe, is the daughter of Britten's friend Erwin Stein (see Letter 394).

[5] This portrait by Edmund Hugh Nelson (1910–   ) is owned by King's College. R.A.: Royal Academy.

393   To William Plomer

129 Wendell Road [London] W. 12
27 May 1950

Dearest William,

Eliot does care about the soul, but the question of how he handles or would handle it is, I think, an important one, which the critics ignored. One of them rightly said that The Cocktail Party is a religious play, but it is also something more specific, namely priest-ridden.[1]

You will gather from the above that I am at Bob's, feeling somewhat brighter, and listening in to what's interesting. I hope to get on to Cambridge and Aldeburgh; hope springs eternal in the human breast, even at my age and in this.

Johnny Simpson looked in the other day, as delighted with your introduction to him as I am with yours to me. I wonder what you say about him. His career had such a fair, and strange, start: unmeasured praise of his detachment, for instance, from Roger Fry.[2] But he has not kept up as I hoped; too good and unselfish, perhaps.

Much love from   Morgan

ALS: Durham University

[1] T. S. Eliot's *The Cocktail Party: A Comedy* (1949), first performed at the 1949 Edinburgh Festival. It opened at the Henry Miller's Theatre, New York, on 21 January 1950; and at the New Theatre, London, on 4 May.

[2] Fry's enthusiasm for Simpson's novels encouraged the Woolfs to publish his *Saturday Night at the Greyhound*.

394   To Benjamin Britten

King's College, Cambridge
Tuesday [early December 1950]

Dearest Ben

Very glad of what you say about the monologue. It is *my* most important piece of writing and I did not, at my first hearings, feel it sufficiently important musically. The extensions and changes you suggest in the last lap may make the difference for me, besides being excellent in themselves.

With the exception of it, all delighted me. Most wonderful.

Returning to ⓘⓣ, I want *passion*—love constricted, perverted poisoned, but nevertheless *flowing* down its agonising channel; a sexual discharge gone evil. Not soggy depression or growling remorse. I seemed turning from one musical discomfort to another, and was dissatisfied. I looked for an aria perhaps, for a more recognisable form. I liked the last section best, and if it is extended so that it dominates, my vague objections may vanish. "A longer line, a firmer melody"—exactly.[1]

I leave it to you to fix our next meeting. I should love to come to Aldeburgh for a couple of nights (so much there draws me). Alternatively there is London. I go there this Thursday, and probably stop over the 5th—day of the boy's audition, I think. Bob is good to ring. My phone CHI 2407. My address 9 Arlington Park Mansions, Chiswick, W. 4.

Love to yourself and to Peter—Morgan.

Has it any inverted relationship to Vere's music when he moves towards the inner cabin, end of Act III?[2]

ALS: Britten Estate

[1] This applies to Claggart's monologue, Act II. EMF did not realise Britten's sensitiveness about criticism of his work. Crozier wrote to Nancy Evans (9 December 1950. Recipient): 'Ben seemed to me definitely peaked and worried. He had received from Morgan a very deflating letter, full of sharply-pointed darts about *BILLY*, and he was still not certain after long discussion with Peter [Pears] and Erwin [Stein (1885–1958), Austrian-born writer and editor of musical works], how much the criticisms were deserved. So, before approaching Morgan again, he wants to have a long talk with me and to go through some of the music. Hence our expedition to Aldeburgh on [next] Tuesday.

'It always distresses me to see Ben seriously worried, and I wish to goodness I could pour oil on the troubled waters. Another snag!—Morgan wants to go and stay at Aldeburgh for a time, but in the present state of affairs between them Ben feels that will be impossible—that he can't have to consult and seek approval for every phrase he writes. . . .

'Oh dear!—when such a misunderstanding begins between two great men, one feverishly busy, the other not busy enough, it is most difficult to bring them to a frank exchange of views and to tolerance of each other's personal need for trust and loyalty. My sympathies are with both—perhaps a little weighted on Ben's side because I have had experience of his problems and his particular methods of working. Morgan said himself, in our radio recording in August [a conversation about the libretto], what remarkable harmony there had been during the collaboration. But now—? A canker seems to have wormed its way into the heart of things. What a terrible pity it is!' On 12 December Crozier wrote to Nancy that Britten was busy rewriting: 'Odd that the trouble with Morgan makes him much more friendly to me.'

² See Britten, Forster, Crozier, *Billy Budd; Opera in Four Acts* (1951 version), p. 308: Vere goes to the inner cabin to communicate the verdict to Billy, an off-stage action that Britten depicted in a succession of thirty-four whole-bar chords, while 'the Curtain remains up until the end of the music, and then slowly falls'.

395   To Eric Crozier

King's College, Cambridge
[19 December 1950]

Dear Eric

I should very much like to come for a drink in Nancy's sitter, and shall ring in hope that a time can be arranged.¹ I go to my flat (CHI 2407) tomorrow, Wednesday eve.

I am most grateful for the hint about Claggart's monologue.² I certainly won't mention it to Ben, and will go carefully if he mentions it to me. He took my still stronger representations about the dirge in Act I so easily that I did not realise that I was here touching him on the raw. It would as you say be lamentable if we came to mistrust each other's judgment, but I think he knows that (except in the two items above) I go with every note he has written. Your suggestion that he should postpone reconsidering the monologue until Act III is done is excellent. Thank you very much again.

I look forward to seeing your redraft of the Shanty, and expect it will now come right. It was a question of shifting the atmosphere. I agree that Moll might shift it too much—especially if Ben uses her in the poem in Act IV. How you do all that tumtity I cannot think.³

Much excited over the prospect of the Queen of Spades on Thursday.⁴

With love to Nancy and yourself.

Morgan.

ALS: Recipient

¹ The singer Nancy Evans (1915–   ) and Crozier had been married on 26 December 1949. She and Kathleen Ferrier alternated creating the title role in Britten's *The Rape of Lucretia* (Op. 37, 1946), and Nancy Evans was Nancy in *Albert Herring* and Polly in Britten's version of Gay's *Beggar's Opera* (Op. 43, 1948). Sitter: Nancy's flat in Cromwell Road.

² See Letter 394.

³ The sailors' shanties that open Act I, Scene 3, were a problem, since words to authentic shanties fitted neither atmosphere nor situation. EMF wrote to Britten (16 December 1950. Britten Estate): 'Black Belinda is lamentable in my judgment. I have written to Eric as unawkwardly as I could, and hinted it wouldn't do as it was, and that it must either be done anew or be altered, and that we must await, my poor Ben, your decision between these two courses, if you decide on alterations only. . . . A shanty about a girl is reasonable, but not when it is spattered with large cold dead smuts.—Cannot you—perhaps with Peter's help—run up some fantasy words as an alternative?' EMF had declined to write the shanties. Crozier tried, but EMF did not like the result. EMF then asked Kenneth Harrison to try, and Britten rejected his effort. Peter Pears also contributed to what was finally a group effort. Moll: 'Bristol Moll', in 'Billy in the Darbies'. 'Black Belinda': source unidentified.

⁴ Tchaikowsky's opera (1890), based on Pushkin's 1834 short story.

396   To Eric Fletcher

129 W[endell] Rd   [London W.12]
9 July 1951

Dear Eric,

Thank you for your welcome letter, with beautiful post card and the interesting news that the Garden of Eden was on the island of Lesbos. That might explain a lot. I once offered another explanation in a little fantasy (neither successful nor printable) in which I made the serpent male and in love with Adam.[1] Theirs was the first emotion on earth—i. e. the first time any created object had forgotten its Creator: hitherto all had ceaselessly praised Him. The Almighty noticed the intermission, chased the serpent underground and created Eve as a helpmate for co-praise. The serpent tempted her, so that she might die, but she handed on the apple to Adam before he could stop her, and Adam died also.—The story of the Fall always fascinates me as a play ground, but I cannot find any profound meaning in it, because of my 'liberal' view of human nature: I cannot believe in a state of original innocence, still less in a lapse from it, and I am always minimising the conception and the extent of Sin and the sinfulness of sex. For St Augustine, who maximised Sin, the Fall was nuts. And perhaps for Michelangelo: in its representation on the ceiling of the Sistine he gives Adam an erection—or gave: it's been a bit blurred over by restorers I think.

But to turn to a more spiritual subject—my ankle—the news is disappointing. The specialist from Barts has come and said I must keep it in plaster until the *beginning of September*.[2] I thought it would be out at the end of this month. You can imagine how upset I am for May's sake, mercifully I am now more mobile on the crutches, can get to the lavatory and even managed yesterday to get down and up stairs. I am going to Cambridge soon with Bob, but he can only stay one night. I wish I could be there longer, to give her a rest from me; may be I can fix something—the doctors want me to get around, and I am to walk with the crutches, not swing on them—much easier.

I have plenty of work and liberal little literary plans, and am recovering my spirits. I am thankful I have any!

Very sorry about Trevor. I suppose I was showing off too, in thinking I could understand Campanology.[3]

How good the Cheltenham Festival sounds![4] I never know about Vaughan-Williams. I know that there is a Vaughan I like and a Williams I dislike, but am uncertain of their proportion and junction.

Have been having some nice visitors. People are awfully kind.

With love,
Morgan

ALS: Recipient

[1] Fletcher was in France, and his postcard showed a carving in the Auch Cathedral, of the serpent with female breasts. EMF's Garden of Eden fantasy has been destroyed.
[2] Barts: St Bartholomew's Hospital, London.
[3] Trevor John Lloyd Martin (1927–) joined the Education Branch of the RAF, 1948–50. From 1956 to 1982 he was an executive with Shell-Mex and British Petroleum. Eric Fletcher does not recall the argument about campanology (the science of bell-ringing or of bell-casting). There may be reference to his accident descending the belfry of Aldeburgh parish church when he broke his ankle (see Letter 397).
[4] Fletcher was living in Hereford when this was written and must have written about the Cheltenham Music Festival, but he does not now recall the remark about Vaughan Williams.

397   To Kenneth Harrison[1]

129 Wendell Road [London] W. 12
17 November 1951

Dear Kenneth { this letter, though signed Tosca, is from morgan }

Here we so far are. I have been intending to write to you, though it should have gradually become evident to you where I was not. Massage and rehearsals combine to keep me at May's—and for the moment at Bob's too, for here he is for the week end. I expect to come up on Friday next or Saturday. I have synovitis, and, since the massage has started and I have stopped walking, am much better. But how shall I be when I start walking and stop massage? The faded-faced pussy-cat who manipulates me does not say.

I went to a rehearsal yesterday. Ben has a bad ear, the producer a septic foot, Eric Crozier an ulcerated stomach, I my ankle, and Krips a nervous break down, but in other ways the prospect is perfect.[2] Billy really splendid—a strong young voice of charming quality, good physique, good enough looks including fair curly hair, some acting power and much natural gaiety. He can throw a somersault and come up singing. Let us hope he does not sprain his neck. Dansker—a Maori—also much pleased me. The two did the end of the 2nd act—when D. warns B. against Claggart—, and the Darbies scene.[3] I cried. I have not heard Claggart yet, but he thanked me for the superb words I had given him, so I think him good too. The smaller parts—officers, &ct—have not been given to hacks. As for the chorus, it filled the foyer where we rehearsed, and lifted all the coffee cups into the air. Quitting this for the auditorium we discovered an immense stage on which lay a stout gent in evening dress, towards whom an *immensely* stout lady was tottering with a pair of candles. These too she placed on the floor and the curtain fell.

Tosca.[4]

ALS: Recipient

[1] Kenneth Harrison (1912–), a fellow of King's 1938–60 and Dean 1945–8. In 1960 he became Professor of Biochemistry at the University of Tehran. See Letter 384, note 2. His rooms adjoined EMF's.

² *Billy Budd*, originally scheduled for the Edinburgh Festival, was now to open instead at Covent Garden on 1 December 1951. The producer was Basil Coleman (1916–   ). Although EMF somewhat exaggerates here, the disabilities were nonetheless real. Britten characteristically suffered from ailments induced by pre-première tension. Crozier's stomach trouble was indeed real. EMF's ankle, broken at Aldeburgh, was still lame. Josef Krips (1902–74), Austrian-born conductor and onetime Professor at the Vienna Academy, was Principal Conductor of the London Symphony Orchestra, 1950–4. His difficulty was with his eyesight and the shortness of time available for learning the score; in the event, he withdrew and Britten conducted.

³ The American baritone Theodor Uppman (1920–   ) sang the role of Billy; he recreated the role at the American television première in 1952, and at its première performance at the Chicago Lyric Opera, in 1970. Inia Te Wiata (1916–71) was Dansker. Frederick Dalberg (1908–   ) was Claggart.

⁴ The scene just described occurs at the end of Act 2 of Puccini's *Tosca*.

398 To Benjamin Britten

King's College, Cambridge
9 December 1951

Dearest Ben,

Thank you for the cheque and letter. Yes, it has been a great event, and I am proud and happy to have been in it and to think of it. You and I have both put into it something which lies deeper than artistic creation, ~~something~~ and which we both understand. It could never have got there but for bóth of us. I hope to live and write on it in the future, but this opera is my Nunc Dimittis, in that it dismisses me peacefully, and convinces me I have achieved.

I wish I could see you and sit about and talk to you. But that is a different achievement. You must be relegated (temporarily) to the position of a great man. Later on we may be near to one another again. We are very near—in the non-physical sense—now.

I like Uppman, and, in the little I have seen of him as a person, found nothing that contradicted the part. What have we not been saved from!

I am snowed under by letters from Mʳˢ Knowsbest, Mʳˢ Knowall, and Miss Nosnibor telling me what we ought to have done.¹ Maybe before the opera's next season you and I and Basil [Coleman] might have a talk, I'm against him being worried further at the moment. How nervous I have been lest you or lest he should collapse!

With love & gratitude

Morgan

ALS: Britten Estate

¹ Nosnibor: Samuel Butler's satirical inversion of 'Robinson', in *Erewhon*.

399   To Norman Prouting

The Reform Club [London]
27 December 1951

Dear Mr Prouting

How good that you cared to tackle the Unobserver, and what a feeble reply Philip Toynbee has returned![1] He is a decent intelligent journalist, who thinks that my reputation is too high and ought to be lowered. But he has never tried to think clearly or to feel *about* me or about any one else; he has never asked himself what he means by 'failure' or 'success' or in what ~~senses~~ circumstances the glib words can be applied to a man's life. I return him to you!—also the draft of your letter, which I am very glad to read.

We must have another meeting soon. I should enjoy it. This in haste. Just off to the final Billy Budd.

Yours sincerely
EMForster

ALS: KCC

[1] Norman Prouting (1924–   ), film writer and director, objected to the viewpoint on Forster in the anonymous 'Profile—E. M. Forster', in *The Observer* for 2 December 1951 (p. 2). This was, that EMF had 'overcome' his long silence 'sufficiently' to produce the libretto of *Billy Budd* after a long time at playing 'that familiar role of inconspicuous public figure and unstrident propagandist of the arts which we had reluctantly resigned ourselves to as a familiar one'. The author went on to say that EMF's attitude toward culture was useful 'as a corrective', but, however liberating, was 'gravely inadequate as an interpretation of life as it is, or as an exhortation to live it differently'. The reply to Prouting's objections came from the writer and occasional columnist for *The Observer*, Philip Toynbee (1916–81). (All letters: KCC.)

400   To John Morris[1]

King's College, Cambridge
12 January 1953

Dear John,

Here's a tiresome letter. I am worried by your rejection of Jack's Chinese-prison script. He has let me see it, also your letter of December 17th. It couldn't of course be broadcast in America, nor (mutatis mutandis, as a sympathetic account of some western prison) would it be broadcast in any Communist country. But I am surprised that it can't be broadcast in England—especially since Jack seems to have been conciliatory and willing to modify or omit where desired, and possibly he might have modified further. I don't agree with the whole of his stuff but then I didn't write it. No more did you. No more did the people to whom you showed it. It was written by a man of integrity, intelligence and distinction who has had an unusual experience which he wants to convey, and he ought to have been given his head.[2]

What puzzles me most is your criticism that he showed 'no sense of engagement'. I haven't met the expression before, and feel bound to comment on its totalitarian tang. Engagement not with the truth as the speaker apprehends it, but with the alleged opinion of the majority of listeners. I do hope that the Third [Programme] is not going to be run on these lines. It hasn't been in the past.

Yours ever
Morgan

TLS: BBC Written Archives

[1] John Morris (1895–1980), soldier and anthropologist, had wide experience of the Far East. He was Head of the Far Eastern Service of the BBC, 1943–52; then, Controller of the Third Programme, 1952–8.

[2] Sprott, who visited China in 1952 with the Britain–China Friendship Association, sent Morris a script on prison reform in China. Morris rejected it (17 December 1952. BBC) because it seemed too partial to the Communist regime, and because it lacked a 'sense of engagement' with an audience 'the majority of whom feel deeply suspicious about these things' and would be 'firmly on the side of those who are fighting against the Chinese forces in Korea'. EMF took up Sprott's case, and on 13 January 1953 Morris wrote in his diary that nobody in the Talks Department 'much cares for it; nor does anybody feel that it can be improved', and that it would have been acceptable if Sprott had given only a tourist's impressions. Morris wrote to EMF (14 January 1953. BBC): 'I think you need have no fear that the Third Programme is now going to be run on totalitarian lines. I share your own views on the liberty of the individual, as indeed do all responsible people here. . . . He went to China as a guest of the government, does not speak the language, and has no first-hand knowledge of previous conditions in China.' EMF was not reassured. At Morris's suggestion they met with Harman Grisewood (1906–   ), who had been with the BBC since 1929 and had preceded Morris as Third Programme Controller. Morris described EMF (diary, 30 January 1953) as being 'in his most puckish mood, sitting rather curled up in my armchair and not at all disposed to see my point of view in the *affaire* Sprott, although thoroughly good-natured and laughing a lot. . . . Harman explained most patiently and at great length that in a broadcast it is not possible to qualify every statement by some such remark as "I was told . . .".' To Florence Barger, EMF wrote (10 February 1953. KCC): 'I have had such a worrying time with the B.B.C., with which you will sympathise. . . . I went up specially to see [Morris] and Harman Grisewood and had an hour's hammer and tongs. It is disgraceful that a man of Jack's intelligence integrity and distinction should be muzzled. They complained he hadn't given a "general picture" of China. I replied "Give me a general picture of England." There was silence.'

401   To Robert J. Buckingham

K[ing's] C[ollege] C[ambridge]
9 February 1953

Dear Bob,

You were much too sharp with me over West Hackhurst. I made a half humourous reference to Fanny Farrer, to find myself instantly in the dock for harbouring class-limitations and obsessions. No doubt our feelings about houses &[ct] differ—if I hadn't mine I shouldn't have written Howards End—but there's no reason we shouldn't talk about them mildly. Don't throw your weight about so![1]

The booksellers promise to post you off the Provost[']s

PASSAGE TO INDIA
By COURTESY OF
HARRINGTONS

*With best
wishes for a
good recovery
EHN.*

*a suggestion for your safety
during the Festival y.B*

A postcard from Edmund Nelson to EMF in 1951. Forster had broken his ankle.

At Castello Montegufoni in 1952;
left to right: Paul Cadmus, Margaret French, Osbert Sitwell, EMF.

Agamemnon to day, and the Provost himself promises you a ticket should I fail. But I'm sure I shan't. I shall enjoy going with you.[2] What a pity Madingly was spoilt by snow! The fire was still nice when I got back and I had a good sleep.[3] This tiredness must be due to my age—it doesn't worry me at all except when I am supposed to be on show, as I should have to be at Paris.

Love
Morgan

ALS: May Buckingham

[1] I.e., over EMF's expulsion from West Hackhurst. Bob Buckingham, in fact, did much to help EMF to overcome his obsession with the loss of his home. Fanny Farrer: Dame Frances Farrer (1895–1977) daughter of Lord Farrer, and the new tenant of West Hackhurst after her London house was bombed.
[2] *The Oresteia of Aeschylus: Agamemnon, Choephori, Eumenides. The Greek Text as arranged for performance at Cambridge, 14th to 18th February 1933, with an English Verse Translation by J. T. Sheppard.* The Agamemnon was produced by the Greek Play Committee, at the Arts Theatre, Cambridge, on 17 February 1953.
[3] Apparently an excursion to Madingley, near Cambridge.

402   To Mary Eleanor Whichelo

as from King's College, Cambridge
14 February 1953

Dearest Nell,
    Just a line to tell you that all went well between myself and the queen yesterday.[1] I was alone with her for about ten minutes—she was quite an ickle thing, very straight and charming, stood with her back to a huge fire, gave me a very handsome decoration in a case which I will bring along when next I see you, and we talked about this and that very pleasantly. She shook hands to start and to finish, and I threw in some bows, and occasionally threw in Your Majesty or Ma'am. She was much better at the chat than I was. I liked her very much indeed. Finally she rang a buzzer in the mantel piece and I retired. It was a state dining room I think, which was gold, and very long. She looked tiny at the end of it, dressed in blue. I drove up to the Palace in a taxi and departed from it on foot.
    Will you tell Percy [Whichelo] the news when he calls—I ought to write now to Agnes and to Bone. I am in the country near Lewes at present with Lydia Lopokova (Lady Keynes), who (intrepid creature) is tramping alone in the snow.[2] Not so your

Morgan
who sends much love from the fireside

ALS: Philip Whichelo

[1] EMF went to Buckingham Palace for investiture as Companion of Honour.
[2] The Russian ballerina Lydia Lopokova (1892–1981) married Maynard Keynes in 1925. EMF writes from Tilton, Sussex.

403   To John Morris

King's College, Cambridge
25 May 1953

Dear John   <u>Private</u>
I should like to do the Penguin Indian Art Book for the Third, especially if I may keep it.[1] Please send instructions with it. I think it is a broadcast script you want, but am not quite sure.—
Very reluctantly I must refuse the Reith lectureship.[2] I was tempted, but I have nothing in my mind on the subject of civilisation that I haven't said before, and don't like the idea of repeating myself. Just a few old gentlemen—Bertrand Russell for instance—have the energy, the ingenuity, the malice, and the complexity of interests that enable them to go on and on in a striking fashion. All the rest of us can offer is 'distilled wisdom'; and often it does not smell too appetising. I might do a talk some time, but a course is too large an order, alas.

Yours ever
Morgan

ALS: KCC

[1] On 6 September 1953, EMF spoke in the Third Programme on Benjamin Rowland, *The Art and Architecture of India: Buddhist, Hindu, Jain* (1953); see that title in *The Listener*, 50 (1953), 419–21.
[2] Morris had been asked to sound EMF as to whether he would give the annual Reith Lectures, founded in honour of the BBC's first Director-General. The 1954 Lectures, 'Britain and the Tide of World Affairs', were given by Sir Oliver Franks (1905–   ), later Baron Franks of Headington.

404   To Robert J. Buckingham

[3 Trumpington Street, Cambridge][1]
28 July 1953
<Read at your leisure>

Dear Bob
I had a worrying lapse of memory yesterday and wonder whether I can venture to go to France. I have decided to unload what worry I can on you. That is what you pay for being you. The thing itself is trivial and merely makes us laugh. I had in a boy for a drink whom I know quite well—name James Carghill-Thompson. Another boy came in, name something-Allen, friend of Florence, and I forgot both names for introduction-purposes and got so flustered that I tried to give the 2nd boy sherry with the stopper in. James Caiger Smith was my shot for the first.[2] This inability has been growing lately. I think there are reasons why it was so bad yesterday—there had been planes all day which always harass me and drive the mind

in. I had had a distressing—if remote—letter from my aged cousin Dolly Whichelo, who is apparently breaking up and being taken away from her dirt and her pet-dogs to a home, my proper spectacles haven't come back, and I've been seeing and touching some snakes and lizards at a lab—creatures which repel me and necessitate forcing of my will.[3] And my swollen ankle compels me to think while I walk. But the real reason—and this is where this letter has the quality of a confessional—is that I have spent too much time of late in writing or trying to perfect an erotic story for my own pleasure—it is about an old person to whom a young one returns. I even thought of it during your visit, and it has been in my mind as an obsession rather than as a creative or a creatable work. I have written several of these stories, and believe that they are impairing my alertness and that I must—on *that* account—give over, and I am going to tear up this particular one in order to prevent continuance, although bits of it are human warm and good.[4]

There's no reason you should answer this latter. The early part is not private. The part about the stories most strictly is. I write to you because I may help myself by doing so. You and I and all ~~my~~ our friends want to stop me from sinking—as poor Arthur Gillett has—into the internal vagueness of which loss of memory is only an external sign. I might have told Francis [Bennett] instead of you, but he may be approaching the same problem.

I shall make no decision about France until I have made the move into College. Robin Caldecote is very busy for the moment, but may see me tomorrow.[5] I don't worry about the move. About France I fear to lose passport, money, be a flustered fool—you know. But I may regain adequate confidence.

I come up to my flat Thursday. A nice letter from Rob and his decision to buy that house. It is his decision and that he should make it is good. I will try to bring along some pounds when I call.[6] I shall probably be seeing you, May &c[t] certainly, and I shall learn what chance of seeing you and the three M[rs] Buckinghams on Sunday*[7]

It is early morning yet. I have been up to the lav. for a little diarrhoea—probably quite a bright idea. Now I hear poor Patrick stumbling around and soon he will announce our usual glum breakfast party.[8] Later I shall ring Nick to see whether we can dust my books together.[9]

Love
Morgan

* May's p. c. Good!

ALS: May Buckingham

[1] Home of the Wilkinsons.
King's College, a bed-sitting room in the home of Patrick Wilkinson and his wife Sydney.
[2] Mark Christopher Caiger Smith (1933–) came up to King's in 1952. William David James Cargill Thompson (1930–78), Reformation historian, taught at the University of Sussex, 1965–9, then joined the Department of Ecclesiastical History, King's College, University of London, where he became Professor and Dean of the Faculty of Theology in 1976.
[3] Dolly was EMF's cousin Ella Mary Louisa Whichelo, sister of Herbert Whichelo. She and her sister May Whichelo lived together for much of their lives, becoming increasingly eccentric. Herbert had helped them from time to time, until his death in 1931, after which EMF gave them a regular allowance.
[4] The story is unidentified and certainly does not survive.
[5] Apparently EMF's physician.
[6] EMF helped Robin and Sylvia Buckingham to buy a house in 1953.
[7] I.e. May Buckingham, Sylvia and Bob Buckingham's mother.
[8] Patrick Wilkinson was recovering from a series of operations.
[9] I.e., P. N. Furbank.

405 To Robert Buckingham

Coimbra[1]
18 September 1953

Dear Bob

I expect you will make trouble if you don't get a letter from Portugal, although you could write a much better one from Coventry. We have been here a week and have already got interested in the Portuguese and like them. They are slow and rather unattractive, but very kind, and will take any amount of trouble to give help as soon as you get across that you want it. Nick—who has done all the work of the expedition—notices this most, and he has had to handle complicated stuff: for instance we never got out here yesterday because our carriage stopped short of the platform, got carried on, but the guard explained all to the station master at the next station and arranged for our gratis return. They neither charm or alarm. We think indeed that they are the Anglo Saxons of the south. Also ~~All the same~~ they once had a great empire, and built out of its spoils a few—not many—wonderful buildings. The *most* amazing is the monastery-church at Belem, which was put up a little before King's [College] Chapel and also has fan vaulting, but has eight gigantic pillars sculptured and writhing from top to bottom, and reminding me of Hindu-Temple stuff. Every ¼ hour or so the light-effects alter[;] we kept coming back to admire them. At sunset there was a round pool of gold on the floor and one pillar rose up from it in gold. The others had vanished. Belem is a suburb of Lisbon. The other marvel—still more difficult to describe—is the *Library of the University* here—that's the main reason of our coming. It is 18th century: the period when Portugal bust herself through building too much[.] Three great halls opening into each other—black, orange-red, and black, all laced together by gold. The poor books looked quite ashamed of themselves. Even the ladders by which one climbed to them were of rare wood, also adorned with gold. The rest of the University has been destroyed or spoiled: this gasping marvel of a Library survives.—We go on to Oporto on Monday, then trickle back to Lisbon. Each has confessed to the other that he prefers trains to buses, so we shan't see some of the out of the way things. Still there is plenty left to see in Lisbon (same hotel, the Lis, though we don't like it.). We are there 24th–27th, when we return and I may sleep that night at your house. Nick has been very kind and a marvel at the language, which is difficult though it often sounds like English. They speak without much gesture or animation.

That is about enough. I have had some interesting talk about the state of the country, which I will keep until we meet. Rose [Macaulay]'s friends did a nasty one on me by saying they would specially invite Roy Campbell to meet me—the chap who blacked Stephen Spender's eye when he was giving a lecture.[2] I had to say I didn't want to meet him and to explain. The British Council people here and at Lisbon have been kind, but no one has suggested taking one out in a car. Give me India.

Food good and well cooked, but a bit heavy. I have upset myself a little with too much fruit—what else is to happen with melons, peaches, figs, grapes &[ct] rolled up against you twice a day? We thought at lunch that the waiters were making us eat too much for a joke, though I don't suppose they would be so disrespectful. They brought much more than was on the menu—a large onion omelette, black blood sausages with potatoes (creamed), two fillets of a super-sole, and a vast meat dish which we waved away with shrieks. Then the fruit course. The wine is rather funny—we keep experimenting.—It's not a dear country, cheaper than England that's to say, and far cheaper than hard grasping France.

Nick sends his love. We share a room here. He is writing too, midnight from the University Clock which stands on the summit of the precipitous town. We ought to turn in, though it'll be an easy day tomorrow I hope.

Love
Morgan

ALS: May Buckingham

[1] EMF and PNF went to Portugal for a holiday in the summer of 1953.

[2] Roy Dunnachie Campbell (1901–57), poet and translator of South African origin. A colourful and controversial personality, he lived a great deal in Spain and Portugal and in 1955 settled in Sintra. The punching episode took place in London on 14 April 1949, when Campbell, who resented Spender's referring to him as a 'fascist', went to hear Spender read his verses at a meeting of the Poetry Society in the crypt of the Ethical Church in London. Campbell, who had drunk a good deal of beer, shouted defiance at Spender, climbed onto the platform and punched his nose, which bled. Spender, who refused to press charges to the police, continued with his reading. See Peter Alexander, *Roy Campbell: A Critical Biography*, pp. 213–14.

406 To P. N. Furbank

[N. p.   c. 20 October 1953]

The confidential Clerk has snubbed us.[1] I have replied to him with all civility and dignity and friendliness, but on a p. c., which is brilliant I think. With love from M. See you when I come back

ALS: Lilly Library

[1] When in Portugal that summer, EMF and PNF made an acquaintance who asked for a photograph of the Queen. The 'snub' was a Palace official's letter of refusal. 'Confidential Clerk': allusion to T. S. Eliot's play of that name (1953).

407 To Leonard Woolf

King's College, Cambridge
5 December 1953

Dear Leonard

I am enjoying the Journals enormously and feel so close to her.[1] I did not feel that in our meetings, as she knew, and she has explained a bit why, but this new contact is very intimate, and I get not only pleasure but *relief* that some things can be expressed and be got off a page on to a reader.[2] Again and again the sensation received seemed new, never received before. A little like what she says about the sensations periodically engendered by the married life which Arnold Bennett laid down must be humdrum.[3]

I wish there could have been more about other people: but there you must have been hung up in various directions indeed from every direction.

Morgan

ALS: Sussex University

[1] *A Writer's Diary: Being Extracts from the Diary of Virginia Woolf*, ed. Leonard Woolf (1953).
[2] Perhaps the entry for 6 November 1919 (pp. 20–1) in which she comments on EMF not only as friend but as *critic*-as-friend.
[3] Bennett's statement, quoted on p. 98 of *A Writer's Diary*: '"The horror of marriage lies in its dailiness. All acuteness of relationship is rubbed away by this: . . . ."'

408 To John Morris

King's College, Cambridge
30 December 1953

Dear John,

Despite post-Christmas fluster, I must drop a line to say how much I ~~enjoyed~~ liked that review in Encounter.[1] Yes—the book entailed a good deal of trouble, which most readers of course do not see. The booksellers—including Bumpus—were against it, and it is only through the good offices of critics that it came across. An extended final section would have made my job easier, but unfortunately most of the material had been destroyed; there were letters from Malcolm's wife to her mother and sister which would have been invaluable.—So I am particularly glad that you quoted from the final section.—Then there is an unpublishable section, which would have made H.H.'s claims to sainthood clearer.[2] That couldn't go in because it couldn't.—His claims to genius are most difficult to document: he was always on to a point before I was and into it deeper, but that is only a start-off.

Love and loyalty <loyalty of *one's own choosing* that's to say> certainly do need a leg up in these days, and I am proud to hear I may have helped. Trouble is, they can only be hoisted indirectly. Direct attempts only result in the sermon or the political harangue.

Here is another piece of paper which reminds me John—why ever do you accuse me of inefficiency?[3] *Quite* fantastic. I make far more money than you do or than any other of my friends do, and in a capitalist society———and I cannot suppose that you are considering any other type of society———the only possible test of efficiency is the ability to make money—. — — So there. Income Tax return against Income Tax return, I'll take on the lot.

But now I really must stop. It is a great pleasure to have such a reader and to realise the care and sensitiveness that have gone to the writing of it.

All good wishes for 1954

Morgan

ALS: KCC

[1] Morris, review of *The Hill of Devi*: 'Love and Loyalty', *Encounter*, 2 (1954), 67–70.
[2] This was 'Kanaya': see Letter 233.
[3] Morris wrote in his review: 'I hope he will not feel offended if I also note that he is not very efficient in the ordinary affairs of everyday life. It has never mattered overmuch since there have always been, there always will be, friends to take over the bothersome details. But the idea of Mr. Forster being charged with looking after someone else's affairs seems to me uproariously funny; there could hardly have been a less efficient private secretary.'

409   To Lady Keynes

King's College, Cambridge
4 March 1954

Dear Mrs Keynes,

How very kind of you to send me Aunt Laura's letters! I have read through them with much interest, have destroyed most of them, since you say I may, and am keeping the remainder. If any more turn up, I should enjoy seeing them too.

I don't know when our aunts first met, but there were plenty of

links—the most probable being through the Wedgewoods. Hensleigh Wedgewood was the brother of Mrs Charles Darwin, and M^{rs}
H. W. was a friend of Marianne Thornton, my aunt's aunt. Aunt
Laura came up constantly to Clapham to stay with her aunt, and as
a child she became friends with the Hensleigh Wedgewood
daughters. So the road towards your aunt was easy.[1]

I don't know *what* was wrong with Aunt Laura's health. She had
nursed five or six of her brothers and sisters who died of
consumption, also her father and mother, and I fancy it broke her
nerve. Heart trouble, gastritis, hysteria perhaps—great energy
between times, much work done, much good done. She lived till
1924. Your Aunt Etty declared at the end she was kept an invalid by
her doctor "nasty vulgar sneering little man." But when the same
doctor said to her, apropos of something or other, "Now M^{rs}
Litchfield what do *you* think? It is such a thing to have the opinion
of a really clever woman", my mother observed that your Aunt Etty
bridled and preened. "Oh well— —", and she gave her opinion.

Many of the references in the letters awoke memories in me. The
'Weenie' who travelled back from France with your Aunt Bessie
became in later years my beloved Mrs Aylward.[2] The Fragonard
paintings, visited in their original setting near Grasse, were
unexpectedly encountered by me in the Frick Gallery, in New
York, and administered a strange shock.

I have photographs of my aunt here, also some of her sketches,
&^{ct}. If when you are in Cambridge any time you would care to come
and see them I should be very pleased.

Yours sincerely
EMForster

ALS: Richard D. Keynes

[1] EMF has embarked upon writing *Marianne Thornton*. Margaret Elizabeth Darwin
(1890–1974) was the daughter of Sir George Howard Darwin (1845–1912); granddaughter of
Charles Darwin; and the wife of Sir Geoffrey Keynes (1887–1982), distinguished surgeon,
bibliographer, and authority on William Blake. 'Effie', 'Snow' and Hope Wedgwood were
daughters of Charles Darwin's brother-in-law Hensleigh Wedgwood and his wife Fanny
Mackintosh (see Letters 1 and 158). Lady Keynes's aunt was Charles Darwin's sister,
Henrietta Emma Litchfield (Letter 28).
[2] 'Aunt Bessie': Susan Elizabeth Darwin (1803–66), sister of Charles Darwin.

410 To J. R. Ackerley

K[ing's] C[ollege,] C[ambridge]
13 September 1954

D.M.J. I have read your novel and liked it.[1] I also started reading
your letter but dropped it like a hot bun, for would you believe me it
started to tell me what Geoffrey Gorer thought I ought to think. I
have read it since and do not agree that the situation as regards

Johnny is at fault. You have established his charm, and consequently Frank as no fool; though it may be unwise nay tragic to fall for a morally worthless charmer it is a sound situation for a book. I did regret the paucity of pleasure—you only accorded one scene, and being self indulgent and lustful I should have liked more.[2]

Johnny's entourage is another matter and I wonder whether some of the later scenes displaying it might not be cut down or summarised. The earlier scenes were brilliant and very funny. I laughed "aloud". I here felt as I have with your work before, that usually it sails ahead freshly, but sometimes gets becalmed upon a not too-translucent patch of sea and revolves there. Example: Abdul in Hindoo Holiday. He was revolving. The analysis of a bore did not bore you. Then you cut him down, to the great advantage of the book. The epilogue of Muriel should certainly be cut down. You are very absolutely right to have one, the form requires it, and it underlines Evie's naughtiness. But it should be of footnote dimensions. For Muriel can provide nothing new—only cobwebs from yet another third-rate spider.[3]

It could—from a literary point of view—be published just as it is, and I hope you'll soon be discussing it with a publisher. I don't advise adding to it—you have been at it so long that you might get it smeary.—Bits of Millie and Maureen might go—their bests are marvellous, and Frank's quarrel with Millie excellent. By curtailing the home-spinners you will incidentally make Johnny more prominent. One doesn't require him to be nice but one wants him to be *there*: a problem in the book—not a defect in it—is that while he is in prison Frank scarcely sees him.

The above after one hasty read-through. I will read it again and return.[4]

I am so glad you have done it Joe.

I expect to be up for a couple of nights next Monday. With love from Morgan.

ALS: HRC

[1] Ackerley, *We Think the World of You* (1960), still in manuscript and being circulated to various friends for comment. Ackerley's letter to EMF does not survive. Geoffrey Edgar Solomon Gorer (1905–   ), anthropologist, author of books on Africa and America.

[2] The novel is the fictionalised account of how Ackerley acquired his dog Queenie, here called Evie, whose later life he describes in *My Dog Tulip: Life with an Alsatian* (1956). Johnny, the jailed young man in the novel, was her former owner; Frank, his friend, is the Ackerley-figure.

[3] Abdul: Ackerley's 'tutor' in *Hindoo Holiday*, described on pp. 68–70. 'The epilogue of Muriel': apparently the last section of the novel, in which Frank's cousin, now called Margaret, moves in to help care for Evie.

[4] For Ackerley's reaction to EMF's reaction, see his *Letters*, p. 122. The novel was finally accepted in 1959 by the Bodley Head.

411 To Lionel Trilling

King's College, Cambridge
1 August 1955

Dear Lionel Trilling

I am very glad to have your book—especially for the Keats which I hadn't seen. I have been reading in his letters ever since. He is almost the only great man I have ever wanted to be with—as opposed to the unsatisfactory "meet". The other one was Thomas Hardy, with whom I was a little and still miss. Keats would have been like friends one knows—plus a greatness which would not have been attached to him but part of him. Your references to his senses delighted me, and I started considering why sight and hearing have more prestige than the others.[1] Once I had a theory that they were held to be superior because they could be shared with other people: several people can look at the same Grecian Urn, but they cannot swallow the same drop of claret. This leaves out poor old smell, though: no sense is morally inferior to smell.—Well this is one of the things one could have talked about with Keats. What couldn't one have talked about, and no need to be at one's best when one did it either: not Conversation, which, tensed up all over, one would [have] offered to Goethe or Johnson or Proust.

I also came across my old, or rather new, friend in your pages. I allude to the Sense of Sin. He is much around here, and in the Universities generally. I went to our Theological College lately, Westcott House, and we had a sort of chat. He told me that without him it was impossible to understand the universe, and I came away having forgotten to reply that it did not occur to me to try to understand the universe. I must not run on like this so. Or rather what I mean is I have just finished the biography of my great aunt. Understanding, or partially understanding, her has been quite a large enough job. I have enjoyed the work very much, and there have been masses of family material for it which only I could handle, so that I have a pleasant illusion of originality.

I am going for a fortnight at the end of the month to the Dordogne, &c, in a car, and when I come back must attack the revision.[2] All going well the book will come out on both sides in the spring[.] Marianne Thornton: a domestic biography, will be its title. (Quite long.)[3]

I hope you are well. I heard a rumour that you were off to Oxford. Indeed you may be there already. I hope not. I am all right myself—except for the checks inevitable at my age. Going back to Keats—what a time he had with all their illnesses and money worries, and how *heroically* in the true sense he bore it all: no stern clenching of the jaws, no Rodinesque contortions. Thank you very much again. Please give my kind remembrances to Mrs Trilling and to James though this last cannot remember me, and be sure to let me know if ever you come this way.

Yours very sincerely
EMForster

ALS: Columbia University

¹ EMF, reading Keats's *Letters* in 1905, felt that Keats must have been nearly the best person in the world. For Trilling's references, see his *Freud and the Crisis of Our Culture*, pp. 22–6.
² He went to France with Bob and May Buckingham.
³ Published in 1956, preceded by two excerpts: see Kirkpatrick, p. 73.

412   To John McCallum

King's College, Cambridge
19 April 1956

Dear Mr McCallum:

It occurs to me to make further reference to *My Dog Tulip*, which I regard as a most original and remarkable little book.¹ Parts of it "put me off", and I have told the author so, ~~and~~ but I would not have those parts removed, for they ~~come up~~[?] contribute to a well-written and well-considered whole.

Ackerley has a high reputation with writers over here, not only because of his own two books (*Prisoners of War* and *Hindu* [*sic*] *Holiday*), but because as literary editor of the Listener for the past twenty years he has consistently encouraged good work in poetry and in prose. He is a most unobtrusive and selfless person, and this may perhaps be the reason why he has not a wider reputation with the general public.

Please excuse this rough piece of paper. I am resting a bit in bed after two active days in town. It was very nice seeing you, and I look forward to seeing the American Marianne [*Thornton*] over whom you have taken so much trouble.

With good wishes

Yours sincerely,
EMForster

ALS: Harcourt, Brace Archives

¹ John McCallum, of Harcourt, Brace, EMF's American publisher, was apparently considering publication of Ackerley's book. It was published in New York in 1965 by the Fleet Publishing Corporation.

413   To Wilfred Stone

King's College, Cambridge
30 August 1956

Dear Professor Stone

Thank you for your interesting and sympathetic letter.[1] I am so glad that you enjoy my work, and I am flattered, as an author must be, by your detailed knowledge of it.

I thought at first that you were planning a critical study of my books (such as Trilling worked out attempted some years ago), and I should have been most happy to give you what help I could over that. I think though that what you actually have in mind is a Biography, and I am afraid I feel that, if that is done at all, it had better be done after my death. I don't myself ever find biographies of living authors interesting, and I don't want to be the occasion of adding another to their number. Biographies of living men of action, public figures &[ct] fall into another category, for they have the support of the events with which they are connected, and this enhances their appeal.

I am so sorry to be unhelpful over this. It is not that I have any doubts as to your competence for the work suggested by you. It is that I doubt my own suitability as a subject.

With many regrets, and again thanking you.

Yours sincerely
EMForster.

You mention your Mark Rutherford book; if you would be so kind as to send me a copy of it, I should feel most grateful. My sympathy for him is somewhat limited, but so I gather is yours?[2]

ALS: Recipient

[1] Wilfred Healey Stone (1917–), Professor of English at Stanford University since 1963, first visited England in 1949–50, while writing his *Religion and Art of William Hale White* *("Mark Rutherford")* (1954). By 1953 Stone, after reading Trilling's study of EMF, had begun to think about writing on him, but his first approaches brought the above response.

[2] Stone presents Hale White as a Victorian oppressed by the rigidity of Christianity as it was preached and practised in his particular time and place. Stone discusses it dispassionately but sympathetically.

414   To Wilfred Stone

King's College, Cambridge
9 January 1957

Dear Professor Stone,

I have just been seeing Professor Willey. We talked of your research-projects, and I am concerned to think that I may be incommoding them.[1]

I wonder whether we could devise a compromise. As you know, I cannot favour either a biography or a literary study with biographical emphasis. I wonder whether you would think it worth while to undertake a purely literary study. This can be done, as has been shown by Professor Trilling who has already done it (from his point of view), and who—as he has since told me—deliberately avoided contacting me until his book was finished. You would of course be doing it from your own point of view, and as far as contacts are concerned I should be happy to see you if you came to Cambridge, when I might be able to show you pamphlets, articles etc. which would otherwise have escaped your notice.

It may well be that you will think the above suggestion inappropriate. Still I make it on the chance.

Yours sincerely,
EMForster

TLS: Recipient

[1] Stone had met Basil Willey (1897–1978), Edward VII Professor of English Literature at Cambridge, in 1949. Willey interceded on his behalf, and Stone wrote to EMF (21 January 1957): 'I am quite agreeable to the compromise you suggest, and far from regarding your suggestion as "inappropriate," I welcome it. The real inappropriateness, to say the least, would have been my proceeding in a "biographical emphasis" against your wishes and without your sympathetic encouragement.' He promised to proceed along 'purely critical lines. I think there is room and need for a literary study beyond that by Professor Trilling, and although I am not sure I am the man to do it, I am gratified to know I shall have your interest in my attempt.' Stone sympathised, he wrote, with EMF's 'desire for privacy (in and out of books).' On 22 January he wrote to Professor Willey: 'I cannot believe that I would be better served by refraining from any contact with him (as Trilling did) until the book is finished.' Stone wanted to see, not only any papers that EMF might make available, but also 'I want to see him, hear his voice, absorb impressions which would never be quite so valid at second hand.' Trilling, he wrote, had 'stolen much of my thunder, for I disagree with him on a number of points', but 'whatever the result, it will be a good adventure'. (Both letters: Stephen Wildman.) The result: Stone's *The Cave and the Mountain*.

415   To Timothy Leggatt[1]

King's College, Cambridge
3 August 1957

Dear Tim

If we don't take care we shall never write to each other, which would be a pity, so here is a line though I don't know your address and have not indeed much to say. The visit to Austria with the Buckinghams is my show-bit of news I suppose; a crowded and rewarding fortnight during which I sometimes felt hot and tired. Climax in Vienna—(to which we went in a boat down the Danube) —where my one Austrian friend has been so good as to become head of all the antiquities and monuments in his country.[2] This meant having a super-guide to the museums, churches, castles,

sceneries, and the only difficulty is now, when we are trying to sort
them out and keep ten baroque abbeys and twelve Breughels apart.

Here at Cambridge the chief piece of news is a mouse, which I
saw dancing in our bathroom fender, and the very same morning M^r
Scholfield saw a second mouse, upstairs.[3] This was a graver matter.
It resulted in the arrival of a Rodent-Exterminator, a trim grey
haired military-looking man whom the bed-makers found irresis-
table. I detested him. He ascribed the invasion to the Hungarian
underneath, who occupies one of Pigou's rooms.[4] "Dirt, sir—
Central Europe and similarly the Middle East, and they don't like it
when you tell them of it." Then he put down some crystals, and the
smell of rodents who have been exterminated in the wainscot is
gradually gathering strength. Two have been found entangled in
Mrs Blackwell's lavatory brush.

You see the dimensions of my news: mice. There are probably
actually rats in Canada and rat catchers who catch them, and I look
forward to a reply on the grand scale. I haven't much gossip of the
human sort, and am indeed not good at accumulating it. (*You* are
usually reported as knowing a good deal and not passing it on).
Norman—to go to the other extreme—exults in his hush-hush work
at the Observatory, and is now off for six weeks to the States. Ian
Stephens shakes off our dust permanently in order to reside at
Rawal-Pindi and write the official history of the Pakistani Army.[5]
He will enjoy this and be among people whom he likes, but a less
rewarding and I must add a more foolish job I find it hard to
imagine. He won't even be able to tell the truth.

I am so glad that your own work seems opening in such an
interesting and promising way, and wish you all good fortune in it.
The snag should be the difference between your political attitude
and that of your colleagues and superiors—the more different since
the politics are likely to be foreign politics. I haven't myself any
great quarrel with the Conservatives over home affairs. Sometimes
they seem to me right. It's when they look abroad that they go
wrong and are bound to do so—especially when they look at
non-white people.

I have just written a short article on Old Age which is rather
funny, unlike most other essays on that solemn subject, and will
some day appear in the London Magazine.[6] I am now reviewing a
Life of Harriet Martineau, and you may imagine me falling asleep
over it in the Fellows Gardens.[7]

No one is in your room for the moment. Kenneth should return
to it next month.[8] A pity you are not both there. You have between
you made my life here very pleasant, and I am grateful indeed.

Affectionate greetings from

                                                              Morgan

ALS: Recipient

[1] Timothy William Leggatt (1933–), after his degree at King's College, went on to receive a PhD from the University of Chicago in 1966. In 1957 he had a summer job in Canada before taking up academic and publishing appointments in India and Africa. He was a Lecturer in Sociology at the University of Sussex, 1966–73; Senior Tutor at King's, 1973–81; and Deputy Principal of the Central School of Speech and Drama in London, from 1982.
[2] Otto Demus (1902–), Austrian art historian, was Monuments Officer to the Austrian Federal Government, 1936–9. He emigrated voluntarily to England, 1939–46, and on his return to Austria resumed his old position and joined the faculty of the University of Vienna, where he became Professor of the History of Art, in 1951.
[3] Alwyn Faber Scholfield (1889–1969), a Fellow of King's, was Keeper of the Records of the Government of India, 1913–19; Librarian of Trinity College, Cambridge, 1919–23; and University Librarian, from 1923.
[4] Arthur Cecil Pigou (1877–1957), Professor of Political Economy at Cambridge, 1877–1957, died on 15 July.
[5] Norman Routledge (1938–) mathematician and Fellow of King's College, 1951–60, worked at the Department of Geophysics; he became an assistant master at Eton in 1959. Ian Melville Stephens (1903–84), journalist and foreign correspondent; with the Government of India Bureau of Information, 1930–7; Assistant Editor, then Editor, of *The Statesman of India*, 1937–51. He retired to England in 1951. Author of *Pakistan* (1963).
[6] Forster, 'De Senectute', *The London Magazine*, 4 (1957), 15–18.
[7] See Forster, 'Neglected Spinster', *The Observer*, 25 August 1957, p. 12; review of Vera Wheatley, *The Life and Work of Harriet Martineau* (1957).
[8] Kenneth Harrison: see Letter 397.

416   To P. N. Furbank

as from 11 Salisbury Avenue
STYVICHALE, Coventry[1]
4 September [1957]

Dear Nick

I am naturally delighted with your letter which I answer at once, though not posting till the end of the week. I don't know how to thank you for your suggestion of typing. It would be wonderful, but oh the time! The MS. must be "finalised" first. I return from Scotland to Coventry on Sept 17. How would it be if I came on to London on the 18th or 19th, got the M.S. for you and let you have it back at the week end? I do feel most grateful, and if the typing is as good as your letters it would be more than I ever hoped. I will get Miss Pate's to do the First Part and Lionel's letter in Part II. Makes a start.[2]

To take your queries—I am anxious for more of them.

"War had not even assumed its colonial aspect." An unwise sentence and in print. Raises the question of their ages and the date of Part II. I can't have Lionel more than 23 or Coco less than 19. That's how I see them together. Ten years off makes them 13 and 9—L. too old. Twelve years off will be better. 11 and 7 I then see them. But the dates? I must cut them and head 'Part II' "Twelve years" or get the years quickly implied—well they are in L's opening letter.

"The end of the chase" Merely bye play. L is the (physical) hunter who takes a little time to get under way. C is the (psychological) hunter who nearly gets his quarry at the end of the long conversation. Essentially they are both hunters. That is how they both get trapped.

"Implicated" caused me much thought and since this is evident had better revert to 'entangled'.

"Depassed": precious, can with advantage be scrapped.[3]

"Egyptian image": Scrap Egyptian perhaps.

I think I must alter and simplify C's rhetorical outpour. It connects with the general problem of conveying what he sees and feels. I have had such nice meditations for him. Such helpful residences in his interior. Notably after L. went on deck, when there were several pages about him and his magic, his trouble with his accounts, his dread of full-nakedness when alone. All had to go, and why? Because it held up the movement. In a story of this type the movement dares not stop. There is that much sense in Percy Lubbock's plea for "the point of view."[4]

The movement, as you have seen, falls into (i) Profane love (ii) the Long conversation culminating almost but not quite in (iii) a sort of Sacred Love—by the way all sensuousness, acceptable elsewhere, must be ~~cut away~~ removed here (iv) Mutual destruction.

L. is trapped by devices he doesn't recognise. At the same time, he wouldn't have been trapped if C. had been a dusky replica of Colonel Arbuthnot. He found physical charms in him and I have not yet indicated them adequately. That dumb boy in "The Medium" had the necessary limbs: on to which the funny shaped head has to be screwed.[5]

Will now sign this, with love and gratitude for your offer. I may add more later.

Morgan

ALS: Lilly Library

[1] The Buckinghams' address.

[2] During his move to Cambridge EMF had come on the manuscript of the opening pages of an abandoned novel, depicting an 'Anglo-Indian' family, a widow and two young children, returning on a boat from India. He had shown it to Ackerley, explaining how the novel had gone wrong: 'The story broadened into several deltas and got dull and bogged. I had not really decided what to make with it' (letter to Ackerley [c. 1948]. HRC). Ackerley published the fragment as 'Entrance to an Unwritten Novel', *The Listener*, 40 (1948), 3, 31. This set EMF's mind running once more on the story's protagonists, Lionel March and the young half-caste 'Cocoa' and on how they might meet again as adults. As a result, in 1957 he composed the novella 'The Other Boat'. PNF typed it, and various revisions, for him. Miss Pate's was a typing agency in Cambridge.

[3] PNF had questioned this, as seeming Frenchified.

[4] I.e. for the Jamesean method of restricting the narrative to one character's viewpoint at a time; see Lubbock, *The Craft of Fiction*, pp. 156–71.

⁵ Colonel Arbuthnot: character in the story. *The Medium*: melodramatic opera (1946) by Gian-Carlo Menotti, which EMF had seen and liked in the United States.

417   To P. N. Furbank

not from Upper Terrace House
Hampstead, N. W. 3
Saturday [7 September 1957]

Dear Nick,

Thank you for your phone message and letter, both very reassuring.

As you do typing so quickly, I will come up quite soon, suggest you come with typescript to the Club after your work is over, and that this time we have some dinner there.

I will ring you at your office Monday afternoon about 3.30. and enquire whether *Tuesday* or *Wednesday* would suit you. If you have not yet come to "They that seek fire shall find rest," miss it out, and I am almost inclined to add miss out anything else that strikes you as a hold up. Yes that tiresome violence. Words don't suit it. On the screen it could be done so well—have two human beings disintegrating into what they felt and did, and reintegrating after it had been done.

Such a dreadful lot missed out, too. Lionel's assegai nearly escaped you, and who will remember that Cocoa, who bit, had once hoped never to shed blood. It is my nearest approach to tragedy, and that is a reason—obviously not the only one, why I have been so enthralled by it. I did not plan it as tragic but now that it has looked at me for some time I see that the two heroes, with their different sorts of strength and weakness were likely to destroy one another. No wonder they both felt afraid near the end.

What a mercy, as well as a pleasure, that you and Joe liked it. I could so easily have been put off.

Hope to get you Monday afternoon. I have your extension.

Love
Morgan

ALS: Lilly Library

418   To James R. McConkey

King's College, Cambridge
21 September 1957

Dear Mr McConkey

Thank you for the book about me, which I have read of course with much pleasure (for it praises most acceptably) and also with much interest. It is curious to find oneself approached so understandingly: for instance, one or two critics have told me lately, that nothing in *A Passage to India* has any importance after the trial scene. One can but bow and smile a little wanly.[1]

I expect you are right in thinking *that* my best book. The one I like by far the best is *The Longest Journey*. I see it has terrible weaknesses, and was fascinated when you approached them. So much depends on Stephen. I never showed (except perhaps through his talk with Ansell) that he could understand Rickie, and scarcely that he could be fond of him. So that, in the end chapter, he lies as a somewhat empty hulk on that hillside. Who cares what he thinks, or doesn't think of? All the same I'm proud of creating him and do not consider him a minor character.

I meant to write you a more ordered response, but have a frightful cold.—In the *L. J.* (and elsewhere) you saw connections that never occurred to me, but they seem to work ~~very~~ quite well—e.g. the tea cup of experience and broken cup at the close: Ansell's 'circles' and Cadbury Rings. The connection I have *had* to reject is one of Lionel Trilling's for *Howards End*: he still feels that Margaret & Helen hint at the 1st and 2nd parts of Faust.[2]

Much entertained by that letter of D. H. Lawrence to Russell.[3] I had not known of it. I remember the quarrel—partly because I scarcely ever do quarrel. We corresponded on and off, but I never felt inclined to repeat the heart-to-heart experience: a disinclination of which he would have disapproved.

Thank you very much

Yours sincerely
EMForster

Eleanor Lavish, not Lydia—but she would be too delighted to be mentioned at all to mind.[4]

Yes—I hope we meet some day. Good wishes.

EMF

ALS: Recipient

[1] James R. McConkey (1921–   ), Professor of English at Cornell University. In *The Novels of E. M. Forster* (1957) he writes (p. 113) that '*A Passage to India* marks the perfection of a technique and a philosophy, the perfect union of rhythm and voice.'

[2] See Trilling, *E. M. Forster: A Study* (p. 116): 'Not for nothing do Margaret and Helen bear the names of the heroines of the two parts of *Faust*, one the heroine of the practical life, the other of the ideal life: Henry Wilcox bears Faust's Christian name and he and Leonard together, the practical man and the seeker after experience, make up the composite hero.'

[3] In *D. H. Lawrence's Letters to Bertrand Russell*, ed. Harry T. Moore, pp. 29–35.

[4] Eleanor Lavish: a character in *A Room with a View*.

419   To William Plomer

King's College, Cambridge
12 December 1957

Dearest William

Thus begins a letter that has been lying around for a long time now, but what is the use of Dearests if they never reach their Williams? I wrote in it that I was glad to hear of your better health, also to sympathise with you and Charles over your problem of living in a built-up area that is being further built up. And all the time the value of money falls. I wonder whether you have decided on a move. As far as amenities go, I think you could now certainly do as well nearer London.

I am lucky to be established here comfortably, and not yet a visible nuisance to others. You will have observed that I have already underlined two words in this letter, though: I am told it is a sign. For the moment I am 'busy' sending off 100 Christmas Cards. Last year I had over 100 friends. This year I seem to have less, and I am wondering who has dropped by the way side. Christmas I spend at Coventry, which thank heaven still stands, unattractive though is the house, and squashed though we shall be in it with the addition of the baby.[1] It sleeps with its grandparents, and May throws biscuits at it through the bars of its cot to stop it from waking up Bob.

I had an interesting day's reading yesterday, with the sudden sensation of being in close contact with what I was reading. It doesn't often come to me. What I read is not important, but it radiated ("believe it or not") from Freud. Trilling[']s cluttered-up meditation on him switched me over to Auden's poem, which I hadn't known and think fine, and thence I switched to the Trojan Women, being partly switched there from another direction, namely from Greece.[2] For Bob May and I are planning to go there again next spring.—But as for reading how curious it is: all these books, their lore of the ages, waiting to be embraced but usually slipping out of one's nerveless hands on to the floor. When one reads properly it is as if a third person is present.

I had reached this point when the enclosed arrived. Probably you have had one too, but I send it on the chance. I hope to see them either here or in London.—How many years can it be since you introduced me to Christopher, and Christopher was wearing a bowler hat. You called his mother a grey iron clad. What can she be compared to now?[3]

My life here goes on comfortably as I say. I see a great deal of Francis Bennett, a good deal of my neighbour Kenneth Harrison, and the young as they come in and out. They are accessible enough, more so I imagine than in most places, but there is no point in seeing much of them, and I expect they feel the same. One of them took me

to The Entertainer in London the other week—certainly a high light
in friendliness, and I wish I had been more entertained[.][4]

Well dear William I must draw to my close. Love to you. Love to
Charles and I hope I may see you both again before long. Write
again William when you feel inclined.

Morgan.

Bob and I rang up Leo when we were driving through
Northumberland in September, but unluckily he was away. The
telephone directory was peppered with Charltons—bye-blows he
would have it of a more fertile age.

ALS: Durham University

[1] Clive Morgan Buckingham (1956–   ), son of Robin Buckingham and his wife Sylvia.
[2] Trilling, *Freud and the Crisis of Our Culture*; cf. Letter 411. W. H. Auden, 'In Memory of
Sigmund Freud' (1948), in his *Another Time*, pp. 116–20.
[3] Isherwood and his friend Don Bachardy (1925–   ) were ending a round-the-world tour
during which Isherwood collected materials for his *Ramakrishna and His Disciples* (1965).
On his mother, Kathleen Machell Smith Isherwood (1868–1960), see his *Kathleen and Frank*
(1971). The 'enclosed' item, from Isherwood, is not now with Plomer's papers (University of
Durham).
[4] John Osborne's play, *The Entertainer*, opened in April 1957 at the Royal Court Theatre
and transferred in September to the Palace Theatre. It was a Laurence Olivier hit, in which
three generations of declining music-hall entertainers and a broken-down hall, the Empire,
suggest the decay of England.

420   To William Roerick

Flat [London].—As from K[ing's] C[ollege],
C[ambridge].   17 May 1958

Dearest Bill,

My article was very good except for its foolish title, which I did
not write. It was called over here "De Senectute", but Harper's
Bazaar, thinking I suppose that this would not shine amongst the
lingerie, changed it to "One Cheer for Old Age" and created quite a
false impression thereby. If they wanted to change it and had asked
me *I* should have suggested "*Four* Cheers for Old Age." But they
did not ask me.[1]

Greece plus Istanbul plus Venice was a great success, not as
romantic as our cruise of two years ago, but introducing even more
remarkable objects to us.[2] I will not describe them to you, since I
wish to address Tom and you on the subject of my 80th Birthday. In
your letter to Bob, more hopefully than in your letter to me, you
speak of the possibility of your both being over here for it. My
GOODNESS, my LOVENESS since you regret that my article
does not mention love, how happy that would make me. A plan is
afoot for a party in Cambridge, and another is atoe for a party in
London. To both you are both instantly invited. I will write again

later, and will touch (of course in a very refined way) on the subject of finance. For I should very much like to offer each when he gets here the sum of ·001ꝝ —you allowed me to do something of the sort once before, and I do assure you it is now exactly a hundred times easier for me to do it. So, although the subject has not been mentioned by me, will you please keep it in mind?[3]

Bob is at the present moment reviving old memories at the Hammersmith Boathouse, Rob and Sylvia are at the Chiswick Empire seeing the Summer of the Seventeenth Doll, May is in their house, taking care of Clive Morgan Buckingham, I am in my flat.[4] We have spent the day together and I hope the same will hold true of tomorrow. This afternoon Bob drove me to Abinger to see my much beloved gardener, Bone—I don't expect you will remember him—and on our way back we called on my Aunt Nellie, aged 96, whom you won't have seen because she has only recently gone into society.[5] She was reading a most terrible looking shocker, "Bloodshed galore" she remarked complacently. And now I must get a little food together—bread, butter, boiled eggs and wine. It somehow doesn't read quite right, but I am looking forward to it. I go back to Cambridge on Monday. I have much more to say—perhaps will put into a letter to Tom to whom I ~~always~~ also owe a letter. He wrote me such a nice one, too. Much love to him and much to you from

Morgan.

ALS: Recipient

[1] On 'De Senectute', see Letter 415; for 'One Cheer for Old Age', see *Harper's Bazaar*, American edition, April 1958, pp. 186–7, 212.

[2] EMF, with Bob and May Buckingham, left on 1 April for this cruise. He had prepared 'by reading about-and-looking-at-Greek-and Turkish things right and left till I can scarcely tell a metope from a mosaic', and he was fascinated by parallels between the 'Greek Experiment' and 'our complications today. They were worse than we are in their open approach of revenge, on the other hand they didn't get bogged down in Original Sin. I don't exactly dislike Christianity, but it is such a relief to get away into a world that isn't coloured by it. One writer (forget which) divides people into those who care for knowledge, those who care for fame, and those who care for money—a non-A. D. division, and a satisfying one. And Pindar says life is bloody awful, but occasionally a light shines in it and makes it comfortable and gentle. This comes in one of his Pythian Odes, and I shall try to remember it if I get to Delphi' (EMF to Eric Fletcher, 25 March 1958. Recipient). The eighth Pythian Ode was a kind of talisman for him (cf. *EMF*, I, 101), and he kept a copy of the passage, in his handwriting, in his rooms.

[3] Tom Coley (1917–   ) and Roerick had paid for EMF's trip through France with them in 1953.

[4] *Summer of the Seventeenth Doll*: film based on the 1955 play by the Australian Ray Lawler (1922–   ), performed in New York in 1958; filmed in Australia, released in the United States as *Season of Passion*.

[5] Aunt Nellie: i.e. Eleanor Mary Whichelo.

421   To P. N. Furbank

King's College, Cambridge
16 July 1958

Dear Nick, 🖋 Round this important blot let me say how much I should like to come for a night on Friday. I will ring you at your office, but if we should not contact I will call for you there a little before 4.30. How very nice that will be.

If there seems time, I want to tell you of a strong experience or rather re-experience that I have just had. I am destroying or rearranging letters, and came across those from Mohammed el Adl—I may not even have mentioned his name to you, he was a tram-conductor whom I met in Alex[andria] 1917–1919, and again saw in 1922, soon before his death. I assumed the letters would be nothing much, but gave a glance before destroying them and was amazed—all the things I most adore glimmering in them.[1] He had gone underground in the interval, and there is no doubt that a little of him reemerged in Cocoa.[1] They have given me the oddest feeling, and one which I am very fortunate to have. (Something like 100 letters). I was an awful nuisance to one or two friends at the time, and no wonder. If I talk about him to you, you will anyhow not have to find him a job.

Morgan

ALS: Lilly Library

[1] Transcribed by EMF into his 'Memoir of Mohammed' (AMS: KCC).
[2] I.e. in 'The Other Boat': see Letters 416, 417.

422   To George Savidis[1]

K[ing's] C[ollege,] C[ambridge]
25 July 1958

Dear George
I have just finished, with a good deal of excitement and occasional doubts, Marguerite Yourcenar's "Cavafy".[2] I don't like the translation, the preface has not the authoritative tone I found in her "Hadrian", and the Parisian interventions of Mallarmé, Utrillo &[ct], rather jar. But she says many good things, and when I have written to you I must try to write to her and tell her so. (Not but what she is likely to know about them already.) One of them is her discovery that Cavafy is, and always potentially was, an *old* poet, another her suggestion that his own erotic life may never have been continuous or strong. And she does bring out, though without stating it, his triumph—a triumph that has nothing to do with success. Sick of getting through my final years by British jokiness, I have had a timely reminder of another method.

I turned from her translation to Wooden cordato's, which is reliable rather than inspired.[3] Then I tried to turn to Cavafy himself, but where can I have put him?

I heard from someone, Noel I think, that you might be allowed to see the unpublished papers.[4] I should be interested in them and in anything about him, but, with his type of mind, I should doubt whether he had anything to conceal beyond names places and dates. How very proud I am, George, that I ever got to know him; it is certainly one of my 'triumphs'. R. A. Furness took me to see him in 1916–17.

Above is a letter from

Morgan

ALS: Recipient

[1] George P. Savidis (1929–   ) was on the faculty of the University of Salonika until 1971; he then became Professor of Modern Greek Literature at Aristotle University, Thessaloniki.

[2] Marguerite Yourcenar (1903–   ), Belgian novelist, essayist, and translator, became a member of the Académie Française in 1981. Her Cavafy volume: *Présentation critique de Constantin Cavafy, 1863–1933* [*par*] *Marguerite Yourcenar* [pp. 7–64]. *Suivie d'une traduction intégrale de ses poèmes par Marguerite Yourcenar et Constantin Dimaras* (1958). Her 'Parisian intervention': 'Couleur du ciel mise à part, nous ne sommes pas si loin du Paris d'Utrillo' (p. 16). On Cavafy as an 'old poet': 'La poésie de Cavafy est une poésie de veillard dont la sérénité a eu le temps de mûrir' (p. 37). 'Hadrian': *Mémoires d'Hadrian* (1951), translated by the author, as *Memoirs of Hadrian* (1954).

[3] John Nicolas Mavrogordato (1882–1970) was Bywater Professor of Byzantine and Modern Greek Language and Literature, and Fellow of Exeter College, Oxford, from 1939. See Cavafy, *Poems*, translated by Mavrogordato, with introduction by Rex Warner (1951). Wooden cordato: EMF seems to be punning on μαυρόω: 'to make dim or obscure, to darken, to blind'—stretching it to include something on the lines of 'to make wooden'.

[4] This was Noël Gilroy Annan (1916–   ), later Lord Annan; Fellow of King's College from 1944; Lecturer in Politics, and Provost, 1948–66; Provost, University College, University of London, 1966–78, and Vice-Chancellor, 1978–81.

423   To Sir John Wolfenden[1]

King's College, Cambridge
19 October 1958

Dear Sir John,

I have now heard from Miss Sands.[2] Many thanks for arranging everything in a way so convenient to me, and I look forward to our talk.

One of our suggested topics was "principles", but I think that if this comes up you will have to handle it. I am clear as to their importance in private life, but am vague as to the part they play or can be expected to play in national life. (For instance individuals can apologise to each other when they have done wrong. Nations never)

I am also pessimistic, or as you would perhaps say cynical, about the foreseeable future of the east, and of the world, and here again is a topic on which I had better not be 'drawn'. I should only depress listeners, and perhaps annoy them.

The things that have most interested me in life are personal relationships and the arts, and I don't, at the age of 80, find my interest in either flagging. This may come in if we discuss "communications".

Yours sincerely
EMForster

ALS: KCC

[1] Sir John Frederick Wolfenden (1906–   ), created Baron Wolfenden in 1974, was Vice-Chancellor of Reading University, 1950–63, and Chairman of the University Grants Commission, 1963–8. He was Chairman, 1954–7, of the Departmental Committee on Homosexual Offences and Prostitution that published *The Wolfenden Report* (1957), implemented in 1967 as the Sexual Offences Act, which revised and liberalised the legal definitions of homosexual offences.

[2] Rose-Mary Sands, a producer of English Talks for Asia in the BBC Overseas Service, was in charge of a 'First Meeting' series, in which Sir John and EMF would discuss topics of their choosing. Miss Sands suggested (5 August 1958. BBC) to EMF the possibilities of his perspective of India, or a kind of 'continuation in time' of *Passage*, or his views on the 'angry young men' of the day. He replied (13 August 1958. BBC): 'Something about India, I think; and not the angry young men.' The programme, 'Sir John Wolfenden Meets E. M. Forster', was broadcast on 13 November 1958.

424   To John Meade[1]

Sunday [*c.* 1959]. King's College, Cambridge

Dear John

I now wish I had accepted your suggestion of driving me down to Chiswick, since—easy though it is by train—it would have given us some more time together.[2]

I did enjoy yesterday evening so much, indeed I shall never forget it. It was such a happiness to find that after long separation we were still in close touch and had so much to communicate. I have been wondering whether our first meeting may be partly responsible for this happy state. We introduced *ourselves*: in nearly all meetings one is introduced by a third person, who subtly presides in the background.

Well anyhow we've met and to me it's a great pleasure.

I mentioned to you that I no longer think sadly of West Hackhurst. About two years ago I realised that if I was still living there, aged 80, without my mother, and without a family—which would have made all the difference—I should have been in an awful fix. I still feel angry with those Farrers who turned me out of a house my own father built: his one achievement as an architect for he died young—and no doubt this has made me more critical than I should be of Farrers generally.

The annotated Passage to India is a very different matter, and a scream. I do hope you find it.[3]

Well I must finish now, John. I do hope that you will both be able to drive over here for a meal before long.

Yours affectionately
Morgan

ALS: Shelagh Meade

[1] John Meade (1921–71) was the son of the Rector of Abinger. Late in 1938 he and EMF struck up a conversation on the London train, and EMF moved into Meade's compartment to continue it. More than once he recalled this as a better way of getting to know people. He kept up with Meade, who entered the Army and went through the African campaign, and arranged for him to meet Judge Brinton in Egypt. Meade remained in the regular army, the family tradition of Shelagh Lugard, whom he married in 1950. Her father was Major Cyril Edward Lugard (1894–1970), son of Major Edward James Lugard (1865–1957) and nephew of Lord Lugard (1858–1945, soldier in African colonial wars, then colonial administrator in Africa and Hong Kong.

[2] To Chiswick: i.e., to his London flat.

[3] Shelagh Meade's grandfather, Major E. J. Lugard, lived at Abinger Common and was said to have a copy of *A Passage to India* that was covered with his furious comments. Apparently EMF never succeeded in seeing this.

425   To Enzo Crea[1]

King's College, Cambridge
12 January 1960

Caro Enzo
Che farà, che dirà il suo Morgano? Le fotografie sono veramente *magnifiche*. A Palestrina io sono gran scrittore, sono serioso, solido, non ho ancora mangiato, forse non mangiero mai. A Roma nel giardino con Nicola tutta si cambia: sono felice, sono contento, ho mangiato il cinghiale, ho bevuto il vino, sono il suo amico.
E lei viene in Inghilterra? Francis dice che è possibile. Quando viene? Se non viene à Cambridge io vengo à Londra, salutarla.—E di nuovo, grazie tante per le fotografie,—

Suo amico affetuoso,
Saluti à tutti

M.[2]

ALS: Recipient

[1] Enzo Crea (1927–), Roman publisher, founded the Edizioni dell'Elefante in 1964. He met EMF in 1959, when EMF visited Italy on a British Council conference tour. Crea was then head of the iconographical section of the *Encyclopedia Universale dell'Arte*, and Francis J. H. Haskell (1928–), Fellow of King's College, 1954–67, and Professor of Art History at Oxford since 1964, asked him to look after EMF. They toured the city together for a week, and Crea visited EMF during annual trips to England.

[2] 'Dear Enzo / What shall your Morgan do, what shall he say? The photographs are truly *magnificent*. At Palestrina I am the great writer, I am serious, solid, I haven't eaten yet, maybe I shall never eat. At Rome in the garden with Nicola everything is different: I am happy, I am cheerful, I have eaten wild boar, I have drunk wine, I am your friend. / And are you coming to England? Francis [Haskell] says that it is possible. When will you come? If you don't come to Cambridge I will come to London, to greet you.—And once again, thank you so much for the photographs. / Your affectionate friend / Greetings to all / M.'

With Tim Leggatt, c. 1962.   With Christopher Isherwood.

With May and Bob Buckingham, 1968.

426   J. R. Ackerley

[N. p.]   Thursday [10 March 1960]

Darling Joe

I have just rung up Walter, invited him to dine at the Reform Tuesday, and told him you will be there too.[1] Will you?

I am here till Sunday, probably sleep Sunday night at young Rob's, and Monday and Tuesday at my flat. Let me know accordingly.

I am very much pleased indeed by your broadcast about the play. Good Newby has sent me a script.[2] What welcome things you say, and even if they aren't true about me they make everything more important[.]

Florence Barger has died in her sleep.[3] She has been as if dead for months, but these things are shocks. I have suddenly wanted to think or look at warm obscenities—this has happened to me when upset all my life, right back to Alexandria. All I can lay my eyes on here is a Poem of Ausonius called "Imminutio"—it's unlikely that you or any other Latin scholar knows of it, it is very much my own discovery, and only has one drawback,—It is made up of extracts from Virgil which as A. says doubles its temperature.—[4]

Love from Morgan

ALS: HRC

[1] Walter Baxter (1915–), author of a controversial novel, *Look Down in Mercy* (1951); at one time a London restaurateur.

[2] Percy Howard Newby (1918–), novelist and critic, joined the BBC in 1949 and was, successively, Controller of the Third Programme, 1958–69; of Radio Three, 1969–71; Director of Programmes, Radio, 1971–5; and Managing Director, Radio, 1975–8. J. R. Ackerley broadcast his commentary on 19 January 1960. EMF offered to send him to New York for the opening there on 31 January of Santha Rama Rau's stage adaptation of *A Passage to India*; see Letter 427. Ackerley went to New York, but not until 1 March, and he saw the play on 5 March. See Ackerley, *Letters*, pp. 163, 170, 201, 202, 204, 206–7.

[3] Florence Barger died on 8 March 1960.

[4] 'Imminutio': Section VIII, of Ausonius, *Cento Nuptialis*. In his introduction, Ausonius warns that if anything in it is shocking, the fault is Virgil's.

427   To Santha Rama Rau[1]

K[ing's] C[ollege,] C[ambridge]
27 April 1960

Dear Miss Santha Rama Rau

I went to the opening performance at the Comedy. Very splendid; everything tightened and clarified, good reception and *most* enthusiastic press. I think all must be now set fair for New York[.]

M[rs] Pundit [*sic*], who ignored the letter I wrote her about the Oxford performance, arrived at this one late, and informed the actors afterwards that she had advised you not to dramatise the novel![2] Well content with herself, she then departed. More important, I managed to have a glimpse of your mother and sister in the general confusion.

Well we are doing well. The pity is we are never together.

Yours very sincerely
EMForster

ALS: Houghton Library

[1] Santha Rama Rau (1923–), daughter of the Indian diplomat Sir Benegal Rama Rau, dramatised *Passage*, in part as response to a dinner-party challenge; see her 'A Passage to Broadway', *Theatre Arts*, 46 (1962), 66–7, 75. To her 'incredulous delight' EMF approved her script. On 5 October 1956 Cheryl Crawford (1902–), of the New York Theatre Guild, received formal approval, contingent on necessary changes' not deviating radically from the book; Miss Rama Rau was authorised to approve any such changes. The script circulated for some five years and was finally taken up by Frank Hauser (1922–), who had reopened the Oxford Playhouse in 1956. *A Passage to India* opened there on 19 January 1960 and received a favourable but qualified review in *The Times* ('A Passage to India by No Means a Novelist's Play,' 20 January, p. 6). Principals were the Pakistani actor Zia Mohyeddin (1933–) as Aziz, Norman Wooland (1905–) as Fielding, Enid Lorimer (died 1982) as Mrs Moore, and Dilys Hamlett (1928–) as Adela. On 20 April, with the same cast, the play moved to the Comedy Theatre, London, under management of Donald Albery (1914–), then Chairman and Managing Director of Wyndham Theatres. Lawrence Langner (1890–1962), of the New York Theatre Guild, flew to England and negotiations began. Helen Strauss, of the William Morris Agency, represented Miss Rama Rau and EMF in New York; see Strauss, *A Talent for Luck*, pp. 261–3, 269. From the outset, EMF's attitude toward a film version was a problem—to EMF because he distrusted Hollywood, to agents and theatrical directors because a film advance would help to defray production costs. Miss Strauss, writing to John Cadell of the Christopher Mann Agency in London (11 December 1959. HL) quoted a letter from EMF: ' "I am surprised that this should crop up yet again. I have no intention whatsoever of having the play filmed, and, if contrary to every expectation, it should be filmed, I have no intention of paying the Oxford Playhouse any percentage on the sale." ' (Correspondence, scripts, contracts, and rehearsal notes are among Miss Rama Rau's papers in the Houghton Library at Harvard, and in the Boston University Library.)

[2] Miss Rama Rau's relative, Mrs Vijaya Lakshmi Pandit (1900–), Nehru's sister and a prominent diplomat; in 1960 she was High Commissioner for India in London. On the family, see Santha Rama Rau, *Home to India* (1945).

428 To Santha Rama Rau

King's College, Cambridge
25 May 1960

Dear Miss Santha Rama Rau

Thank you so much for your letter and for "Nina's" charming one[.][1] I can't remember the curtain rising and falling all that often[.]

Your words are confirmed most agreeably; I have just had the papers about the New York production and will work through them tomorrow. I do hope they will let Frank Hauser produce, and as for Zia Mohyeddin—they are <u>mad</u> if they don't have him. He *is* the part—please tell them so from me, with all the eloquence at your disposal. I think too that they ought to have Norman Wooland. For the two women['s] parts they will probably insist on substituting ~~people in~~ actresses with names.[2]

Here the play goes better and better, and the College Porter has just rushed up to tell me that "Women's Hour" says it is the only play worth seeing in London.[3]

With much admiration and gratitude:

Yours very sincerely
EMForster

I hope you are well. I am, but on the tired side, and am clear that I shall not be coming over for the U. S. production.

ALS: Houghton Library

[1] Nina: Miss Rama Rau's niece, now Mrs Jonathan Marks, delighted EMF by being the only member of the family who remembered to count curtain calls.

[2] Hauser wrote to Miss Rama Rau (27 April 1960. HL): 'I am dead certain that Forster will blow his top if anything happens to the script which you and I haven't initiated. I think you can tell [Lawrence] Langner that if he really wants to have a scandal on his hands, with the aged author denouncing the production in advance, he is going the right way about it. Forster is obviously very happy about it all now: . . . You will be glad to hear the two Broadway types who attended with [American actor] Sam Wanamaker said in the first interval that the play was slow in coming to its point. As one of them put it, "We all know this Indian guy is going to fall in love with the girl, so why don't they get down to it." As a friend of mine remarked, they had come to see "Up in Quested's Room".'

[3] By mid-April profits were over £1500. Early reviews in leading London papers expressed considerable admiration. Private opinions were encouraging. Victor Gollancz, Miss Rama Rau's publisher, wrote to her (29 July 1960. HL): 'This is the first play I have really enjoyed for a very long time. . . . It is so witty, subtle, humane and moving.'

429   To William Plomer

King's College, Cambridge
17 August 1960

Dearest William,

What agreeable news Jack brought back with him! not agreeable in all ways, since, by the terms of our reference, I shall never read the book. But that you have consented, and on the particular lines reported by him, gives me great predeceased pleasure. It is exactly what I should wish. I am most grateful.[1]

I was also glad of your other news. He and Joe seem to have enjoyed themselves much. The next day I went to Coventry, and paid a saddish call on Margery in the pouring rain, and on what is left of Ron. May took a grave view of his health, and courageously said so. He was not, when we saw him, in pain or gloom. Margery also poorly. The irony of that pleasant room—I don't remember whether you know it. If only Johnny Simpson had lived! But every thing there has collapsed in the wrong order.[2]

Weird journey from Coventry today, as so often. Line blocked by derailment south of the station. Bob drove me like lightening [*sic*] to Rugby, whence a train missed all the connections, but gallantly took on a life of its own and never gave up until it touched Ely.

Love & renewed appreciation from Morgan

ALS: Durham University

¹ William Plomer had agreed, through the mediation of Sprott, who at that time was EMF's appointed literary executor, to write a biography of EMF, not to be published until after his death. Over the subsequent years Plomer collected a certain amount of material, which he handed to PNF.

² At the death of John Simpson in 1955, Margery Wilson was left to care for her mentally-handicapped brother Ron, to whom Simpson had been a nurse: see Letter 283.

430   To William Plomer

King's College, Cambridge
[21 June 1961]

My dear William:
 Can I ask your advice?
 ("I *think* perhaps....")
 No but dear William do listen. It is something unusual and odd. My kind stockbrokers sent me yesterday a cheque of unexpected proportions. I had staggeringly underestimated what would be realised by a sale of 'rights'. The result is that I have at least £1000 for "charities". You are more in touch than I am with struggling young writers or indigent old ones and perhaps with societies that assist them—though societies have the drawback of premises, secretaries &ᶜᵗ who sop up the donations.—Here's my first impulse coupled with a preference for writers who seem likely to do, or who have done good work.
 My second impulse is more questionable. I would dearly like to give a donation to the Homosexual Law Reform Society if it was an efficient body, but know nothing about it, and it seems to have lost influential or fashionable support since it was founded. People bother over homosexuality much less—except for the many, and I suppose there are as many as ever, who get persecuted and prosecuted quietly.—I wonder whether you have more information about this soc[iety] than can be gained from the remarks of J. B. Priestley.¹
 I wonder how Joe is—no recent news. Or indeed how you are. Is Charles back yet? I am back two days from Coventry—a restful fortnight there livened by wisecracks from May. Such as: "I can always sleep if I'm left alone" or "I consider a hot bath is a remedy for every ill, particularly if it's of the spirit."

Don't let my questions bother you. I thought of you as one who might have a suggestion close to his hand.—I am also writing to K. Clark (though not knowing him nearly so well) in case he had any suggestions about artists.[2]

Before my windfall I bought a picture without seeing it. Dashingness justified, I think.

Much love from
Morgan

Your caviare was consumed at Bob's board with great delight.

ALS: Durham University

[1] This Society was founded in 1958 and ceased its activities in 1969. It was instrumental in the passage of the Sexual Offences Act of 1967, which legitimised homosexual acts between consenting adults. Priestley was one of thirty-three signatories to a letter expressing 'general agreement with the recommendations of the Wolfenden Report that homosexual acts committed in private between consenting adults should no longer be a criminal offence', and that the present law represented neither Christian nor liberal opinion. (See 'Homosexual Acts: Call to Reform Law', *The Times*, 7 March 1958, p. 11.)

[2] Kenneth Mackenzie Clark, created Lord Clark in 1969 (1903–83), was Keeper of the National Gallery, 1934–45; Slade Professor of Fine Art at Oxford, 1946–50 and 1961–2; and Chairman of the Arts Council, 1953–60.

431   To Santha Rama Rau

King's College, Cambridge
23 October 1961

Dear Miss Rama Rau,

I have been able to talk over your letter at once with Mr Rylands.[1] All seems fairly well. Here are some notes[:]

Donald McWhinny [*sic*] *not* preferred to Tony Richardson, but acceptable. I saw The Caretaker over here—an odd little affair I thought it, and not nearly as good as The Birthday Party, still what there was to direct in it went all right.[2]

Gladys Cooper—not really right, but I've always admired her greatly, and if she would be so good as to get herself up as dumpy as she can bear and to mug up a little mysticism or poetry she would do, for M^rs M[oore]

E. Portman preferred to R. Richardson, on the whole.

Now for our questions and comments,:—

Who does Adela? Immensely important, we think. Please may I be informed before it is settled.[3]

Very important: Scenery. The Court Scene unsuccessful in ~~London~~ the original, is said to have been most impressive in one of the provincial shows—Bristol I think—where the building was flimsy, made as it were of wattle, which the tropical sunshine pierced. And in connection with this scene

MOST IMPORTANT OF ALL

the nude beautiful punkah wallah. Without him, Mr Rylands says, the play must be cancelled! He can easily be contrived—he was at Nottingham, though neither beautiful nor nude there, and a punkah was seen working which blew off no one's wig. Will you please impress this on all whom it may concern[.][4]

Zia—we all repeat—is important and must remain so even if poisoned by some aspiring Porto Rican[.]

> With all good wishes
> EMForster

ALS: Houghton Library

[1] George Humphrey Wolferstan Rylands (1902–), Fellow, and administrator in various capacities, of King's College; University Lecturer in English Literature; Chairman, Cambridge Arts Theatre; Governor of the Old Vic, 1945–78.

[2] Donald McWhinnie (1920–), Head of Sound Drama, BBC; first stage production was *Krapp's Last Tape*, by Samuel Beckett (1958). He directed Pinter's *The Caretaker* (1960) and the New York production of *Passage* (1962). Pinter's *The Birthday Party* opened in London in 1958. Tony Richardson (1928–) also began in BBC television and had produced in both England and the United States.

[3] In New York the English actress Dame Gladys Cooper (1888–1971) was Mrs Moore; Eric Portman (1903–69), not Sir Ralph Richardson, was Fielding; and the American actress Anne Meacham (1925–) was Adela. EMF wrote to Miss Rama Rau (12? November 1961: HL): 'The news sounds good, my only outstanding anxiety being Adela. She is difficult and essential—strange her part should not be listed as "star"—though when I come to think of it stars have no necessary connection with parts.'

[4] EMF wrote to Miss Rama Rau (10 January 1961. HL): 'My only disappointment is over the Punkah: there is not to be one in the Third Scene, for technical reasons.' The play opened at the Ambassador Theatre on 31 January. It got a bad review from John Simon: 'A Passage to India', *Theatre Arts*, 46 (1962), 57–8. Most of the other New York reviews echoed the admiration of the British press; see, for example, Howard Taubman, 'Worth Adapting', *The New York Times*, 11 February 1962, Section 2, p. 1.

432 To Benjamin Britten

> King's College, Cambridge
> 31 August 1962

Dearest Ben

Your letter does not bring much comfort, I knew you were ill but hadn't realised the extent. It is dreary news indeed. I hope — — &^ct and so on, — — but it is scarcely worth finishing the sentence.[1]

I saw darling Rob this morning. He is always in bed now, temperature 103–4, discomfort rather than pain, can still be amusing, and, though I loathe the word "purified", his face, with its thinness and the splendid darkness of the eyes, has now an etherial [*sic*] beauty. Dignity has taken charge of the floundering athlete we once tolerated, and he says nothing that is not impressive, though scarcely above his breath. He will leave us for certain, what concerns me is May. Bob, though the tragedy has altered him, is more resilient. We are all four helped I think by our disbelief in the existence of god. We should keep worrying otherwise why such a catastrophe had occurred.[2] As soon as one realises that the universe is neither for us or against us one feels steadier. Hardy weakened himself by supposing it was hostile, and set traps.

To turn to easier matters, I hope to go to France in a fortnight's time for about a fortnight. I shall have to travel alone this time but shall stay in [sic] friends.

I will write again, and I shall be getting news of you, even if you aren't writing to me yourself.

Your loving and grateful Morgan, as always.

ALS: Britten Estate

[1] Britten had just finished a very heavy schedule of composition.
[2] Robin Buckingham, now father of two sons, fell ill in 1961 and the diagnosis, after taking many wrong turnings, finally indicated that he was dying of Hodgkin's disease. He died on 8 September 1962.

433   To Eric Fletcher

King's College, Cambridge
6 January 1963

Dearest Eric,

Just as I am about to reply to your lovely letter I lose it—all except its last page, brilliantly terminated by the signatures of Marianne and Mark.[1] I seem losing everything to day and knocking most things over—the milk has just gone on to the poems of George Herbert. Your letter gave me great happiness as have one or two others of this 1962–3 festival [Christmas Season] when the weather has been so discouraging and the public encouragements matching it. You make me feel that I have done and been something in my life and that on the top of that you have managed to respect and love me, I respect, I love, you. There's a great deal to be grateful for and proud of—I very much hope I shall end up feeling this about many things. And I am ~~very sorry for~~ moved when I see little Clive and Paul [Buckingham], accepting family and personal affection as ~~things of course~~ assumptions, but possibly surviving them. I want general education. I want economic security for all. But neither of these guarantees what I most want.

I forget when or what I wrote last. I was at Coventry Dec. 19–Jan. 2 with an interval at Rockingham of three days which was prolonged into four, as I was snowed up.[2] Bob extricated me, also brought me here. 'Here' has been mainly this room—a beautifully warm one. Really how lucky I am to have crept into it. Where and how does an old man live otherwise? Every comfort, and agreeable servants. I should have had to tack on to or near friends—never a good move—or had a small and centrally heated service flat in London.

This leads me to enquire after Woodside. I do hope it works tolerably.[3]

I had an unusual and welcome experience yesterday. As the result of reading a poem aloud to myself, my mind concentrated and I was able to write a little, intently and intensely. The poem, believe it or not was *Little Gidding*. What I wrote was not in its praise, was indeed a denunciation of its main idea that there is something specially real in pain.[4] I believe in pain of course—(one has to, looking around one, e. g. at Rob, or at the newspapers)—but as an interruption not as an essential. I side indeed with all the other animals. It takes a human animal of Christian perversity to announce that the rose and the fire are one.

But what I want to ~~impress~~ convey is the effect that the intonation of poetry in a solitary room had on me. Have you ever tried it? I tried the following night with no success, though the poet was Auden—his threnody on Freud—and the emotions congenial. Repetition often does fail, but my conclusion was that Eliot was the better poet in one way—he had more staying power and did not weaken himself by whimsies.

I am hoping the cold will not prevent my going up to the Albert Hall for Ben's Requiem on Wednesday—the fog did for the Abbey performance.[5] I have a few more engagements in January, but they are here. When is the hope of seeing *you* again? Perhaps the letter I can't find says. As for the future, Bob *and* May plan to go abroad at the end of May and assume I shall come too, and I shall if I feel mobile enough.

Well this shall now be posted with my love to Vicky and the children and to yourself with what's aforesaid.

Morgan

ALS: Recipient

[1] EMF replies to a birthday letter from Fletcher, who was living at the time in Keighley. Marianne (1956–) and Mark (1952–) are his children.

[2] EMF had been at Rockingham Castle, Northamptonshire, visiting Lady Faith (1911–83) and Commander Sir Michael Culme-Seymour, 5th Baronet (1909–).

[3] I.e. Woodlands, the South Yorkshire mining village where Fletcher was born, still his parents' home. EMF asks about the illness of Fletcher's father.

[4] T. S. Eliot's *Little Gidding* (1942) was published as the fourth of his *Four Quartets* (1944). EMF wrote on it in *CB*, pp. 266–7.

[5] Benjamin Britten's *War Requiem* (Op. 66) was first performed 30 May 1962 at the rebuilt Coventry Cathedral. It was performed on 6 December 1962 at Westminster Abbey, in one of the worst London fogs for many years, and again at the Royal Albert Hall on 9 January 1963.

434   To Wilfred Stone

[N. p.]   9 February 1963

Dear Professor Stone

I was so pleased to get your letter the other day. I had as a matter of fact been recently thinking of you and wondering how you and your work had been faring. I knew that you had been ill, and was hoping for news of your health.

But to begin with your questions. Of course you are *most* welcome to quote from my published works and equally welcome to quote from my letter to Wedd. He was *certainly* the leading influence on me when I was an undergraduate, and a permanent one since. He taught me—most important in my case—that I knew more than I thought I did. It is he who said, in a gentle drawling voice 'I don't see why you shouldn't write.' After leaving Cambridge I got to know him socially, and remember a holiday in Yorkshire lodgings with him, his mother and his sister. I remember his marriage, his illness, and after his return to Cambridge his occupancy of this room ~~where you and I met~~, while Mrs Wedd sat in the entry-room, a scholarly Cerberus, writing her history of Universal Religion. (This did not do so well.)[1]

Of the others whom you mention in Wedd's group I knew Roger Fry well, but not till later years, McTaggart not at all, and I saw something of G. E. Moore but at the end of his life.[2] Wedd was the formative figure and I am so glad that this should be emphasised.

I have stupidly (an octogenarian's privilege) mislaid your recent letter, and I should have liked to have it by me when I replied. But I haven't forgotten to give your messages to Noel Annan and Patrick Wilkinson and both of them are pleased and reciprocate.[3] Nor shall I ever forget your considered opinion about the *Passage*. I wonder whether you are right, and needless to add I ~~think so~~ hope so.[4]

My own health continues satisfactory for my age and I continue to live in the pleasant surroundings which you have seen, and to be cared for by good friends. I much look forward to the publication of your book and if there's anything else about it which you want to write to me over please don't hesitate. I send you my best wishes, and please also convey them to your wife, who may remember me, to your son, who might, and to your daughter who can't!

EMForster

ALS: Recipient

[1] Rachel Wedd's encyclopaedic history was never published. For EMF's letters quoted by Stone, see *The Cave and the Mountain*, pp. 400–2.

[2] George Edward Moore (1873–1958), ethical theorist, was a Prize Fellow at Trinity College, Cambridge, 1898–1904; then Professor of Philosophy at Cambridge, 1925–39. He edited *Mind*, 1921–47, and he received the Order of Merit in 1951. His most widely-known work is *Principia Ethica* (1903). John McTaggart Ellis McTaggart (1866–1925), author of

commentaries on Hegelian philosophy, was a Fellow of Trinity College, Cambridge, from 1891, and Lecturer, 1907–23. He is best known for his two-volume *The Nature of Existence* (1921–7).
³ Noël Annan was very helpful to Stone in England in 1957.
⁴ Perhaps, in *The Cave and the Mountain*, p. 346: 'In short, the book is a masterpiece of *understanding*.'

435　To Noël Gilroy Annan

King's College, Cambridge
21 February 1963

Dear Noel,

I have been reading your lively speech as reported, partly with sympathy and partly with a personal interest, for it has led me to ask myself why I am so often reluctant to agree with you. I don't write "disagree" for that entails a knowledge of facts and a ~~grasp~~ capacity for arguement that are beyond me.[1]

I have come to the conclusion that the barrier between us is temperamental. I have a growing—perhaps *in*growing!—respect for smallness, and you are increasingly attracted by largeness. I think our high table, college, university, are all too large and deprecate further ~~ext~~ distensions, and I jib at grandiose projects outside them.

Such is my reaction, though in expressing it I can command neither the prolixity of Sheppard nor the profundity of Goldie. I am further hindered by my inability to think nationally for more than ten minutes at a time whereas your speech sounds to have been consistently national—in the super-democratic sense of the word of course—and to have ignored such adjuncts as meditation and the arts.

All the best from
Morgan

ALS: Recipient

[1] On 18 February 1963, Annan spoke at Cambridge, at the inaugural meeting of the East Anglian branch of the 1963 Campaign for Education. He called for, among other measures, a quarter of the population to receive full-time training, for priorities in educational needs, and for improvement of technical institutions. Citing the 'brain drain' to the United States, he described the present plan as 'peanuts'. See 'Higher Education Plan "Peanuts"', *The Times*, 19 February 1963, p. 12. EMF had recently opposed an increase in the size of King's College, while Annan as Provost supported a moderate increase. On this letter, Lord Annan comments: 'Typical Morgan block-buster . . . Morgan's letter on this matter is *excellent*—his wisdom at its best.' (Letter to PNF, 20 April 1982. Recipient.)

436   To Benjamin Britten

King's College, Cambridge
12 April 1963

Dearest Ben,

I have been thinking so much about you lately and have often composed a good letter to you in my head in my bed, but it vanished when facilities arrived.

It began about a fortnight back, after a drive to Little Dunmow. It is some way in your direction and I began to wonder whether you had seen the odd lean church and the exquisite 'altar' tomb jammed against its left wall. There is a photograph of this in Pevsner but the man turned out to be far finer in his actual alabaster.[1] One could reach him by scrambling over pews and touch his face with one's own. He was either young or middle aged according to the shifting of the curves, and neither a saint nor a quack[?] churl; very strong. She outlived him by twenty years; they cannot have been pleasant. She has been given too bright a new nose; otherwise all seems untouched and I got that sense of *uninterrupted* communication which I think you know about. I thought of you as we drove back, in some huge and far away public place, getting the acclaim you so deserve and I sent you a sort of dove. Aren't the crowds a curse, Ben! How they spread death without intending to do so! Isn't it significant that the innocent tourists, merely by breathing are destroying the Lascaux paintings![2] Crowds will not follow me over the Little Dunmow pews. You may, and I can't think of you as ever bringing spreading any thing but the right sort of life. It is one of my reasons for loving you.

M.

ALS: Britten Estate

[1] Walter Fitzwalter (d. 1432) and his wife (d. 1464), in the Church of St Mary, Little Dunmow, Essex. Nikolaus Pevsner, in *Essex* (1954), finds them effigies 'of the highest quality available', with an appeal rare in English fifteenth-century funeral sculpture (p. 278, Plate 33a).

[2] In 1963 the prehistoric paintings in the Lascaux cave in the Dordogne had to be sealed up because visitors and exposure to the outside air were causing rapid deterioration.

437   To K. N. Natwar-Singh

King's College, Cambridge
17 June 1963

Dear Natwar,

I received your kind letter on my return from France—a particularly agreeable France.

I don't think I ought to edit a tribute to myself——or indeed to contribute to it except by my long-ago tribute to Gandhiji which I am very glad should appear.

So I am not reading what Mulk writes about me.[1]

I have not heard from H. B. of this pleasant project and do not see why I should.[2] I am not interested, (here) in that side of the thing. It has my affectionate approval and I shall be glad if it contains an element of surprise. Tell them *not* to send me any contracts. I require *no payment* for the Gandhi speech or for anything else. I should feel it unseemingly [unseemly].

Yours ever,
Morgan

TTr supplied by recipient

[1] In *E. M. Forster: A Tribute, with Selections from His Writings on India*, edited by K. Natwar-Singh; see Mulk Raj Anand, 'Recollections of E. M. Forster', pp. 41–9; Forster, 'Mahatma Gandhi', pp. 79–81.

[2] H.B.: Harcourt, Brace.

438 To William Plomer

King's College, Cambridge
Wednesday 20 November [1963]

Dearest William,

How lovely to be asked whether Oniton is any where. No one but you has ever asked, and those chapters of the book have always given me a particular feeling.

It is *Clun*. I can't be sure of the date from my diary, but my map shows that I walked there, over Clun Forest, from Newton (Montgomery), and walked on next day to Ludlow. I was alone, except for the dubious accompaniment of A. E. Houseman. There are breaths from him in those chapters, the best I think being at the end of ch. 29.[1]

This little matter has set me thinking of the past which is sometimes evoked by smallness. A big matter—Mohammed el Adl—has occurred to me. I think you know that the scraps ~~serving~~ surviving from him are gathered in a box, together with some "memories" of him, shymaking and threnodic. With one exception—and that a tremendous one—he has been the greatest thing in my life. Poor FitzGerald—for I have been reading your thorough and *most* admirable contribution—I can see most of my tendencies in him but in my case they seem to have blessed.[2]

I have now neatly—and not designedly—reached Nov. 22, when I hope both to see and hear you. Through the kindness of Marion I am being taken to Gloriana and back to the party.—And to complete the pleasant prospect, Bob will be picking me up at it.[3] I do hope he sees you.

Love   Morgan

ALS: Durham University

¹ EMF refers here to the part of *Howards End* set in Oniton and dealing with Evie Wilcox's marriage. Chapter 29 ends (p. 246): 'Day and night the river flows down into England, day after day the sun retreats into the Welsh mountains and the tower chimes "See the Conquering Hero".' For Housman's 'Clun' see *A Shropshire Lad*, No. 50.

² See Plomer, 'Edward Fitzgerald (A Lecture Delivered at the First Festival of Music and the Arts in [8] June 1948 [at Aldeburgh])', in *Orpheus: A Symposium of the Arts*, 2 (1949), 57–72; reprinted in Plomer, *Electric Delights*, pp. 87–105. Fitzgerald (1809–83), poet and man of letters, is remembered principally as trans-creator of *The Rubaiyat of Omar Khayyam* (1859).

³ This was a concert performance of Britten's *Gloriana* (Op. 53, 1951), with libretto by Plomer, for Britten's fiftieth birthday, 22 November 1963, at the Royal Festival Hall. A party at the Harewoods' home followed. News of President Kennedy's assassination came during the concert but was kept from Britten so as not to spoil the birthday celebrations. For Plomer's libretto, see *The Operas of Benjamin Britten*, ed. David Herbert, pp. 207–30.

439 To P. N. Furbank

K[ing's] C[ollege] C[ambridge]
7 March 1964

Dear Nick

I have been dipping all day, pleased, into Hardy, opening at a poem I did not know, *Night in November*, and making other welcome discoveries. I differ strongly with you only on one point—your rejection of *My Cicely*.¹ I have always found it so moving and solemn. The human anecdote, as so often with him, does not work well, and the opening stanzas <which are *not* the stanzas you quote> are certainly clumsy. But what does the anecdote distil? One of the great homages to England, the reel or "riband" westward as far as Exeter, and, after disillusionment there, the eastward return, touching briefly what had been traversed in another mood—And in the last stanza the human happens to go right and allows what might have been an imperfect poem to be called by me a great one. Goldie Dickinson thought it was, and so did a still remoter figure, Sydney Waterlow. It is very much mixed up with my own "Wessex" past, though it doesn't enter into the *L.J.*, and may not have been written at that date. I think of it always when I rush by the House of Long Sieging in a train.² It gathers up so much scenery and history, and does so with effortless power.

I'll write again soon. I had forgotten Tim N.'s good offices over Maurice.³

Love and thanks from Morgan

I too find Fitzwilliam Hall definitely forgivable, but have only seen it from the Highway.⁴

ALS: Lilly Library

¹ 'Night in November', in Hardy, *Selected Poems*, ed. P. N. Furbank, pp. 56–7. In his Introduction (pp. xi–xxii), PNF wrote: 'When writing a narrative poem he often makes the

characters talk the most incredible and unnatural mish-mash of language: what is one to make of the opening of "My Cicely", for instance?... "My Cicely", despite some fine passages, *is* bad, as bad as it seems.' See *The Complete Poems of Thomas Hardy*, ed. James Gibson, pp. 51–4.

² Hardy's 'House of Long Sieging' is Old Basing House near Basingstoke, scene of a Civil War siege.

³ O. W. Neighbour, a friend of PNF, had been lent a copy of *Maurice* and had raised a query that caused EMF to rewrite the conclusion.

⁴ PNF had said that he liked the architecture of Fitzwilliam College's new buildings, which include a striking dining hall with a clerestory.

440   To Wilfred Stone

King's College, Cambridge
18 February 1966

Dear Will

thank you for your further letter of January 26. You must think my silence strange, but I have been ill and was indeed in hospital for a little. The hospital did me no harm and I'm now enjoying life again.[1] But my eye-sight has been affected and I now read or write very little. I commandeer friends to work for me and this line is being written by one of them. He is also reading some of your book aloud to me and I have read some of it myself, but not straightforward. My admiration remains great and is shared by others who have read it.

First to answer your question: Why did I stop writing fiction after *The Passage* came out? To that question there is no answer at all; I have been racking my brains and can find no reply to this very reasonable question. I can only suggest that the fictional part of me dried up. As far as I can remember I did not even think of writing either a novel or short stories. I did not dry up entirely, for when the war broke out in 1939 my hatred and fear of the Nazis inspired me to do a great deal of propaganda. I wrote a pamphlet which official red tape forbade me to publish. There was nothing special in it, and most of it has appeared in broadcasts &ᵗᶜ.[2] The Germans anyhow listened to it and I was put on their list for annihilation. I remember Rose Macaulay ringing me up when the War ended to announce the delightful news that we should be punished together. I wish we could meet and talk it over together. Is there any chance of you coming?

To turn to the more satisfactory subject of your book. My only point of disagreement is your lengthy criticism of Lowes Dickinson. I wish you could have made it not softer (it would be wrong to ask you that) but shorter, and I do not think this would have damaged the book.[3]

The care and the insight of your work are both remarkable. Yesterday we read 'A Room with a View' and 'The Longest Journey'. As you know I am very fond of the latter and you have shown me reasons why I should not be. I do not withdraw my fondness, nor would you wish me to.[4]

I hope to be writing again to you later and perhaps in my own hand. My own hand spells a good many words wrong, though what does that matter.

I appreciate your writing so affectionately and I venture to return the affection.

Morgan

ALS: Recipient. J. R. Ackerley's hand, signature by EMF

[1] EMF had had a slight stroke in 1965.
[2] This pamphlet is unidentified.
[3] Stone, in *The Cave and the Mountain* (pp. 80–5), assesses humanism as being unrealistic and utopian.
[4] *Ibid.*, 184–215.

441   To Robert J. Buckingham

King's College, Cambridge
Tuesday [Autumn 1966]

Dear Bob

I have just received your letter of Saturday[.] I wonder how you found dear Ted. The news sounds bad.[1] *There* is a person who appears to do nothing, but has actually done all he can for everyone all his life.—You will see him of course next week end, too. Give him my love, if he can receive it. I suppose things are all right for money.

I have been annoyed with you for planning to go to the Boat Race without me. We have seen it together, when we could, since 1930, and this sort of thing hurts. I have indeed written you a letter ~~about this~~, which I now tear up.—Don't do it again, please, if there is an again. Life is never very long.

Love
Morgan

ALS: May Buckingham

[1] Bob's brother Edward lost his voice in 1966; the cause was cancer, and he was ill until his death on 20 April 1968.

442   To Santha Rama Rau

King's College. 20 July 1967

Dear Miss Santha Rama Rau

I didn't and I don't want *A Passage* filmed. I am so sorry.[1]

I do hope that your health continues on a better level. Natwar

EMF's room at King's, Cambridge, 1969 (bottom picture shows Tom Coley with EMF).

EMF on the beach at Aldeburgh.

gave me a fairly favourable account of it. I hope too that your tiresome domestic trouble has softened itself.

Yours very sincerely
Morgan Forster

ALS: Boston University; J. R. Ackerley's hand, signature by EMF

[1] Miss Rama Rau had written ([mid-summer 1967] HL), asking permission for herself and Natwar-Singh to write a film script for Hollywood: 'Always, before, when you didn't wish to consider the idea of such a film both of us understood and agreed with your refusal to "sell" a work of art to "barbarians"—which is, indeed, the only appropriate word for the world of the Hollywood movie types.' Proposals now came from 'one of India's leading movie stars—an actor, not just a glamour-boy', and from the distinguished Bengali director, Satyajit Ray. She pointed out that the final section of the book, omitted from the play, could be included in a film to 'make a whole of what on the stage was only a part of a great novel'. She completed a film script. In 1984 a film version of *A Passage to India* was in production.

443   To Edward Buckingham[1]

King's College, Cambridge
Wednesday [March 1968]

Dear Ted

I send you a line, as I hear you are feeling poorly—though it doesn't do *me* much good when I feel poorly myself[.] Have had a nice line from Bob and I think he is going to see you himself. I go on all right myself, and, as you may have heard, we hope to go to Aldeburgh in the summer, for the Music—he, May, and I. It is generally a pleasant place, but for the visit it will be buzzing with musicians, all jabbering about music, and each thinking the other plays badly.

Well I must stop now, for I must not bore you about the Arts

Much love as usual, and all my hope that you will improve in health

Morgan

ALS: Shirley Buckingham

[1] Bob Buckingham's brother; see Letters 342, 441

444   To William Plomer

King's College, Cambridge
[17 March 1968]

Dearest William

Your charming and welcome letter of March 7th should have been answered sooner, but neither my head nor my pen are as much on the spot as they should be, and here is March 17th. I was so pleased with your kindness and your readiness to help Nick. He has just been here, and duly grateful. I have certainly fallen among useful as well as charming friends.[1]

Ben's collapse is indeed wretched, and unexpected. I had a cheerful card from Venice, just before he returned, and am now full of anxiety for the future.[2] I am thankful that he is being looked after at Ipswich. I am well myself, but shattered by the money trouble which Nick has just been trying to explain to me. It is the sort of trouble which I had never expected, short of a war, and due solely to French wickedness, as far as I can gather.[3]—But my brain is not too bright, and I had been better [sic] stop. I can only repeat how much I liked your letter, and to send my best love to you and to Charles. I shall hear in good time how the Prodigal Son stands. I heard such cheerful news of it from Venice.

Best love as afore said from

Morgan

to you ~~all~~ both[4]

ALS: Durham University

[1] PNF was beginning to collect information for *E. M. Forster: A Biography*.
[2] This was the start of Britten's heart trouble, for which he had open-heart surgery in May 1973. He had gone to Venice in January 1968 to work on *The Prodigal Son*, the third of his Church Parables, libretto by Plomer. See *The Operas of Benjamin Britten*, edited by Donald Herbert, pp. 309–18.
[3] Britain was in a severe financial crisis in the first three months of 1968 as a result of the devaluation of sterling in November 1967. In mid-March De Gaulle's government precipitated a panic-stricken rush on gold, which appeared likely to destroy the international monetary system based on sterling and the dollar.
[4] Both: Plomer, and his friend Charles Erdman.

445   To Duncan Grant[1]

King's College, Cambridge
17 October [1968?]

Dearest Duncan

thank you for your letter, and how I do *agree* with you about Joe's books, though no one else will. It seems so ill-tempered, and such a reproach to all his friends. Did any of his friends (except of course Queenie) love him or appear to love him? I wish I could give him a good smack![2]

Love to yourself from

Morgan

ALS: Columbia University

[1] The painter (1885–1978), member of the London Group and of the Bloomsbury circle.
[2] EMF refers in particular to Ackerley's *My Father and Myself*, published in 1968. The intended sense of EMF's third sentence is plainly: 'He writes as if none of his friends . . . loved

him.' EMF was suffering from the effects of a minor stroke when he wrote this, and Duncan Grant later denied having written to EMF on the subject.

446   To May Buckingham

King's College, Cambridge
Sunday [postmark 24 October 1969]

Darling
    Silence cannot mean peace. Send me a line. (All right here)

Morgan

ALS: Recipient

BIBLIOGRAPHY
Volumes One and Two

BOOKS BY E. M. FORSTER

—— *Abinger Harvest*. London: E. Arnold; New York: Harcourt, Brace, 1936.

—— *Alexandria: A History and a Guide*. Alexandria: Whitehead Morris, 1922; 2 vol. ed., revised: Whitehead Morris, 1938; Gloucester, Mass.: Peter Smith, 1968.

—— Arctic Summer *and other fiction*. Ed. Oliver Stallybrass and Elizabeth Heine. Abinger Editions (Vol. 9). London: E. Arnold, 1980.

—— *Aspects of the Novel*. London: E. Arnold; New York: Harcourt, Brace, 1927.

—— Aspects of the Novel *and related writings*. Ed. Oliver Stallybrass and Elizabeth Heine. Abinger Editions (Vol. 10). London: E. Arnold, 1974.

—— *Avec vue sur l'Arno* [A Room with a View]. Trans. Charles Mauron. Paris: Robert Laffont, 1947.

—— *The Celestial Omnibus and Other Stories*. London: Sidgwick & Jackson, 1911; New York: Knopf, 1923.

—— *Commonplace Book*. London: Scolar Press, 1979.

—— *The Development of English Prose between 1918 and 1939*. W. P. Ker Memorial Lecture, 1944. Glasgow: Jackson, Son and Company, 1945.

—— *The Eternal Moment and Other Stories*. London: Sidgwick and Jackson; New York: Harcourt, Brace, 1928.

—— *Goldsworthy Lowes Dickinson*. London: E. Arnold; New York: Harcourt, Brace, 1934.

—— Goldsworthy Lowes Dickinson *and related writings*. Ed. Oliver Stallybrass. Abinger Editions (Vol. 13). London: E. Arnold, 1973.

—— *The Government of Egypt; Recommendations by a Committee of the International Section of the Labour Research Department, with Notes on Egypt, by E. M. Forster*. London: The [Fabian] Labour Research Department [1920].

—— *The Hill of Devi, being Letters from Dewas State Senior*. London: E. Arnold; New York: Harcourt, Brace, 1953.

—— The Hill of Devi *and other Indian writings*. Ed. Elizabeth Heine. Abinger Editions (Vol. 14). London: E. Arnold, 1983

—— *Howards End*. London: E. Arnold; New York: Putnam, 1910.

—— *Howards End*. Ed. Oliver Stallybrass. Abinger Editions (Vol. 4). London: E. Arnold, 1973.

—— *Indiske Dage* [A Passage to India]. Trans. Paul Laessøe Müller. Copenhagen: Berlingske Forlag, 1935.

—— *Le Legs de Mrs Wilcox* [*Howards End*]. Trans. Charles Mauron. Paris: Plon, 1950.

—— *The Life to Come and Other Stories.* Ed. Oliver Stallybrass. Abinger Editions (Vol. 8). London: E. Arnold, 1975.

—— *The Longest Journey.* Edinburgh and London: Blackwood, 1907.

—— *The Longest Journey.* Ed. Elizabeth Heine. Abinger Editions (Vol. 15). London: E. Arnold. In progress.

—— *Marianne Thornton. A Domestic Biography, 1797–1887.* London: E. Arnold; New York: Harcourt, Brace, 1956.

—— *Maurice: A Novel.* London: E. Arnold; New York: Norton, 1971.

—— *Monteriano* [*Where Angels Fear to Tread*]. Trans. Charles Mauron. Paris: Plon, 1954.

—— *The New Disorder.* New York: privately printed, 1949.

—— *Nordic Twilight.* War Pamphlets (No. 3). London: Macmillan, 1940.

—— *Pageant of Abinger.* In aid of the Parish Church Preservation Fund, 14 and 18 July 1934. Dorking: A. A. Tanner, 1934.

—— *A Passage to India.* London: E. Arnold; New York: Harcourt, Brace, 1924.

—— *A Passage to India.* Introduction by Peter Burra. Everyman's Library (No. 972). London: J. M. Dent, 1942.

—— *A Passage to India.* Ed. Oliver Stallybrass. Abinger Editions (Vol. 6). London: E. Arnold, 1978. See also: Rama Rau, Santha.

—— *Pharos and Pharillon.* London: Hogarth Press; New York: Knopf, 1923.

—— *Le plus long des voyages* [*The Longest Journey*]. Trans. Charles Mauron. Paris: Plon, 1952.

—— *A Room with a View.* London: E. Arnold, 1908; New York: Putnam, 1911.

—— *A Room with a View.* Ed. Oliver Stallybrass. Abinger Editions (Vol. 3). London: E. Arnold, 1977.

—— *Route des Indes* [*A Passage to India*]. Trans. Charles Mauron. Paris: Plon, 1927.

—— *Two Cheers for Democracy.* Ed. Oliver Stallybrass. Abinger Editions (Vol. 11). London: E. Arnold, 1972.

—— *What I Believe.* Sixpenny Pamphlets (No. 1). London: Hogarth Press, 1939.

—— *Where Angels Fear to Tread.* Edinburgh and London: Blackwood, 1905; New York: Knopf, 1920.

—— *Where Angels Fear to Tread.* Ed. Oliver Stallybrass. Abinger Editions (Vol. 1). London: E. Arnold, 1975.

—— *W Słońcu Indy* [*A Passage to India*]. Trans. H. Myslakowska. Warsaw: Towarzystwo Wydawnicze „Rój", 1938.

—— and Eric Crozier. *Billy Budd, Opera in Four Acts. Music by Benjamin Britten. Libretto by E. M. Forster and Eric Crozier. Adapted from the story by Herman Melville.* London: Boosey & Hawkes, 1951. Revised version: *Billy Budd: Opera in Two Acts* (1961).

OTHER WORKS

Abercrombie, Lascelles. *Emblems of Love, Designed in Several Discourses.* London and New York: John Lane, 1912.

Ackerley, J. R. *Hindoo Holiday, An Indian Journal.* London: Chatto & Windus; New York: Viking, 1932.

—— *The Letters of J. R. Ackerley.* Ed. Neville Braybrooke. London: Duckworth; New York: Harcourt Brace Jovanovich, 1975. American title: *The Ackerley Letters.*

—— *My Dog Tulip.* London: Secker & Warburg, 1956; New York: Fleet Publishing, 1965.

—— *My Father and Myself.* London: The Bodley Head; New York: Coward McCann, 1968.

—— *The Prisoners of War: A Play in Three Acts.* London: Chatto & Windus, 1925.

—— *We Think the World of You.* London: The Bodley Head: New York: I. Obolensky, 1960.

Aeschylus. *The Oresteia of Aeschylus: Agamemnon, Choephori, Eumenides.* Trans. J. T. Sheppard. Cambridge: The University Press, for Bowes and Bowes, 1933.

Aksakov, Sergei Timofieevich. *A Russian Gentleman.* Trans. J. D. Duff. London: E. Arnold, 1917.

—— *A Russian Schoolboy.* Trans. J. D. Duff. London: E. Arnold; New York: Longmans, Green, 1917.

—— *Years of Childhood.* Trans. J. D. Duff. London: E. Arnold; New York: Longmans, Green, 1916.

Alain-Fournier (pseud. of Henri-Alban Fournier). *Le grand Meaulnes.* Paris: Emile-Paul Frères, 1913; London: Barnard & Westwood, 1944.

—— *The Lost Domain (Le grand Meaulnes).* Trans. Frank Davison. London: Oxford University Press, 1959.

—— *The Wanderer (Le grand Meaulnes).* Trans. Françoise Delisle. Boston and New York: Houghton Mifflin, 1928.

Alexander, Peter. *Roy Campbell: A Critical Biography.* Oxford and New York: Oxford University Press, 1982.

Ali, Ahmed. *Twilight in Delhi: A Novel.* London: Hogarth Press, 1940.

Ali, Mohammed. *My Life: A Fragment: An Autobiographical Sketch.* Ed. Afzal Iqbal. Lahore: Sh. Muhammed Ashraf, 1942.

Allen, Walter. *As I Walked Down New Grub Street: Memories of a Writing Life.* London: Heinemann; Chicago: University of Chicago Press, 1982.

—— *Innocence Is Drowned.* London: Michael Joseph, 1938.

All-India Writers' Conference. *The Indian Literatures of To-Day: A Symposium. Essays presented at Jaipur, October 20th–22nd, 1945.* Bombay: P.E.N. All-Indian Centre, 1947.

Angell, Norman. *Shall This War End German Militarism?* London: Union of Democratic Control, 1914.

Anstey, F[rederick] (pseud. of Thomas Anstey Guthrie). *The Travelling Companions: A Story in Scenes.* London and New York: Longmans, Green, 1892.

Antonius, George. *The Arab Awakening: The Story of the Arab National Movement.* London: Hamish Hamilton; Philadelphia and New York: J. B. Lippincott, 1939.

Archer, William. *India and the Future.* London: Hutchinson, 1917; New York: Knopf, 1918.

Arnim-Schlagentin, Elizabeth von. See Russell, Mary.

Auden, Wysten Hugh. *Another Time: Poems by W. H. Auden.* London: Faber and Faber; New York: Random House, 1940.

—— and Christopher Isherwood. *The Ascent of F6: A Tragedy in Two Acts.* London: Faber and Faber, 1936; New York: Random House, 1937.

—— and Christopher Isherwood. *Journey to a War.* London: Faber and Faber; New York: Random House, 1939.

Austen-Leigh, Augustus. *King's College.* Cambridge College Histories. London: F. E. Robinson, 1899.

Barbusse, Henri. *Le Feu: (journal d'une escouade).* Paris: Flammarion, 1916.

Basham, A. L. *The Wonder That Was India.* London: Sidgwick and Jackson, 1954; New York: rev. ed., Hawthorn Books, 1963.

Basileona: A Magazine of King's College, Cambridge, 1900–14. Introduction by Sir Charles Tennyson. London: Scolar Press, 1974.

Baxendall, Lee, and Stefan Morawski, eds. *Marx & Engels on Literature and Art: A Selection of Writings.* New York: International General, 1977.

Baxter, Walter. *Look Down in Mercy.* London: Heinemann; New York: Putnam, 1951.

Beckett, Samuel. *Krapp's Last Tape, and* Embers. London: Faber and Faber, 1959; New York: Grove Press, 1960.

Beddoes, Thomas Lovell. *The Works of Thomas Lovell Beddoes.* Ed. H. W. Donner. London: Humphrey Milford for Oxford University Press, 1935.

Bedford, Sybille. *Aldous Huxley: A Biography.* 2 vols. London: Chatto & Windus/Collins; New York: Knopf/Random House, 1974.

Beerbohm, Max. *Zuleika Dobson: or an Oxford Love Story.* London: Heinemann, 1911; New York: John Lane, 1912.

Begbie, Lionel F[rank]. *Boshtan Ballads: Flotsam from the Isis and Other Verses.* Oxford: Alden & Company; London: Marshall, Hamilton, Kent, 1901.

Bernhardi, Friedrich Adam Julius von. *Britain as Germany's Vassal, together with Kriegsbrauch—The Customs of War,* . . . . Trans. J. Ellis Barker. London: W. Dawson; New York, Doran, 1914.

—— *Germany and the Next War.* Trans. Allen H. Powles. New York: Longmans, Green, 1914.

—— *On War of Today.* Trans. Karl von Donat. 2 vols. London: H. Rees, 1912–13.

Bevan, Edwyn. *Indian Nationalism: An Independent Estimate.* London: Macmillan, 1913.

Blunt, Wilfrid. *Cockerell*. London: Hamish Hamilton, 1964; New York: Knopf, 1965.

Blunt, Wilfrid Scawen. *My Diaries: Being a Personal Narrative of Events, 1888–1914*. 2 parts. London: M. Secker, 1921.

Bone, Gertrude Helena. *Women of the Country*. London: Duckworth, 1913.

Brailsford, H[enry] N[oel]. *The Origins of the Great War*. London: The Union for Democratic Control, 1914.

Brenan, Gerald. *Personal Record, 1920–1972*. London: J. Cape, 1974; New York: Knopf/Random House, 1975.

Bridges, Robert. *The Spirit of Man: An Anthology in English & French from the Philosophers & Poets made by the Poet Laureate in 1915 & dedicated by gracious permission to His Majesty The King*. London: Longmans, Green, 1916.

—— *The Testament of Beauty: A Poem in Four Books*. Oxford: The Clarendon Press; New York: Oxford University Press, 1929.

Briggs, Asa. *The History of Broadcasting in the United Kingdom*. 3 vols. London: Oxford University Press, 1961–70.

Britten, Benjamin. *Billy Budd* [opera]: see Forster, E. M. and Eric Crozier.

—— *The Operas of Benjamin Britten: The Complete Librettos Illustrated with Designs of the First Productions*. Ed. David Herbert. London: Hamish Hamilton, 1979.

Browning, Hilda. *Women under Fascism and Communism*. London: M. Lawrence, 1934.

Bryce, James. *The Holy Roman Empire*. Arnold Prize Essay, 1863. Oxford: T. & G. Shrimpton; London and Cambridge: Macmillan, 1864.

Burdekin, Catherine. *The Rebel Passion*. London: T. Butterworth; New York: W. Morrow, 1929.

Burlingham, Russell. *Forrest Reid: A Portrait and a Study*. London: Faber and Faber, 1953.

Burra, Peter. *Baroque and Gothic Sentimentalism, An Essay*. London: Duckworth, 1931; New York: Folcroft, 1970.

—— *Van Gogh*. Great Lives (No. 29). London: Duckworth; New York: Macmillan, 1934.

—— *Wordsworth*. Great Lives (No. 63). London: Duckworth; New York: Macmillan, 1950.

Butler, Samuel. *Erewhon, or Over the Range*. London: Trübner, 1872; New York: Dutton, 1910.

—— *Life and Habit*. London: Trübner, 1878; London and New York: Longmans, Green, 1890.

Carey, Hugh. *Duet for Two Voices: An Informal Biography of Edward Dent compiled from his Letters to Clive Carey*. Cambridge: The University Press, 1979.

Carpenter, Edward. *My Days and Dreams: Being Autobiographical Notes*. London: Allen & Unwin; New York: Scribner, 1916.

Cavafy, Constantine Peter. *Collected Poems*. Trans. Edmund Keeley and Philip Sherrard. Ed. George Savidis. Princeton, N. J.: Princeton University Press; London: Hogarth Press, 1975; London: Chatto & Windus, 1978.

—— *The Poems of C. P. Cavafy, translated into English with a few notes by John Mavrogordato*. London: Hogarth Press, 1951; New York: Grove Press, 1952.

Cecil, Lord David. *The Stricken Deer; or, The Life of Cowper*. London: Constable, 1929; New York: Oxford University Press, 1930.

Charlton, L[ionel] E[velyn] O[swald]. *Charlton*. London: Faber and Faber, 1931; London and New York: Longmans, Green, 1940.

—— *More Charlton*. London and New York: Longmans, Green, 1940.

—— *War from the Air: Past, Present, Future*. London: Thomas Nelson, 1935; London and New York: Longmans, Green, 1940.

Chevrillon, André. *Dans L'Inde*. Paris: [Hachette?] 1891.

Chirol, Valentine. *Indian Unrest*. London: Macmillan, 1910.

Church, Richard, and M. M. Bozman, comps. *Poems of Our Time 1900–1942*. Everyman's Library (No. 981). London: J. M. Dent, 1945.

Churchill, Randolph S. *Winston S. Churchill*. 4 vols. London: Heinemann; Boston: Houghton Mifflin, 1966–77.

Clayden, P[eter] W[illiam]. *[Samuel] Rogers and His Contemporaries*. 2 vols. London: Smith, Elder, 1889.

Clutton-Brock, Arthur. *Are We to Punish Germany, If We Can?* London and New York: Oxford University Press, 1915.

—— *More Thoughts on the War*. London: Methuen, 1915.

—— *Thoughts on the War*. London: Methuen, 1914.

—— *The Ultimate Belief*. New York: Dutton, 1916.

Cobbold, Richard. *The History of Margaret Catchpole, A Suffolk Girl*. London: H. Colburn, 1845; New York: Appleton, 1846.

Collier, John. *His Monkey Wife: or, Married to a Chimp*. London: P. Davies, 1930; New York: Appleton, 1931.

—— *Tom's a-cold, A Tale*. London: Macmillan, 1933.

Conrad, Joseph. *The Arrow of Gold: A Story between Two Notes*. London: T. F. Unwin; Garden City, N. Y.: Doubleday, Page, 1919.

—— *Tales of Unrest*. London: T. F. Unwin; New York: Scribner, 1898.

—— *'Twixt Land and Sea, Tales*. London: J. M. Dent; New York: Hodder & Stoughton/Doran, 1912.

Crabbe, George. *The Life of George Crabbe, by His Son, with an Introduction by E. M. Forster*. The World's Classics. London: Oxford University Press, 1932.

Cramb, John Adam. *Germany and England*. London: J. Murray; New York: Dutton, 1914.

Crockett, Samuel Rutherford. *The Surprising Adventures of Sir Toady Lion . . . .* London: Gardner, Darton; New York: F. A. Stokes, 1897.

Crozier, Eric, ed. *Benjamin Britten: Peter Grimes*. Sadler's Wells Opera Books

(No. 3). London: John Lane, The Bodley Head, 1945. See also: Britten, *The Operas of Benjamin Britten*; Forster, E. M., and Eric Crozier.

Darling, Sir Malcolm Lyall. *Apprentice to Power: India 1904–1908*. London: Hogarth Press; Toronto: Clarke, Irwin, 1966.

Day-Lewis, C[ecil]. *Overtures to Death and Other Poems*. London: J. Cape, 1938.

—— *Poems in Wartime*. London: J. Cape, 1941.

Dent, Edward Joseph. *Mozart's Operas: A Critical Study*. London: Chatto and Windus, 1913.

Dickinson, Goldsworthy Lowes. *Appearances: Being Notes of Travel*. Garden City, N. Y.: Doubleday, Page, 1914.

—— *The Autobiography of G. Lowes Dickinson and Other Unpublished Writings*. Ed. Dennis Proctor. London: Duckworth, 1973.

—— *An Essay on the Civilisations of India, China & Japan*. London: J. M. Dent, 1914.

—— *The Greek View of Life*. London: Methuen, 1895; New York: McClure, Phillips, 1896.

—— *Letters from John Chinaman*. London: R. B. Johnson, 1901; New York: McClure, Phillips, 1903. American title: *Letters from a Chinese Official, Being an Eastern View of Western Civilisation*.

—— *The Meaning of Good, A Dialogue*. Glasgow: MacLehose, 1901; London: Brimley Johnson, 1902; New York: McClure, Phillips, 1906.

—— *A Modern Symposium*. London: Brimley Johnson & Ince; New York: McClure, Phillips, 1905.

Dickson, Lovat. *Radclyffe Hall at the Well of Loneliness: A Sapphic Chronicle*. London and Toronto: Collins, 1975.

Dimbleby, Jabez Bunting. *The New Era at Hand (1898-¼); or, The Approaching Close of the Great Prophetic Periods,* .... 13th ed. London: E. Nister, 1897.

Dimock, Edward C., and Denise Levertov, trans. *In Praise of Krishna: Songs from the Bengali*. Garden City, N. Y.: Doubleday Anchor Books, 1967.

Dostoievsky, Feodor. *An Honest Thief and Other Stories*. Trans. Constance Garnett. London: Heinemann; New York: Macmillan, 1919.

Doughty, Charles Montagu. *Travels in Arabia Deserta*. 2 vols. Cambridge: The University Press, 1888. New edition, with Introduction by T. E. Lawrence. 2 vols. London and Boston: A. P. L. Warner and J. Cape, 1921.

Douglas, Norman. *South Wind*. London: M. Secker, 1917; New York: Dodd, Mead, 1918.

Drinkwater, John. *Abraham Lincoln: A Play*. London: Sidgwick & Jackson, 1918; Boston and New York: Houghton Mifflin, 1919.

Ede, Harold Stanley. *Savage Messiah*. London: Heinemann; New York: Knopf, 1931. Also as *A Life of Gaudier-Brzeska*.

Eliot, T. S. *The Cocktail Party: A Comedy*. London: Faber and Faber; New York: Harcourt, Brace, 1950.

—— *The Confidential Clerk: A Play*. London: Faber and Faber; New York: Harcourt, Brace, 1954.

—— *Four Quartets*. New York: Harcourt, Brace, 1943; London: Faber and Faber, 1944. Includes *Little Gidding* (1942).

—— *Murder in the Cathedral*. London: Faber and Faber; New York: Harcourt, Brace, 1935.

'Elizabeth': see Russell, Mary Annette Beauchamp (Countess).

Escombe, Edith. *Phases of Marriage*. London: Elkin Mathews, 1897.

Essays offered to G. H. Luce . . . in honour of his Seventy-fifth birthday. Ed. Ba Shin et al. Ascona: Publishers Artibus Asiae, 1966.

Fay, Eliza. *Original Letters from India 1779–1815*. Ed. E. M. Forster. London: Leonard and Virginia Woolf/Hogarth Press, 1925.

Fielden, Lionel. *The Natural Bent*. London: André Deutsch, 1960.

Finney, Brian. *Christopher Isherwood*. London: Faber and Faber; New York: Oxford University Press, 1979.

Flecker, James Elroy. *Hassan: A Play in Five Acts*. London: Heinemann; New York: Knopf, 1922.

Fletcher, C. R. L., and R. Kipling. *A School History of England*. Oxford: Clarendon Press, 1911.

Foemina (pseud. of Augustine Bulteau). *L'âme des Anglais*, Paris: B. Grasset, 1910.

—— *The English Soul* [*L'âme des Anglais*]. Trans. H. T. Porter. London: Heinemann, 1914.

Ford, Ford Madox. *The English Novel, from the Earliest Days to the Death of Joseph Conrad*. Philadelphia and London: J. B. Lippincott, 1929; London: Constable, 1930.

Forster, Charles. . . . *The One Primeval Language Traced Experimentally through Ancient Inscriptions* . . . 3 vols. London: R. Bentley, 1851–4.

Foster, Birket. *Birket Foster's Pictures of English Landscape* . . . London: Routledge, 1862.

France, Anatole (pseud. of J. A. F. Thibault). *Thaïs*. Paris: Calman Lévy, 1891.

Frazer, J[ames] G[eorge]. *The Golden Bough: A Study in Magic and Religion*. 2 vols. 3rd ed. London and New York: Macmillan, 1911.

Furbank, P. N. *E. M. Forster: A Life*. 2 vols. London: Secker and Warburg, 1977–8; New York: 1 vol., Harcourt Brace Jovanovich, 1978.

Galsworthy, John. *The Silver Box*. New York: Putnam, 1909; London: Duckworth, 1910.

Garnett, Edward. *A Censored Play: The Breaking Point, with preface and a letter to the Censor*. London: Duckworth, 1907.

—— *The Feud: A Play in Three Acts*. London: A. H. Bullen, 1909.

Gaye, Phoebe Fenwick. *John Gay: His place in the Eighteenth Century*. London: Collins, 1938.

General Index to the Bills, Reports and Papers printed by Order of the House of

Commons and to the Reports and Papers presented by Command. London: H.M.S.O., 1900/1948–9.

George, Walter Lionel. *Blind Alley; . . . the way of the world through the great war into the unexplored regions of peace.* London: T. F. Unwin; Boston: Little, Brown, 1919.

Gibbon, Edward. *The Autobiographies of Edward Gibbon.* Ed. John Murray. London: J. Murray, 1896.

Gibbon, Lewis Grassic (pseud. of James Leslie Mitchell). *A Scots Quair: A Trilogy of Novels: Sunset Song, Cloud Howe, Grey Granite.* London and New York: Jarrolds, 1934–7.

Gide, André. *Les Caves du Vatican, sotie.* Paris: Nouvelle Revue Française, 1914.

Giraudoux, (Hyppolyte–) Jean. *Electre: Pièce en deux actes.* Paris: B. Grasset, 1937.

Gittings, Robert. *The Older Hardy.* London: Heinemann; Boston: Atlantic-Little, Brown, 1978. American title: *Thomas Hardy's Later Years.*

Gosse, Edmund. *The Life of Algernon Charles Swinburne.* Bonchurch Edition, vol. 19. London: Heinemann; New York: Gabriel Wells, 1925–7.

Graham, George Farquhar Irving. *The Life and Works of Syed Ahmed Khan.* Edinburgh: Blackwood, 1885; London: Hodder & Stoughton, 1909.

Graves, Robert. *Lawrence and the Arabs.* London: J. Cape, 1927; Garden City, N. Y.: Doubleday, Doran, 1928. American title: *Lawrence and the Arabian Adventure.*

—— *On English Poetry: Being an Irregular Approach to the Psychology of This Art, from Evidence Mainly Subjective.* London: Heinemann; New York: Knopf, 1922.

—— *Poems 1928–1930.* London: Heinemann, 1931.

—— *Welchman's Hose.* London: The Fleuron, 1925.

[Grelling, Richard] *I accuse! (J'accuse!). By a German.* Trans. Alexander Gray. New York: H. Doran, 1915; London and New York: Hodder and Stoughton, 1916.

[——] *J'Accuse! von einem Deutschen.* Lausanne: Payot, 1915.

Grey, Edward (1st Viscount). *The League of Nations.* London: Oxford University Press, 1918; New York: G. H. Doran, 1919.

Grierson, Mary. *Donald Francis Tovey: A Biography Based on Letters.* London and New York: Oxford University Press, 1952.

Grove, Lady Agnes. *The Social Fetich.* London: Smith, Elder, 1907.

Hall, (Marguerite) Radclyffe. *The Well of Loneliness.* London: J. Cape; Garden City, N. Y.: Blue Ribbon Books, 1928.

Halward, Leslie. *Let Me Tell You.* London: M. Joseph, 1938.

Hamilton, Gerald B. F. *Mr. Norris and I: An Autobiographical Sketch.* London: Allan Wingate, 1956.

Hampson, John (pseud. of John Hampson Simpson). *Saturday Night at the Greyhound.* London: L. and V. Woolf, 1931.

Hanley, James. *Boy.* London: Boriswood, 1931.

—— *A Passion before Death*. London: privately printed, 1930; New York: subscribers' edition, 1935.

Hardy, Thomas. *Complete Poems*. Ed. James Gibson. New Wessex Edition. London: Macmillan; New York: St. Martin's Press, 1976.

—— *Late Lyrics and Earlier, with Many Other Verses*. London: Macmillan, 1922

—— *Selected Poems*. Ed. with an Introduction by P. N. Furbank. Macmillan's English Classics—New Series. London: Macmillan, 1964; New York: St. Martin's Press, 1966.

—— *The Well-Beloved: A Sketch of a Temperament*. London: Osgood, McIlvaine; New York: Harper, 1897.

Harris, Frank. *The Man Shakespeare and His Tragic Life Story*. London: Frank Palmer; New York: M. Kennerley, 1909.

Havell, Ernest B. *Indian Sculpture and Painting; . . . their Motives and Ideals*. London: J. Murray, 1908. Rev. ed., 1928.

Heard, Gerald. *The Creed of Christ: An Interpretation of the Lord's Prayer*. London, Toronto, and New York: Cassell, 1941.

—— *Pain, Sex and Time: A New Outlook on Evolution and the Future of Man*. New York: Harper; London: Cassell, 1939.

Herringham, Lady C[hristiana] J[ane] P[owell]. *Ajanta Frescoes; . . . copies taken in the years 1909–1911* . . . . London and New York: Oxford University Press, 1915.

Hewlett, Maurice. *The Forest Lovers: A Romance*. London: Macmillan; New York: Scribner, 1898.

Hölderlin, (J. C.) Friederich. *Hyperion*. 2 vols. Tübingen: Cotta, 1797–9.

Holmes, Edmond Gore Alexander. *All Is One: A Plea for the Higher Pantheism*. London: Richard Cobden-Sanderson; New York: Dutton, 1921.

Horne, E[ric] A[rthur]. *The Political System of British India, with Special Reference to the Recent Constitutional Changes*. Oxford: The Clarendon Press, 1922.

Housman, A. E. *Last Poems*. London: Richards Press; New York: Holt, 1922.

—— *A Shropshire Lad*. London: K. Paul, Trench, Trübner, 1896; New York: John Lane, The Bodley Head, 1897.

Housman, Laurence. *All-fellows: Seven Legends of Lower Redemption with Insets in Verse*. London: K. Paul, Trench, Trübner, 1896.

Hsüan-Tsang. *Si-yu-ki. Buddhist Records of the Western World*. Trans. Samuel Beal. 2 vols. London: Trübner, 1884; Boston: Osgood, 1885.

Hudson, Derek. *Munby: Man of Two Worlds: The Life and Diaries of A. J. Munby, 1828–1910*. London: J. Murray; Boston: Gambit, 1972.

Huxley, Aldous. *Brave New World: A Novel*. London: Chatto & Windus; New York: Doubleday, Doran, 1932.

Huysmans, Joris-Karl. *La Cathédrale*. Paris: P. V. Stock, 1898.

Hynes, Samuel. *The Edwardian Turn of Mind*. Princeton, N. J.: Princeton University Press, 1968.

Ibsen, Henrik. *Collected Works.* Trans. William Archer. 11 vols. London: Heinemann; New York: Scribner, 1906–8.

Institute for International Cooperation. *Le Destin prochain des lettres.* 2nd Paris Entretien. Bulletin No. 8. Paris: League of Nations, 1938.

Irving, Robert Grant. *Indian Summer: Lutyens, Baker, and the Building of New Delhi.* New Haven, Conn.: Yale University Press, 1981.

Isherwood, Christopher. See also Auden, W. H., and Isherwood.

—— *Christopher and His Kind.* London: Eyre Methuen; New York: Farrar, Straus, Giroux, 1977.

—— *Kathleen and Frank.* London: Methuen, 1971; New York: Simon and Schuster, 1972.

—— *The Memorial: Portrait of a Family.* London: L. and Virginia Woolf, Hogarth Press; Norfolk, Conn.: New Directions, 1946.

—— *Mr. Norris Changes Trains.* London: L. and Virginia Woolf, Hogarth Press; New York: W. Morrow, 1935. American title: *The Last of Mr. Norris.*

—— *My Guru and His Disciple.* London: Eyre Methuen; New York: Farrar, Straus, Giroux, 1980.

—— *Prater Violet: A Novel.* New York: Random House, 1945; London: Methuen, 1946.

—— *Ramakrishna and His Disciples.* London: Methuen; New York: Simon and Schuster, 1965.

Jackson, Holbrook. *The Story of Don Vincente.* Limited edition. London: Corvinus Press, 1939.

James, Henry. *The Middle Years.* Ed. Percy Lubbock. Glasgow and London: Collins; New York: Scribner, 1917.

—— *The Sense of the Past.* London: Collins; New York: Scribner, 1917.

James, William. *Memories and Studies.* New York and London: Longmans, Green, 1911.

—— *Pragmatism: A New Name for Some Old Ways of Thinking: Popular Lectures on Philosophy.* New York: Longmans, Green, 1907.

Jones, Ebenezer. *Studies of Sensation and Event. Poems.* London: Charles Fox, 1843.

Jones, Sidney. *The Geisha: A Story of a Teahouse. A Japanese Musical Play.* London: Hopwood & Crew; Boston: White-Smith, 1896.

Keats, John. *The Letters of John Keats.* Ed. Hyder E. Rollins. 2 vols. Cambridge: The University Press; Cambridge, Mass.: Harvard University Press, 1958.

Keynes, John Maynard. *The Economic Consequences of the Peace.* London: Macmillan, 1919; New York: Harcourt, Brace and Howe, 1920.

Kilvert, Francis. *Kilvert's Diary: Selections from the Diary of the Rev. Francis Kilvert, chosen, edited, and introduced by William Plomer.* 3 vols. London: J. Cape, 1938–40; New York: Macmillan, 1947.

Kipling, Rudyard. *Stalky & Co.* London: Macmillan; New York: Doubleday, 1899.

Kirkpatrick, B[rownlee] J[ean]. *A Bibliography of E. M. Forster*. 2nd rev. ed. Soho Bibliographies. London: Rupert Hart-Davis, 1968. 3rd rev. ed., Oxford: Clarendon Press; New York: Oxford University Press, 1985.

[Knighton, William] *The Private Life of an Eastern King. By a member of the household of his Late Majesty, Nussir-u-Deen, King of Oude*. London: Routledge; New York: Redfield, 1855.

Koestler, Arthur. *Darkness at Noon*. Trans. Daphne Hardy. London: J. Cape, 1940; New York: Macmillan, 1941.

—— *Scum of the Earth*. Trans. Daphne Hardy. London: J. Cape; New York: Macmillan, 1941.

Koss, Stephen, ed. *The Pro-Boers: The Anatomy of an Anti-War Movement*. Chicago: University of Chicago Press, 1973.

Kugler, Franz Theodor. *Handbook of Painting. The Italian Schools*. Trans. 'by a lady' [Mrs Margaret Hutton]. Ed. Sir Charles L. Eastlake. 2 vols. London: J. Murray, 1842.

Lacouture, Jean. *André Malraux*. Trans. Alan Sheridan. London: André Deutsch; New York: Pantheon Books, 1975.

Lago, Mary, comp. *A Calendar of the Letters of E. M. Forster*. London: Mansell, 1984.

——, ed. *Imperfect Encounter: Letters of William Rothenstein and Rabindranath Tagore, 1911–1941*. Cambridge, Mass.: Harvard University Press, 1972.

Landor, Walter Savage. *The Complete Works*. Ed. T. Earle Welby. 16 vols. London: Chapman and Hall, 1927–36.

Lawrence, A[rnold] W[alter], ed. *Letters to T. E. Lawrence*. London: J. Cape, 1962.

——, ed. *T. E. Lawrence by His Friends*. London: J. Cape; New York: Doubleday, Doran, 1937.

Lawrence, D. H. *D. H. Lawrence's Letters to Bertrand Russell*. Ed. Harry T. Moore. New York: Gotham Book Mart, 1948.

—— *The Letters and Works of D. H. Lawrence*. Cambridge Edition. Ed. George T. Zytaruk and James T. Boulton. 2 vols. Cambridge: University Press, 1979–

—— *The Prussian Officer, and Other Stories*. London: Duckworth, 1914; New York: B. W. Huebsch, 1916.

—— *The Rainbow*. London: Methuen; New York: B. W. Huebsch, 1915.

—— *The White Peacock*. London: Heinemann; New York: Duffield, 1911.

Lawrence, T. E. *The Letters of T. E. Lawrence*. Ed. David Garnett. London and Toronto: J. Cape, 1938; New York: Doubleday, Doran, 1939.

—— *Seven Pillars of Wisdom: a triumph*. Oxford: private edition, 1922; London: 'Subscribers' Edition', 1926.

—— *The Seven Pillars of Wisdom*. New York: Doran, 1926; London: J. Cape, 1935.

Lehmann, John. *New Writing in Europe*. Pelican Books. Harmondsworth, England, and New York: Penguin, 1940.

Liddell Hart, Basil Henry. *'T. E. Lawrence': In Arabia and After*. London: J. Cape, 1934; New York: Doubleday, Doran, 1938.

Longford, Elizabeth. *A Pilgrimage of Passion: The Life of Wilfrid Scawen Blunt*. London: Weidenfeld and Nicolson; New York: Knopf/Random House, 1979.

Lothar, Ernst. *Little Friend* [*Kleine Freundin*]. Trans. Willa and Edwin Muir. London: M. Secker, 1933.

Louÿs, Pierre. *Byblis changée en fontaine*. Paris: Borel, 1898.

—— *Les Chansons de Bilitis*. Paris: Michel, 1894.

Lubbock, Percy. *The Craft of Fiction*. London: J. Cape; New York: Scribner, 1921.

Lucretius Carus. *Translations from Lucretius, by R. C. Trevelyan*. London: Allen & Unwin, 1920.

Lucas, Frank Laurence. *Journal under the Terror, 1938*. London: Cassell, 1939.

Lyall, Sir Alfred C. *Asiatic Studies: Religious and Social*. London: J. Murray, 1882.

—— *The Rise and Expansion of the British Dominion in India*. London: J. Murray: 1882; New York: Scribner, 1893.

Macaulay, Rose. *The Writings of E. M. Forster*. London: Hogarth Press; New York: Harcourt, Brace, 1938.

McConkey, James R. *The Novels of E. M. Forster*. Ithaca, N. Y.: Cornell University Press, 1957.

McDowell, Frederick P. W. *E. M. Forster: An Annotated Bibliography of Writings about Him*. Dekalb, Illinois: Northern Illinois University Press, 1976.

McKenna, Marian C. *Myra Hess: A Portrait*. London: Hamish Hamilton, 1976.

McLagan, Bridget (pseud. of Mary Borden-Turner). *The Mistress of Kingdoms; or Smoking Flax*. London: Duckworth, 1912.

MacLeish, Archibald. *Land of the Free—USA*. New York: Harcourt, Brace; London: Boriswood, 1938.

McTaggart, John McTaggart Ellis. *The Nature of Existence*. 2 vols. Cambridge: The University Press, 1921-7.

Maeterlinck, Maurice. *Pelléas et Mélisande*. Brussels: Paul Lacomblez, 1892.

Malgonkar, Manohar. *The Puars of Dewas Senior*. Bombay: Orient Longmans, 1963.

Mallarmé, Stephane. *Poems*. Trans. Roger Fry, with commentaries by Charles Mauron. London: Chatto & Windus, 1936; New York: Oxford University Press, 1937.

Mallon, Thomas. *Edmund Blunden*. Twayne English Authors. Boston: G. K. Hall, 1983.

Mansfield, Katherine. *Journal of Katherine Mansfield*. Ed. J[ohn] Middleton Murry. London: Constable; New York: A. A. Knopf, 1927.

Manucci, Niccolo. *Storia do Mogor; or, Mogul India, 1653–1708*. Trans. William Irvine. 4 vols. London: J. Murray, 1907-8.

Marsh, Sir Edward Howard, ed. *Georgian Poetry.* 5 vols. London: The Poetry Bookshop, 1913–22.

Masefield, John. *The Tragedy of Nan, and Other Plays.* London: Grant Richards; New York: M. Kennerley, 1909.

—— *The Tragedy of Pompey the Great.* London: Sidgwick & Jackson; Boston: Little, Brown, 1910.

Matson, Norman Häghejm. *Flecker's Magic.* London: Ernest Benn; New York: Boni & Liveright, 1926.

Mauron, Charles. *L'Homme triple.* Paris: R. Laffont, 1947.

—— *Poèmes en prose de Charles Mauron.* Argenteuil: Coulouma, 1930.

Mayor, Joseph B. *A Sketch of Ancient Philosophy from Thales to Cicero.* Cambridge: The University Press, 1885.

Melville, Herman. *Billy Budd, Foretopman: A Novel.* Introduction by William Plomer. London: J. Lehmann, 1946.

Menotti, Gian-Carlo. *The Medium.* New York: G. Schirmer, 1947.

Meredith, Hugh Owen. *Week-Day Poems.* London: E. Arnold, 1911.

Meynell, Viola, ed. *Friends of a Lifetime: Letters to Sydney Carlyle Cockerell.* London: J. Cape, 1940.

Michelangelo (Buonarrroti). *The Sonnets of Michael Angelo Buonarroti . . . .* Trans. John Addington Symonds. Portland, Maine: T. B. Mosher, 1897; New York: Putnam, 1902; London: Smith, Elder, 1904.

Middleton, Richard Barham. *The Ghost Ship and Other Stories.* London: T. F. Unwin, 1912.

Millgate, Michael. *Thomas Hardy: A Biography.* London: Oxford University Press; New York: Random House, 1982.

Millin, Sara Gertrude. *God's Stepchildren.* London: Constable, 1924; New York: Boni and Liveright, 1926.

Mitchell, Donald, and John Evans, comps. *Benjamin Britten: Pictures from a Life 1973–1976.* New York: Scribner, 1978.

Mitter, Partha. *Much Maligned Monsters.* Oxford: Oxford University Press, 1977.

Moore, George. *Ave.* Part I of *Hail and Farewell.* 3 vols. London: Heinemann, 1911; New York: Appleton, 1912.

Moore, G[eorge] E[dward]. *Principia Ethica.* Cambridge: Cambridge University Press, 1903.

Moore, Harry. T. *The Priest of Love: A Life of D. H. Lawrence.* Rev. ed. Carbondale: Southern Illinois University Press, 1977.

Morel, E[dmond] D[ene], *et al. The Morrow of the War.* London: Union of Democratic Control, 1914.

Morrell, Ottoline. *Memoirs of Lady Ottoline Morell: . . . 1873–1915.* Ed. Robert Gathorne-Hardy. London: Faber and Faber, 1963; New York: Knopf, 1964.

[Munby, Arthur Joseph] *Dorothy: A Country Story, in Elegiac Verse.* London: C. Kegan Paul, 1880; Boston: Roberts Brothers, 1882.

—— *Verses New and Old.* London: Bell and Daldy, 1865.

—— *Vestigia Retrorsum. Poems.* London: J. Macqueen, 1891.

Murray, Constantine (pseud.). *Proud Man.* London: Boriswood, 1934.

Murray, Rosalind. *The Leading Note.* London: Sidgwick & Jackson, 1910.

National Gallery. *National Gallery Concerts.* London: National Gallery, 1944.

Natwar-Singh, K. ed. *E. M. Forster: A Tribute, with Selections from His Writings on India.* New York: Harcourt, Brace & World, 1964.

Newsome, David. *On the Edge of Paradise: A. C. Benson: The Diarist.* London: J. Murray; Chicago: University of Chicago Press, 1980.

Osborne, John. *The Entertainer: A Play.* London: Evans Brothers, 1959; New York: Bantam Books, 1960.

O'Sullivan, Maurice. *Twenty Years A-Growing.* Trans. Moya Llewelyn Davies and George Derwent Thomson. Introductory note by E. M. Forster. London: Chatto & Windus; New York: Viking, 1933.

Ould, Hermon, ed. *Writers in Freedom: A Symposium based on the XVII International Congress of the P.E.N. Club held in London in September 1941.* London and New York: Hutchinson, 1942.

Ouspensky, Petr Dem'yanovich. *A New Model of the Universe: . . . .* London: K. Paul, Trench, Trübner; New York: Knopf, 1931.

Owen, (William) Harold. *Aftermath.* London and New York: Oxford University Press, 1970.

Parry, Benita. *Delusions and Discoveries: Studies on India in the British Imagination, 1880–1930.* London: Allen Lane; Berkeley: University of California Press, 1972.

Pater, Walter. *Marius the Epicurean: His Sensations and Ideas.* London: Macmillan, 1885; New York: Macmillan, 1891.

Perey, Lucien, and Gaston Maugras. *La Vie intime de Voltaire aux Délices et à Ferney 1754–1778, d'après des lettres et des documents inédits.* Paris: Michel Lévy Frères, 1885.

Perrin, Alice. *Idolatry.* London: Chatto & Windus; New York: Duffield, 1909.

Pevsner, Nikolaus. *Essex.* 2nd ed., rev. by Enid Radcliffe. Buildings of England. Harmondsworth, England: Penguin, 1965.

Pinter, Harold. *The Caretaker: A Play.* London: Methuen, 1960; New York: Grove Press, 1961.

—— *The Birthday Party and Other Plays.* London: Methuen, 1960; New York: Grove Press, 1961.

Plomer, William. *At Home: Memoirs.* London: J. Cape, 1958.

—— *The Autobiography of William Plomer.* London: J. Cape, 1943; New York: Taplinger, 1976.

—— *The Case Is Altered.* London: Leonard Woolf, Hogarth Press, 1932.

—— *Cecil Rhodes.* London: Peter Davies; New York: Appleton, 1933.

—— *Double Lives: An Autobiography.* London: J. Cape, 1943.

—— *Electric Delights*. Selected by Rupert Hart-Davis. London: Rupert Hart-Davis, 1978.

—— *The Invaders*. London: J. Cape, 1934.

—— *Sado*. London: L. and Virginia Woolf, 1931.

—— *Turbott Wolfe*. London: Hogarth Press; New York: Harcourt, Brace, 1926.

Pound, Reginald. *Sir Henry Wood: A Biography*. London: Cassell, 1969.

Prawer, Siegbert Salomon. *Karl Marx and World Literature*. Oxford: The Clarendon Press, 1976.

Priestley, J. B. *I Have Been Here Before: A Play in Three Acts*. London and New York: Harper; London: Heinemann, 1938.

Proust, Marcel. *Contre Sainte-Beuve*. Paris: Gallimard, 1954.

—— *Du côté de chez Swann*. Ed. P. Clarac and André Ferre. 3 vols. Pléiade Edition. Paris: Gallimard, 1954.

Quennell, Peter. *John Ruskin: The Portrait of a Prophet*. London: Collins; New York: Viking, 1949.

Rama Rau, Santha. *Home to India*. New York and London: Harper, 1945.

—— *A Passage to India: A Play by Santha Rama Rau from the Novel by E. M. Forster*. London: E. Arnold; New York: Harcourt, Brace & World, 1960.

Raverat, Gwen. *Period Piece: A Cambridge Childhood*. London: Chatto & Windus, 1952.

Raymond, Ernest. *Tell England*. London and New York: Cassell; New York: Doran, 1922.

Read, Herbert. *Henry Moore: Sculpture and Drawing*. New York: Curt Valentin, 1944.

Reeves, Amber. *The Reward of Virtue*. London: Heinemann, 1911.

Reid, Forrest. *The Bracknels: A Family Chronicle*. London: E. Arnold, 1911. Re-written as *Denis Bracknel*.

—— *Brian Westby*. London: Faber and Faber, 1934.

—— *Denis Bracknel*. London: Faber and Faber, 1947.

—— *Following Darkness*. London: E. Arnold, 1912. Re-written as *Peter Waring*.

—— *A Garden by the Sea: Stories and Sketches*. Dublin: Talbot Press; London: T. F. Unwin, 1918.

—— *The Gentle Lover: A Comedy of Middle Age*. London: E. Arnold, 1912.

—— *Illustrators of the Sixties*. London: Faber & Gwyer, 1928.

—— *The Kingdom of Twilight*. First Novel Library (No. 9). London: T. F. Unwin, 1904.

—— *Peter Waring*. London: Faber and Faber, 1937.

—— *Pirates of the Spring*. London: T. F. Unwin, 1919; Dublin: Phoenix, 1920; New York: Houghton Mifflin, 1920.

—— *Private Road*. London: Faber and Faber, 1940.

—— *The Retreat; or The Machinations of Henry*. London: Faber and Faber, 1936.

—— *The Spring Song*. London: E. Arnold, 1916; Boston and New York: Houghton Mifflin, 1917.

—— *Tom Barber*. Introduction by E. M. Forster. Contains *Young Tom; The Retreat; Uncle Stephen*. New York: Pantheon, 1955.

—— *Uncle Stephen*. London: Faber and Faber, 1931.

—— *Walter de la Mare: A Critical Study*. London: Faber and Faber; New York: Holt, 1929.

—— *W. B. Yeats: A Critical Study*. London: M. Secker; New York: Dodd, Mead, 1915.

—— *Young Tom, or Very Mixed Company*. London: Faber and Faber, 1944.

Richards, I. A. *Principles of Literary Criticism*. London: Kegan, Paul, Trübner; New York: Harcourt, Brace, 1924.

Richards, Philip Ernest. *Indian Dust; being Letters from the Punjab*. London: Allen & Unwin, 1932.

Roberts, S. C. *Zuleika in Cambridge*. Cambridge: Heffer, 1941.

Rolland, Romain. *Au-dessus de la mêlée*. Paris: Paul Ollendorff, 1915; Chicago: Open Court, 1916. American title, trans. C. K. Ogden, *Above the Battle*.

—— *Musiciens d'aujourd'hui*. Paris: Hachette, 1917.

—— *Vie de Michel Ange*. Paris: Hachette, 1907.

Rostand, Edmund. *Chantecler: Play in Four Acts*. Trans. Gertrude Hall. New York: Duffield, 1910.

Rothenstein, William. *Men and Memories; Recollections of William Rothenstein*. 3 vols. London: Faber and Faber, 1931–9. Abridged and annotated by Mary Lago, 1 vol. London: Chatto and Windus; Columbia: University of Missouri, 1978.

Rowland, Benjamin. *The Art and Architecture of India; Buddhist, Hindu, Jain*. Pelican History of Indian Art. London and Baltimore: Penguin, 1953.

Russell, Bertrand. *The Principles of Social Reconstruction*. London: G. Allen & Unwin; New York: Century, 1916. American title: *Why Men Fight*.

—— *War--The Offspring of Fear*. London: Union of Democratic Control, 1914.

Russell, Mary Annette Beauchamp (Countess). *The Adventures of Elizabeth in Rügen*. London and New York: Macmillan, 1904.

—— *The April Baby's Book of Tunes*. London and New York: Macmillan, 1900.

—— *The Benefactress*. London and New York: Macmillan, 1901.

—— *Elizabeth and Her German Garden*. London and New York: Macmillan, 1898.

Sargeson, Frank. *I Saw in My Dream*. London: John Lehmann, 1949.

—— *That Summer, and Other Stories*. London: John Lehmann, 1946.

Sassoon, Siegfried. *Collected Poems*. London: Faber and Faber, 1942; New York: Viking Press, 1949.

—— *Counter-Attack, and Other Poems*. London: Heinemann; New York: Dutton, 1918.

—— *Sherston's Progress*. London: Faber and Faber; Garden City, N. Y.: Doubleday, Doran, 1936.

—— *Siegfried's Journey 1916–1920*. London: Faber and Faber; New York: Viking, 1945.

[Schreiner, Olive]. *The Story of an African Farm: A Novel*. 2 vols. London: Chapman and Hall; Boston: Little, Brown, 1883.

Scott, Peter. *The Eye of the Wind*. London: Hodder and Stoughton; Boston: Houghton, Mifflin, 1961.

Seeley, Sir John Robert. *The Growth of British Policy. An Historical Essay*. Cambridge: The University Press, 1895.

Shahani, Ranjee Gudarsing. *Shakespeare Through Eastern Eyes*. London: H. Joseph, 1932.

Shaw, G. B. *Plays: Pleasant and Unpleasant*. London: Grant Richards; Chicago and New York: A. S. Stone, 1898.

Sheppard, J. T. *Greek Tragedy*. Cambridge: University Press, 1911.

Sherwood, Mary Martha. *The History of the Fairchild Family: or, The Child's Manual* . . . . London: Hatchard, 1818.

Sinclair, May. *Mary Olivier: A Life*. London: Cassell; New York: Macmillan, 1919.

Sitwell, Constance. *Flowers and Elephants*. Foreword by E. M. Forster. London: J. Cape; New York: Harcourt, Brace, 1927.

Sitwell, Osbert. *Left Hand, Right Hand*. 5 vols. London: Macmillan, 1945–50.

Sleeman, Sir William Henry. *Rambles and Recollections of an Indian Official*. 2 vols. London: Hatchard, 1844.

Spalding, Frances. *Roger Fry: Art and Life*. London and New York: Elek, 1980.

Spender, Stephen. *Collected Poems, 1928–1953*. London: Faber and Faber; New York: Random House, 1955.

—— *Poems*. London: Faber and Faber; New York: Random House, 1934.

Sophocles. *Sophocles: The Plays and Fragments with Critical Notes, Commentary, and Translation in English Prose, by R[ichard] C[laverhouse] Jebb*. 7 vols. Cambridge: The University Press, 1892–1900.

Spinoza, Benedict. *Ethic: demonstrated in geometrical order and divided into five parts*, ... Trans. W. Hale White. Oxford: Oxford University Press, 1910.

Sprott, W. J. H. *Human Groups*. Pelican Original. Harmondsworth, England: Penguin, 1958.

Stallybrass, Oliver, ed. *Aspects of E. M. Forster: Essays and Recollections written for his Ninetieth Birthday 1st January 1969*. London: E. Arnold; New York: Harcourt, Brace & World, 1969.

Stawell, Florence Melian, and G. Lowes Dickinson. *Goethe & Faust, An Interpretation, with Passages newly translated into English Verse*. London: G. Bell, 1928.

Stephens, Ian Melville. *Pakistan*. Nations of the Modern World. London: Ernest Benn; New York: Praeger, 1963.

Stone, Wilfred. *The Cave & The Mountain: A Study of E. M. Forster*. Stanford: Stanford University Press, 1966.

—— *Religion and Art of William Hale White ('Mark Rutherford')*. Stanford University Publications; Language and Literature, vol. 12. Stanford: Stanford University Press, 1954.

Strachey, Giles Lytton. *Landmarks in French Literature*. Home University Library. London: Williams and Norgate; New York: Holt, 1912.

Strauss, Helen. *A Talent for Luck: An Autobiography*. New York: Random House, 1979.

Struther, Jan (pseud. of Joyce Maxtone Graham). *Mrs. Miniver*. London: Chatto & Windus, 1939; New York: Grosset and Dunlap, 1940.

Swinnerton, Frank. *The Georgian Literary Scene: A Panorama*. New York: Farrer & Rinehart, 1934; London: Heinemann, 1935. American title: *The Georgian Scene: A Literary Panorama*.

—— *Swinnerton: An Autobiography*. Garden City, N. Y.: Doubleday, Doran, 1935; London: Hutchinson, 1937.

Symonds, John Addington. *Sketches in Italy and Greece*. London: Smith, Elder, 1874.

Symonds, Margaret, and Lina Duff Gordon. *The Story of Perugia*. Medieval Towns. London: J. M. Dent; New York: Dutton, 1927.

Synge, John Millington. *In Wicklow, West Kerry, and Connemara*. Dublin: Maunsel, 1911.

—— *The Playboy of the Western World: A Comedy in Three Acts*. Dublin: Maunsel, 1907; Boston: J. W. Luce, 1911.

Syrett, Netta. *Three Women*. London: Chatto & Windus, 1912.

Tagore, Devendranath. *The Autobiography of Maharshi Devendranath Tagore*. Trans. Satyendranath Tagore and Indira Devi. Calcutta: S. K. Lahiri, 1909; London: Macmillan, 1914.

Tagore, Rabindranath. *Gitanjali. Song-Offerings*. London: The India Society, 1912; London and New York: Macmillan, 1913.

Taylor, Brian. *The Green Avenue: The Life and Writings of Forrest Reid, 1875–1947*. Cambridge: The University Press, 1981.

Tennyson, Hallam. *Alfred Lord Tennyson; a Memoir, by His Son*. 2 vols. London and New York: Macmillan, 1897.

Thomas, Edward. *Beautiful Wales*. London: A. and C. Black, 1905.

—— *The Icknield Way*. London: Constable, 1913.

—— *Last Poems*. London: Selwyn & Blount, 1918.

—— *Richard Jefferies, His Life and Work*. London: Hutchinson, 1908; Boston: Little, Brown, 1909.

Thompson, Edward [John]. *Robert Bridges 1844–1930*. London: Oxford University Press, 1944; New York: Oxford University Press, 1945.

Thomson, George H. *The Fiction of E. M. Forster*. Detroit: Wayne State University Press, 1967.

Tolstoy, Leo. *Resurrection: A Novel*. Trans. Louise Maude. New York: Crowell, 1889; London: Francis R. Henderson, 1900.

Tovey, Donald Francis. *A Companion to Beethoven's Pianoforte Sonatas (Complete Analysis)*. London: Royal Academy of Music, 1931.

Tremaine, Herbert. *The Feet of the Young Men: A Domestic War-Novel*. London: C. W. Daniel, 1917.

Trevelyan, Robert Calverley. *The Bride of Dionysus, A Music-Drama, and Other Poems*. London and New York: Longmans, Green, 1912.

—— *The Collected Works*. 2 vols. London: Longmans, Green, 1939.

—— *The Pterodamozels: An Operatic Fable*. London: privately printed at the Pelican Press, 1916.

Trevelyan, Raleigh. *A Pre-Raphaelite Circle*. London: Chatto & Windus; New York: Rowman and Littlefield, 1978.

Treves, Sir Frederick. *The Other Side of the Lantern: An Account of a Commonplace Tour Round the World*. London and New York: Cassell, 1905.

Trilling, Lionel. *E. M. Forster: A Study*. Norfolk, Conn.: New Directions 1943; London: Hogarth Press, 1944.

—— *Freud and the Crisis of Our Culture*. Boston: Beacon Press, 1955.

—— *The Middle of the Journey*. New York: Viking; London: Secker and Warburg, 1947.

[Upanishads] *The Thirteen Principal Upanishads. . . . Trans. Robert Ernest Hume*. Madras: Oxford University Press, 1949.

Van Rysselberghe, Maria. *Les Cahiers de la Petite Dame. Notes pour l'histoire authentique d'André Gide*. Vols. 4–7 of *Cahiers André Gide*, 11 vols. Paris: Gallimard, 1969–82.

Virgil. *The Aeneid of Virgil*. Trans. E. Fairfax Taylor. Introduction and Notes by E. M. Forster. The Temple Classics. G. Lowes Dickinson and H. O. Meredith, eds. 2 vols. London: J. M. Dent, 1906.

Wadia, Ardaser Sorabjee N. *Reflections on the Problems of India*. London and Toronto: J. M. Dent, 1913.

Wallas, Graham. *The Great Society: A Psychological Analysis*. London and New York: Macmillan, 1914.

Walpole, Hugh. *Maradick at Forty: A Transition*. London: Smith, Elder; New York: Duffield, 1910.

—— *Reading: An Essay; Being one of a series of essays edited by J. B. Priestley and entitled: These Diversions*. London: Jarrolds; New York and London: Harper, 1926.

—— *The Wooden Horse*. London: J. Murray, 1909; New York: Dutton, 1914.

Warburg, Fredric. *All Authors Are Equal. The Publishing Life of Fredric Warburg 1936–1971*. London: Hutchinson, 1973; New York: St. Martin's Press, 1973.

Waugh, Alec. *The Loom of Youth*. London: Grant Richards, 1917; New York: Doran, 1920.

Wedgwood, A. Felix. *The Shadow of a Titan*. London: Duckworth; New York: John Lane, 1910.

Weekley, Ernest. *The Romance of Names*. London: J. Murray; New York: Dutton, 1914.

—— *The Romance of Words*. London: John Murray; New York: Dutton, 1912.

Wells, H. G. *An Englishman Looks at the World. Being a Series of Unrestrained Remarks upon Contemporary Matters*. London and New York: Cassell, 1914.

—— *Mr. Britling Sees It Through*. London: Collins; New York: Macmillan, 1916.

—— *The New Machiavelli*. New York: Duffield, 1910; London: John Lane, 1911.

Wharton, Edith. *Ethan Frome*. London: Macmillan; New York: Scribner, 1911.

Wheatley, Vera. *The Life and Work of Harriet Martineau*. London: Secker & Warburg; Fair Lawn, N. J.: Essential Books, 1957.

White, Newman Ivey. *Shelley*. 2 vols. New York: Knopf, 1940; London: Secker & Warburg, 1947.

Wilder, Thornton. *The Bridge of San Luis Rey*. London and New York: Longmans, Green; New York: A. & C. Boni, 1927.

Wilkinson, L. P. *A Century of King's 1873–1972*. Cambridge: King's College, 1980.

—— *Kingsmen of a Century 1873–1972*. Cambridge: King's College, 1980.

Willcocks, Sir William. *The Nile Projects*. Cairo: Printing Office of the French Institute of Archaeology, 1919.

Williams, Tennessee. *A Streetcar Named Desire*. London: John Lehmann, 1949; New York: New American Library, 1951.

[Wolfenden Committee] *Report of the Committee on Homosexual Offences and Prostitution*. London: H.M.S.O., 1957.

Wood, Joseph. *Ediscenda*. London: Rivington, 1893.

Woolf, Leonard. *The Village in the Jungle*. London: E. Arnold, 1913; New York: Harcourt, Brace, 1926.

Woolf, Virginia. *The Diary of Virginia Woolf*. Ed. Anne Olivier Bell, assisted by Andrew McNeillie. 5 vols. London: Hogarth Press; New York: Harcourt, Brace, 1977–84.

—— *Freshwater: A Comedy*. Ed. Lucio P. Ruotolo. London: Hogarth Press; New York: Harcourt Brace Jovanovich, 1976.

—— *Jacob's Room*. London: L. and V. Woolf, Hogarth Press, 1922; New York: Harcourt, Brace, 1923.

—— *The Letters of Virginia Woolf*. Ed. Nigel Nicolson and Joanne Trautmann. 6 vols. London: Hogarth Press; New York: Harcourt, Brace, 1975–80.

—— *Night and Day*. London: Duckworth, 1919; New York: Harcourt, Brace, 1920.

—— *To the Lighthouse*. London: L. and V. Woolf, Hogarth Press; New York: Harcourt, Brace, 1927.

—— *The Voyage Out*. London: Duckworth; New York: Doran, 1920.

—— *The Waves*. London: Hogarth Press; New York: Harcourt, Brace, 1931.

—— *A Writer's Diary: Being Extracts from the Diary of Virginia Woolf*. Ed. Leonard Woolf. London: Hogarth Press, 1953; New York: Harcourt, Brace, 1954.

—— *The Years*. London: Hogarth Press; New York: Harcourt, Brace, 1937.

Wortham, H[ugh] E[velyn]. *Oscar Browning*. London: Constable, 1927.

Yazdani, Ghulam. *Ajanta: The Colour and Monochrome Reproductions* .... 4 vols. Oxford: Oxford University Press, 1930–5.

Yeats, W. B. *Cathleen ni Houlihan: A Play in One Act and in Prose*. London: A. H. Bullen, 1902.

Yeats-Brown, Francis Claypon. *Bengal Lancer*. London: Victor Gollancz; New York: Viking, 1930. American title: *The Lives of a Bengal Lancer*.

Young, Edward Hilton. *By Sea and Land: Some Naval Doings*. London: Methuen, 1920.

—— *The Evidence You Shall Give*. Privately printed, 1939.

—— *A Muse at Sea; Verses*. London: Sidgwick & Jackson, 1919.

Yourcenar, Marguerite. *Memoires d'Hadrian*. Paris: Plon, 1951.

—— *Présentation critique de Constantin Cavafy, 1863–1933 [par] Marguerite Yourcenar. Suivie d'une traduction intégrale de ses poèmes par Marguerite Yourcenar et Constantin Dimaras*. Paris: Gallimard, 1958. See also Cavafy, C. P., works by.

INDEX
Volumes One and Two

Number in *italics* indicates a letter or letters from EMF to the person concerned.
Works by his correspondents are listed under their names, as well as by title.